Contributions to Finance and Accounting

The book series 'Contributions to Finance and Accounting' features the latest research from research areas like financial management, investment, capital markets, financial institutions, FinTech and financial innovation, accounting methods and standards, reporting, and corporate governance, among others. Books published in this series are primarily monographs and edited volumes that present new research results, both theoretical and empirical, on a clearly defined topic. All books are published in print and digital formats and disseminated globally. This book series is indexed in Scopus.

Steven Meighan

Money Laundering and Crypto-Assets

A Socio-Technical Approach to Financial Intelligence

Springer

Steven Meighan
High Rock Consultancy
Dublin, Ireland

ISSN 2730-6038 ISSN 2730-6046 (electronic)
Contributions to Finance and Accounting
ISBN 978-3-032-13480-6 ISBN 978-3-032-13481-3 (eBook)
https://doi.org/10.1007/978-3-032-13481-3

This Springer imprint is published by the registered company Springer Nature Switzerland AG
The registered company address is: Gewerbestrasse 11, 6330 Cham, Switzerland

To Laura, with all my love.

Preface

Money laundering and organised crime go hand-in-hand. Most crime is committed for financial gain, which affords criminals a lavish lifestyle far beyond their legitimate means. Money is also powerful: it enables criminal organisations to extend their reach and range of criminality, increasing their societal harm. It is no exaggeration to say that money is the life-blood of organised crime and the motivation behind most crimes.

However, this dirty money also exposes them. It links its possessor to the predicate offence that generated it, providing law enforcement an opportunity to investigate and prosecute, as well as seizing the criminal assets. A most unwelcome outcome for criminals. To avoid this, they need a process that breaks the link with the predicate offence, obscures the criminal source, and leaves them free to enjoy the fruits of their criminality or to re-invest into further criminal acts. That process is money laundering, a challenging *wicked problem* for civil society to address.

Public understanding of these issues is often shaped, oversimplified, and glamorised by the media. One television series that portrayed the true nature of money laundering and its role in organised crime was *The Wire*. In it, the older, more methodical detective offers a blunt but enduring truth: 'You start to follow the money, you don't know where the f—it's gonna take you'. That principle remains the foundation of financial investigations to this day.

My first book explored this 'follow the money' idea as a strategy to understand and disrupt organised crime. It focused on Ireland's historical, legislative, and policing context. This new book continues that journey, this time in a space where money becomes code. Drawing on my background in computer science, law, and enforcement, I examine crypto-laundering: the use of crypto-assets to move and conceal illicit wealth, and the challenges posed to traditional AML systems at every level. It draws on socio-technical systems theory to explore if we can better understand this challenge in a more holistic manner.

As part of my work with FIU Ireland, I observed first-hand how crypto-laundering, and the regulatory efforts to prevent and detect it, affected real-world AML practice. With privileged access to both the pre- and post-regulation period, and to rare primary data, I gained valuable empirical insight into the operational challenges facing FIUs. This research uses that insight to develop models that can explain, and potentially improve, the regulation and detection of crypto-laundering.

This book forms part of the Springer Contributions to Finance and Accounting series. It aligns with the series' mission by addressing the interface of financial crime, technological innovation, and institutional response. It is written for both researchers and practitioners. For academics, it provides theoretical models grounded in systems thinking and field data. For FIU professionals, AML practitioners, and policy makers, it offers practical models that can be adapted across national and international AML contexts, particularly those aligned to FATF standards.

Completing this book would not have been possible without the support of many people. In particular, I thank my wife Laura, and our children Grace, Olivia, and Jamie. Thank you for your love, patience, and unwavering support in this and all our shared endeavours. To my parents, Derek and Teresa, thank you for your encouragement throughout my career. I am deeply grateful to my colleagues and friends in An Garda Síochána, especially the Garda National Economic Crime Bureau (GNECB) and FIU Ireland, thank you for your trust and insights. Special thanks to (Retired) Detective Chief Superintendent Patrick Lordan—a giant in Irish AML—who understood the value of opening the door to academic research in the traditionally closed policing space. To Dr. Dionysios Demetis, my PhD supervisor and friend, whose guidance shaped both my thinking and this project. To my editor, Rocio Torregrosa, and all the team at Springer Nature, thanks for trusting me to deliver this work and be part of the publishing family.

Over the past 25 years in policing, I have worked across multiple jurisdictions and continents. While the laws and tactics differ, one truth remains: hitting criminals in the pocket still hurts them the most. This book is a small contribution to understanding and improving how we do that in the age of crypto-assets.

The views expressed in this book are my own and do not represent those of An Garda Síochána or any other organisation with which I am affiliated. All errors are mine alone. The content is current as of 1 August 2025. As this is a fast-evolving field, readers are encouraged to consult the latest legal and regulatory updates before relying on any material herein.

Dublin, Ireland
31 August 2025

Steven Meighan

Declarations

Ethics Approval

The original research presented in this book was carried out as part of the author's doctoral studies in Systems Science at the University of Hull. Formal ethics approval was granted in writing in February 2022 by the Faculty of Business, Law, and Politics Ethics Committee. The research was conducted in accordance with the conditions of that approval and the safeguards outlined in the submitted research ethics documentation. It fully complied with the University's Research Ethics Policy, the EU GDPR, and the Irish Data Protection Act.

Permissions

The author received written approval to observe FIU operations, interview staff, and analyse anonymised Suspicious Transaction Reports (STRs) from the Head of FIU Ireland in April 2022. No de-anonymised data was removed from the secure FIU and Garda IT infrastructure. All sources cited in this book are either open-access or cited with full attribution. No copyrighted or proprietary materials were reproduced.

Informed Consent

Prior to their participation, the author gave all interview and focus group participants clear written information on the purpose of the research, the adopted research procedures, details of their confidentiality safeguards, and their right to withdraw at any stage. All participants gave their written informed consent. The interviews and focus groups were audio-recorded, anonymised during transcription, and the written record was reviewed for accuracy by the participants before being used. All participants in this study have been anonymised to protect individual identities to the greatest extent possible.

Competing Interests The author has no competing interests to declare that are relevant to the content of this manuscript.

About This Book

This book explores the use of crypto-assets to conceal the origins of criminal proceeds—known as *crypto-laundering*—through a socio-technical systems view of *financial intelligence* and Ireland's *Financial Intelligence Unit (FIU)*. It examines how dynamic, decentralised technologies challenge traditional *Anti-money Laundering (AML)* systems and frames crypto-laundering as a *wicked problem*. Drawing on rare empirical access to 2719 *Suspicious Transaction Reports (STRs)*, the book develops a series of socio-technical models to explain both the laundering process and the institutional response to it. It introduces dual 2D frameworks to represent the criminal and regulatory systems, and a combined 3D model illustrating their structural coupling. This study offers technical insights and practical guidance for FIUs, regulators, and policy makers in FATF-aligned jurisdictions. The book contributes to the fields of financial intelligence, crypto-crime, and crypto-regulation by offering a transferable framework for understanding and addressing crypto-laundering in an ever-changing complex world.

Contents

1 Introduction 1
1.1 The Modern Complex World 1
1.2 Introducing Crypto-Assets 4
1.2.1 Cybercrime 5
1.3 Money Laundering 6
1.4 Anti-Money Laundering 7
1.5 A Wicked Problem 10
1.6 Book Outline 11
References 14

2 The Evolution of the Global AML System 17
2.1 Money Laundering 18
2.1.1 Categories of Money Laundering 19
2.1.2 Three Stages of Money Laundering 20
2.1.3 The Corrosive Effect of Money Laundering 21
2.1.4 The Scale of Money Laundering 22
2.1.5 Money Laundering Methods and Processes 23
2.1.6 Cyber-Laundering 25
2.1.7 Terrorist and Proliferation Financing 26
2.2 The Regulation of Money Laundering 28
2.2.1 The Development of Anti-Money Laundering (AML) 29
2.2.2 Hierarchy of AML Rule-Making 31
2.2.3 The International Dimension: The Financial Action Task Force 32
2.2.4 The Supranational Dimension: The European Union 39
2.2.5 The National Dimension: Ireland 46
2.2.6 An Imperfect System? 53
References 54

3 Crypto-Assets: Technology, Adoption, and Criminal Exploitation 59
3.1 Money 59
3.2 Towards Crypto-Assets 60

3.3 Bitcoin ... 62
3.4 Crypto-Crime ... 73
3.5 Crypto-Laundering ... 74
References ... 79

4 Regulating Crypto-Assets: AML Systems and Enforcement ... 83
4.1 Choices to Be Made ... 83
4.2 Regulating Crypto-Assets ... 84
4.2.1 The International Dimension: The FATF and the Regulation of Crypto-Assets ... 86
4.2.2 The Supranational Dimension: The EU and the Regulation of Crypto-Assets ... 88
4.2.3 The National Dimension: Ireland and the Regulation of Crypto-Assets ... 91
4.3 Observations ... 94
References ... 96

5 Socio-Technical Systems Theory in AML Context ... 99
5.1 A Theoretical Scaffold ... 100
5.2 Why Systems? ... 100
5.2.1 What Is a System? ... 103
5.3 Organisations and Phenomena as Systems ... 109
5.4 Socio-Technical Systems Theory ... 111
5.5 Criticisms of Systems Theory ... 114
5.6 Application of Systems Theory to AML ... 115
5.6.1 The Irish AML System ... 115
5.6.2 FIU Ireland as a Socio-Technical System ... 118
5.7 Alternative Theories Considered ... 121
References ... 124

6 The Case of FIU Ireland ... 129
6.1 Introduction to the Case Study ... 129
6.1.1 Crypto-Laundering ... 130
6.1.2 The Role of FIUs in the AML System ... 130
6.1.3 Data Sources ... 131
6.2 FIU Ireland ... 131
6.2.1 Establishment of FIU Ireland ... 132
6.2.2 Role of FIU Ireland ... 135
6.2.3 Legislative Framework ... 137
6.2.4 Structure of FIU Ireland ... 139
6.2.5 Training of FIU Staff ... 140
6.3 Receipt of STRs and Other Information ... 141
6.4 Analysis of STRs and Crypto-STRs ... 148
6.4.1 International STRs ... 157
6.5 Intelligence Store ... 159
6.6 Recap of Current Situation in FIU Ireland ... 160
References ... 160

7 Analysis of Crypto-Related STRs 161
7.1 General Analysis 161
7.2 Insights from VASP Reporting of STRs 171
7.3 Insights from Crypto-STRs Submitted by Non-VASPs 174
7.4 Leading the Way: Noteworthy 2021 Crypto-STRs 175
7.5 Final Observations 179
Reference 182

8 AML Socio-Technical Systems Models 183
8.1 Socio-Technical Systems Modelling 184
8.1.1 Crypto-Laundering Socio-Technical Systems Model 185
8.1.2 FIU Ireland Socio-Technical Systems Model 192
8.2 3D Model to Understand and Address Crypto-Laundering 197
8.3 Practical Contributions 202
8.3.1 Improving Quality of Crypto-STRs 203
8.3.2 The Exploitation of Crypto-ATMs 205
8.3.3 Ransomware Investigation 207
8.3.4 Summary of Practical Contributions 209
8.4 Randomness, a New Approach? 209
8.5 General Applicability and Limitations 210
References 213

9 Conclusion and Future Directions 215
9.1 Introduction 215
9.2 Summary of Key Findings 216
9.3 Theoretical Contributions 216
9.4 Practical and Policy Implications 217
9.5 Limitations 217
9.6 Future Research Directions 218
9.7 Closing Reflection 218
References 219

Appendices 221

Glossary 245

About the Author

Steven Meighan has extensive national and international experience in the investigation of money laundering and organised crime. He was part of the Financial Action Task Force (FATF) team that undertook Indonesia's membership evaluation, with responsibility for the evaluation of their money laundering investigation and asset recovery systems. He previously served as a United Nations peacekeeper in Cyprus. His work with Europol, Interpol, and the European Commission has taken him around the world working with numerous international law enforcement and government agencies. He is a member of An Garda Síochána, was called to the Irish Bar in 2015, and holds a PhD in Anti-money Laundering.

Acronyms

AML	Anti-Money Laundering
AMLA	Anti-Money Laundering Authority (EU)
AMLD	Anti-Money Laundering Directive (EU)
AMLR	Anti-Money Laundering Regulation (EU)
BEC	Business E-mail Compromise
BO	Beneficial Owner
BZG	Byzantine Generals
CAB	Criminal Assets Bureau (Ireland)
CASP	Crypto-asset Service Provider
CBDC	Central Bank Digital Currency
CBI	Central Bank of Ireland
CDD	Customer Due Diligence
CFT	Countering the Financing of Terrorism
CSE(M)	Child Sexual Exploitation (Material)
dAPP	Decentralised Application
DeFi	Decentralised Finance
DEX	Decentralised Exchange
DLT	Distributed Ledger Technology (Blockchain)
DNFBPs	Designated Non-financial Businesses and Persons
EDD	Enhanced (Customer) Due Diligence
EU	European Union
FATF	Financial Action Task Force
FIU	Financial Intelligence Unit
FSRB	FATF-Style Regional Body
GNECB	Garda National Economic Crime Bureau (Ireland)
GST	General Systems Theory
ICT	Information and Communications Technology
IOCTA	Internet Organised Crime Threat Assessment (Europol)
IRPU	International Relations and Policy Unit (FIU Ireland)
KYC	Know Your Customer
LEA	Law Enforcement Agency

MiCA/MiCAR	Markets in Crypto-Asset Regulation (EU)
ML	Money Laundering
MLRO	Money Laundering Reporting Officer
MMORPG	Massively Multi-player Online Roleplaying Game
NFT	Non-fungible Token
OCG	Organised Crime Gang/Group (Criminal Organisation)
OSINT	Open-Source Intelligence
PEC	Privacy-Enhanced Coin
PEP	Politically Exposed Person
PF	Proliferation Financing
PNC	Police National Computer
SAR	Suspicious Activity Report
SOCTA	Serious and Organised Threat Assessment (Europol)
STR	Suspicious Transaction Report
STST	Socio-Technical Systems Theory
TF	Terrorist Financing
TFR	Transfer of Funds Regulation (EU)
TM	Transaction Monitoring
UN	United Nations
UTXO	Unspent Transaction Output
VASP	Virtual Asset Service Provider
VOIP	Voice Over Internet Protocol

Chapter 1
Introduction

1.1 The Modern Complex World

The modern world is complex. It is difficult to deconstruct and is resistant to traditional analytical methods. *Complexity* is arguably the overwhelming issue facing society in the twenty-first century. It is, inter alia, caused by:

1. The acceleration of societal changes at the global, economic, social, legal, technological, and ecological levels.
2. The increased size, interconnectivity, and diversity of the world and its inhabitants.
3. The rapid rate of continuous change.
4. The increased differentiation of society, leading to divergent stakeholder perspectives.
5. The loss of 'faith' in traditional theories and institutions such as religion, progress, economic growth, and economic theories (Reynolds and Holwell 2020).

Even well-intentioned interventions in a complex system have unintended and unpredictable consequences (Lane, 2020).

Two key drivers emerge from the discussion of complexity: *globalisation* and *technology*. The first is the process that transforms world order, turning the world into a (complex) global village through the multiplication and intensification of linkages and interconnections (Meighan, 2004, p. 14). Indisputably, *technology* amplifies and accelerates this transformation.[1] As an example, consider that

[1] Technology is "the application of scientific knowledge for practical purposes" and can be thought of as "the way humans apply science to do things or solve problems." This problem-solving is often achieved by using an *artefact*, which is defined as an "object produced or shaped by humans for a particular end and to solve a practical problem" (Oxford University Press 2022). Another useful definition of technology is the "methods, systems, and devices, which are the result of scientific knowledge being used for practical purposes" (Collins English Dictionary 2020). Both defi-

S. Meighan, *Money Laundering and Crypto-Assets*, Contributions to Finance and Accounting, https://doi.org/10.1007/978-3-032-13481-3_1

information and communications technology (ICT)[2] has become engrained in society. The world has become dependent on it in daily life, as it offers access to a global and universal communication medium (Barrett, 1997, p. 1). It affects every major institution of society (Grabosky, 1998, 2001), if not society itself.

As is readily apparent, technology can range from simple artefacts, such as hammers or microscopes, to broader *socio-technical* instances, such as *crypto-assets*, which will be introduced presently.

Important
This book adopts a socio-technical systems perspective, drawing on the foundational work of Bostrom and Heinen (1977), which views *systems* (Wiener, 1948; Von Bertalanffy, 1950, 1968; Trist and Bamforth, 1951; Boulding, 1956; Trist, 1981; Bogdanov and Dudley, 1996; Mumford, 2006; Emery, 2016) as comprised of two interdependent subsystems (Chap. 5).

The *social subsystems*—human actors, organisational roles, structures, processes, and relationships—and the *technical subsystem*—technology, tools, artefacts, workflows, and procedures.

The key principles of this approach are:

1. **Joint optimisation**: effective performance arises when both subsystems are balanced and aligned, not optimised independently (Trist and Bamforth, 1951; Bostrom and Heinen, 1977).
2. **Mutual causality**: changes in technology affect social behaviours and structures, and vice versa (Bostrom and Heinen, 1977; Mumford, 2006).
3. **Contextual adaptability**: Socio-technical systems evolve through interaction with their environment, requiring continuous realignment (Bostrom and Heinen, 1977; Mumford, 2006).

This book describes the Anti-money Laundering (AML) system, when dealing with crypto-asset-related intelligence, as an integrated socio-technical entity, operating in a much more complex environment, interacting across technological infrastructure, human agents, and regulatory frameworks.

nitions involve social and technical elements combining to solve a practical issue, which indicates that a *socio-technical* approach to understanding is required.

[2] ICT can be understood as including (1) devices such as computers and mobile phones, including the software and hardware they are made up of, (2) the tools provided by and techniques that are possible through the use of these devices, and (3) any Internet and web-based information/communications systems and protocols, including their constituent software and hardware (modernised from Meighan 2004, p. 14).

The introduction of any technology influences society, in both positive and negative ways. Gary Kasparov[3]—the chess grandmaster eventually beaten by a chess computer called *Deep Blue* (the epitome of technology?)—writes of the effect that technology has on society and how society should respond to it. His views, although given in the context of artificial intelligence, are applicable to thinking about how the emergence of any novel technology, including crypto-assets, should be interpreted:

> Every disruptive new technology, any resulting change in the dynamics of society, will produce a range of positive and negative effects that shift over time, often suddenly… You cannot discard the downsides of globalisation while keeping the benefits… Our attitude matters, and not because we can stop the march of technological progress even if we wanted to, but because our perspective on disruption affects how well prepared for it we will be. There is plenty of room between the utopian and dystopian visions of the future—which we are heading into at rapidly increasing speed. Each of us has a choice to make: to embrace new challenges, or to resist them. Will we help shape the future and set the terms of our relationship with new technology, or will we let others force the terms upon us? (Kasparov, 2018, pp. 25, 43).

Similarly, Kranzberg's first law,[4] "technology is neither good nor bad, nor is it neutral," is the most apt and interpreted for this book as meaning that technology always interacts with and affects the social ecology (Kranzberg, 1986). As technology develops, there are often environmental, social, and human consequences necessitating a socio-technical mindset to understand and evaluate. Oftentimes, these consequences go beyond the immediate purpose of the technology and can have unforeseen consequences, especially if the technology is being used in a way not intended by its creator (Kranzberg, 1986, pp. 545–546).

Combining these insights, we can say that (digital) technology is a tool that, depending on the intention of the user, can be used as easily for illicit purposes as for legitimate ones (Meighan, 2004, p. 16), a true *double-edged sword.*

> Technology can be of great benefit to society and be a force for good, *and* it can contribute to criminality that destabilises our common global security (Goodman, 2015, p. 13 emphasis added).

Technology can spur innovation, efficiency, and even improve financial inclusion, but can concurrently create new opportunities for criminals who exploit the rapid mobility of people, information, ideas, and money (Grabosky, 2001).

The potential for *cybercrime* is a negative consequence of globalisation and any emergent technology, such as *crypto-assets.*

---

[3] As an avid admirer and follower of chess, albeit a very poor player, the author is delighted to be able to bring some insight into this book from one of his favourite players. Kasparov has taken his experiences from chess and extrapolated them to many management and life scenarios in a very creative and insightful way.

[4] An American historian and technologist who wrote six laws or truisms for the study of how technological development affects sociocultural change. Despite their vintage, they are still relevant today (Sacasas, 2011; Mims, 2017; Turner, 2018).

1.2 Introducing Crypto-Assets

The discussion thus far has, in abstract terms, explored the positive and negative effects of new technology on society. The technology of particular interest to this book is *crypto-assets,*[5] and of significance is how society seeks to understand the phenomenon and regulate their usage to prevent money laundering and other types of criminality.

The first crypto-asset, *Bitcoin*, was introduced in 2009. It is a digital asset that operates on a peer-to-peer network, recording each transaction on a cryptographically secured digital ledger called a *blockchain*. Each user accesses their assets by means of a public–private pair of cryptographic keys. Transactions are verified by miners who expend massive computational power and resources, such as electricity to power and cool computers, to solve complex mathematical puzzles. Miners receive a reward, in the form of newly created assets (limited to 21 million bitcoin), and a transaction fee from the sender for their efforts. Once they are verified, transactions are added together in blocks that are joined to form a chronological, tamper-evident chain of every transaction that has ever taken place. This digital data structure, the blockchain or digital ledger, allows for transparency, security, and aspires to eliminate the need for trusted intermediaries such as banks (Nakamoto, 2008; Franco, 2015; Popper, 2016; Clohessy, 2019).

Definition Crypto-assets are private digital assets that: (1) are recorded on some form of a digital distributed ledger secured with cryptography—a blockchain, (2) are neither issued nor guaranteed by a central bank or public authority, and (3) can be used as a means of exchange and/or for investment purposes and/or to access a good or service (Houben and Snyers, 2020, p. 17). Additionally, legal definitions will be explored in later chapters.

Crypto-assets have become a global phenomenon that has emerged from obscurity to almost universal acceptance. At the time of printing, there are over 20,000 types of crypto-assets, made up of almost 19.33 million coins or tokens, trading through over 838 known exchanges, with a market capitalisation of $3.98 trillion and a daily volume of $190.96 billion. The two biggest crypto-assets are Bitcoin (the first and the most adopted) and Ethereum, with market shares of 59.9% and 12.8%, respectively. The remainder are derivatives of either Bitcoin or Ethereum.[6]

The potential benefits of crypto-assets are attractive. They are exciting and have many potentially beneficial applications, e.g. as an efficient, reliable, and cost-effective (despite rising transaction costs) international payment service that

[5] The underlying software, hardware, and ICT—together with the devices that users interact with the asset (e.g. mobile telephones, computers, Crypto-ATMs)—can be considered technological artefacts, as discussed earlier; however, for the sake of simplicity, they will be collectively referred to using the overarching term technology.

[6] See the Coin Market Cap website for the most up-to-date figures (www.coinmarketcap.com). The website was accessed on 11 August 2025 for the figures in this book.

provides increased international access to financial markets, particularly for the "unbanked" in the developing world (O'Sullivan, 2020, pp. 20–21), or they can be obtained and used for speculative and investment purposes. Aside from the economic potential, their technical capacity may extend into political, humanitarian, social, and scientific domains to address real-world problems (Swan, 2015, p. viii). However, like all technology, crypto-assets can be exploited by criminals.

1.2.1 Cybercrime

Cybercrime is the misuse or exploitation of digital technology in the planning, commissioning, or concealing of a crime. It is transnational in nature due to the inherent make-up of the underlying ICT, transcending sovereign frontiers and national law enforcement efforts (Meighan, 2004, p. 15). Technology is attractive to criminals due to:

1. The massive earning potential, with little investment of resources or knowledge.[7]
2. The perceived anonymity made possible by techniques and tools such as encryption, access control, and steganography.
3. A fast, secure, and anonymous means of communication and value transfer.
4. A perceived low chance of being detected and apprehended due to the apparent intractability of jurisdictional and enforcement issues.
5. The ubiquitous nature of the technology with the associated benefits of speed, ease of use.
6. Ready access to a global audience (Meighan 2004, p. 16).

For these reasons, criminals embrace emerging technology, frequently being the earliest adopters of it. Crypto-assets were no exception to this trend of early criminal adoption.

Traditionally, cybercrime is divided into two categories: *cyber-dependent* or *cyber-enabled crimes*. Cyber-dependent crime includes any type of crime that can be committed using ICT. The target of these crimes is the ICT itself, and without it, these crimes would be impossible to commit. The most common of these crimes today are denial of service attacks and ransomware. Conventionally, these crimes are investigated by the specialist cyber department of a police force. Cyber-enabled crimes are any traditional, real-world crime that is facilitated, and made more effective, using ICT. The technology increases the scale, speed, and reach of the crime. Examples include economic crimes such as romance scams, investment frauds, CEO frauds, and phishing. ICT can be misused by criminals to carry out social

[7] For example, crime as a service (CAAS) is readily available on the Dark Web. This allows people with no technical knowledge to purchase malicious software or other criminal services that can be easily deployed by the purchaser. Oftentimes, the provider will supply a help desk or support function if the purchaser runs into difficulties using the software. These services are usually anonymous and paid for in crypto-assets.

engineering on individuals and deceive them into providing confidential information, such as passwords and bank account details, which are later used to commit lucrative frauds. These crimes are investigated by financial investigators in a police force's economic crime department.

Unfortunately, crypto-assets can be used to procure, commit, and finance criminal activity—a phenomenon referred to as *crypto-crime*. For example, pirated content, drug trafficking, counterfeit currency, stolen credit card numbers, false documents, identity theft, child sex abuse images, human trafficking, prostitution, and crime-as-a-service are all obtainable on dark web marketplaces where crypto-assets are accepted and expected as payment (Goodman, 2015, pp. 287–327).

All crimes, traditional, cyber, or crypto, have the potential to generate significant profits for those committing them, but unfortunately for the criminal, those profits connect them to the crime that generated them. To avoid adverse law enforcement attention, a method is required to break that linkage. That method is *money laundering*.

Before discussing money laundering, one final distinction needs to be made. The cross-cutting nature of crypto-assets and their criminal ubiquity has shifted the traditional cybercrime dichotomy. When discussing crypto-crime, the crimes need to be divided into *off-chain* or *on-chain*. On-chain refers to any activity within the crypto-asset system, while off-chain refers to anything in the real world. For example, off-chain refers to criminal activity that is committed traditionally, and the criminal proceeds can be subsequently converted into crypto-assets to be laundered. Conversely, on-chain activity can refer to when the proceeds of a wide spectrum of cyber-criminality are received in the form of crypto-assets; therefore, they do not have to be converted from fiat currency to be laundered. This distinction is important as on-chain activities are pseudonymous yet transparent and traceable, while off-chain activity requires traditional investigative methods. In many cases, criminals adopt a hybrid strategy—conducting crimes off-chain and then using on-chain transfers to obscure the criminal origin of the funds—meaning law enforcement must embrace both domains and challenge the traditional investigative dichotomy.

On-chain activity is interesting as, for the first time, reasonably reliable estimates of the amount of crime can be made by the private companies operating in the blockchain analysis space (see Chap. 3).

1.3 Money Laundering

Money laundering, in its broadest sense, is the process by which criminals legitimise "dirty" money, generated as profit from organised or regular crime (referred to as *predicate offences*), by exploiting the normal, legitimate business channels (adapted from Martin, 2009, p. 357). Money laundering is a worldwide, transnational crime that has the potential to negatively affect the integrity of the business and financial services marketplace, dampen the economic development of a country, and potentially cause further damage to society at large and the rule of law by allowing crime to go unpunished (Financial Action Task Force, 2020). While traditional criminality operates in the shadows of the physical world and in the dark corners of the financial system, cyber-criminality and new digitally enabled forms of crime operate in ways that challenge the study of these phenomena and their prevention and detection. The exploitation of crypto-assets plays an important role in facilitating the transfer of criminal profits across all cybercrime areas. Crypto-assets have become the de facto method of victim-to-criminal payments in ransomware and exploitation schemes, as well as criminal-to-criminal payments on the dark web (Europol, 2020). With this change, criminals are using a crypto-asset specific variant of cyber-money laundering, namely *crypto-laundering*, i.e. laundering the proceeds of crime through crypto-related digital assets.

Definition Crypto-laundering is the process by which criminal assets are laundered through the medium of crypto-assets.

To address crypto-laundering, a regulatory *intervention* is required, namely anti-money laundering (AML). Effectively addressing crypto-laundering involves integrated socio-technical strategies combining regulatory tools, blockchain analytics, and public–private collaboration.

1.4 Anti-Money Laundering

New digital technology, therefore, requires intervention in the form of regulation to protect society from the harmful effects of its illicit use. The regulation of any new technology, especially technology being manipulated for cyber-criminality, is challenging. Organisations in civil society are attracted to the benefits of the new technology but grapple with understanding it, especially how it is being (ab)used by criminals. Society often initially ignores the problem and is only spurred into action when the misuse becomes too ostensible to ignore. Regulation and law enforcement awareness, training, and capability eventually catch up to the pace of technological development, some individual "victories" are achieved by civil society, but criminal actors rapidly adapt to exploit newly emergent vulnerabilities in the regulatory environment, thus continuing the cycle ad infinitum. Regulation can be seen merely as a disruptor that leads to displacement or the use of newer (better, more secure, and privacy-enhanced) technology. This process plays out with all technology and can be perceived as the interplay of technology, organisations, regulation, and policing that together create a complex *cycle of criminality* (Fig. 1.1).

In essence, and consistent with the basic concepts of systems theory, there is a complex and dynamic interplay between various systems and their evolving environment, especially regarding emerging technology. Kasparov suggests that addressing complex issues, such as the regulation of technology, requires a societal effort to work together to achieve something difficult. He calls this a *Sputnik*

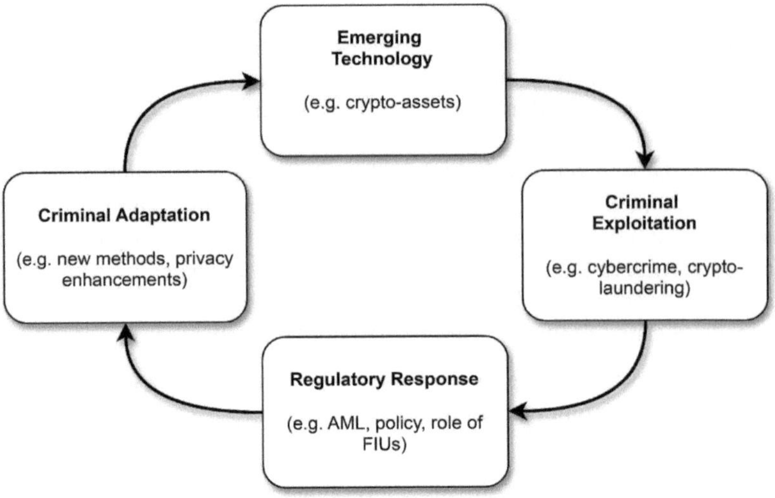

Fig. 1.1 Technology-crime-regulation cycle

moment,[8] which is a "transformative effort on a global scale requiring the focused minds of politicians, business leaders, and a plurality of citizens to support it" with the necessity of "government regulation that promotes innovation instead of trying to limit it" (Kasparov, 2018, pp. 44–45).

Definition *Anti-money laundering* (AML) is the series of preventative and repressive measures put in place by governments, in cooperation with international organisations and private entities, which aim to prevent, disrupt, detect, and prosecute money laundering. Ideally, money laundering investigations should be carried out, by appropriately trained specialist investigators, in parallel with the investigation of the underlying predicate offences that generated the proceeds of crime. The goal of such investigations is the confiscation of the criminal's ill-gotten gains to deny them their enjoyment or prevent the reinvestment into further and more harmful criminality.

At the heart of any AML system is a country's financial intelligence unit (FIU). The FIU is the central, national agency responsible for receiving, requesting, and analysing disclosures of *financial intelligence* by private entities concerning suspected money laundering, which are developed into actionable intelligence for law enforcement (The Egmont Group, 2020). The FIU is therefore a crucial link between private entities and law enforcement, responsible for gathering disparate data from multiple sources into a usable intelligence package (information) for investigators.

[8] Or, from an American perspective, the Apollo Moon Programme initiated by President John F. Kennedy in 1962 (see, for example: https://spacecenter.org/this-day-in-history-jfk-delivers-iconic-we-choose-to-go-to-the-moon-speech/, accessed: 21 August 2025).

Important *Financial Intelligence* refers to information about a person, their financial activities and assets, and any suspected links to criminality. It is gathered by private sector organisations that are obliged to conduct due diligence and transaction monitoring of their customers. Where activity is considered suspicious, it is sent to and processed by FIUs that collect, analyse, and disseminate financial data to detect criminality and money laundering.

Collection: FIUs receive Suspicious Transaction/Activity Reports (STRs/SARs) and other data from obliged entities.

Analysis: FIUs use a variety of techniques and multiple data sources to re-establish the triparty person–property–crime relationship that the laundering process attempted to obscure.

Dissemination: Intelligence packages are reported to law enforcement and supervisory bodies.

FIUs function as the central connection within the socio-technical AML system and the primary processors of *financial intelligence*.

This book is one of the few that enjoyed unrestricted access—albeit subject to some reporting constraints due to confidentiality, security, and data protection legislation—to data, processes, and documentation within the FIU as the author was an embedded practitioner–researcher, working in a senior position in the Irish FIU whilst undertaking this research at a time of significant regulatory change.

The efforts to combat money laundering over the past 40 years through international organisations including, inter alia, the Financial Action Task Force (FATF) and the European Union (EU) can be viewed as a *Sputnik-like* collective effort. Whether all participants are willing and fully engaged in the task, and what its overall effectiveness is remains unclear, especially when addressing crypto-laundering using traditional banking and business rules.

Unfortunately, criminals have shown themselves to be extremely imaginative in creating new money laundering schemes to circumvent the AML system. To counteract this ongoing threat, the AML system *should* be sufficiently agile to detect such changes and respond appropriately (Financial Action Task Force, 2020), but is it? Due to the emergence of crypto-laundering as a criminal phenomenon to launder the proceeds of cyber and regular crime through the medium of crypto-assets, new regulation was required to expand the scope of the AML system to bring crypto-assets into their remit. Demetis and Angell (2006) rightly argue that the introduction of any new technology to the AML domain is a "systemic risk, inherently problematic and must be recognised as non-trivial", further increasing the complexity of the issue, a truly *wicked problem.*

1.5 A Wicked Problem

Crypto-assets also have the potential to change the very nature of money, a common element of money laundering and AML, and the global financial system. The FATF (2020) estimates that digital transactions are rising by 12.7% annually and account for approximately 60% of the global GDP.

This is significant as it (potentially) encompasses the disintermediation of traditional financial intermediaries such as banks and allows for transactions to occur without the need for human intervention, a central control of the current AML systems (Clohessy, 2019, pp. 7–8). *Know your customer* (KYC) and *customer due diligence* (CDD), two of the key AML approaches, are potentially rendered redundant as all communication is at a distance without physical interactions. In response, financial and credit institutions turn to technology in the battle against money laundering and crypto-laundering. Onboarding, transaction monitoring, and the identification of Suspicious Transaction/Activity Reports (STRs/SARs) are now often computerised processes utilising artificial intelligence and other machine learning techniques. Consequently, this has led to an increase in the number of STRs/SARs filed with FIUs, making the identification of actual money laundering even more difficult. Again, technology and its regulation are a complex issue akin to a proverbial double-edged sword.

Given these issues, we can say that the regulation of crypto-assets to combat their misuse by criminals, i.e. *understanding and addressing crypto-laundering*, can be considered a complex or wicked problem. Midgley (2021) describes these matters as consisting of the following elements:

1. There are many interlinked issues, cutting across silos, e.g. economy, politics, law, making for a high degree of complexity.
2. There are multiple agencies involved, across the public, private, and voluntary sectors, trying to account for multiple scales (local, regional, national, and global).
3. There are many different views on the problem and potential *solutions.*[9]
4. There is conflict over desired outcomes or the means to achieve them, and power relations make change difficult.
5. There is uncertainty about the possible effects of action.

[9] The very concept of solution itself is problematic as solutions in turn can become the basis for even more decisions to solve, leading to more problems, ad infinitum (Demetis, 2010, pp. 39–40). Solutions always seem to "multiply, proliferate, disperse, circulate, diversify, and diffuse the original problem" (Rossbach, 1993).

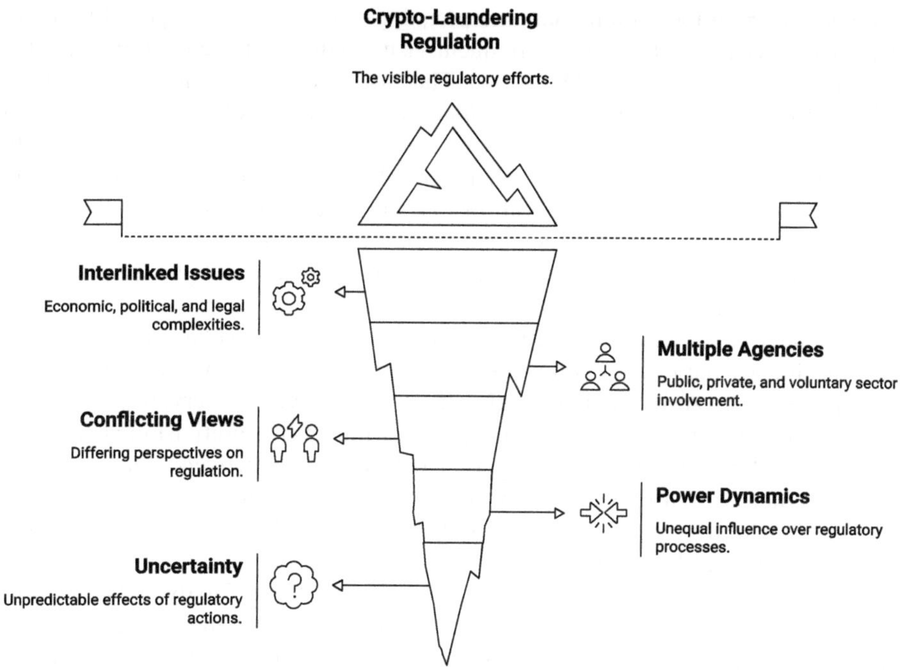

Fig. 1.2 Crypto-laundering regulation as a wicked problem

Cabrera and Cabrera agree by stating that wicked problems are caused by complexity; many interdependencies, multiple people involved, with much disagreement on the problem and possible "solutions", and a lack of reliable information (2018, p. 15). Fig. 1.2 shows the scale of difficulty in addressing crypto-laundering diagrammatically.

What is therefore required is a way for understanding the world to make effective strategic decisions to understand and manage its complexity (Reynolds and Holwell, 2020, p. ix). This book provides one such way to examine the effect that crypto-asset technology is having on the regulation of money laundering by organising *crypto-laundering* (as a criminal phenomenon) and its *pursuit and detection* (i.e. AML, with a focus on the role of the FIU) as complex, interacting socio-technical systems that exist in and are heavily influenced by their dynamic, complex environment (Angell and Demetis, 2005; Demetis, 2010).

1.6 Book Outline

Today's systems researchers are faced with complex and intertwined socio-technical structures which are difficult to grasp and understand (Walsham, 1995, p. 75; Jackson, 2019, 2020). To make sense of this complexity, researchers have adopted approaches which focus on human interpretations and meanings, especially the in-depth case study, which "involves frequent visits to the field site over an extended period of time" (Walsham, 1995, p. 74). The case study is considered particularly suitable for research involving a *practitioner–researcher* which the author was as a senior manager in the FIU during the research (Saunders et al., 2009; Creswell, 2013). Interpretative case studies, when carried out and written up carefully, can make a valuable contribution to both theory and practice (Walsham, 1995, p. 80) and can help researchers to understand human thought and action in social and organisational contexts, with the potential to produce deep insights into systems phenomena (Klein and Myers, 1999, p. 67).

The underlying theoretical scaffold of this book is *socio-technical systems theory*, specifically the intersection of management and technology, while its domain of exploration is AML, and the technology under review is crypto-assets. The research was based on a realist ontology, following an interpretivist epistemology (Walsham, 1995, 2006; Klein and Myers, 1999) with an inductive/deductive double loop of reflective reasoning (Dewey, 1910) that is theoretically underpinned by socio-technical systems theory (Trist and Bamforth, 1951; Bostrom and Heinen, 1977; Trist, 1981; Mumford, 2006; Emery, 2016).

There were two main primary data sources for this book. Firstly, a dataset containing the 2719 anonymised crypto-STRs received by FIU Ireland in 2021 that concerned suspected crypto-laundering. Secondly, several semi-structured interviews and focus groups were conducted to capture individuals' experiences and develop themes that assist in the interpretation of the data collected. The secondary sources utilised included AML legislation, FATF and Central Bank of Ireland documentation, and various internal procedure and process manuals.

The central research question and purpose of this case study research is to understand crypto-laundering and how crypto-assets are regulated for the purposes of AML using a socio-technical systems view of FIU Ireland. The case study research period was September 2020 to March 2023, which covered the period immediately before and immediately after the AML regulation of crypto-assets was introduced. Ireland is a suitable site for study as it is a member of the EU, the FATF, and is a recognised hub for fintech (digital technology supporting banking and financial services) innovation. Arising from the central research question, several theoretical contributions are anticipated:

1. The development of a socio-technical systems model of the crypto-laundering phenomenon.
2. The development of a socio-technical systems model describing how crypto-laundering is pursued and detected.
3. Examining how these two models, interact together and with their complex environment, and considering whether a unified or combined model to capture the crime and its detection is more appropriate.

This book can be considered to be divided into three parts: foundations, the evolution of AML systems, and the case study and its analysis.

This short chapter introduced the research topic underlying the book, set out some key definitions, justified the need for research on the topic, and set out the research questions. Each subsequent chapter progressively builds an integrated understanding of crypto-laundering and AML anchored in socio-technical systems thinking.

Chapter 2 (*The Evolution of the Global AML System*) explores the nature of money laundering and its regulation by means of anti-money laundering (AML) rules. It looks at the development of AML over the past 40 years through international, supranational, and national analysis. This hierarchical approach allows the main organisations at each level—the United Nations (UN), the Financial Action Task Force (FATF), and the European Union—to be introduced, and their AML impact explored. This three-level analysis is followed throughout the book when discussing major topics of interest, such as crypto-asset regulation (Chap. 4) and FIU requirements (Chap. 6). The chapter continues by setting out an indicative or model National AML system that each and every country is obliged to establish according to the soft-law requirements set by the UN, the FATF, and, where applicable, the EU. The chapter concludes by highlighting some of the current challenges of the current AML system.

Chapter 3 (Crypto-assets: Technology, Adoption, and Criminal Exploitation) explores the changing nature of money and the circumstances which allowed crypto-assets to emerge from obscurity to almost universal acceptance. It then highlights some of the specific crypto-crimes that can be committed through the misuse of crypto-assets, before concluding with an introduction to the concept of crypto-laundering, the cyber-enabled variant of money laundering through the medium of crypto-assets.

Chapter 4 (*Regulating Crypto-Assets: AML Frameworks and Enforcement*) focuses on the regulatory response put in place to prevent, detect, disrupt, and investigate crypto-laundering. It does this through the three-level approach previously taken, namely international, supranational, and national. It concludes by providing an overview of the investigation powers provided for crypto-laundering investigations and some of the many challenges faced by investigators.

Chapter 5 (*Socio-Technical Systems Theory in AML Context*) sets out the theoretical framework used in this book, namely socio-technical systems theory, and defends the choices taken from among the many alternatives used by other researchers to examine the AML domain. This chapter will be a natural extension of the preceding literature chapters and will detail the theories and concepts used to address or make sense of the research question under investigation. One of the major outputs from this chapter, and this book, will be a novel, combined systems model to illustrate a complex phenomenon or organisation on both the macro- and micro-levels.

Chapter 6 (*The Case of FU Ireland*) introduces the case study of the Irish FIU, which is sensitised by socio-technical systems theory so that the disparate data collected through observations, interviews, focus groups, and document analysis can be considered together. The chapter concludes by pulling together some of the key findings that emerge from the specific case described.

Chapter 7 (*Analysis of Crypto-Related STRs*) describes the exploration of the 2719 crypto-STRs received by FIU Ireland in 2021. This gives a unique perspective on how crypto-laundering and the misuse of crypto-assets is perceived and reported by the private sector entities obliged to report the suspicious activity of their customers. The access to this level of data was unprecedented, given the usual secrecy of the FIU. It also offers a unique window as it straddles the introduction of crypto-asset regulation in Ireland.

Chapter 8 (*AML Socio-Technical Systems Models*) builds upon the case study described in Chap. 7. Further analysis allows for the development of two customised, equivalent, and structurally coupled theoretical frameworks in the socio-technical tradition to represent the phenomenon being studied, crypto-laundering, as well as its pursuit and detection from the perspective of the FIU. These models will be described using the combined model developed in Chap. 5. To help reflect on the interacting components of the two models and how they interact with each other and with the wider environment, a 3-D version of the combined model will be described. This will be another of the major outputs of this book and will allow complex phenomena or organisations to be explored as structurally coupled systems. This approach will allow further inductive progression to identify patterns and theoretical dimensions/abstractions.

Chapter 9 (*Conclusion and Future* Directions) closes the book and provides some final observations, discusses the limitations of the research, and offers some suggestions for further research.

Go n-eirí an bóthar leo! (A traditional Irish greeting literally translated as "May the road rise up to meet us" or good luck to us all on our journey together).

References

Angell I, Demetis D (2005) Systems thinking about anti-money laundering: considering the Greek case. J Money Launder Control 8:271–284

Barrett N (1997) Digital crime, policing the cybernation. Kogan Page Ltd, London

Bogdanov A, Dudley P (1996) Bogdanov's Tektology: 1996. Centre for Systems Studies, University of Hull

Bostrom RP, Heinen JS (1977) MIS problems and failures: a socio-technical perspective, part II: the application of socio-technical theory. MIS Q 1:11–28

Boulding KE (1956) General systems theory—the skeleton of science. Manag Sci 2:197–208

Clohessy T (2019) Blockchain: the business perspective. NovoRay, Galway

Collins English Dictionary (2020) Technologies definition and meaning. https://www.collinsdictionary.com/dictionary/english/technologies. Accessed 21 Aug 2025

Creswell JW (2013) Qualitative inquiry and research design: choosing among five approaches, 3rd edn. SAGE Publications, Los Angeles

Demetis D (2010) Technology and anti-money laundering: a systems theory and risk-based approach. Edward Elgar, Cheltenham

Demetis DS, Angell IO (2006) AML-related technologies: a systemic risk. J Money Launder Control 9:157–172. https://doi.org/10.1108/13685200610660970

Dewey J (1910) How we think. D. C. Heath, Lexington, MA

Emery F (2016) Characteristics of socio-technical systems. In: The social engagement of social science, a Tavistock anthology, Volume 2. University of Pennsylvania Press, pp 157–186
Europol (2020) Internet Organised Crime Threat Assessment. European Union Agency for Law Enforcement Cooperation, The Hague
FATF (2020) 12 month review of the revised FATF standards on virtual assets and virtual asset service providers. FATF-GAFI, Paris
Financial Action Task Force (2020) Money laundering. FATF-GAFI
Franco P (2015) Understanding bitcoin: cryptography, engineering and economics. Wiley, West Sussex
Goodman M (2015) Future crimes: everything is connected, everyone in vulnerable and what we can do about it. Corgi, London
Grabosky P (1998) Crime in cyberspace. In: Combating transnational crime: Concepts, activities and responses, pp 195–208
Grabosky PN (2001) Virtual criminality: old wine in new bottles? Soc Leg Stud 10:243–249
Houben DR, Snyers A (2020) Crypto-assets–Key developments, regulatory concerns and responses. 77
Jackson M (2020) Critical systems practice and Covid-19 in the UK: diagnosing a lack of resilience in the health system
Jackson MC (2019) Critical systems thinking and the management of complexity: responsible leadership for a complex world. Wiley Blackwell, Hoboken, NJ
Kasparov G (2018) Deep thinking: where machine intelligence ends and human creativity begins, 1st edn. John Murray
Klein HK, Myers MD (1999) A set of principles for conducting and evaluating interpretive field studies in information systems. MIS Q 23:67–93
Kranzberg M (1986) Technology and History: "Kranzberg's Laws.". Technol Cult 27:544–560. https://doi.org/10.2307/3105385
Lane O (2020) Mastering systems theory in practice. Open University
Martin EA (2009) Oxford dictionary of law, 7th edn. Oxford University Press, Oxford
Meighan S (2004) Ireland's response to internet child pornography: a critical examination. In: M.Sc. In international police science. University of Portsmouth
Midgley G (2021) An Introduction to Systems Thinking for Tackling Wicked Problems
Mims C (2017) The six Laws of technology everyone should know. Wall Street J
Mumford E (2006) The story of socio-technical design: reflections on its successes, failures and potential. Inf Syst J 16:317–342
Nakamoto S (2008) Bitcoin: a peer-to-peer electronic cash system. 9
O'Sullivan J (2020) After the gold rush. Gazette Law Soc 114:20–25
Oxford University Press (2022) English dictionary (online). Oxford University Press
Popper N (2016) Digital gold: the untold story of bitcoin. Penguin
Reynolds M, Holwell S (2020) Systems approaches to making change: a practical guide, 2nd edn. Springer
Rossbach S (1993) The Author's Care of Himself on Friedrich Nietzsche, Michel Foucault, and Niklas Luhmann. European University Insitute, Florence
Sacasas LM (2011) Kranzberg's six Laws of technology, a metaphor, and a story. In: L.M. Sacasas. https://thefrailestthing.com/2011/08/25/kranzbergs-six-laws-of-technology-a-metaphor-and-a-story/. Accessed 21 Aug 2025
Saunders MNK, Lewis P, Thornhill A (2009) Research methods for business students, 5th edn. Prentice Hall, New York
Swan M (2015) Blockchain: blueprint for a new economy, 1st edn. O'Reilly, California
The Egmont Group (2020) Financial Intelligence Units (FIUs). https://egmontgroup.org/en/content/financial-intelligence-units-fius. Accessed 21 Aug 2025
Trist EL (1981) The evolution of socio-technical systems. Ontario Quality of Working Life Centre, Toronto

Trist EL, Bamforth KW (1951) Some social and psychological consequences of the longwall method of coal-getting: an examination of the psychological situation and defences of a work group in relation to the social structure and technological content of the work system. Hum Relat 4:3–38

Turner N (2018) Is Kranzberg Still Right? https://web.colby.edu/st112a2018/2018/02/13/is-kranzberg-still-right/. Accessed 21 Aug 2025

Von Bertalanffy L (1950) An outline of general system theory. British Journal for the Philosophy of science, Br J Philos Sci

Von Bertalanffy L (1968) General system theory: foundations, development, applications. G. Braziller

Walsham G (1995) Interpretive case studies in is research: nature and method. Eur J Inf Syst; Abingdon 4:

Walsham G (2006) Doing interpretive research. Eur J Inf Syst 15:320–330

Wiener N (1948) Cybernetics or control and communication in the animal and the machine. Technology Press

Chapter 2
The Evolution of the Global AML System

Activities such as drug trafficking, economic crime, cybercrime, and most other serious offences have the potential to generate enormous amounts of illicit proceeds for those that perpetrate them (Government of Ireland 2016; Conteh 2018, pp. 2–4). It is an often overlooked truism that criminals engage in crime because of the *profits* their illegal activities generate (Newburn 2017; Cassara 2020, pp. 2–3). For the most part, the aim and motivation for committing these *predicate offences*[1] is not the guilty act itself, but greed for the money that is generated, and a thirst for the subsequent opportunities that come from the purchasing power of the *dirty* money. The proceeds of crime enable criminals to enjoy lavish lifestyles—well beyond their legitimate means—and cause further harm to society by enabling additional criminality. In that manner, money serves as the lifeblood of organised crime groups (OCGs).

However, the dirty money links back to its illicit origins, potentially exposing its possessor to criminal investigation, prosecution, imprisonment, and asset forfeiture. For criminals and organised crime groups, this unwanted state attention can disrupt and dismantle their criminal enterprises. Therefore, from the criminal perspective, a process to legitimise dirty money and give it the *appearance* of legitimacy is required (Stessens 2000, p. 16; Martin 2009, p. 357; OECD 2009, pp. 11–13). That process is known as money laundering. Until 40 years ago, money laundering went virtually unchecked. A collective effort between the public and private sectors, at international and national levels, introduced anti-money laundering (AML) to challenge the pretentious legitimacy of dirty money and address societal concerns about the corrosive effect of organised crime.

Section 2.1 introduces the topic of money laundering, its methods and processes, and why society must act against it. Section 2.2 explains the regulation of money

[1] A predicate offence is any crime that generates money or assets which subsequently must be laundered in order to make them appear legitimate.

S. Meighan, *Money Laundering and Crypto-Assets*, Contributions to Finance and Accounting, https://doi.org/10.1007/978-3-032-13481-3_2

laundering and the system put in place to protect society and the legitimate financial systems.

2.1 Money Laundering

Money laundering is the illegal process of making dirty money generated from criminal activity appear to have come from a legitimate source. This *cleaning* or *laundering* uses the legitimate financial and business system—including the professions that work in and around it, referred to as designated non-financial businesses and professionals (DNFBPs)—to break the link between the money and the criminality that generated it. This allows the criminal to enjoy the fruits of their ill-gotten gains or reinvest them in crime without adverse attention from the state (Walsh 1999, pp. 204, 212, 216; Schott 2006, pp. I1–7).[2] Money launderers "succeed largely to the extent that they are able to conceal the criminal origins of their money and sanitise it by moving it through national and international financial systems" (Schott 2006, pp. I1–I2; OECD 2009, p. 15).

A succinct definition of money laundering is:

> the process of creating the appearance that money, which was obtained from criminal conduct, originated from a legitimate source. It involves a practice of engaging in financial transactions to conceal the identity, source, or destination of the proceeds of crime, either to disguise the fact that the property is the proceeds of crime or to obscure the true beneficial owner of it (Horan 2011, p. 23.01).

A more granular definition is doing one of the following three distinct, alternative acts:

> (1) the conversion or transfer of funds, knowing that such property represents the proceeds of crime, (2) the concealment or disguise of the true nature, location, movement, or ownership of or rights with respect to property, knowing that such property is the proceeds of crime, or (3) the acquisition, possession or use of property, knowing that, at the time of receipt, that such property is the proceeds of crime (Connell 2018, p. 71).

Practically speaking, money laundering is doing one of these three acts with property that represents, directly or indirectly, the proceeds of crime. Of course, to be guilty of an offence of money laundering, one must have the requisite *mens rea* or guilty mind, namely knowing, believing, or being reckless as to whether the property is actually the proceeds of crime (see Meighan 2025).

In Ireland, money laundering first became a criminal offence with the enactment of the *Criminal Justice Act, 1994*. The current legal definition was created by Section 7of the *Criminal Justice (Money Laundering and Terrorist Financing) Act, 2010*, which states that:

> A person commits an offence if:

[2] Indeed, some criminals have been known to happily pay legitimate tax to clean their dirty assets, which may be considered a small price to pay.

(a) The person engages in any of the following acts in relation to *property*[3] that is the *proceeds of criminal conduct*[4]:
   (i) Concealing or disguising the true nature, source, location, disposition, movement or ownership of the property, or any rights relating to the property
   (ii) Converting, transferring, handling, acquiring, possessing or using the property
   (iii) Removing the property from, or bringing the property into, the state

(b) The person knows or believes (or is reckless as to whether or not) the property is the proceeds of criminal conduct

In effect, there is a three-way relationship between the person doing one of three acts with property that is generated, directly or indirectly, by the crime (Fig. 2.1). These links are what the criminal hopes the money laundering process will obliterate, while the criminal investigator hopes to discover using a *follow-the-money* approach. In effect, there are two opposing processes occurring, depending on the perspective taken, which shows the duality and structural coupling of two complex phenomena or systems (Chap. 5).

2.1.1 Categories of Money Laundering

There are three broad categories of money laundering, dependent on how closely the person laundering the property is connected to the predicate offence. They are:

1. *Third-party money laundering*—the laundering of proceeds by a person who was not involved in the commission of the predicate offence.

Fig. 2.1 Money laundering tri-party link

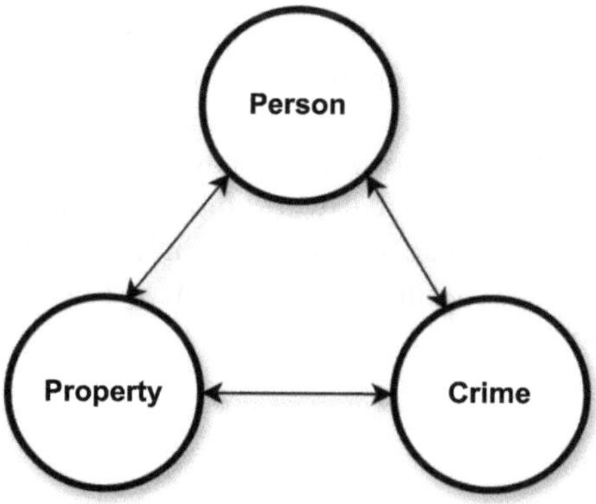

[3] *Property* means all real or personal property, whether heritable or moveable, and includes money, choses in action, and any other intangible or incorporeal property (Section 2, Criminal Justice (Money Laundering and Terrorist Financing) Act, 2010 as amended).

[4] *Proceeds of criminal conduct* means any property that is derived from or obtained through criminal conduct, whether directly or indirectly, or in whole or in part (ibid., Section 6). In Ireland, every criminal offence is a predicate offence for money laundering.

2. *Self-laundering*—the laundering of proceeds by a person who was involved in the commission of the predicate offence.
3. *Stand-alone money laundering*—the prosecution of money laundering offences independently without prosecuting the predicate offence.

The final category could be particularly relevant when there is insufficient evidence of the particular predicate offence—but there must be some criminality evident—that gives rise to the criminal proceeds, or in situations where there is a lack of territorial jurisdiction over the predicate offence or offences (Financial Action Task Force 2019a, p. 116).

2.1.2 Three Stages of Money Laundering

Money laundering is generally described using a clichéd, but universally advanced, three-stage model as shown in Fig. 2.2 (Martin 2009, p. 357; OECD 2009, pp. 11–17). The funds are introduced into the legitimate business and financial system (*Placement*), creating a complex set of transactions that obfuscate the link with the illicit source of the funds (*Layering*), and making the funds appear to be from a legitimate source or business (*Integration*). The integration phase may be further divided into two sub-phases: justification (creating an apparent legal origin for the criminal proceeds) and investment (using the criminal proceeds for personal benefit). Once the *dirty* money has been *cleaned*, the criminal is free to enjoy the fruits of their criminality or to reinvest in further criminal enterprises. This re-entry to crime is important as it is the primary mechanism of why crime pays, and how it gains its sustainability (OECD 2009, p. 13; Demetis 2010, pp. 11–12).

While this model is a generally accepted but simplistic representation of a complex phenomenon, it has been criticised by many for failing to consider the reality of the phenomenon and of white-collar crime types such as VAT carousel frauds and crypto-asset investment scams (Bakowski 2012, p. 2). Walsh argues, quite rightly, that the traditional three-stage model does not represent the non-linear and contingent nature of real-world money laundering, for example money may already be in the legitimate system, criminals may immediately consume their profits, or they may be comingling with enterprises that have substantial cash revenues (1999, pp. 206–208).

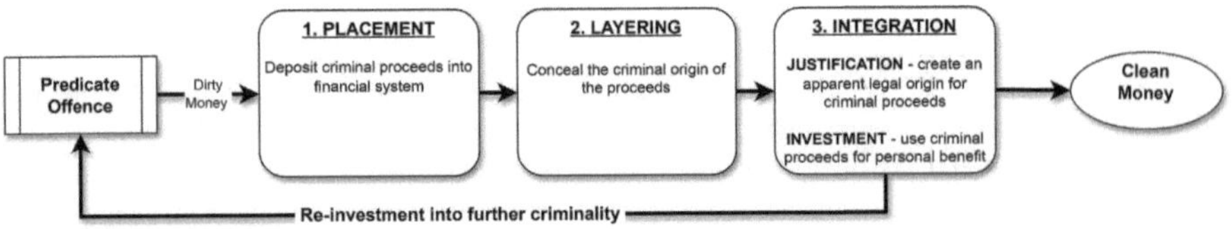

Fig. 2.2 Traditional three-stage money laundering process

Various authors have speculated about which is the most effective stage of the money laundering process to focus law enforcement resources on. For example, Handoll (as cited in Stessens 2000, p. 146) argues that enforcement should be concentrated on the placement stage, while Duff (2019, p. 85) argues that, due to the shortcomings of the three-stage model in describing real-world money laundering, the other stages should receive more focus than they do. In reality, and more accurately, money laundering transactions cannot easily be distinguished from the millions of similar transactions or transfers of value. This is what criminals desire: to be the so-called illegal *needle* hidden in the giant *haystack* of near-identical legitimate transactions. What makes a transaction money laundering is if its origin is criminal in nature. Likewise, for terrorist financing and proliferation financing (Sect. 2.1.7), the destination or usage is what distinguishes these from their legitimate counterparts. The fact that nearly every transaction is identical is what makes detecting money laundering and terrorist financing so difficult. How do we pick out the illegal transaction when they all look nearly identical?

2.1.3 The Corrosive Effect of Money Laundering

Money laundering is recognised as "an important contemporary phenomenon and a challenging problem area, with few prosecutions and convictions" (Demetis 2010, p. 1). It is a worldwide, transnational crime that has the potential to affect the integrity of the business and financial services marketplace negatively, dampen the economic development of a country, and potentially cause further damage to and corrupt society at large by allowing crime to go unpunished (Stessens 2000; Schott 2006; Bakowski 2012; Terry and Robles 2018, p. 630; Duff 2019, p. 90; Financial Action Task Force 2020a; Rae 2020; Al-Tawil and Younies 2021).

The effect of money laundering on a nation state can lead to imbalances in the exchange rate, increased crime and corruption, a bad international reputation affecting trade and foreign investment, and a negative effect on international banking relationships (Schott 2006, Chap. 3; Forsman 2020, p. 26). According to the International Monetary Fund (IMF), money laundering can result in the discouragement of foreign investment and can distort international capital flows.

> This can result in substantive welfare losses, the draining of resources from more productive economic activities, and can even have de-stabilising effects on other countries. This means that money laundering is a direct threat to the integrity and stability of the financial sector and the economy as a whole and must be treated as such (Connell 2018, p. 71).

Nigeria in the early 2000s is a prime example of the corrosive effect that money laundering has on civil society. Due to large-scale corruption and money laundering, it experienced negative attitudes of other countries, undermining the integrity of the financial and private sectors, loss of control of national economic policy, economic distortion, and loss of revenue (Inter-Governmental Action Group against Money Laundering in West Africa 2008; Aluko and Bagheri 2012).

There are many socially important reasons to understand and combat money laundering, namely to: identify tax crimes, identify other crimes and criminals, demonstrate to the public that crime is being addressed, and locate and confiscate criminal assets (OECD 2009, pp. 15–16; Duff 2019, p. 88; Forsman 2020, p. 26). Also, money laundering is a criminal offence that must be prevented, detected, disrupted, and prosecuted by the authorities to maintain faith in the rule of law and the legal system (see generally Bingham 2011). The suppression of money laundering also disrupts the benefits of money being available to criminals to reinvest in further criminality. For these reasons, money laundering features highly on the international and domestic political agenda (Stessens 2000, pp. xiii, 90).

2.1.4 The Scale of Money Laundering

Nobody knows the size and scale of the problem of money laundering. Because of its secretive, illegal, and hidden nature, money laundering is an activity carried out by criminals outside the scope of regular economic, financial, and statistical measurement, albeit some stages of the process necessarily converge with the formal economic system.

The aim of money laundering is to get the dirty money deeper into the legitimate financial system, making it more difficult to find its origin and classify it accordingly. These basic facts make it an extremely difficult task to estimate the amount of money that is laundered each year (Schott 2006, p. I–6; Financial Action Task Force 2020a; UNODC 2021). Initially, when money laundering was defined solely in relation to profits from drug trafficking, the scale was approximated on the estimated size of the drug market; guesses upon guesses using figures from hidden black or grey economies. As the scope of predicate offences captured by the money laundering definition increased, coupled with the distorting effect that money laundering may have on some economic indicators, the task of measurement went beyond our capacity to estimate it (Demetis 2010, pp. 13–16; Terry and Robles 2018, pp. 630–634). What we have are some rough estimates of the scale of the activity made by international organisations such as the United Nations Office on Drugs and Crime (UNODC) and the IMF, for example. They estimate the range of money laundered per year to be between $600 billion and $2 trillion US dollars in monetary terms, or the often-touted metric of 2–5% of Global GDP (Demetis 2010, p. 13; Bakowski 2012, p. 1; Financial Action Task Force 2020a; UNODC 2021). For Ireland, with a 2024 GDP of approximately €538 billion, the figures could be extremely large and worrying (Central Statistics Office 2025). Anecdotally, some claim that money laundering is the world's third-largest market (see for example Robinson 1995). However, such figures and opinions need to be treated with extreme caution as precise statistics are very difficult to produce for the reasons discussed above and the illegal, hidden nature of the phenomenon (Business Insider 2011; Financial Action Task Force 2020a).

Nevertheless, it is well accepted that the scale of money laundering is sufficiently large to require action to be taken to mitigate its negative effects. Another issue with our inability to know the scale of the problem is outlined by Pol, who argues that the paucity of credible data about the scale and scope makes it difficult to measure the effectiveness of any policies introduced to address the perceived problem (2019, p. 838). Beyond the scope of this research but a hot topic among certain financial institutions is the often cited complaint about the cost of mitigation measures being higher than the real (monetary) "damage" caused by money laundering (see for example Saperstein et al. 2015). Logically, the size of the money laundering market increases as wider-ranging predicate offences are added to the definition of money laundering, albeit there may be increases and decreases in the amount of money laundered from different crime areas over time (Demetis 2010, p. 13; Unger 2013, p. 658). The position taken in this book is that, despite not knowing the size of the problem, it is a significant societal problem deserving of our attention, even more so considering the effect of technological advances such as crypto-assets.

2.1.5 Money Laundering Methods and Processes

There are myriad ways that criminals commit money laundering, ranging from small cash deposits in unremarkable bank accounts to the purchase of luxury items or property. It is a constantly changing criminal phenomenon, with updated *modus operandi* and business models (Schott 2006, pp. I9–I10; Demetis 2010, pp. 11–12; van Wegberg et al. 2018, p. 421; Foley et al. 2019, pp. 3–4). For example, money can be laundered by OCGs purchasing exclusive London properties through (criminal) special purpose vehicles that operate through the exclusive, elite private banking system (see for example Burgis 2020), via various online schemes that can be purchased from other criminal groups on the dark web (Goodman 2015; see for example Bartlett 2015; White 2020) or through more *traditional* cash-based schemes (see for example Robinson 1995).

In his career as a financial investigator, the following are three of the common money laundering schemes that the author has investigated. Firstly, the receipt of invoice redirection and romance frauds into Irish money mule bank accounts. These accounts were gathered by a mule herder for the benefit of a highly organised West African Organised Crime Group (OCG). The proceeds were then used to purchase goods in China that were directly shipped to Nigeria in a form of Trade-based Money Laundering.[5] Secondly, fictitious Irish companies stated that they shipped (non-existent) goods through a legitimate company to fictitious Northern Irish companies availing themselves of a VAT refund as a (then) EU border was crossed in the

[5] *Operation Joggle*, see for example https://www.thejournal.ie/two-arrested-over-west-african-money-laundering-investigation-5260981-Nov2020/ (Accessed: 7 April 2025).

form of Vat-Carousel Fraud by a subversive OCG.[6] Finally, investment frauds where elderly people were duped into opening accounts with legitimate exchanges in the presence of the scammers. Lured by the false pretence of profit, they lodged their money into the account, from where it was whisked away and laundered by the criminal through the crypto-system.[7]

One must distinguish between money laundering methods and processes. The processes of money laundering can be considered the traditional three-stage model that was discussed above. Methods or techniques of laundering money, known as *typologies*, are ever-changing and are regularly published and updated by intergovernmental bodies (Schott 2006, pp. I9–I10; Demetis 2010, pp. 12–13). Some of the recently published[8] typologies include:

- Trade-Based Money Laundering (2006)
- Laundering through VAT Carousels (2007)
- Laundering and the Real-Estate Sector (2007)
- Laundering through Commercial Websites (2008)
- Laundering through Internet-Based Payment Services (2008)
- Laundering through Gambling and the Football Sectors (2009)
- Laundering through Trust and Company Service Providers (2010)
- Laundering through Corruption (2011)
- Laundering through Human Trafficking (2011)
- Laundering through the Illicit Tobacco Trade (2012)
- Laundering through the Legal Profession (2013)
- Laundering through the Hawala System (2013)
- Laundering through Afghan Opiates (2014)
- Laundering through the Non-Profit Organisation Sectors (2014)
- Laundering through ISIL and the Islamic State in Iraq (2015)
- Laundering through Crypto-Assets (2020)
- Countering Ransomware (2023)
- Illicit Financial Flows from Cyber-Enabled Fraud (2023)
- Misuse of Citizenship and Residency by Investment Programmes (2023)
- Detecting, Disrupting, and Investigating Online Child Sexual Exploitation (2025)
- Sanctions Evasion (2025)

Traditional money laundering methods have centred on the use of cash, for example cash-based businesses. While these remain an important area, as seen during their re-emergence during the recent COVID-19 global pandemic, criminals continue to seek new and innovative ways to exploit weaknesses in financial

[6] *Operation Myriad*, see for example https://www.garda.ie/en/about-us/our-departments/office-of-corporate-communications/news-media/2017-garda-annual-report.pdf (Accessed: 7 April 2025).

[7] See for example https://www.independent.ie/irish-news/crime/retired-man-scammed-out-of-250k-as-garda-report-120pc-increase-in-investment-fraud-40171685.html (Accessed: 7 April 2025).

[8] See FATF Website, https://www.fatf-gafi.org/publications/methodsandtrends/ (Accessed: 7 April 2025).

systems in an attempt to stay ahead of law enforcement (OECD 2009, p. 14). This includes the use of ICT and crypto-assets (Chap. 3).

2.1.6 Cyber-Laundering

As discussed in Chap. 1, transformative technologies have always been accompanied by optimistic and pessimistic visions of how they will change humanity and society. For example, the Internet has acted as a canvas onto which we have painted both positive and negative pictures of our future. It is a world of power and freedom: of expression, of creativity, of information, of ideas. It fosters breathtaking creativity, adaptiveness, and innovation, but outsiders, radicals, pariahs, and criminals are often the first to find and use new technology in shrewd ways, and the rest of us have much to learn from them (Bartlett 2015, pp. 219, 237; van Wegberg et al. 2018, p. 421). It has been opined that the Internet is a great tool that can be exploited and misused by people to commit crime (Grabosky 1998; Meighan 2004a, b; Goodman 2015).

The advancement of technology and financial globalisation makes it easier to transfer illegal funds through the legitimate banking and business systems (Joveda et al. 2019; Al-Tawil and Younies 2021). Enforcement efforts are caught in a game of catch up with modern, rapidly changing, and sophisticated means of financial transfers including the threats posed by crypto-assets (Duff 2019, p. 85). The problem of ensuring that legal definitions and instruments are not outstripped by technological and entrepreneurial developments is not a new one, but a reminder that legislators should be ever willing to react to such developments, and any measures introduced should be framed in a technology-neutral manner to provide an element of future proofing (Clark 2020, p. 5).

Cyber-laundering is a cyber-enabled crime where the Internet and ICT are used to launder money (Filipkowski 2008, pp. 16–17; Demetis 2010, p. 15). Some of the features of ICT that are attractive to launderers, according to Filipkowski (2008, pp. 16–17), are:

1. (Pseudo-)anonymity—the use of encryption and other methods to hide one's identity and frustrate the efforts of law enforcement to attribute a transaction to a person in real life.
2. Disintermediation—the ability to conduct transactions in a peer-to-peer manner, without having to be physically present at a location, removes a valuable source of identification through which law enforcement might identify a person in a money laundering transaction.
3. Open network—available in every location across the world.
4. Speed of transactions—technology allows for money to be moved rapidly and effortlessly introduce many layers of transacting complexity.
5. Globalisation / Cross-border—technology allows payments to rapidly and easily cross borders and make international payments which frustrates law enforce-

ment due to the sovereign nature of criminal law and criminals exploit regulatory differences between legal systems.

One can easily apply the three-stage money laundering process to cyber-laundering and make the following observations. For the placement stage, one must look at how to get cash into the Internet-based system; this is usually through an intermediary such as a financial institution, but in some cybercrimes this stage is not required, as the money/value may already be in cyberspace, for example with ransomware payments. ICT allows for the layering process to be carried out quickly and effectively by creating complex layers of financial transactions to distance the ill-gotten gains from the criminal source and break the audit trail that would identify the criminal, who is exploiting the beneficial features of ICT (perhaps in a way not envisioned by its creators). Finally, it is possible to integrate the laundered proceeds through a variety of legitimate and illegal online services, e.g. preloading credit and debit cards, online gambling, darknet marketplaces, online auctions, and online games (Filipkowski 2008, pp. 18–24). Using ICT, the three stages become less clearly defined, and the same techniques can be used at multiple points in the process.

The advantages offered by the (mis-)use or exploitation of technology are obvious to see, and cyber-laundering is another example of the technological double-edged sword (Chap. 1).

2.1.7 Terrorist and Proliferation Financing

The companion to money laundering is terrorist financing (TF), as countering the financing of terrorism (CFT) is to AML. The concepts have become merged together such that the phrase AML/CFT is in daily use and breathlessly mentioned by many compliance officers in their work. *Terrorism* is the use or threat of violence for political, religious, or ideological ends (Martin 2009, p. 546), and terrorist financing is the direct or indirect funding of terrorist acts, terrorists, and terrorist organisations (Financial Action Task Force 2019b, p. 125).

To discuss terrorist financing, we must first mention the international organisation that brought the concept to the fore, the *Financial Action Task Force*. FATF, of which more later, is an intergovernmental body that was set up in 1989 by the then G7. It is considered to be the standard-setting AML body and, in the wake of the 9/11 terrorist attacks, extended its remit in 2001 to cover terrorist financing and again in 2012 to counter the financing of proliferation of weapons of mass destruction (Financial Action Task Force 2020b). Since then, countering terrorist financing has been wedded to AML in an unsatisfactory way.[9]

[9] The author spoke with a senior member of the FATF who attended the late-night meeting where TF and CTF were added to FATF's mandate. They described a chaotic, lengthy discussion where

Many have criticised FATF for this expansion of its remit, which, due to the hysteria and panic that followed the events in the United States, meant there was no proper review of the existing AML regime, including the first two EU AML directives, carried out. The imposition of new measures imposed additional time and monetary costs on financial institutions and DNFBPs and had an arguably greater effect on civil society than on the terrorists (Culley 2006, pp. 173–174).

Surprisingly, most terrorist acts are committed for small sums of money, and therefore terrorist organisations can achieve their aims with micro-financing. The 1993 World Trade Centre bombing cost $400.00, the 2013 Boston Marathon bombing cost $500, and the 2005 London 7/7 bombing campaign cost £7000. Most terrorist acts are carried out with low-capability weapons, from knives to bombs, and are "cheap" terrorism (Ryder 2020). Financing terrorism also includes activities such as recruitment, financing, procurement, and coordination which can be carried out effectively using the tools readily available on the Internet and by crypto-assets (Meighan 2004a, p. 27).

Demetis argues that using the AML framework in the fight against terrorist financing is a severe contradiction or paradox (2010, pp. 31–35). Money laundering takes money, usually large amounts, from illegal sources and attempts to give it legitimacy through the financial system. Terrorist financing, on the other hand, takes small amounts of money (usually) from legitimate sources and directs it towards an illegal end, oftentimes through legitimate channels, such as charitable organisations and non-profit organisations (NPOs) (Ryder 2020).

This difference in structure between money laundering and terrorist financing presents challenges to the AML regime. Outside of checking sanctions lists, it is extremely difficult to identify small sum transactions from legitimate sources inside the financial system, the proverbial needle in the haystack, unless the financial institution knows its customer is a terrorist, which is, hopefully, most unlikely. Most private financial institutions profile their customers and transactions so that they can attempt to recognise what is unusual or suspicious. But if one introduces a profile for terrorist financing, there is a risk of "resorting to discriminatory practices that impinge on the sensitive issues of race, country of origin, and religion" (Demetis 2010, pp. 31–35; Ryder 2020). What is known to be of assistance to financial institutions in detecting terrorist financing are briefings from law enforcement and intelligence agencies (Demetis 2010, p. 33), but given the sensitivity of the information involved and data protection/privacy concerns, this type of activity does not occur often enough.

Ryder (2020) identifies a number of emerging threats in the terrorist financing sphere:

1. Social media platforms, including encrypted messaging capability.
2. The use of prepaid cards.

---

it was accepted that adding terrorist financing to the AML system was the incorrect approach. However, the United States gathered sufficient support to eventually get the proposal accepted.

3. Crypto-assets.[10]
4. Exploitation of natural assets.
5. The continued use and desirability of cash.
6. Self-financing from legitimate sources (e.g., wages, savings, money from parents/family) or from other crime (e.g., ransomware attacks purchased on the dark web).

Terrorist financing is a worthy topic of study, especially when crypto-assets are being used as a funding method, but it is beyond the scope of this research. Similarly, the next iteration of AML/CFT now includes preventing the financing of the proliferation of weapons of mass destruction (PF), which is also beyond the scope of this research but a worthy topic for future examination. It should be remembered that any discussion of money laundering from this point in the book onwards, especially when AML is mentioned, equally applies to terrorist and proliferation financing.

2.2 The Regulation of Money Laundering

Anti-money laundering (AML) can be considered the series of preventative and repressive measures and efforts put in place by governments, in cooperation with international organisations and private entities, which aim to prevent, disrupt, detect, and prosecute money laundering and organised crime.

Money laundering investigations should be carried out, where possible, in parallel with investigating the offences that generated the proceeds of crime in the first place, and with a view to confiscating those proceeds (FATF, 2020b). Such confiscation is most likely post-conviction based (PCB), but some countries, including Ireland, have an additional non-conviction-based (NCB) confiscation regime.

Prevention is a crucial element of AML, in which activities are not only in the domain of the state but increasingly involve international organisations and the private sector. The collaborative efforts of the United Nations (UN), the Financial Action Task Force (FATF), the European Union (EU), and self-imposed rules established by private institutions make up this aspect of the AML regime (Bakowski 2012).

Acting as the central link between the private and public sectors is the Financial Intelligence Unit (FIU) (Chap. 6).

The interplay between money laundering, AML, and its constituents is part of a complex sociopolitical and economic environment in which changes introduced oftentimes have unintended or unforeseen consequences that may present practical difficulties to the financial and non-financial sectors (Demetis 2010, pp. 1–3) (Chaps. 5 and 6).

[10] The recent events in the Middle East show that Hezbollah utilise crypto-assets to raise funds (see for example https://www.chainalysis.com/blog/israel-nbctf-hezbollah-iran-quds-crypto-seizure/, accessed: 21 August 2025).

2.2.1 The Development of Anti-Money Laundering (AML)

Up until the last 40 years, society did not take notice of, or indeed take action, regarding criminals enjoying their ill-gotten gains. Those at the higher end of criminal organisations were effectively insulated from state action if they kept their hands clean. This attitude of inaction can be conceptualised by the Latin phrase *pecunia non olet* (Walsh 1999; Stessens 2000, pp. 3–4; Gleason and Gottselig 2004). The phrase is attributed to the Roman Emperor Vespasian who ruled from 69 to 79 AD, and supposedly reintroduced a tax on the sale of urine from public urinals (*vectigal urinae*), which was used for several commercial purposes including (ironically) by launderers as a source of ammonia to whiten woollen togas. In response to his son Titus's complaints about the disgusting source of his father's income, Vespasian held up a gold coin and said that it did not stink, yet it came from urine, hence was not tainted by its origins (Hill 2015; Handwerk 2016). Of benefit to money launderers, and echoing the burden of modern financial investigators frustrated in their "follow-the-money" investigative efforts, Marx similarly observed that:

> since every commodity disappears when it becomes money it is impossible to tell from the money itself how it got into the hands of the possessor, or what article has been changed into it (Marx and Mandel 1990, p. 205).

Although the laundering of money has probably been done since money first existed, it was not a (stand-alone) criminal offence in any country until the mid-1980s; until then, the criminal law only prosecuted the perpetrator of the predicate offence. There were no mechanisms in existence to confiscate the proceeds of crime or prevent the legal business world from being misused by criminals. In many cases, the higher echelons of drug trafficking and OCGs were well insulated, escaped punishment, and got the benefit of the dirty money. This situation posed a threat to global financial and social integrity and is starkly illustrated by several examples from around the world. From the 1970s to the 1990s, the Americas experienced a massive flow of illegal drugs northwards and a corresponding flow of money and arms to the south, especially concerning the Escobar and Cali cartels (Forsman 2020, p. 24). Lord Diplock in an English drug trafficking case—*R v. Cuthbertson* [1981] AC 470— stated:

> With considerable regret, the power of forfeiture … did not apply … and could not be used to provide a means of stripping professional drug-traffickers of the whole of their ill-gotten gains or the total profits of their unlawful enterprises.[11]

The infamous Irish criminal Martin "The General" Cahill purchased a house in 1984 in an affluent area on the south side of Dublin for IR£80,000.00 in cash, despite being in receipt of social welfare and having had no paid employment since the late 1960s. The equally notorious drug trafficker John Gilligan won his 2005 case in the Irish Supreme Court, preventing the Irish State from seizing €17 million

[11] See Stessens (2000, p. 4) and case record that is available from https://swarb.co.uk/regina-v-cuthbertson-hl-1981/ (Assessed: 21 August 2025).

worth of assets from him after his conviction (Williams 1995, 2001). Ironically, the exploits of Cahill, exacerbated by the murder of the crime journalist Veronica Guerin in 1996 on the orders of John Gilligan, contributed to the introduction of money laundering and criminal asset seizure legislation in Ireland and the establishment of the NCB asset seizure agency, the Criminal Assets Bureau (CAB).

The magnitude of societal problems created by this serious criminality, and the apparent inability of civil society to take action as part of their *war on drugs* and later on all serious crimes, demanded action (Walsh 1999, p. 204; Stessens 2000, p. 3).

The UN *Convention against Illicit Traffic in Narcotic Drugs and Psychotropic Substances*, adopted in Vienna on 19 December 1988 (the *Vienna Convention*), was the first instrument that required states to criminalise the laundering of the proceeds of drug trafficking. The Convention recognised that criminals using these proceeds posed a serious threat to the welfare of people and could adversely affect the economic, cultural, and political foundations of society. The Convention also required each ratifying country to adopt legislation to identify, trace, and seize the proceeds of crime and to introduce measures to overcome banking secrecy rules. Extradition and mutual legal assistance were also covered in the treaty (Demetis 2010, pp. 18–19).

The UN *Convention against Transnational Organised Crime*, adopted in Palermo in December 2000 (the *Palermo Convention*), expanded the scope of money laundering to all serious offences that carried a penalty on conviction of imprisonment for 4 years or more (Article 6). It also required the setting up of regulatory and supervisory regimes for institutions susceptible to money laundering, based on customer identification, record keeping, and the reporting of suspicious transactions. International cooperation and information exchange were stressed in the convention (Stessens 2000, pp. 135–136; Bakowski 2012, pp. 1–4; Financial Action Task Force 2019a, p. 27; UNODC 2021).

Following these international treaties, international and supranational bodies such as the UN, the FATF, and the EU devised a series of initiatives to tackle money laundering (Demetis 2010, pp. 16–31). These initiatives can collectively be referred to as the AML regime, a combination of preventative and repressive components working in cooperation with each other (Gleason and Gottselig 2004, p. 82).

AML refers to the processes or activities that aim to prevent, disrupt, detect, investigate, and prosecute money laundering and to seize criminal assets. It can be broadly summarised as being concerned with the following three main activities:

1. The criminalisation of money laundering, which is to be investigated in parallel to the predicate offence.
2. The tracing, freezing, and confiscating of the proceeds of crime to deny the criminal the benefit of them.
3. Implementing a regulatory regime to protect the legitimate financial and business system from being misused for money laundering.

Essentially, AML aims to reduce criminal activity and to challenge the pretentious legitimacy of dirty money. This requires a high level of international cooperation to make AML efforts work and requires law enforcement to *follow-the-money* in order to attribute suspicious transactions to identify the criminal(s) behind them (Irwin and Dawson 2019; Al-Tawil and Younies 2021). It is vital to remember that, given the transnational nature of money laundering, any effective solution must be devised and implemented on an international and supranational level. However, criminal law is the exclusive sovereignty of national courts and parliaments. It remains the prerogative of governments to adopt and implement measures of a legislative and regulatory nature. Any interference with that sovereignty is limited to guidance and setting minimum required standards in the form of *soft-law*, which has seen impressive development in the AML sphere (Stessens 2000, pp. 15–16).

Some of the contemporary trends in worldwide AML are:

1. A revamping of AML laws (in the EU and United States, for example).
2. Developing ultimate beneficial ownership (UBO) registers to show the true owner of companies and property.
3. The use of technology, especially artificial intelligence and machine learning, in combatting money laundering.
4. Bringing crypto-assets into the scope of AML regulation (Academy of European Law 2021).

The final trend identified represents the focus of this book.

2.2.2 Hierarchy of AML Rule-Making

The primary approach of AML is to gather as much *financial intelligence* for the national authorities as possible, using the FIU as a conduit between the private and public sectors, allowing the identification of the owner of the assets or attributing the transaction (Haffke et al. 2020, pp. 130–131).

AML rules are typically derived from what is referred to as the (traditional) three-tier model of AML rule-making, although it now has an additional layer to account for the EU's supranational role (Fig. 2.3). The international organisations, primarily the FATF, set *soft-law* such as conventions, recommendations, standards, principles, technical assessments, and guidelines on an AML regime (*The International Layer*). These standards are adopted and enacted into *hard-law* by EU supranational and Irish national legislation (*The Supranational and National layers*), which impose a set of requirements, with punitive sanctions for non-compliance, on private entities, usually credit and financial institutions but also including many professional classes, called *obliged entities* or *designated persons* (*The Private Sector Layer*).[12]

---

[12] EU law refers to these private entities as *obliged entities*, emphasising the requirement for money laundering *gatekeepers* to protect the European Financial System, while Irish law refers to them as *designated persons*. The terms are interchangeable, which is an example of where loose terminology is rather unhelpful.

Fig. 2.3 Three-level hierarchy of AML rule-making

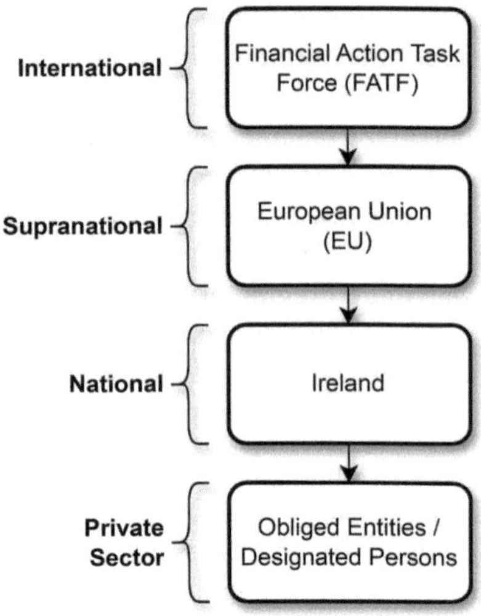

Each level of the hierarchy will now be examined in turn, describing the AML system that has been put in place to prevent and detect money laundering and organised crime. This three-level analysis will be followed in other sections of the book when introducing important topics.

2.2.3 The International Dimension: The Financial Action Task Force

The FATF is the global standard-setting AML watchdog (Financial Action Task Force 2019b, p. 7).

Money laundering schemes often include transnational elements such as transfers to financial institutions in different jurisdictions. This facet of money laundering, and the ease of cross-border transfers using modern technology, means that money laundering has to be addressed efficiently at the international level (Bakowski 2012, p. 2).

The FATF currently has 40 *full members*. They are: Argentina, Australia, Austria, Belgium, Brazil, Canada, China, Denmark, the European Commission, Finland, France, Germany, Greece, the Gulf Cooperation Council, Hong Kong China, Iceland, India, Indonesia,[13] Ireland, Israel, Italy, Japan, Korea, Luxembourg, Malaysia, Mexico, Netherlands, New Zealand, Norway, Portugal, Russian

[13] Indonesia's application for full membership was contingent on a satisfactory evaluation of its AML/CFT regime. The 2022–2023 evaluation found deficiencies to such an extent that its membership was deferred until an action plan for remedying the deficiencies was satisfactorily completed. The author served as the police expert on the evaluation team, with responsibility for IO7 and IO8, see FATF (2023) for further details. Indonesia completed its action plan and was granted full membership during the October 2023 plenary.

Federation,[14] Saudi Arabia, Singapore, South Africa, Spain, Sweden, Switzerland, Türkiye, United Kingdom, and the United States.

Several international organisations[15] are classified as *observer organisations*. There are nine FATF-style regional bodies (FSRBs)[16] that have *associate member* status.

While all the above can attend the quarterly plenary meetings, contribute to the debate, and sit on ongoing project groups, only full members have voting and decision-making rights. In all, more than 200 countries around the world have agreed to abide by the FATF recommendations via membership of the FATF, a FATF-style regional body (FSRB), or by being FATF observers (Terry and Robles 2018, p. 627), although the vast majority affected by the FATF play no part in the decision-making process (Academy of European Law 2021).

Currently, the FATF's mandate is to lead decisive, coordinated, and effective global action to counter the threat of abuse of the financial and business system by criminals and terrorists. It achieves this by:

1. Developing and refining international standards (the FATF recommendations).
2. Assessing and monitoring member countries in a peer-review process called a mutual evaluation and using a standard methodology.
3. Identifying and engaging with countries that have strategic AML difficulties.
4. Identifying and analysing threats to the integrity of the financial system, including the methods and trends involved.
5. Ensuring clear understanding of the FATF Recommendations and processes, by providing guidance, training, and strengthening FSRBs (FATF, 2019c, p. 7).

---

[14] FATF suspended the Russian Federation's membership on 24 February 2023 following the invasion of Ukraine.

[15] African Development Bank, Anti-Money Laundering Liaison Committee of the Franc Zone (CLAB), Asian Development Bank, Basel Committee on Banking Supervision (BCBS), Camden Asset Recovery Inter-agency Network (CARIN), Egmont Group of Financial Intelligence Units, European Bank for Reconstruction and Development (EBRD), European Central Bank (ECB), Eurojust, Europol, Group of International Finance Centre Supervisors (GIFCS), Inter-American Development Bank (IDB), International Association of Insurance Supervisors (IAIS), International Monetary Fund (IMF), International Organisation of Securities Commissions (IOSCO), Interpol, Organization of American States/Inter-American Committee Against Terrorism (OAS/CICTE), Organization of American States/Inter, American Drug Abuse Control Commission (OAS/CICAD), Organisation for Economic Cooperation and Development (OECD), Organization for Security and Cooperation in Europe (OSCE), United Nations (various representatives including UNODC), World Bank, and World Customs Organization (WCO).

[16] Asia/Pacific Group on Money Laundering (APG), Caribbean Financial Action Task Force (CFATF), Council of Europe Committee of Experts on the Evaluation of Anti-Money Laundering Measures and the Financing of Terrorism (MONEYVAL), Eurasian Group (EAG), Eastern and Southern Africa Anti-Money Laundering Group (ESAAMLG), Financial Action Task Force of Latin America (GAFILAT), Intergovernmental Action Group against Money Laundering in West Africa (GIABA), Middle East and North Africa Financial Action Task Force (MENAFATF), and Task Force on Money Laundering in Central Africa (GABAC).

The UN and the EU have asserted that the FATF recommendations should be recognised as the international standard against money laundering (Demetis 2010, pp. 20–22; FATF, 2020b). As the FATF:

> has no law-making function, it is incumbent on each jurisdiction to transpose the Recommendations into national law to operationalise them (FATF, 2020a, p. 6).

Thus, the FATF imposes its will on the assessed countries by way of *negative incentivisation*, that is it makes non-binding proposals that carry indirect consequences if not implemented effectively and efficiently (Academy of European Law 2021). The Recommendations set out a comprehensive framework of measures that define the foundation of every country's AML regime. They represent a set of legal, regulatory, and operational measures necessary to tackle money laundering and to ensure that criminals and terrorists cannot exploit regulatory gaps between countries (FATF, 2019c). They also demand that each country impose specified activity-based AML requirements on financial institutions and DNFBPs and ensure compliance with those obligations (FATF, 2019b, p. 7).

While the original *FATF Forty Recommendations* were drawn up in 1990, they have been revised from time to time to reflect ever-changing money laundering trends and techniques, evolving technology, and to broaden their scope well beyond drug–money laundering (FATF, 2019c, p. 6).

Some argue that, to account for new technologies, the continued adaptation of rules that are no longer fit for purpose and were designed for a twentieth century banking system is not appropriate to deal with the challenges posed by new forms of criminality and money laundering (Academy of European Law 2021).

While the Recommendations set out a comprehensive and consistent AML framework that a country should implement to combat money laundering, just having this foundation in place does not automatically mean that a country has an effective AML regime. Therefore, FATF requires that not only is a country technically compliant by having the measures outlined in the Recommendations in place, but also that those measures must operate effectively to combat money laundering (FATF, 2019c, p. 7).

Technical compliance (Table 2.1) measures how the FATF recommendations are legislated for. Effectiveness (Table 2.2) measures the successful AML outcomes that are achieved as a result. Effectiveness is assessed through 11 immediate outcomes (IOs), leading to intermediate outcomes, and:

> ultimately to the high level objective of ensuring that financial systems and the broader economy are protected from the threats of money laundering and the financing of terrorism and proliferation, thereby strengthening financial sector integrity and contributing to safety and security" (FATF, 2019c, pp. 15–22).

By necessity, the Recommendations must be described in broad terms, but some intended clarity is provided by accompanying guidance and information contained in the methodology. This additional information is more specific in scope but is not binding. This leaves gaps for countries when implementing their AML laws, which could lead to further fragmentation and criminal arbitrage (Academy of European Law 2021).

Table 2.1 FATF recommendations (technical compliance)

A—AML/CFT policies and coordination *Assess ML/TF risk, coordinate a risk-based approach to mitigate these risks*	
Rec 1	Assessing risk and applying a risk-based approach
Rec 2	National cooperation and coordination
B—Money laundering (ML) and confiscation *Criminalise ML and have authority to confiscate dirty money/property from criminals*	
Rec 3	Money laundering offence
Rec 4	Confiscation and provisional measures
C—Terrorist financing (TF) and proliferation financing (PF) *Criminalise TF, sanctions for TF and PF*	
Rec 5	Terrorist financing offence
Rec 6	Targeted financial sanctions related to terrorism and terrorist financing
Rec 7	Targeted financial sanctions related to proliferation
Rec 8	Non-profits organisations (NPOs)
D—Preventative measures *Ensure that the private sector, including gatekeepers to the financial system, takes measures to prevent criminals from misusing the financial system*	
Rec 9	Financial institution secrecy laws
	Customer due diligence and record keeping
Rec 10	Customer due diligence
Rec 11	Record keeping
	Additional measures for specific customers and activities
Rec 12	Politically exposed persons (PEPs)
Rec 13	Correspondence banking
Rec 14	Money or value transfer services (MVTS)
Rec 15	New technologies
Rec 16	Wire transfers
	Reliance, controls, and financial groups
Rec 17	Reliance on third parties
Rec 18	Internal controls and foreign branches and subsidiaries
Rec 19	Higher risk countries
	Reporting of suspicious transactions
Rec 20	Reporting of suspicious transactions
Rec 21	Tipping-off and confidentiality
	Designated non-financial businesses and professions (DNFBPs)
Rec 22	DNFBPs: Customer due diligence
Rec 23	DNFBPs: Other measures

(continued)

Table 2.1 (continued)

E—Transparency and beneficial ownership of legal persons and arrangements *Ownership of legal persons and arrangements to be transparent*	
Rec 24	Transparency and beneficial ownership of legal persons
Rec 25	Transparency and beneficial ownership of legal arrangements
F—Powers and responsibilities of competent authorities and other institutional measures *Create institutions and provide existing institutions with powers to combat ML/TF/PF*	
	Regulation and supervision
Rec 26	Regulation and supervision of financial institutions
Rec 27	Powers of supervisors
Rec 28	Regulation and supervision of DNFBPs
	Operational and law enforcement
Rec 29	Financial intelligence units (FIUs)
Rec 30	Responsibilities of law enforcement and investigative authorities
Rec 31	Powers of law enforcement and investigative authorities
Rec 32	Cash couriers
	General requirements
Rec 33	Statistics
Rec 34	Guidance and feedback
	Sanctions
Rec 35	Sanctions
G—International cooperation *As ML/TF/PF are transnational offences, the sharing of information and providing legal assistance through supervisors, law enforcement, prosecutors, and the entire AML/CFT regime is vital*	
Rec 36	International instruments
Rec 37	Mutual legal assistance
Rec 38	Mutual legal assistance: Freezing and confiscation
Rec 39	Extradition
Rec 40	Other forms of international cooperation

Periodically, experts from other member countries evaluate each country against a standard methodology. The outcome of this process is a Mutual Evaluation Report (MER). This process holds all countries to the same standard by ensuring that all are evaluated in the same way. Shortcomings are identified, and recommended actions are set out to improve compliance and effectiveness. With regard to technical compliance, there are five ratings ranging from *Compliant* to *Non-compliant*, and there are four ratings for effectiveness ranging from *High* to *Low* (Financial Action Task Force 2019a, pp. 13, 21). Despite this process being well established and accepted, it does not escape all criticism (Terry and Robles 2018; Pol 2018, 2019, 2020). It

Table 2.2 FATF immediate outcomes (effectiveness)

High-level Objective: Financial systems and the broader economy are protected from the threats of money laundering, terrorism financing, and proliferation, thereby strengthening financial sector integrity and contributing to safety and security.

Intermediate outcomes	**Immediate outcomes**	
Policy, coordination, and cooperation mitigate the money laundering and financing of terrorism risks.	IO1	Money laundering and terrorist financing risks are understood and, where appropriate, actions are coordinated domestically to combat money laundering and financing of terrorism and proliferation.
	IO2	International cooperation delivers appropriate information, financial intelligence, and evidence, and facilitates action against criminals and their assets.
Proceeds of crime and funds in support of terrorism are prevented from entering the financial and other sectors or are detected and reported by these sectors.	IO3	Supervisors appropriately supervise, monitor, and regulate financial institutions, DNFBPs and VASPs for compliance with AML/CFT requirements commensurate with their risks.
	IO4	Financial institutions, DNFBPs and VASPs adequately apply AML/CFT preventive measures commensurate with their risks and report suspicious transactions.
	IO5	Legal persons and arrangements are prevented from misuse for money laundering or terrorist financing, and information on their beneficial ownership is available to competent authorities without impediments.
Money laundering threats are detected and disrupted, and criminals are sanctioned and deprived of illicit proceeds. Terrorist financing threats are detected and disrupted, terrorists are deprived of resources, and those who finance terrorism are sanctioned, thereby contributing to the prevention of terrorist acts.	IO6	Financial intelligence and all other relevant information are appropriately used by competent authorities for money laundering and terrorist financing investigations.
	IO7	Money laundering offences and activities are investigated, and offenders are prosecuted and subject to effective, proportionate, and dissuasive sanctions.
	IO8	Proceeds and instrumentalities of crime are confiscated.
	IO9	Terrorist financing offences and activities are investigated and persons who finance terrorism are prosecuted and subject to effective, proportionate, and dissuasive sanctions.

(continued)

Table 2.2 (continued)

	IO10	Terrorists, terrorist organisations, and terrorist financiers are prevented from raising, moving, and using funds, and from abusing the NPO sector.
	IO11	Persons and entities involved in the proliferation of weapons of mass destruction are prevented from raising, moving, and using funds, consistent with the relevant UNSCRs.

does, however, produce a common assessment of all jurisdictions to the same standards and using the same procedures, albeit with different assessors who may view adherence and effectiveness subjectively. The debate and approval of an MER by a full plenary session of the FATF before publication, in theory, smooth out any inconsistencies. Depending on the outcome of a county's mutual evaluation, it will be placed in a system of regular or enhanced follow up. Each outcome comes with a different level of *pressure* or follow up. The ultimate sanction is grey-listing or black-listing uncooperative countries with deficient AML regimes, meaning that other countries may decline to carry out *business* with them if they are listed, which can have an enormous effect on the economy of the non-compliant country (Forsman 2020, pp. 30–31). At the time of writing, the following countries are currently on the FATF's grey list and subject to increased monitoring: Algeria, Angola, Bolivia, Bulgaria, Burkina Faso, Cameroon, Côte d'Ivoire, Democratic Republic of Congo, Haiti, Kenya, Lao People's Democratic Republic, Lebanon, Monaco, Mozambique, Namibia, Nepal, Nigeria, South Africa, South Sudan, Syria, Venezuela, Vietnam, Virgin Islands (UK), and Yemen.[17]

To address the strategic deficiencies identified in these jurisdictions, the FATF states that it will continue to work closely with the concerned country and their inclusion on the list does not indicate a call to avoid that country or to automatically apply enhanced due diligence; however, the inclusion on the list should feed into the risk analysis of a country or business intending to do business with the listed country or a company within. Only three jurisdictions are currently on the FATF blacklist: Iran, Myanmar, and the Democratic People's Republic of Korea.[18] As significant strategic AML deficiencies have been identified, the FATF calls for enhanced due diligence and the implementation of appropriate countermeasures to protect the financial system when dealing with these jurisdictions. Placing a country on or removing it from these lists can be seen as a political act that may not influence reducing real-world money laundering; however, it must be accepted that a grey- or black-listed country will often face concurrent EU and/or UN sanctions, which have a real effect.

[17] https://www.fatf-gafi.org/en/countries/black-and-grey-lists.html (Accessed: 13 August 2025).

[18] Ibid.

2.2.4 *The Supranational Dimension: The European Union*

The European Union (EU) is an economic and political union of 27 European countries.[19]

The EU is a full member of the FATF and fully endorses its aims and objectives. It has implemented the majority of FATF recommendations into EU law, meaning that these recommendations are binding on EU member states and represent a common EU approach. The EU has also acceded to the relevant UN AML conventions (Bakowski 2012, pp. 5–6; Forsman 2020, p. 29).

This positions the EU as a significant actor in the AML rule-making hierarchy. The lens of analysis for this book is the Irish Financial Intelligence Unit (FIU), and Ireland has been a member of the European Union since 1973.[20] In the context of this research, the EU is important as it adds a layer of AML rule-making. European legislation is superior to Irish law and, in many cases, has direct effect. Therefore, it is important to understand the EU and how it makes its laws. From an AML point of view, it should not matter which country is chosen, as each country is required to implement the FATF standards, and each EU country is required to adhere to European law.

2.2.4.1 History of the European Union

The EU was created in 1958 against the backdrop of the devastating aftermath of World War II, to foster economic cooperation and trade. By making neighbouring countries economically interdependent, it was hoped that future conflicts could be avoided.

The EU has evolved from a purely economic union into an organisation that spans numerous policy areas such as climate, finance, environment, health, and security (Kirk 2021). For this book, one of the areas of common concern is money laundering and anti-money laundering. People can travel, live, study, and work frictionlessly throughout the Union. The so-called *Single Market*—the engine of the Union—enables goods, services, money, and people to move freely (*the free*

---

[19] The current member states of the EU are Austria, Belgium, Bulgaria, Croatia, Cyprus, the Czech Republic, Denmark, Estonia, Finland, France, Germany, Greece, Hungary, Ireland, Italy, Latvia, Lithuania, Luxembourg, Malta, the Netherlands, Poland, Portugal, Romania, Slovakia, Slovenia, Spain, and Sweden.

[20] Ireland signed a Treaty of Accession to join the then European Economic Community (EEC) in 1972. As European law would have effect in Ireland as a result, a referendum was necessary to amend *Bunreacht na hÉireann* (the Irish constitution) to state that the Oireachtas (Irish Parliament) was no longer the sole maker of Irish law. On 10 May 1972, 83.09% of the electorate (from a high turnout of 70.3%) voted in favour of the referendum. After a period of preparation, Ireland joined the EEC on 1 January 1973 (https://www.oireachtas.ie/en/inter-parliamentary-work/european-union/brief-history/, accessed: 12 April 2025).

movements). A total of 19 member states use a single currency, the Euro (European Commission 2020). Approximately 448 million people (5.5% of the global population) live in the EU, and it generates approximately 15% (€14.5 trillion) of the world's economic output (European Commission 2025).

The main decision- and law-making bodies at the EU level are:

1. The *European Parliament*, elected directly by EU citizens every 5 years.
2. The *European Council*, made up of the heads of state of all EU members.
3. The *Council*, made up of the government ministers from each member state responsible for the policy area under discussion.
4. The *European Commission*, the administrative body of the EU who are responsible for the day-to-day running of the EU.

There are also various EU agencies that assist the Union by carrying out specific functions for the Union, including the Anti-Money Laundering Authority (AMLA), which will be introduced shortly.

The Court of Justice of the European Union ensures that EU legislation is interpreted and applied the same way in each member state and has the power to settle disputes between member states, EU institutions, businesses, and individuals (European Commission 2020).

Every action taken by the EU is founded on treaties that have been approved voluntarily and democratically by all EU countries (Table 2.3). These set out the objectives of the Union, the EU institutions and how they operate, the relationship between the EU and its members, and how EU law is made, implemented, and enforced. These treaties represent the *primary legislation* of the Union; the main two are the Treaty on the Functioning of the European Union (TFEU) and the Treaty on European Union (TEU). The TFEU and TEU are considered the constitutional basis of the EU and determine how it operates.

Table 2.3 EU primary legislation: the treaties

Date	Treaty	Effect	In force from
1957	Treaty of Rome *Treaty on the functioning of the European Union (TFEU)*	Founding treaty of the European economic community (now EU).	1 January 1958
1986	Single European act	Amended other treaties.	1 July 1987
1992	Treaty of Maastricht *Treaty on European Union (TEU)*	Amended the TFEU giving it more significance; one of the treaties that forms the constitutional basis of the EU.	1 November 1993
1997	Treaty of Amsterdam	Amended other treaties.	1 May 1999
1999	Treaty of Nice		1 February 2003
2001	Treaty of Lisbon		1 December 2009

2.2.4.2 EU Law

EU law is *sui generis*, separate from international and national law—truly *supranational*, with the goal of integrating member states into a cohesive legal system (Halloran 2025).

The EU has built up a considerable body of legislation and case law, created through the EU treaties and their amendments (*primary legislation*)—which are adopted with the agreement of all member states in inter-governmental conferences—or through legislative powers given to the EU institutions which are enforceable in the countries of the EU (*secondary legislation*, see for example Table 2.4).

EU law has supremacy over the laws of the individual member states but only in the limited and specific areas where the member states have ceded their national sovereignty. This is done when agreeing to the EU treaties and granting the EU the exclusive right to make law in those areas. These areas are usually important to the proper functioning of the EU and EU rights, for example the fundamental freedoms and the single currency. For this reason, unlike other international law, EU law is *supranational* in nature, as it has an enforcement mechanism, and the political will, to ensure that its laws are followed (European Commission 2020; Kirk 2021, pp. 3–9).

Under the *Principle of Conferral*, the EU can only act within the powers granted to it by member states in the treaties. The areas of competence where the member states have granted the EU the right to make law are listed in Articles 3–6 of the TFEU. Article 3 contains the areas where the EU has been granted exclusive competence to make law, while the other articles set out areas where the EU shares competence with the member states, supports competence, or coordinates policies.

Secondary legislation is made by the EU institutions under powers granted to them under Article 288 of the TFEU, which states that "to exercise the Union's competences, the institutions shall adopt regulations, directives, decisions, recommendations, and opinions" (Art. 288(1) TFEU). Regulations are generally applicable across the Union and automatically become law in all member states (Art. 288(2) TFEU). Directives are applicable to all member states but require the national parliaments to put national enabling legislation in place to give effect to the directive (Art. 288(3) TFEU). Decisions are binding in their authority, but only on the parties to whom they are addressed (Art. 288(4) TFEU). Recommendations and opinions are non-binding acts; nevertheless, they are influential and serve as guidance rather than enforceable rules (Halloran 2025).

Interestingly, there is no reference to the supremacy of EU law in any of the treaties. This principle emerged from the Court of Justice of the European Union (CJEU) in a case called *Costa v. ENEL* [1964] ECR 585, which arose from several conflicts between Italian law and certain treaty provisions. The CJEU recognised that by joining the EU, member states had limited their sovereignty in certain areas and transferred that power to the EU to give effect to the Union's primary

Table 2.4 EU AML legislation*

1991	European Council Directive (91/308/EEC) on prevention of the use of the financial system for the purpose of money laundering (10 June 1991) *Now repealed*	1st EU Anti-Money Laundering Directive (1AMLD)
2001	European Parliament and Council Directive (2001/97/EC) amending Council Directive 91/308/EEC on prevention of the use of the financial system for the purpose of money laundering (4 December 2001) *Now repealed*	2nd EU Anti-money Laundering Directive(2AMLD)
2005	Directive (2005/60/EC) of the European Parliament and of the Council of 26 October 2005 on the prevention of the use of the financial system for the purpose of money laundering and terrorist financing (26 October 2005) *Now repealed*	3rd EU Anti-money Laundering Directive(3AMLD)
2015	European Parliament and Council Directive (2015/849/EU) on the prevention of the use of the financial system for the purposes of money laundering or terrorist financing, amending Regulation (EU) No 648/2012 of the European Parliament and of the Council, and repealing Directive 2005/60/EC of the European Parliament and of the Council and Commission Directive 2006/70/EC (20 May 2015)	4th EU Anti-money Laundering Directive(4AMLD)
2018	European Parliament and Council Directive (2018/843/EU) amending Directive (EU) 2015/849 on the prevention of the use of the financial system for the purposes of money laundering and terrorist financing, and amending Directives 2019/138/EC and 2013/36/EU (30 May 2018)	5th EU Anti-money Laundering Directive(5AMLD)
2018	European Parliament and Council Directive (2018/1673/EU) on combating money laundering by criminal law (23 October 2018)[a]	Money Laundering Directive
2023*	Regulation (EU) 2023/1113 of the European Parliament and of the Council of 31 May 2023 on information accompanying transfers of funds and certain crypto-assets and amending Directive (EU) 2015/849 (recast)	Recast Transfer of Funds Regulation (TFR)
2023	Regulation (EU) 2023/1114 of the European Parliament and of the Council of 31 May 2023 on markets in crypto-assets	Markets in Crypto-Assets Regulation (MiCA)
2024*	Regulation (EU) 2024/1620 of The European Parliament and of the Council of 31 May 2024 establishing the Authority for Anti-Money Laundering and Countering the Financing of Terrorism	Anti-money Laundering Authority Regulation (AMLA)
2024*	Regulation (EU) 2024/1624 of The European Parliament and ff the Council of 31 May 2024 on the prevention of the use of the financial system for the purposes of money laundering or terrorist financing	EU Anti-money Laundering Directive (AMLR)
2024*	Directive (EU) 2024/1640 of The European Parliament and of the Council of 31 May 2024 On the mechanisms to be put in place by member states for the prevention of the use of the financial system for the purposes of money laundering or terrorist financing,	6th EU Anti-money Laundering Directive(6AMLD)

*Denotes being part of the EU AML Package that was first proposed in May 2020

[a]Almost universally incorrectly referred to as 6AMLD, which caused substantial misunderstanding when the actual sixth directive was introduced in 2024

legislation. In effect, member states had agreed to prioritise EU law, which is a treaty obligation under Article 4(3) of the TEU and made it superior to their own legislation. This case was followed by *International Handelsgesellschaft mbH* [1970] ECR 1125, which further clarified that secondary law, for example regulations and directives, is also superior to the constitutional and national law of a member state (European Commission 2020; Kirk 2021, pp. 1–9; Academy of European Law 2021).

2.2.4.3 EU Anti-Money Laundering Law

The EU considers that money laundering poses a serious threat to the integrity of the EU economy and financial system and to the security of its citizens. To facilitate their criminal activities, money launderers are likely to take advantage of the free movement of capital within the Union and exploit any weaknesses caused by the inconsistent application of legislation within member states.

Since 1991, the EU has enacted many AML directives to protect the Union's citizens and institutions from the threat of money laundering and organised crime (Table 2.4). Based on a yearly supranational AML risk assessment, the EU has attempted to identify and mitigate risks affecting the EU Internal market. The AML directives introduced a series of measures intended to implement an effective and efficient EU AML regime that is in line with the FATF recommendations.

As directives, there is a requirement for member states to transpose the legislation into national law. Due to the principle of *Minimum Harmonisation*, the states have only met a minimum standard, and regulatory gaps allow criminal arbitrage of legal systems to avoid detection. This leaves the EU having to review the transposition of enabling national legislation and make frequent amendments to its own directives. Various pieces of EU legislation are rapidly being introduced for this reason and to keep pace with technological developments, such as crypto-assets (Houben and Snyers 2018, 2020; Wiewiorówski 2020). The rapid pace of change could give an indication to the public that the contents of previous directives are not sufficient to handle modern-day AML, thereby reducing overall trust in the efficiency and reliability of the previous legislation, especially without a thorough cost–benefit and effectiveness analysis of the existing legislation being carried out (Culley 2006, pp. 167–168, 170–173; Khan 2019a, b, p. 41).

In 2015, the EU adopted a consolidated, modernised AML framework with the adoption of Directive (EU) 2015/849 on preventing the use of the financial system for money laundering or terrorist financing, the Fourth Anti-Money Laundering Directive (4AMLD). It fully considered the then FATF recommendations and went further in several areas to promote the highest standards for AML (Forsman 2020, p. 33; European Commission 2021). 4AMLD places a significant emphasis on the implementation of policies and procedures (Duff 2019, p. 86). 4AMLD and its successor (discussed in Chap. 4) were considered innovative pieces of legislation, although certain aspects, e.g. beneficial ownership registers, have faced criticism from a privacy/GDPR perspective, the tension between AML and GDPR is still not addressed and resolved despite attention from the European Data Protection Supervisor (Finck 2018; Khan 2020a, b, c, d; Wiewiorówski 2020). EU law went further than the FATF recommendations that were in force at the time. FATF subsequently adopted the EU position on the topic of crypto-assets and revised its own recommendations, which then went somewhat further than 5AMLD, which is somewhat of a vicious circle or evidence of self-referential systemic feedback (Forsman 2020, pp. 32–33).

Subsequently, the EU adopted Directive (EU) 2018/1673 of the European Parliament and of the Council of 23 October 2018, almost universally mistakenly referred to as 6AMLD, to establish minimum rules concerning the definition of criminal offences (*predicate offences*) and sanctions related to money laundering.

In May 2020, the EU Commission introduced an extensive *Action Plan* for a comprehensive EU AML regime that aims to strengthen the rules and their consistent implementation across the Union (2020/C 164/06). The plan outlined six pillars or priorities as follows:

1. Ensuring effective implementation of the existing EU AML framework.
2. Establishing an EU single AML rulebook.
3. Bringing about EU-level AML supervision in certain sectors.
4. Establishing a support and cooperation mechanism for EU FIUs.
5. Enforcing EU-level criminal law provisions and information exchange (on an inter-community basis).
6. Strengthening the international dimension of the EU AML regime (3rd country basis, treating the EU as a single bloc).

The EU put forward four legislative proposals, considered by them as one coherent whole, to achieve their *Action Plan*, namely:

1. Establishing a harmonised EU-wide AML regime by way of regulation to overcome the lack of direct applicability and fragmented implementation of 4AMLD and 5AMLD across EU member states.
2. Establishing an EU Anti-Money Laundering Authority (AMLA) by way of regulation to provide EU-level supervision of certain parts of the EU AML regime.
3. Updating the parts of 4AMLD and 5AMLD that are not covered by the new proposed regulation.
4. Recasting Regulation EU 2015/847 the Transfer of Funds Regulation (TFR) to include crypto-assets.

The plan was approved by the Parliament on 24 April 2024 and adopted by the Council on 30 May 2024. Those pieces of legislation have been enacted and will take effect over 5 years; the resulting substantial changes will alter the EU landscape and represent interesting times for compliance officers, FIUs, law enforcement, and criminals.

Important
The current EU AML regime consists of eight pieces of legislation: 4AMLD (2015/849), 5AMLD (2018/843), the money laundering directive (2018/1673), the (recast) TFR (2023/1113), the MiCA regulation (2023/1114), the AMLA regulation (2024/1620), the AMLR (2024/1624), and 6AMLD (2024/1640). Other pieces of legislation also deal with parts of money laundering and crypto-assets; however, these eight form the main corpus of EU law on the subject.

Parts of each of these concern the AML regulation of crypto-assets, which will be discussed in Chap. 4.

The *Single Rulebook*, or the first EU AML Regulation (AMLR), is set out in Regulation (EU) 2024/1624. The regulation states that although EU AML rules have existed for over 30 years, they are still inconsistently implemented and in a way that is not fully consistent with the requirements of an integrated internal market. Therefore, the EU considered it necessary that parts of 4AMLD be set out in a regulation to achieve the desired uniformity of application across the Union. It sets out the measures to be applied by obliged entities to prevent money laundering, the rules around the transparency of beneficial owners, and measures to limit the misuse of anonymous instruments. It also covers reports made to the FIU and information sharing. When fully operational, it will repeal 4AMLD. The date of application for this regulation is *10 July 2027*, except for football agents and professional football clubs which take effect on 10 July 2029. The effect of this regulation on current national AML systems—which are set out in national law to transpose the current EU AML directives—is uncertain.

Regulation (EU) 2024/1620 establishes a new EU AML Authority (AMLA). Its key responsibilities will include:

1. Directly supervising selected financial sector entities that operate on a cross-border basis and present a high risk of money laundering and terrorism financing, as well as indirectly supervising other entities in the financial and non-financial sectors.
2. Supporting and coordinating Financial Intelligence Units (FIUs) by facilitating joint cross-border case analyses, enabling controlled information exchange, providing capabilities, advanced data analytics, and managing the common FIU. net information system.
3. Complementing EU AML/CFT rules by developing regulatory and implementing technical standards and issuing guidelines.

AMLA will be fully staffed and begin directly supervising those selected entities on *1 January 2028*.

Directive (EU) 2024/1640, the Sixth EU AML Directive (6AMLD), sets out the main bulk of the requirements specifying the make-up of a member state's AML system. This Directive lays down rules concerning:

1. The measures applicable to sectors exposed to money laundering and terrorist financing, at a national level.
2. The requirements in relation to registration of, identification of, and checks on, senior management and beneficial owners of obliged entities.
3. The identification of money laundering and terrorist financing risks at the Union and member state level.
4. The set-up of and access to beneficial ownership and bank account registers and access to real estate information.
5. The responsibilities and tasks of Financial Intelligence Units (FIUs).
6. The responsibilities and tasks of bodies involved in the supervision of obliged entities.
7. Cooperation between competent authorities and cooperation with authorities covered by other Union legal acts.

This directive repeals 4AMLD, and it must be transposed by the states by *10 July 2027*, although there is a derogation for some articles until 10 July 2029.

The pieces of EU legislation that specifically apply to crypto-assets will be discussed in Chap. 4.

2.2.5 The National Dimension: Ireland

Ireland has been an independent state since 1921. It is situated in the North Atlantic Ocean on the western edge of Europe with an approximate population of 5 million people.

Ireland is a parliamentary democracy. The National Parliament (the *Oireachtas*) consists of the President and two Houses: a House of Representatives (*Dáil Éireann*) and a Senate (*Seanad Éireann*). The functions and powers of the President, Dáil, and Seanad are derived from the Constitution of Ireland (*Bunreacht na hÉireann*, enacted in 1937 and amended periodically by referendum). All laws passed by the Oireachtas must conform to the Constitution. Ireland's legal system is derived from the English common law tradition. The Constitution establishes the branches of government, the courts, and sets out how those institutions should be run. Ireland is a member of the FATF, the EU, and the Eurozone (Financial Action Task Force 2017).

In 2024, Ireland's GDP was over €500 billion, with financial services playing an important role in its economy.[21] Ireland is the fourth largest exporter of financial services in the EU, and globally, over 40% of hedge fund assets are administered in

[21] https://www.cso.ie/en/statistics/nationalaccounts/quarterlynationalaccounts/ (accessed: 21 August 2025).

Ireland. A majority of the world's aircraft leasing and financing operates through Ireland (Financial Action Task Force 2017, p. 17). Ireland has a thriving fintech sector that is actively engaging in crypto-assets and their service provision. The legal framework for combating money laundering is set out in the *Criminal Justice (Money Laundering and Terrorist Financing) Act, 2010* as amended, which is heavily influenced and guided by the FATF and the EU, particularly 4AMLD and its amending directives. EU Law has supremacy over Irish law within certain competencies (Sect. 2.2.4 and Meighan 2025).

2.2.5.1 Evaluation of Ireland's AML System

Assessors from the FATF visited Ireland in November 2016 to examine its AML measures. A Mutual Evaluation Report, published in September 2017, analysed Ireland's compliance with the FATF Standards (Financial Action Task Force 2017, 2019a, c). The report found that Ireland had a generally sound legislative and institutional AML framework that had seen improvement in recent years. However, despite demonstrating a substantial level of effectiveness in some areas, additional measures and resources were required for a fully effective system commensurate with the money laundering risks faced (Financial Action Task Force 2017, p. 3).

The main crime threats faced in Ireland at the time were organised crime groups—including former local paramilitary groups—involved in drug trafficking, human trafficking and migrant smuggling, fuel laundering, and fraud (including VAT fraud). Cash and cash-intensive sectors (e.g. dealers in high-value goods, currency exchanges) remained important; however, criminal reliance on them was decreasing and moving towards other methods of value transfer, including investment funds, the misuse of complex legal structures, and "instant" payment services (Financial Action Task Force 2017, p. 5). There was a follow-up assessment in 2019, resulting in minor upgrades to several of the 40 recommendations (Financial Action Task Force 2019c). The current rating of Ireland is set out in Tables 2.5 and 2.6. The assessors found that Ireland had a strong legislative framework for pursuing money laundering; however, this had not translated to prosecution and conviction results (Financial Action Task Force 2017, p. 4). Ireland's next MER is due to take place in 2027, with the report issuing shortly afterwards.

Another view of Ireland's AML system is provided by the internationally renowned Basel Institute on Governance. It was established in 2003 in Basel, Switzerland, and works with worldwide partners to advance knowledge, practice, and policy on anti-money laundering, asset recovery, and business integrity. In 2024, Ireland was assigned a Basel AML Index Score of 4.23 out of 10 and was ranked 135 out of 164 countries in the world.[22] The higher the Basel score and ranking, the greater the risk of

[22] https://index.baselgovernance.org/ranking (Accessed: 13 April 2025). The Basel Index measures the risk of money laundering and terrorist financing in countries using data from publicly available sources such as the Financial Action Task Force (FATF), Transparency International, the World Bank and the World Economic Forum. It uses a total of 15 indicators of countries' adherence to

Table 2.5 FATF evaluation of Ireland 2017 (effectiveness)

Immediate Outcome (IO)	Description	Rating
IO.1	Risk, policy, and coordination	Substantial
IO.2	International cooperation	Substantial
IO.3	Supervision	Substantial
IO.4	Preventive measures	Moderate
IO.5	Legal persons and arrangements	Moderate
IO.6	Financial intelligence	Substantial
IO.7	Money laundering investigation and prosecution	Moderate
IO.8	Confiscation	Moderate
IO.9	Terrorist financing investigation and prosecution	Moderate
IO.10	Terrorist financing preventive measures and financial sanctions	Moderate
IO.11	Proliferation financing financial sanctions	Substantial

Table 2.6 FATF Evaluation of Ireland 2017 and 2019 (technical compliance)

R.1	**R.2**	**R.3**	**R.4**	**R.5**	**R.6**	**R.7**	**R.8**	**R.9**	**R.10**
LC	C	C	C	LC	PC	PC	PC	C	LC
R.11	**R.12**	**R.13**	**R.14**	**R.15**	**R.16**	**R.17**	**R.18**	**R.19**	**R.20**
LC	C	PC	LC	LC	C	LC	LC	LC	C
R.21	**R.22**	**R.23**	**R.24**	**R.25**	**R.26**	**R.27**	**R.28**	**R.29**	**R.30**
C	PC	LC	LC	LC	C	C	LC	C	C
R.31	**R.32**	**R.33**	**R.34**	**R.35**	**R.36**	**R.37**	**R.38**	**R.39**	**R.40**
C	PC	PC	C	LC	C	C	LC	C	LC

money laundering, which puts Ireland in a low category of money laundering risk, although most EU countries have a lower score than Ireland.

2.2.5.2 Ireland's AML System

Having examined the development of AML and how the different levels of rule-making interact, it is now possible to develop a model of Ireland's AML system (Fig. 2.4).[23] This is an important step as the model developed will be used to

AML regulations; levels of corruption, financial standards, political disclosure, and the rule of law are aggregated into one overall risk score. By combining these data sources, the overall risk score represents a (so-called) holistic assessment addressing structural as well as functional elements of the country's resilience against ML and Terrorist Financing. The scores are aggregated as a composite index using a qualitative and expert-based assessment in order to form the final country ranking. The index does not measure the actual amount of ML or terrorist financing activity but rather is designed to assess the risk of such activity.

[23] This task is an observer-dependent function and is based on the author's views, experiences, education, opinions, background, biases, etc. The actual model is developed from a review of the prevailing literature which has been synthesised by the author including the FATF recommenda-

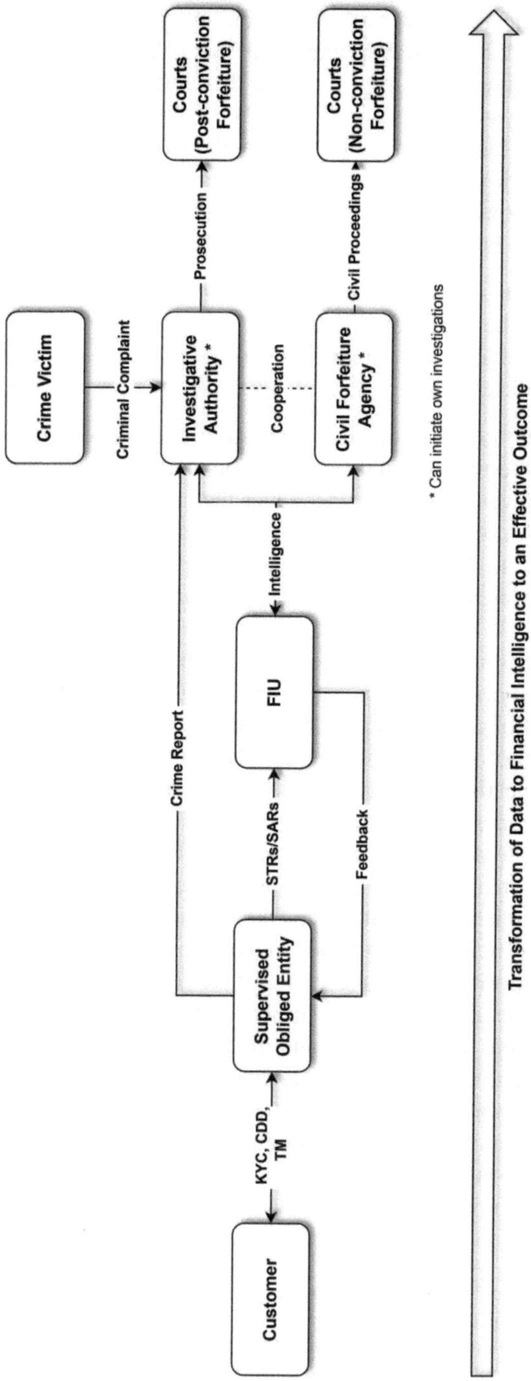

Fig. 2.4 Model of the Irish AML system

illustrate the efficacy, or otherwise, of regulating crypto-assets for the purposes of AML throughout the remainder of this book. As the Irish system follows the International (Sect. 2.2.3) and Supranational (Sect. 2.2.4) rules put in place, the model is equally applicable to any country in the world with minor amendments to account for differences in legislation (Fig. 2.4).

AML in Ireland is the system put in place by the Irish government in consultation with the relevant national and supranational organisations, and the private-sector entities, to address money laundering. It aims to prevent, disrupt, detect, investigate, and prosecute money laundering and organised crime through three pillars:

1. The criminalisation of money laundering and organised crime.
2. The forfeiture of the proceeds of crime.
3. Protecting the financial and business sector from being exploited by criminals and money launderers.

The AML system consists of both repressive and preventative measures. The repressive measures cover the first two functions and generally involve the public sector, while the preventative measures cover the last function and usually involve the private sector. A properly functioning AML system needs to focus equal attention on each pillar, and there should be actual compliance focusing on the true purpose of AML—the prevention of money laundering—rather than merely for the sake of compliance.

Starting with the repressive measures on the public sector side, one can consider the investigative authority, which is usually the police service (*An Garda Síochána*, Ireland's National Police and Security Service), receiving information that a crime has occurred directly from a crime victim. Sometimes, the police may also proactively initiate an investigation based on other information, e.g. from another investigation, good-citizen reports, media reports, or other intelligence reports. The police will investigate the alleged crime, including any accompanying money laundering, by utilising their police powers. These include the power to demand documents, to search premises, and to arrest and interview suspects during an investigative detention. Where sufficient prima facie evidence exists, they will prepare a file for the prosecuting authority (in Ireland, the Director of Public Prosecutions) seeking permission to charge and bring the suspect before the courts. The prosecuting authority will examine the police file and direct such a prosecution where there is sufficient evidence and a public interest to do so. The suspect is then brought before the courts, and the matter is examined and determined during the trial process. Where a person is found guilty of the offence, they are punished, usually by means of a period of imprisonment imposed for serious offences such as money laundering. Where financial investigators have identified criminal assets, these assets may

---

tions, the EU's AMLDs, and the Irish *Criminal Justice (Money Laundering and Terrorist Financing) Act* 2010 as amended. It is also important to remember that the supervision of AML obliged entities, the coordination of national public sector entities, and the development of policy and legislation are vital components of any AML system; however, these are excluded as they fall outside the scope of this book.

be ordered to be forfeited to the state in a post-conviction forfeiture. In Ireland, there is a civil forfeiture agency (The Criminal Assets Bureau or CAB) that focuses on the actual criminal assets and may take civil (*In Rem*) proceedings to ask a judge to forfeit those proceeds to the state utilising a non-conviction-based forfeiture process. The police and civil forfeiture agency cooperate closely to ensure assets are seized even in cases where there is no prosecution or conviction, e.g. due to evidential or territorial difficulties in prosecuting the suspect for a criminal offence. In this way, one ensures that the criminalisation of money laundering and the forfeiture of criminal proceeds are achieved. The additional benefit of the non-conviction approach is that the criminal burden of proof (beyond a reasonable doubt) is replaced by the less onerous civil burden (the balance of probabilities).

As we can deduce from the above, the police must have information that a crime may have taken place. Their job is then to find out who may have committed the crime, who laundered the money, and where the criminal proceeds are now situated. This is where a financial investigator is called in to adopt a *follow-the-money* approach. One can see that aside from the initial input of the crime victim, all the elements on the repressive side of AML are public sector agencies.

The third function of the AML system is to protect the legitimate financial system from being exploited for the purpose of money laundering. This is referred to as the preventative measure of AML and is what most compliance officers consider AML to be, ignoring the first two purposes discussed above. A properly functioning AML system needs to focus on all three functions; otherwise, there may be a tendency for the system to become a bureaucratic "tick the box" exercise for the sake of compliance, rather than a real effort to prevent and detect money laundering. AML preventative measures are characteristic of a trend whereby certain private sector entities (the supervised obliged entities) are coerced, under pain of punishment, administrative sanction, or bad publicity, to carry out investigation-like functions. This *Foucauldian* diffusion of power represents a move away from the traditional command and control government to a form of *governmentality* where authority is diffused throughout and to the lower levels of the system to a form of almost self-regulation with national oversight (Rose et al. 2006; Wong 2013; McGrath 2019). The situation represents a transfer of global norms and practices—the AML "solution"—and enables coherence to a global governance regime (Demetis 2010, pp. 18–19). Some argue that these measures put an excessive burden on the private sector to carry out tasks that the government should be undertaking; however, the counterargument is that the private sector has the required information and the obligation to report it (Stessens 2000, pp. 159–181).

Obliged entities in Ireland must comply with the following broad risk-based, preventative AML rules:

1. Conduct a business risk assessment that takes a holistic view of their organisation and operational environment by looking at their activities, services, groups of clients, and products, especially those that tend to be riskier in nature and susceptible to money laundering.

2. Conduct a client risk assessment, informed by the business risk assessment, on each individual customer and transaction.
3. Have internal AML policies, documented AML procedures, and adequately AML-trained staff.
4. Perform customer due diligence (CDD), or enhanced due diligence (EDD) if appropriate, on each customer by identifying and verifying their customers and beneficial owners (also known as KYC or *know your customer*).
5. Conduct continuous transaction monitoring (TM) and ascertain the background and purpose of certain activities and transactions they carry out, especially to identify those that fall outside of expected customer behaviour.
6. File suspicious transaction/activity reports (STR/SARs) if they suspect their customer of being involved in money laundering.
7. Keep records of all the above for inspection by their AML supervisor (a public sector body who ensures AML and prudential compliance and has the power to impose sanctions in the case of identified AML failures).

Located in the middle, as the crucial link between the private and public sectors, and the preventative and repressive functions of AML, is the FIU (Chap. 6). As was discussed in the Introduction (Chap. 1), the FIU is the central, national agency responsible for receiving STRs/SARs from the obliged entities, developing them with other sources of information, and where a criminal indicator is present, disseminating an intelligence package to law enforcement for possible investigation. This is one of the main ways that law enforcement becomes aware of money laundering activity, other criminality, and the location of the proceeds of crime (Stessens 2000, pp. 143–145; Gleason and Gottselig 2004).

> ***Important*** *The reporting of STRs/SARs is one of the main pillars of the preventative AML system*, accepting that they are not the only source of money laundering investigations which may be initiated directly by law enforcement agencies.

Effective law enforcement activity invariably depends on information that offences have been committed, which is not always readily available to law enforcement, is often distributed across entities, and, in the past, was obscured by banking secrecy rules, and efforts may be taken to hide the identity of the person behind the transaction. This is sometimes referred to as the AML *information deficit* (Stessens 2000, pp. 159–181; Odedra 2020), which FIUs, as an integral part of the AML regime, seek to overcome. The need for a specific FIU was only recognised by FATF with the introduction of their 2003 version of the Recommendations on the basis of work done by the Egmont Group (Gleason and Gottselig 2004, pp. 17, 19). There are several different types of FIU, classified by their nature and staff makeup, e.g. police based, administrative, or judicial (Stessens 2000, pp. 185–190; Gleason and Gottselig 2004). Two reporting models to the FIU can be distinguished: a blind system of objective threshold reporting, and a subjective suspicion-based model.

Both have advantages and disadvantages and, although some countries use a combination of the two, the suspicion-based model is favoured despite a lack of criteria around the definition of suspicion (Stessens 2000, pp. 161–162, 164–171).

It is worth expanding on the important concept of suspicion, as it is the threshold for an obliged entity to make an STR/SAR to the FIU in the first place. Regarding the AML system, the construction of suspicion refers to the process by which obliged entities identify, assess, and report suspicious activities that may be indicative of money laundering. They are, in fact, creating or nominating "suspects" based on their customer's financial activity. At each stage of the AML system, up until the moment a person is found guilty beyond a reasonable doubt, that suspicion is being examined and built upon. Given its importance as a concept, it is surprising that (legal) suspicion is not defined in international, supranational, or national AML rules. The UK Court of Appeal in *R v Da Silva* [2006] EWCA Crim 1654 defined "suspicion of money laundering" as "the possibility, which is more than fanciful, that the person was or had been engaged in, or benefited from criminal conduct". In the Irish case of *DPP v. Farrell* [2009] 4 IR 689, Clark J. held that "the suspicion must be fair and reasonable and honestly held on the basis of information available … at the time". It appears that the threshold is relatively low.

Definition An SAR/STR is defined as an information report submitted to the FIU on what an obliged entity considers to be suspicious transactions or activity, indicative of money laundering, which is made available to the public sector in order to initiate and assist investigations, and help identify assets that have been obtained through criminality (Cook 2019, p. 238).

These concepts will be fleshed out in Chaps. 6 and 7 when the role of the FIU is discussed in depth.

2.2.6 An Imperfect System?

It is important at this juncture to recognise that the AML and STR/SAR system is far from perfect, and many have suggested a need for its reform. Nevertheless, it is a remarkable international experiment whereby a common standard, against which each country is measured and held to account, was put together in four decades across turbulent geopolitics.

Some of the areas in need of reform and clarification can be summarised as follows:

1. Measuring the effectiveness of the AML regime, given a reported impact of 0.01% on criminal finances (Pol 2018, 2019, 2020). It must be stated that studies of this kind rely upon unreliable measures of the size of the money laundering market; equally, one cannot be blinded by anecdotal successes that may mask the reality of an overall policy failure.

2. Poor-quality STRs from the private sector and little or no feedback from the FIU contributing to defensive, automatic reporting (Angell and Demetis 2005; Demetis and Angell 2006, 2007; Demetis 2010; Odedra 2020).
3. The futility of adopting a risk-based approach (Demetis and Angell 2006).
4. No definition of suspicion—this is a nebulous, subjective concept—combined with the ambiguity and looseness of the *risk-based approach* (Demetis and Angell 2006; Demetis, 2010; Odedra 2020).
5. AML is considered a cost of doing business with little buy-in or engagement from stakeholders who are merely looking to do the minimum ("box ticking") to avoid regulatory fines and negative press. Equally, the money spent by the hundreds of thousands of businesses and professionals comprising the compliance system might be spent better elsewhere (Pol 2018, 2019, 2020).
6. The burgeoning compliance cost inflicted upon private companies, meaning the impact of AML is felt more by legitimate businesses and citizens than criminals (Pol 2020, pp. 85, 87).
7. The expansion of the number of regulated entities creates an ever-increasing volume of financial data, yet some regulated sectors rarely, if ever, make an STR (Forsman 2020, p. 49).
8. Little or no guidance from supervisors.
9. Data protection and privacy issues being used as a shield to avoid reporting and cooperation with law enforcement (Finck 2018; Wiewiorówski 2020).
10. The use of technology in the identification of STRS leads to an increase in noise and reports to an already over-whelmed FIU (The World Bank 2009; Demetis 2010; Academy of European Law 2021).

References

Academy of European Law (2021) Annual conference on financial compliance in the EU 2021

Al-Tawil TN, Younies H (2021) The implications of the Brexit from EU and bitcoin. J Money Launder Control 24:137–149

Aluko A, Bagheri M (2012) The impact of money laundering on economic and financial stability and on political development in developing countries: the case of Nigeria. J Money Launder Control 15:442–457

Angell I, Demetis D (2005) Systems thinking about anti-money laundering: considering the Greek case. J Money Launder Control 8:271–284

Bakowski P (2012) Combatting money laundering: EU law in an international context. In: Library of the European Parliament. Accessed 21 Aug 2025

Bartlett J (2015) The dark net. Windmill Books, London

Bingham RHLB of CKPFT (2011) The rule of law,. Reprint edition. Penguin, London

Burgis T (2020) Kleptopia: how dirty money is conquering the world. William Collins

Business Insider (2011) The economics of money laundering. https://www.businessinsider.com/the-economics-of-money-laundering-2011-6?op=1. Accessed 1 Mar 2025

Cassara JA (2020) Money laundering and illicit financial flows: following the money and value trails. Independently published

Central Statistics Office (2025) Gross domestic product. CSO, Dublin

Clark R (2020) UK jurisdiction taskforce publishes legal statement on status of crypto-assets and smart contracts—Observations from Ireland. C L P 27:3–9
Connell D (2018) Do EU regulations combating money laundering and the financing of terrorism adequately tackle cryptocurrencies? The case of Ireland. I J E L 21:68–90
Conteh JD (2018) Anti-money laundering and combating the financing of terrorism. Sondiata Global Media Ltd, London
Cook T (2019) Blackstone's senior investigating officers' handbook, 5th edn. Oxford University Press, Oxford
Culley AC (2006) The third EU money laundering directive: a banker's tightrope? I J E L 13:161–174
Demetis D (2010) Technology and anti-money laundering: a systems theory and risk-based approach. Edward Elgar, Cheltenham
Demetis D, Angell I (2006) AML-related technologies: a systemic risk. J Money Launder Control 9:157–172
Demetis D, Angell I (2007) The risk-based approach to AML: representation, paradox, and the 3rd directive. J Money Launder Control 10:412–428
Duff C (2019) "Dirty money"–an overview of the Irish anti-money laundering landscape. C L P 26:85–90
European Commission (2020) The European Union: what it is and what it does. Publications Office of the European Union, Luxembourg
European Commission (2021) Anti-money laundering and counter terrorist financing. https://ec.europa.eu/info/business-economy-euro/banking-and-finance/financial-supervision-and-risk-management/anti-money-laundering-and-counter-terrorist-financing_en. Accessed 1 Mar 2025
European Commission (2025) Key figures on the EU in the world: 2025 Edition. Publications Office of the European Union, Luxembourg
Filipkowski W (2008) Cyber laundering: an analysis of typology and techniques. Int J Criminal Justice Stud 3:15–27
Financial Action Task Force (2017) Anti-money laundering and counter-terrorist financing: Ireland fourth round mutual evaluation report. FATF-GAFI, Paris
Financial Action Task Force (2019a) Methodology for assessing technical compliance with the FATF recommendations and the effectiveness of AML/CTF systems. FATF-GAFI, Paris
Financial Action Task Force (2019b) International standards on combatting money laundering and the financing of Terrorism & Proliferation: the FATF recommendations. FATF-GAFI, Paris
Financial Action Task Force (2019c) Anti-money laundering and counter-terrorist financing measures: Ireland, enhanced follow-up report & technical compliance re-rating. FATF-GAFI, Paris
Financial Action Task Force (2020a) Money laundering. FATF-GAFI, Paris
Financial Action Task Force (2020b) Report to the G20 finance ministers and central Bank governors on so-called Stablecoins. FATF-GAFI, Paris
Finck M (2018) Blockchain regulation and governance in Europe. Cambridge University Press, Cambridge, United Kingdom; New York, NY, USA
Foley S, Karlsen JR, Putniņš TJ (2019) Sex, drugs, and bitcoin: how much illegal activity is financed through cryptocurrencies? Rev Financ Stud 32:1798–1853
Forsman M (2020) 30 years of combating money laundering in Sweden and internationally—does the system function as intended? Sveriges Econ Rev 1:24–55
Gleason P, Gottselig G (2004) Financial intelligence units: an overview. International Monetary Fund: World Bank Group, Washington, D.C
Goodman M (2015) Future crimes: everything is connected, everyone in vulnerable and what we can do about it. Corgi, London
Government of Ireland (2016) National Risk Assessment for Ireland: money laundering and terrorist financing. Government Publications, Dublin
Grabosky P (1998) Crime in cyberspace. In: Combating transnational crime: concepts, activities and responses, pp 195–208

Haffke L, Fromberger M, Zimmermann P (2020) Cryptocurrencies and anti-money laundering: the shortcomings of the fifth AML directive (EU) and how to address them. J Bank Regul 21:125–138
Halloran D (2025) Understanding EU law: research matters–key insights for the 34th Dáil and 27th Seanad. Government of Ireland, Dublin
Handwerk B (2016) Feeling overtaxed? The romans would tax your urine. In: National Geographic News. https://www.nationalgeographic.com/news/2016/04/160414-history-bad-taxes-tax-day/. Accessed 21 Aug 2025
Hill B (2015) Money does not stink: the urine tax of ancient Rome | ancient origins. In: money does not stink: the urine tax of ancient Rome. https://www.ancient-origins.net/history-ancient-traditions/money-does-not-stink-urine-tax-ancient-rome-003408. Accessed 21 Aug 2025
Horan S (2011) Corporate crime. Bloomsbury Professional
Houben DR, Snyers A (2018) Cryptocurrencies and Blockchain. 103
Houben DR, Snyers A (2020) Crypto-assets–Key developments, regulatory concerns and responses. 77
Inter-Governmental Action Group against Money Laundering in West Africa (2008) Mutual evaluation report of Nigeria. GIABA, Dakar
Irwin ASM, Dawson C (2019) Following the cyber Money Trail: global challenges when investigating ransomware attacks and how regulation can help. J Money Launder Control 22:110–131
Joveda N, Khan MT, Pathak A (2019) Cyber laundering: a threat to banking industries in Bangladesh: in quest of effective legal framework and cyber security of financial information. Int J Econ Financ 11:54
Khan S (2019a) Anti-money laundering/counter terrorism financing efforts and forecasts for Ireland–part I. I L T 37:23–25
Khan S (2019b) Anti-money laundering/counter terrorism financing efforts and forecasts for Ireland–part II. I L T 37:38–41
Khan S (2020a) Anti-money laundering: a practitioner's insight into complying with the AML directive and GDPR–part 1. Irish Law Times 38:30–32
Khan S (2020b) Anti-money laundering: a practitioner's insight into complying with the AML directive and GDPR–part 2. I L T 38:45–48
Khan S (2020c) Anti-money laundering: a practitioner's insight into complying with the AML directive and GDPR–part 3. I L T 38:58–60
Khan S (2020d) Anti-money laundering: a practitioner's insight into complying with the AML directive and GDPR–part 4. I L T 38:86–88
Kirk E (2021) Law express: EU law, 7th edition. Pearson, Harlow, England u.a
Martin EA (2009) Oxford dictionary of law, 7th edn. Oxford University Press, Oxford
Marx K, Mandel E (1990) Capital: critique of political economy v. 1, New Edition. Penguin Classics, London; New York, N.Y
McGrath J (2019) 'Walk softly and carry no stick': culture, opportunity and irresponsible risk-taking in the Irish banking sector. Eur J Criminol 17:86–105
Meighan S (2004a) An examination of the concept of cyber-terrorism. Communique: The Manage J An Garda Síochána:24–28
Meighan S (2004b) Ireland's response to internet child pornography: a critical examination. In: M.Sc. In international police science. University of Portsmouth
Meighan S (2025) Money laundering in Ireland: context, History and the Law. Clarus Press, Dublin
Newburn T (2017) Criminology, 3rd edn. Routledge, London New York
Odedra D (2020) The Fault In Our SARs: The importance of realignment towards actionable intelligence | Arachnys. https://www.arachnys.com/the-fault-in-our-sars-the-importance-of-realignment-towards-actionable-intelligence/. Accessed 21 Aug 2025
OECD (2009) Money laundering and terrorist financing awareness handbook for tax examiners and tax auditors. OECD, Paris
Pol RF (2018) Anti-money laundering effectiveness: assessing outcomes or ticking boxes? J Money Launder Control 21:215–230

Pol RF (2019) Anti-money laundering ratings: uncovering evidence hidden in plain sight. J Money Launder Control 22:836–857
Pol RF (2020) Response to money laundering scandal: evidence-informed or perception-driven? J Money Launder Control 23:103–121
Rae S (2020) International fraud prevention conference. In: International fraud prevention conference. Croke Park, Dublin
Robinson J (1995) The laundrymen, New edition. Pocket Books, London
Rose N, O'Malley P, Valverde M (2006) Governmentality. Annu Rev Law Soc Sci 2:83–104
Ryder N (2020) Countering the financing of terrorism: sources of terrorism financing
Saperstein L, Sant G, Ng M (2015) The failure of anti-money laundering regulation: where is the cost-benefit analysis? Notre Dame Law Rev Online 91:1–11
Schott PA (2006) Reference guide to anti-money laundering and combatting the financing of terrorism: second edition and supplement on special recommendation IX, 2nd edn. The International Bank for Reconstruction and Development, The World Bank, The International Monetary Fund, Washington
Stessens G (2000) Money laundering: a new international law enforcement model. Cambridge University Press, Cambridge
Terry LS, Robles JCL (2018) The relevance of FATF'S recommendations and fourth round of mutual evaluations to the legal profession. Fordham Int'l L J 42:627–728
The World Bank (2009) Module 2 role of the financial intelligence unit. http://pubdocs.worldbank.org/en/834721427730119379/AML-Module-2.pdf. Accessed 21 Aug 2025
Unger B (2013) Can money laundering decrease? Public Financ Rev 41:658–676
UNODC (2021) Money laundering. United Nations Office on Drugs and Crime, Vienna
van Wegberg R, Oerlemans J-J, van Deventer O (2018) Bitcoin money laundering: mixed results? An explorative study on money laundering of cybercrime proceeds using bitcoin. J Financ Crime 25:419–435
Walsh EJ (1999) The enforcement of money laundering legislation. I C L J 9:204–217
White G (2020) Crime dot com: from viruses to vote rigging, how hacking went global, New Edition. Reaktion Books
Wiewiórowski W (2020) Opinion 5/2020 on the European Commission's action plan for a comprehensive policy on preventing money laundering and terrorism financing. European Data Protection Supervisor, Brussels
Williams P (1995) The general: godfather of crime. The O'Brien Press, Dublin
Williams P (2001) Evil empire: John Gilligan, His Gang and the Execution of Journalist Veronica Guerin. Merlin Publishing, Dublin, Ireland
Wong L (2013) Money-laundering in Southeast Asia: liberalism and governmentality at work. Contemp Polit 19:221–233

Chapter 3
Crypto-Assets: Technology, Adoption, and Criminal Exploitation

3.1 Money

Money is almost as old as civilisation. Different forms or types of money have been used as (fungible) assets throughout the history of humanity to overcome the limitations of the barter process (Weatherford 1997; Davies 2002). Modern economists assign money with the following functions:

1. *A medium of exchange*—money can be exchanged for goods and services.
2. *A means of payment*—money can be used to pay debts.
3. *A store of value*—money can be used to transfer purchasing power from the present to the future.
4. *A unit of account*—goods and services are quoted in terms of the money unit (Demetis 2010a, b, pp. 6–7; Franco 2015, p. 21)

Typically, three evolutions of money are recognised:

1. *Commodity money*—money backed by gold or other valuable materials.
2. *Contract money*—pieces of paper that promise to pay the bearer an equivalent value in gold or other valuable materials.
3. *Fiat money*—money that is not attached to gold or any other valuable material but is backed by a government and accepted by them for payment of tax debts (Demetis 2010a, p. 6)

A fourth evolution can be considered, namely *virtual money*. Virtualisation is defined as creating a virtual rather than an actual version of something at the same level of extraction. Some examples of virtual money include plastic money, mobile money, or crypto-assets, which will be discussed shortly. A good early example of virtual money is in-game money within massively multiplayer online role-playing games (MMORPGs) such as *World of Warcraft* and *Fortnite*. This in-game money could be purchased by exchanging fiat currency through the developer and used

S. Meighan, *Money Laundering and Crypto-Assets*, Contributions to Finance and Accounting, https://doi.org/10.1007/978-3-032-13481-3_3

internally in the game to build up characters and purchase items such as weapons and spells. Initially, the in-game money could not be re-exchanged for fiat money with the issuer (*non-convertible*), but it was possible to sell your developed avatar to another gamer in real life (outside the game, perhaps by exchanging logons/passwords for fiat money) and could potentially be used to launder criminal proceeds (Moiseienko and Izenman 2019). Some games now allow for in-game money to be directly exchanged for fiat money (*convertible*), increasing the opportunities for laundering. MMORPGs are, therefore, a good example of virtual money succumbing to fraudulent activities, being exploited by criminals, and being a *modus operandi* for the laundering of fiat money (Demetis 2010a, pp. 5–12).

3.2 Towards Crypto-Assets

The evolution and development of money detached the actual value of money from a perceived value, as the *money* is now intrinsically worthless. Instead, users rely upon a collective intentionality, or trust, in the item having value and being accepted as such, referred to as *Searle's Theory* (Demetis 2010a, pp. 5–7). By thinking of money as a record of the intended value, we can overcome objectors to Searle's Theory who question the ontological nature of virtual money, i.e. there is no physical backing object serving as the referent (Smit et al. 2011, pp. 16–20).

Definition Money is defined as "any self-referential system of exchange tokens or assets, that may or may not take physical form, that its community of users believes to be valuable, and uses as such" (Demetis, 2010b).

For money to work, "a collective intentionality and mechanisms that will establish trust among the collective" are required (Demetis 2010a, pp. 7–12).

Traditionally, that trust mechanism was provided by possession of physical cash and the digital ledgers of the world's governments and banks (centralised and decentralised networks, see Fig. 3.1). By maintaining a record of all balances and transactions, they guarantee that every transaction (transfers of assets/value) is safe and reliable, thereby maintaining trust in the system (Smit et al. 2011; Werbach et al. 2018). However, recent events such as the 2008 financial crisis, the 2010 PayPal ban on WikiLeaks' donations page, and the 2015 Greek bank restriction on withdrawals have led to that trust being eroded and a reinvigoration of the desire to remove government involvement and that of central authorities such as banks. To replace the traditional system with the desired internet-based payment mechanism (i.e. non-government backed virtual or digital money) required a distributed (see Fig. 3.1) ledger trusted by all participants (Popper 2016; Werbach et al. 2018). However, there were several obstacles that prevented this technology from being developed, namely *the Byzantine generals' problem* (BGP) and *the double-spend problem.*

The first major obstacle arises from the fact that the internet was developed as a global distributed system, built on the assumption that everyone is a trusted

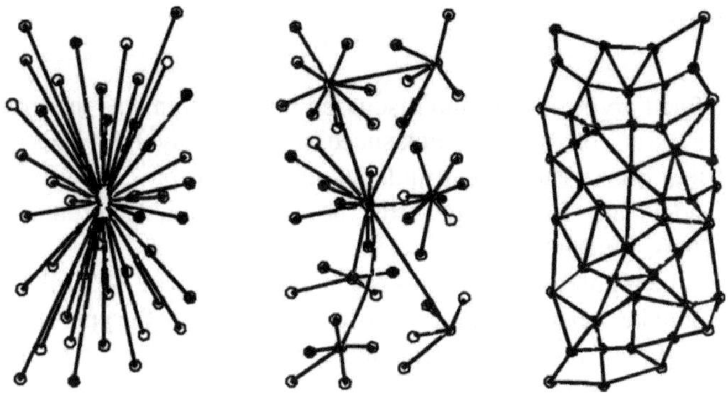

Fig. 3.1 Centralised, decentralised, and distributed networks

user. There was no account made for a user who may have a nefarious purpose, e.g. to change or falsify the digital ledger for their own benefit. Without a central authority to maintain trust in the system, each user must regularly agree, or arrive at *consensus*, on the current state of the ledger in a situation where the users cannot or do not trust each other but instead must trust in the agreed-upon ledger itself (Netflix 2018; Binance 2019). A perennial distributed network theory conundrum called the BGP illustrates this difficulty. In the parable, several generals are laying seize to Byzantium. They have the city surrounded and must collectively decide when to attack, without a means of secure communication. Unless all the generals attack at the same time, they will be defeated. The problem is how can the generals organise their plan and trust the messages they send and receive, which may have been delayed, destroyed, lost, or even falsified by one of the generals for their own gain. Each metaphorical general represents a node in the distributed network, which has their own copy of the ledger, and all nodes need to reach consensus on the current state of the ledger to prove asset ownership, approve transactions, and prevent an unscrupulous person double spending their value (Lamport et al. 1982; Binance 2019; Gatti 2019; Leishman n.d.). This brings us to the second major obstacle to overcome, namely the double-spend problem. Unlike the anti-counterfeiting security features provided on physical cash, digital money (simply a string of 1 s and 0 s) can be easily copied or falsified. In a centralised or decentralised system, a trusted third party could verify if the asset had already been transferred to another person (i.e. spent) by checking the one true ledger. This cannot be done in a distributed system where multiple versions of the ledger exist and where no party trusts the others (Franco 2015, pp. 11–13; Apodaca 2017). Over the years, many projects failed in their attempt to overcome these two obstacles, but in doing so, they developed several interesting technologies, techniques, and algorithms which a mysterious person, or group of people, called Satoshi Nakamoto, innovatively combined to implement the first functioning crypto-asset in 2009, Bitcoin (Nakamoto 2008; Popper 2016).

3.3 Bitcoin

Chapter 1 defined crypto-assets and discussed how Bitcoin was the first fully functioning crypto-asset, followed in quick succession by many thousands more. For the purposes of this book, a technical understanding of crypto-assets is not required. Interested readers are directed towards the Bitcoin and Ethereum Whitepapers (Nakamoto 2008; Buterin 2014).

To explore the regulation of crypto-assets for the purpose of AML, one needs to understand some key terminology, the basic functionality of crypto-assets, how one obtains (buys and sells) crypto-assets, and how crypto-assets compare to fiat currency and the traditional financial system.

Many consider crypto-assets to be a novel concept; however, a very early example of using a shared and agreed-upon ledger (solving the Byzantine generals and double-spend problems) to show the ownership and transfer of assets can be seen in a tiny cluster of islands in the Pacific region of Micronesia. As far back as the thirteenth century, the island of Yap was known for using giant calcite millstones called Rai stones, some of which were up to 4 m in diameter, as their primary currency (Fig. 3.2). They are still used to this day for land trades and marriage dowries. The stones originated from islands many miles away. A large amount of effort and

Fig. 3.2 A Yap stone

energy was expended in the mining, carving, and transportation of these stones. This work and the scarcity of stones contributed to their perceived value among the islanders; in essence, the islanders agreed they were valuable and suitable for trading. The enormity of the stones meant they could not be moved. The islanders kept a mental note of who owned each stone and used simple rules to solve any disputes that arose. After a stone was transferred to another islander, the transaction was broadcast to the entire community so that every person knew that the stone at a particular location belonged to the new owner. Each person kept a mental record (ledger) of all agreed ownership (consensus). This even worked with stones that were at the bottom of Yap's harbour after a shipwreck. Any attempt at misappropriation would be quickly rejected by the rest of the villagers, who had agreed upon who the true owner was (unless a majority of 51% of the villagers were in on the crime, which was unlikely for cultural reasons).

A cautionary tale for modern crypto-assets is the sudden deflation in value of the stones when a nineteenth-century ship's captain from Ireland, David O'Keefe, used modern methods and shipping to bring additional stones to Yap (Dash 2011).

Today, modern blockchain-based crypto-assets, such as Bitcoin, work in almost the exact same manner. The asset is a record of a transaction or transfer of ownership from one person to another, and a record of who currently owns the *value*. The asset, as such, *exists* only as a record on the blockchain and does not move. Its value comes from the fact that each user agrees that it has value to them, and they are willing to accept its value for payment and in exchange for goods and services. New assets are awarded to those (miners) who expend real-world resources (electricity, hardware, cooling, staff, etc.) to verify the transaction and keep consensus regarding the state of the ledger, which is of financial incentive to all participants in the crypto-asset system (Dash 2011; Poole 2018; Furneaux 2018, pp. 3–8).

The terminology[1] describing crypto-assets is under constant change, with various legislation and international recommendations unhelpfully using different terms interchangeably, such as cryptocurrencies, coins, tokens, crypto-assets, etc. It is important to understand several key terms from the broader crypto-asset lexicon, many of which are used differently from their usual everyday meanings and require a paradigm shift, to understand how crypto-assets work. This understanding is important when we analyse the collected data (Chap. 7) and develop socio-technical systems theory models of crypto-laundering and the regulation of crypto-assets (Chap. 8) to decide on the effectiveness, or otherwise, of regulating crypto-assets for the purposes of AML. This book will use Bitcoin as the referent to describe the key terminology. This is appropriately justified as it was the first crypto-asset, is still the most widely used, and its technological structure and operation form the basis for almost every other crypto-asset in existence.

Coins, tokens, and other similar words are often used to refer to the valuable part, or what the community of users perceived to be valuable, of a crypto-asset, e.g. 1

[1] The terminology and description were synthesised by the author from the following valuable sources: Nakamoto (2008), Franco (2015), Popper (2016), Antonopoulos (2016, 2017, 2019), Furneaux (2018), Finck (2018), Clohessy (2019), Spithoven (2019), and Bleakley (2020).

BTC or bitcoin. This value is what is transacted between two users; however, it is important to realise that no such coins or tokens exist. What we think of as such is a concept called an *unspent transaction output* (UTXO).

A *UTXO* is a fundamental concept of a Bitcoin transaction. They are indivisible crypto-asset units cryptographically *locked* to a specific owner and recorded on the blockchain. Whenever a user receives bitcoin (either as a transaction from another user or as a mining reward), that amount is recorded on the blockchain as a UTXO. A user's *balance* may be scattered as UTXO anywhere on the blockchain. The amount of a crypto-asset held by a particular user is calculated by scanning the entire blockchain and aggregating all UTXOs belonging to that user. The UTXO becomes spent when it is transferred to another user.[2]

A (public) *address* is shared or published (as a string of hexadecimal characters, which can be converted to a QR code for ease of use) to receive a transaction or transfer of *value* from another user. The vernacular is to send *tokens* or *coins* to an address. 1A1zP1eP5QGefi2DMPTfTL5SLmv7DivfN is an example of a Bitcoin public address in text format. This is the public address from the very first transaction on the Bitcoin blockchain.

A (private) *key* is required to send a *value* to another user. Possession of the private key proves ownership of the asset, as it is required to unlock the ability to transfer the UTXO onwards to another person. Public and private keys are generated using cryptographic algorithms and are linked to each other. Users can have any number of public keys, and their activity using one set of keys is not inherently tied to their activity using another set or their real-world identity. This is the pseudonymous nature of crypto-assets.

A *wallet* is a piece of software (an algorithm) that stores a user's private key(s) and the associated public addresses. Ironically, a wallet does not store any coins or tokens, as we know that these do not exist—only a record of their ownership exists on the blockchain. A better word for a wallet could be a keyring. One user can have multiple wallets, each of which may contain many private keys and their associated public addresses. There are many different types of wallets: some are stored online (*hot* wallets), while some are stored offline (*cold* wallets in the form of USB keys, written on pieces of paper, etc.). Closely associated with a user's private keys are *seeds* or *seed words*, which are a list of words that allow a user to reconstruct their wallet without having to remember their lengthy, incomprehensible private keys. As a user's "balance" may be scattered as UTXO anywhere on the blockchain, the wallet software scans the blockchain and aggregates all UTXOs belonging to the key pairs that are contained in the wallet.

[2] The other major form of crypto-asset is based on Ethereum. This operates on an account basis, akin to a regular bank account. Its other main application, *smart contracts*, spurred the rapid rise in derivative crypto-assets. The concepts discussed in this chapter, excluding UTXOs, equally apply to Ethereum-based assets; however, the technical differences will not be discussed in this book.

A *transaction* is a record of *value* transferring from one user to another. Transferring bitcoin requires three things: (1) a sending address (that has sufficient UTXOs associated with it), (2) a receiving address, and (3) a private encryption key (to unlock the UTXOs).

Every transaction that has ever taken place is recorded on the Bitcoin *blockchain*. Within the transaction, there is no link to the real-world identity of the person sending or receiving the crypto. This is where crypto-assets have both private and public natures at the same time. On one hand, real-world identities are private and not readily ascertainable from viewing the open blockchain. On the other hand, every transaction is available to any person interested in viewing it. This includes law enforcement who, as part of a criminal investigation, may seek to (1) trace value moving through the system, (2) cluster addresses in a manner that may provide a window into otherwise anonymous activity, and (3) associate those addresses with a single user (attribution).

A *block* is a piece of data that contains several transactions that are bundled together by a process called *mining*. *Miners* verify the legitimacy of transactions and are rewarded for their efforts by the receipt of transaction fees from all transactions within the block they mined, and newly minted assets. They provide security to the network by their proof of work or proof of stake, and in effect, incentivise the continued operation of the network.

A *blockchain* is a chain of blocks linked together *cryptographically*. Despite the hype surrounding it, it is simply a data structure that records transactions in a digital ledger that is distributed across many nodes on a network. This provides a transparent, open-source list of every transaction that has ever occurred, albeit without the real-world identities of the people behind the transactions.

An *exchange* is one of the most popular methods where a user can purchase assets in exchange for fiat currency. A user can also *cash out* their assets in exchange for fiat currency. It is important to note that assets transacted to an exchange are held in the exchange's own wallets; a balance is maintained on account for the user. Assets sent by a user from an exchange will be sent from the exchange's UTXOs, and the user's account will be deducted appropriately. Exchanges are becoming increasingly regulated and are required to collect KYC information on their customers, which can be useful to law enforcement when attempting to attribute transactions in a *follow-the-money* criminal investigation, and with the use of commercial blockchain analysis tools.

These concepts are best explained by means of a rich picture (Fig. 3.3) and a simple description of how one person transacts value to another person. Person A wishes to send 10 BTC to Person B (**1**). To do this, they must first acquire some bitcoin; this usually involves converting fiat currency from a bank account or other sources to bitcoin through an exchange (**2**). The exchange transfers 10 BTC to a public address held by Person A (**3**). Person A, using their wallet or other software, constructs a transaction. They *lock* this transaction using a public address that was supplied by Person B (**4**). This transaction is then joined with other people's

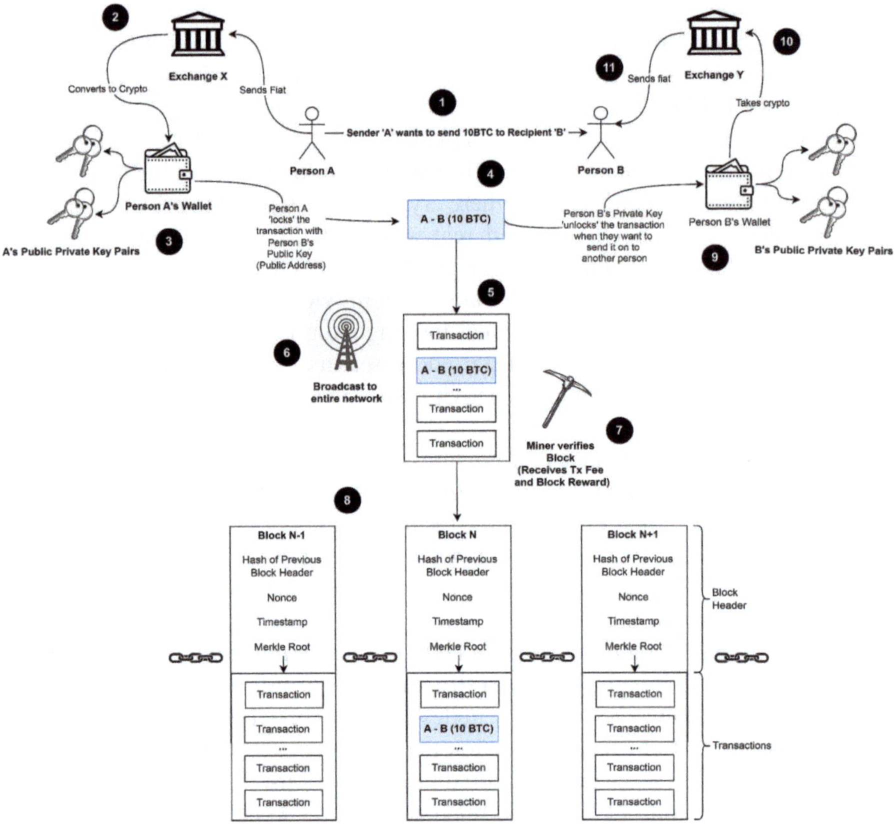

Fig. 3.3 Crypto-asset transaction

transactions and assembled into a candidate block (**5**). This block is broadcast to the entire network (**6**). Miners verify that the transaction is not fraudulent and has not been double spent (**7**). Miners provide processing power and the associated costs of electricity for power and cooling, to the Bitcoin network in exchange for the opportunity to be rewarded with bitcoin in the form of transaction fees and newly "minted" bitcoin. Once the block is verified, the transaction is complete it is added to the blockchain (**8**). Person B, at a later stage, could send this bitcoin to another person or may wish to convert it back to fiat currency. The process is the same. They "unlock" the transaction using the private key that corresponds to their public address and create a transaction to the desired recipient (**9**). In this case, the person wishes to "cash out" their bitcoin, so they send the transaction to an exchange (**10**), which credits their bank account with an equivalent value in fiat currency, minus a fee (**11**).

Although it is a simplistic representation of a complex process, this example covers the main functionality of crypto-asset transactions. It doesn't matter if the user's intention is good or bad, or whether the transaction is for legal or illegal purposes (the doubled-edged swords of technology discussed in Chap. 1); the process is the same, which is another point that makes detecting criminality and crypto-laundering difficult. All transactions look the same on the blockchain!

Initial debates around crypto-assets considered them to be a form of currency with the usual agentive properties given to fiat money (Whelan 2018). Monetary principles, such as deflation and inflation, were theorised by examining the concept of lost passwords, supply limits, etc. (Franco 2015, p. 33). However, given their volatile and virtual nature, a property-based legal definition was soon preferred and generally adopted, hence what were originally called crypto-currencies are now called crypto-assets (Albrecht et al. 2019; Irwin and Dawson 2019; Clark 2020, pp. 4–5). The novelty and technical difficulty of the blockchain need not confuse policymakers with the fact that, for all their strangeness, they quite easily meet all the traditional definitions of property (Maddox 2020, p. 146). Given they are legally considered property, they are subject to taxation (Revenue Commissioners 2020) but exempt from VAT [*Skatteverket v. Hedqvist* C-264/14 Judgment of the Court of Justice (Fifth Chamber) of 22 October 2015]. It is also possible to "seize" criminal crypto-assets; most likely by either serving a freezing order on a compliant exchange[3] or by transferring the impugned assets into a law enforcement wallet (Furneaux 2018, p. 255, b; Duff 2019; Attorney General's Cyber Digital Task Force 2020; CEPOL 2020).

Of more jurisprudential interest is how to define possession of a crypto-asset; is it merely possession of the private key? Unhelpfully, the United Kingdom jurisdiction taskforce (UKJT) concluded that a private key is not in itself to be treated as property because it is information (Clark 2020, p. 4). This shows a fundamental misunderstanding of the nature of crypto-assets; the asset is owned by the possessor of the private key, which cannot be separated from the value of the asset (defined and discussed in the following section). A recent legal notice (Fig. 3.4) in the *Financial Times* (Thursday, 30 June 2022) illustrates the difficulty in using, recovering, or freezing an asset when it has been transferred to an unknown location or unfriendly jurisdiction. It also shows the importance of keeping control of one's private key.

Crypto-assets can generally be considered as a self-governing (information) system that can be used for asset exchange (Chap. 5). The fact that crypto-assets are not backed by a government or central bank and were originally intended not to need any third party or government involvement fitted the cypher-punk, libertarian-inspired view that computer networks (information systems) could create order in society without transaction cost and, in turn, rebalance societal power dynamics. However, the reality is far from this ideal. Regulation and supervision are increasingly required from *trusted* third parties, and fiat money (government-issued money) is needed to enter (purchase crypto-assets) and exit (sell crypto-assets) the system

[3] A compliant exchange can be considered one that will accept a court order or answer an enquiry from law enforcement. These are usually the regulated VASPs or CASPS (see more presently). Examples of non-compliant exchanges are ones in unfriendly jurisdictions where the recognition or enforcement of a court order would be impossible.

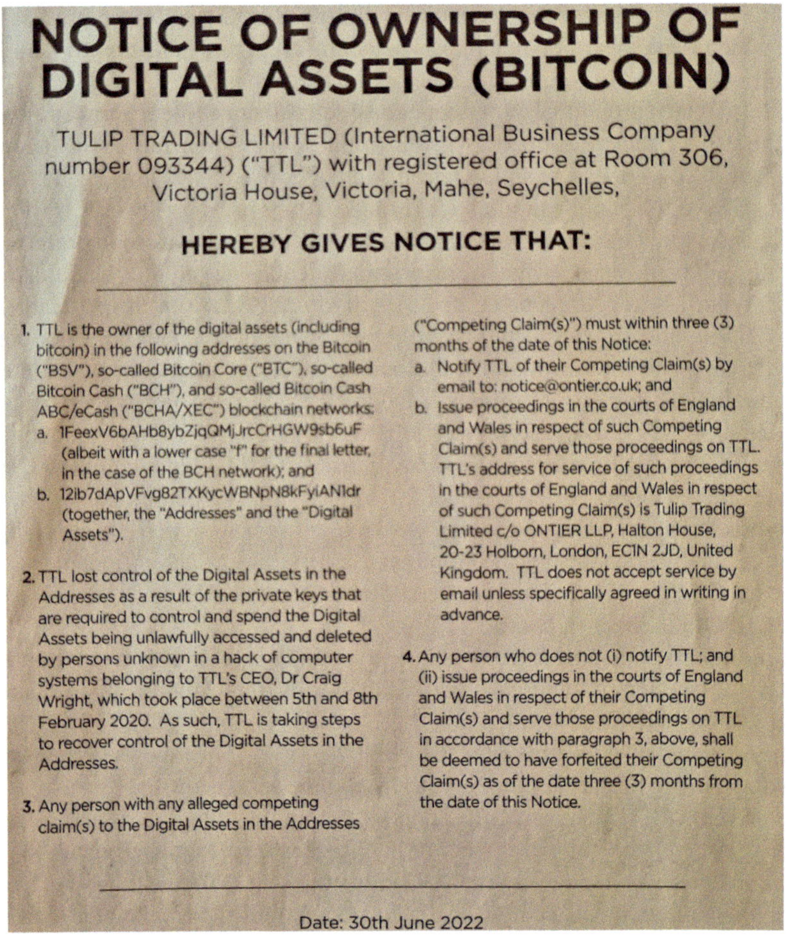

NOTICE OF OWNERSHIP OF DIGITAL ASSETS (BITCOIN)

TULIP TRADING LIMITED (International Business Company number 093344) ("TTL") with registered office at Room 306, Victoria House, Victoria, Mahe, Seychelles,

HEREBY GIVES NOTICE THAT:

1. TTL is the owner of the digital assets (including bitcoin) in the following addresses on the Bitcoin ("BSV"), so-called Bitcoin Core ("BTC"), so-called Bitcoin Cash ("BCH"), and so-called Bitcoin Cash ABC/eCash ("BCHA/XEC") blockchain networks:
   a. 1FeexV6bAHb8ybZjqQMjJrcCrHGW9sb6uF (albeit with a lower case "f" for the final letter, in the case of the BCH network); and
   b. 12ib7dApVFvg82TXKycWBNpN8kFyiAN1dr (together, the "Addresses" and the "Digital Assets").

2. TTL lost control of the Digital Assets in the Addresses as a result of the private keys that are required to control and spend the Digital Assets being unlawfully accessed and deleted by persons unknown in a hack of computer systems belonging to TTL's CEO, Dr Craig Wright, which took place between 5th and 8th February 2020. As such, TTL is taking steps to recover control of the Digital Assets in the Addresses.

3. Any person with any alleged competing claim(s) to the Digital Assets in the Addresses ("Competing Claim(s)") must within three (3) months of the date of this Notice:
   a. Notify TTL of their Competing Claim(s) by email to: notice@ontier.co.uk; and
   b. Issue proceedings in the courts of England and Wales in respect of such Competing Claim(s) and serve those proceedings on TTL. TTL's address for service of such proceedings in the courts of England and Wales in respect of such Competing Claim(s) is Tulip Trading Limited c/o ONTIER LLP, Halton House, 20-23 Holborn, London, EC1N 2JD, United Kingdom. TTL does not accept service by email unless specifically agreed in writing in advance.

4. Any person who does not (i) notify TTL; and (ii) issue proceedings in the courts of England and Wales in respect of their Competing Claim(s) and serve those proceedings on TTL in accordance with paragraph 3, above, shall be deemed to have forfeited their Competing Claim(s) as of the date three (3) months from the date of this Notice.

Date: 30th June 2022

Fig. 3.4 Legal notice regarding missing Bitcoin

(Hughes 1993; Spithoven 2019, p. 385). Given the prohibitively high costs now associated with mining, the only realistic way to obtain crypto-assets is to get ones that are already held by another person by:

1. Exchanging fiat currency for crypto-assets at an exchange.
2. Exchanging cash for crypto-assets at a crypto-ATM.[4]

[4] A crypto-ATM is a machine that allows a user to insert cash and send an equivalent value to either an exchange or a supplied public crypto-asset address (usually in the form of a QR code). Most crypto-ATMs in operation only deal in bitcoin and operate unidirectionally, i.e. fiat to crypto—where the users deposit cash and an equivalent value of bitcoin, minus a fee, is credited to a supplied Bitcoin public address. Less commonly, there are some bidirectional crypto-ATMs and some that deal in more than one crypto-asset.

3. Locating a person with crypto-assets who wishes to sell for fiat currency (P2P or person-to-person exchanges, e.g. localbitcoin.com, ebay.com).
4. Receiving a salary in the form of crypto-assets.
5. Accepting crypto-assets in exchange for goods and services (illegal services are usually found on the dark web).
6. Purchase crypto-assets from a traditional financial institution.[5]
7. Through the proceeds of cybercrime (e.g. ransomware and sextortion received in Bitcoin).
8. Stealing crypto-assets from an exchange (via a hack or exit scam) or from a user's wallet.

Important
These can be considered the interfaces or friction points between the real and the virtual/digital worlds. To exit the system, that is, sell crypto-assets, one must do the opposite of the above or find an exchange that issues some type of credit or debit card that will allow the value of their held crypto-assets to be spent on goods and services in the real world (after conversion to a fiat equivalent value). It is usually at these friction points that AML regulation (Chap. 4) is directed.

In a distributed ledger (blockchain), the complete ledger is fully transparent and can be seen by everyone, including law enforcement. Privacy is maintained by breaking the flow of information in another place when compared with a traditional bank (Fig. 3.5); in effect, by keeping private keys anonymous. The public can see that someone is sending value to someone else, but without information linking or attributing the transaction to a real-world identity (Nakamoto 2008, p. 6). This pseudo-anonymity is one of the most attractive features of the technology for money launderers. Note that we have used the phrase pseudo-anonymity, as blockchain analytics are able to attribute transactions and public addresses to a real-world user, which was thought to be impossible when Bitcoin was first used and exploited by criminals.

To consolidate our understanding of crypto-assets, it is useful to compare them with fiat currency, the traditional banking system, and Rai stones under several key headings (Table 3.1).

As we discussed in Chap. 1, while many users of crypto-assets use them for lawful transactions, criminals were early adopters of them and used their features, in ways (hopefully) unimagined by their creators, to their advantage for nefarious purposes, including money laundering. The focus of this book is a particular form of money laundering, namely crypto-laundering.

---

[5] In most cases, the purchaser is merely buying on option against a stated crypto-asset. The litmus test would be if their bank will transfer the asset to a supplied public address that is not controlled by them.

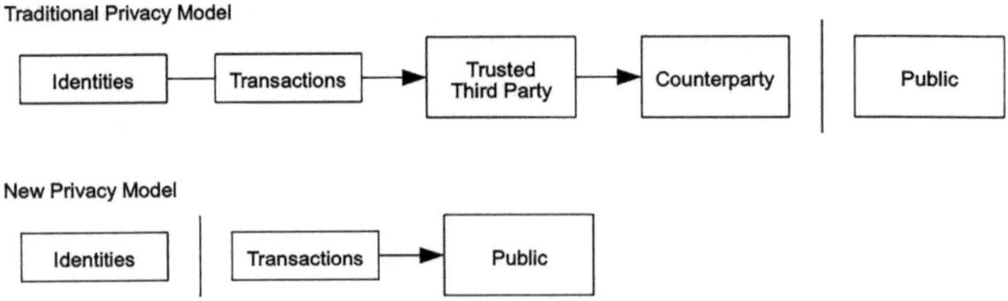

Fig. 3.5 Bitcoin privacy model from the Bitcoin whitepaper (2008)

Table 3.1 Comparison of fiat currency, traditional banking, rai stones, and crypto-assets

Categories	Fiat currency (cash)	Traditional banking System	Rai stones	Crypto-assets
Form	**Physical**—Paper notes and coins issued by central authorities. Only a small proportion of the total money supply is in physical form, with the remainder being in electronic form as part of the banking system. Cash is available from banks and ATMs.	**Virtual**—Digital and physical records in regulated financial and credit institutions. Reliance on computer records, such as databases and ICT.	**Physical**—Large stone discs quarried in Palau and transported by boat to yap.	**Virtual**—No physical form, digital entries on a blockchain that are verified through a process called mining.
Usage	Exchanged for goods and services through banks, financial institutions, businesses, and individuals.	Accounts can be opened at banks and other financial institutions. Value is exchanged through electronic transfers or cash withdrawals/ lodgements.	Acquired through community exchanges and transactions for significant events. Exchanged through oral agreements. Physical movement is not always necessary or possible.	Purchased on exchanges or earned through mining. Possible to exchange in a peer-to-peer fashion, but the majority of usage is through an exchange.
Cultural significance	No inherent cultural significance, but notes and coins may depict cultural symbols or historical figures.	No inherent cultural significance.	Significant cultural and historical importance in Yapese society.	May reflect the cultural significance of technology and libertarianism.

(continued)

Table 3.1 (continued)

Categories	Fiat currency (cash)	Traditional banking System	Rai stones	Crypto-assets
Network type	**Centralised**—Issued, controlled, and regulated through a central bank.	**Decentralised**—Each entity is regulated by a central bank and other government authorities, but is connected to banks in other countries via EFT systems (SWIFT, IBAN, etc.)	**Distributed**—Controlled by the community, trust-based system.	**Distributed**—Each node in the network is connected.
Perceived value	Widely accepted as legal tender. Value is typically stable but is subject to inflation, deflation, and government monetary policy.	Value is linked to the fiat currencies that it transacts.	Value is based on the effort put into bringing the stone to the island, and due to historical and cultural factors. The value is stable as it is based on community trust and historical significance.	Value is based on supply and demand; it is a speculative asset that is highly volatile and sensitive to market fluctuations.
Identity management	None, cash is a fungible asset.	Persons are linked to accounts with verified ownership (high levels of KYC, CDD, TM, and relationship was traditionally face to face).	Community agrees on the ownership of each stone.	Cryptographic keys and wallet addresses are used. It was originally intended that users could autonomously create and manage (multiple) pseudonyms (offering high levels of privacy); however, the majority of persons using crypto-assets now use an exchange which operates in a similar way to a traditional bank account.

(continued)

Table 3.1 (continued)

Categories	Fiat currency (cash)	Traditional banking System	Rai stones	Crypto-assets
Accessibility and method of transfer	Widely accepted as legal tender. Physical exchange and electronic transfers.	Widely accessible. Electronic transfers, checks, debit/credit cards.	Limited accessibility due to physical constraints. Ownership transferred through oral history and community consensus.	Global accessibility is dependent on ICT connectivity; however, peer-to-peer transactions on the blockchain are generally carried out through an exchange or via a crypto-ATM.
Record keeping	Holder of physical cash can use it.	Banks update and track balances and transactions through user accounts using private databases.	Community shared-mental note of ownership.	Transactions are recorded on a publicly available distributed data structure (blockchain) that is transparent, immutable, and tamper evident.
Supply	Regulated and controlled by central authorities.	Regulated by central banks and financial institutions.	Limited supply due to the scarcity of stones and the work required to mine them.	Varies by crypto-asset, for example Bitcoin has a fixed maximum supply, while some others may have inflationary-like mechanisms built in.
Portability	Easily transferable physically and using ICT.	Easily transferable using ICT.	Impractical to transport due to size and weight.	Easily transferable using ICT.
Storage	Physical vaults, bank accounts, digital databases.	Digital databases, records, storage systems.	Stored in public spaces, community recognition.	Digital wallets, hardware wallets, online platforms, offline storage.
Divisibility	Divisible into smaller denominations.	Digital entries allow for precise divisibility.	Not divisible.	Divisible into smaller units with a high level of precision.
Security	Counterfeit protection measures, legal frameworks.	Security protocols, encryption, legal frameworks.	Relied on community trust and oral history.	Relies on cryptographic algorithms.
Taxable	Yes.	Yes.	No, not part of Yapese culture.	Yes, dependent on local legislation.

(continued)

Table 3.1 (continued)

Categories	Fiat currency (cash)	Traditional banking System	Rai stones	Crypto-assets
Siezeable	Yes, subject to local legislation.	Yes, subject to local legislation.	No, due to physical form and cultural significance.	Yes, dependent on local legislation.
Misuse for criminal purposes	Yes.	Yes.	Not usually due to communal trust and oral history.	Yes.
Consensus / trust dependency	Trust in government and central authorities.	Trust in banks and financial institutions.	Relies on communal trust and oral history.	Trust in algorithm, technology, and cryptography (distributed or computational trust).

3.4 Crypto-Crime

Chapter 1 highlighted how the rapid growth and mainstream acceptance of crypto-assets present both significant benefits and serious risks; the classic technological double-edged sword. Positively, crypto-assets offer fast, efficient, global value transfers. Attractive to all in society, but empowering to the unbanked populations in developing nations, fostering financial inclusion and economic growth. Unfortunately, these same attractive attributes—distributed, irreversible, pseudonymous, and rapid global transactions—make crypto-assets equally appealing to organised criminal networks and other illicit actors.

Definition This book defines *crypto-crime* as any crime involving crypto-assets or blockchain technology. It includes both ***on-chain activity*** (e.g. smart contract exploits, ransomware payments, illicit transactions on public ledgers) and ***off-chain activity*** (e.g. fraud, phishing, drug trafficking, or scams using crypto as a payment method but occurring outside the blockchain).

Industry reports, from the major blockchain intelligence companies, estimated that in 2024 between $40 billion and $75 billion were received by public crypto-asset addresses they had identified as illicit, noting that this figure only covers *on-chain* criminality and not the majority of cases where profit is generated *off-chain* and moved into crypto-assets for transfer and laundering purposes (Chainalysis 2025; TRM Labs 2025). In 2023, the Federal Bureau of Investigation received more than 69,000 complaints from the public concerning crimes that had a crypto-asset nexus and estimated losses of $5.6 billion (Federal Bureau of Investigation 2024, p. 3).

Crypto-assets facilitate nearly every crime type, including *cyber-dependent* threats such as ransomware (where Bitcoin dominates due to its accessibility) and *cyber-enabled* crimes such as investment frauds, business email compromise (BEC), and romance fraud (Europol 2024; Federal Bureau of Investigation 2024; Chainalysis 2025).

Europol's Internet Organised Crime Threat Assessment (IOCTA) identifies ransomware attacks, child sexual exploitation (CSE), and economic crime as the primary cyber-threats in the EU. Each one of these is enabled and enhanced by the criminal (mis-)use of crypto-assets (Europol 2024). Europol's Serious and Organised Crime Threat Assessment (SOCTA) further underscores the enabling role played by crypto-assets in sustaining serious and organised crime. The report notes the immense financial gains generated by these illicit activities (Europol 2025). In essence, crypto-assets are seen as a cross-cutting facilitator of cybercrime and a challenger to criminal investigations and asset recovery (Europol 2020). Crypto assets have become the de facto method of victim-to-criminal payments in ransomware and exploitation schemes, as well as criminal-to-criminal payments on the dark web (Europol EC3 2021).

Unfortunately for criminals, the immense criminal profits generated also link the possessor of the funds to the crime. To avoid adverse law enforcement attention, an intricate array of money laundering techniques is required to break that linkage. With the introduction of crypto-assets, criminals are now using a crypto-asset specific version of cyber-money laundering, namely *crypto-laundering*—laundering the proceeds of crime through crypto-related digital assets.

3.5 Crypto-Laundering

Crypto-laundering is a crypto-asset-specific variant of cyber-laundering involving the laundering of the proceeds of crime through the crypto-asset system.

In some cases, the criminal proceeds are generated by real-world criminality such as drug trafficking. This scenario is referred to as "*off-chain*" activity, as the crime is committed outside the crypto-asset system and the proceeds are subsequently converted into crypto-assets to be laundered. "*On-chain*" activity refers to where the proceeds of a wide spectrum of cyber-criminality are received in the form of crypto-assets and are ready to be laundered, as they are already in the crypto-asset system and don't require conversion from fiat.

With the rise in ransomware attacks,[6] and the sale of illegal goods and services through online dark marketplaces,[7] crypto-assets have become a significant method

---

[6] A ransomware attack is where a malicious computer program is inserted into a victim's computer that denies access to the system until a ransom, usually in the form of crypto-assets, is paid. In many cases, the software is developed by a person who sells it to the ultimate criminal user, in a process known as crime-as-a-service (Goodman 2015; White 2020). At the end of 2022, there were estimated to be over 10,000 strains of ransomware available for criminals to purchase (Chainalysis 2023, p. 30).

[7] The dark web is a hidden, encrypted area of the internet accessed by a web browser called The Onion Router or TOR. Users of TOR are difficult to trace, as are the websites, forums, and blogs that exist as TOR hidden services. The dark web has become synonymous with the sale of illicit goods such as drugs, guns, pornography, and child abuse material. These items are sold anonymously on dark web marketplaces where crypto-assets are taken as payment (Bartlett 2015).

of victim-to-criminal and criminal-to-criminal payment; in effect, they have become a cross-cutting enabler of crime and cybercrime (Popper 2016; Europol 2020; White 2020; ElBahrawy et al. 2020; Europol EC3 2021). To be clear, however, the misuse of crypto-assets in this way is not necessarily a new phenomenon or process; it is more like *new wine in old bottles*, utilising traditional money laundering methods but where the value is in the form of virtual money (Grabosky 1998, 2001; Meighan 2004).

The goal of crypto-laundering is to move criminal money to public crypto addresses (incorrectly but colloquially known as wallets) where the predicate offence that generated it cannot be determined, and ultimately to a service that allows crypto-assets to be exchanged for fiat currency, usually via an exchange (Chainalysis 2023, p. 42). Crypto-laundering can be conceptualised by overlaying the traditional three-stage money laundering process (Fig. 2.2) onto a diagrammatic representation of the crypto-asset system (Fig. 3.6).

The process can be summarised as follows: a predicate offence is committed in the real world and the proceeds of criminal conduct are used to purchase crypto-assets in one of the ways discussed earlier, but most likely through an exchange or a crypto-ATM (*placement*). In the case of cybercrimes, such as ransomware attacks, the proceeds from the crime are already in the form of crypto-assets, and the placement stage can be considered the transaction that moves the funds into a public address controlled by the criminal. Like the traditional financial system, a money mule[8] could be used here to defeat any AML controls that the exchange might put

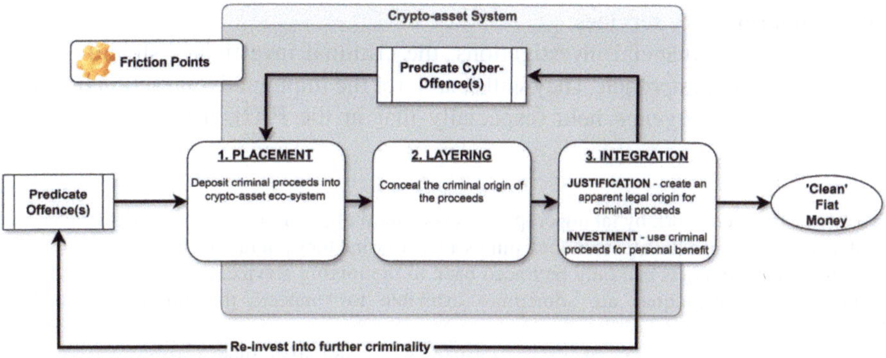

Fig. 3.6 Crypto-laundering process

[8] A money mule is a person who is recruited by criminals to receive money into their (bank) account, withdraw it, and pass it on to the criminal. They are often enticed by a promise of receiving a commission payment in return for the provided services, which often does not materialise. The benefit of using money mules is they have a readily available account and have already supplied identification that satisfies AML controls in the financial institution (Source: https://www.garda.ie/en/about-us/organised-serious-crime/garda-national-economic-crime-bureau/money-muling.html, accessed: 21 August 2025).

in place to prevent illegal activity. There will then be some level of obfuscation, such as mixing or tumbling services,[9] gambling sites,[10] or cross-chain activity[11] (*layering*). The criminal is now free to enjoy the *cleaned* money or reinvest in further criminality (*integration*). In the case of further cyber-crimes, it is not necessary to move the money from the crypto-asset system as it is already in a form that can be reused, but if they want to reinvest in other off-chain crimes or spend the money in the real world they usually must convert the money back to fiat (Christopher 2014; Brenig et al. 2015; Choo 2015; Goodman 2015; de Andrade 2017; Gifari et al. 2017; Mabunda 2018; Custers et al. 2019; Gonçalves 2019). There has also been anecdotal evidence of criminals exchanging private keys, often by exchanging cold wallets; however, the possessor still needs to convert to fiat at some stage to realise the value of the property.

Crypto-laundering typically involves two on-chain entities and services, namely exchanges and intermediary services. We have discussed exchanges previously; they are the important exits or "off-ramps" from the crypto-system that exchange crypto-assets for fiat money. Intermediary services exist within the crypto-asset system and allow criminals to hold funds, obfuscate the movement of funds, or swap between different crypto-assets (referred to as "cross-chain activity"). Examples of these services include mixers/tumblers, dark net marketplaces, and unhosted wallets[12] (Chainalysis 2023, p. 42). The use of these services, together with other encryption or privacy-enhancing technologies, is attractive to criminals and allows for effective integration of funds, layering, and solid cash-out opportunities (van Wegberg et al. 2018; Ishii 2019; Europol 2020). The effectiveness of any AML regulation, therefore, needs to be examined vis-à-vis these real-world friction points and the intermediary services.

In traditional financial investigations, the criminal investigator should adopt a *follow-the-money* approach. They will search for the impugned transaction by utilising *financial intelligence* held (especially that in the FIU), using their coercive

[9] Mixers or tumblers work by taking crypto-assets from multiple users, mixing them together, and sending each user an equivalent amount, minus a fee, to what they put in. The intended result is that each user's crypto-assets can only be traced back to the mixing service; however, special blockchain analytics techniques are sometimes available to "unpeel" this mixing (Chainalysis 2023, p. 45).

[10] There are some gaming sites that take in crypto-assets and allow their users to play games of chance or make bets on live sporting events. The criminal is hoping to create the impression that their assets have come from an apparently legal source. This type of activity has been occurring in the real world for decades, and there is no surprise that it has crossed into the virtual one too.

[11] Cross-chain activity, or hopping, refers to when one swaps their crypto-assets for an equivalent value in another asset, e.g. swopping Bitcoin for Ethereum, hoping to obfuscate the financial trail.

[12] An unhosted wallet is where a user maintains their public/private keypair (de facto possession of crypto-assets) outside of an exchange. This can be on a USB device, a mobile phone app, or even written on a piece of paper. The problem with unhosted wallets is the difficulty in attributing them to a real-world person as no KYC or CDD has taken place. Conversely, a hosted wallet means a keypair that exists on a third-party platform, such as a verified exchange, upon which a court order might be served, or an FIU power utilised.

police investigative powers, or by serving court orders on the relevant financial institution. This allows the analysis of the criminal financial activity and tracing the illicit flow from the predicate offence to its current location. When an asset is located, it may be secured by freezing the account holding it or taking possession of the asset itself. The investigator will then construct a full financial profile of the suspect to show the difference between their legitimate income and assets held. Finally, the suspect can be arrested for the purpose of an investigative interview, which may include statutory reverse onus inference provisions. A similar approach is followed in crypto-asset investigations, with the added advantage that the technology can be leveraged to detect complex crimes, including crypto-laundering, that are committed on the blockchain. Examples include *follow-the-(virtual-)money* on the transparent digital ledger,[13] blockchain-based digital identity schemes to enhance KYC,[14] and other use cases that attempt to implement AML controls on the blockchain at the time of the transfer.[15]

The blockchain is, for the financial investigator, *following-the-money* like having a copy of the bank statement of every person who uses the asset, albeit without a name identifying the real-world identity of the parties. The challenge is therefore in attributing the transaction to a real-world person (Furneaux 2018, p. 67). Using techniques such as open-source intelligence (OSINT), clustering and identifying *change* addresses (Furneaux 2018; CEPOL 2020), address dusting[16] (Europol EC3 2021), cookie tracking and using de-mixing techniques (Goldfeder et al. 2018), data mining and statistical analysis (Irwin and Dawson 2019), and graph network analysis (Weber et al. 2019) it is possible for commercial companies and law enforcement to trace and attribute real-world identities to illicit transactions. These techniques are collectively called blockchain analytics and allow the tracking of public addresses and transactions associated with "ransomware attackers, malware operators, scammers, human traffickers, dark net marketplace operators, and terrorist groups" (BBC, 2022). Unfortunately, the rapid pace of changing technology places significant training demands on law enforcement trying to keep up with the criminals; law enforcement is often only reactive.

The transparent nature of the blockchain also allows estimates to be made about the scale of crypto-asset-related criminality, which is not possible with traditional finance. Companies such as Chainalysis and Ciphertrace produce yearly crypto-crime reports that make for interesting reading and give an *indication* of the scale of the offending and how it evolves over time. It must be stressed that these reports are a snapshot in time with "lower bound estimates … likely to rise as additional illicit activity is discovered" through additional blockchain analysis and do "not include off-chain criminal where the proceeds may have been moved into crypto for

[13] For example: https://www.trmlabs.com/ and https://www.chainalysis.com/

[14] For example: https://tykn.tech/identity-management-blockchain/ (Accessed: 21 August 2025).

[15] For example: The Blockchain Council (2020).

[16] Address dusting is a technique where a tiny amount of a crypto-asset is sent to a suspect address to identify associated addresses using the "change" address. Unfortunately, criminals also use the same method to identify high-value individuals to steal funds from.

laundering" (Chainalysis 2023, p. 8). At the end of 2022, the market cap of all crypto-assets was approximately $1.1 trillion (Ciphertrace 2023). Of that, 0.24% or $20.6 billion has been associated with illegal activity (Chainalysis 2023, p. 6). $5.9 billion is attributed to the proceeds of crypto-scams, $3.8 billion to stolen crypto-assets or hacks, €1.5 billion to dark web marketplace revenue, $457 million to ransomware and extortion pay-outs, and smaller amounts in other areas including child sex abuse material, crime-as-a-service, and terrorist financing (Chainalysis 2023).

Of particular interest to this book is where the funds identified as being associated with on-chain criminality end up. This is important as it may give an indication of where regulation and enforcement need to be concentrated and how effective, or otherwise, any existing intervention is.[17] In 2023, most illicit assets (68%) were transferred to exchanges. This figure reduces to 50% of all illicit assets when we remove exchanges in high-risk jurisdictions (presumably those on the FATF grey and black lists, and those subject to UN and EU sanctions) and high-risk exchanges (those in jurisdictions where no AML controls exist and seen as favourable to launderers). This 68% figure is notable for two reasons. Firstly, as we will see in the next section, it is this area at which AML regulation is directed. Secondly, there is an assumption that a large proportion of illicit funds going to an exchange will be converted to fiat money and removed from the crypto-asset system. When we look at the remaining illicit funds, approximately 8% is sent to mixing services, 6% to other destinations (including gambling services), and 18% to what is known as decentralised finance (DeFi) protocols (Chainalysis 2023, pp. 42–45). DeFi is an emerging financial technology based on distributed digital ledgers and allows users access to "traditional" financial services such as investing, borrowing, or lending. However, it is important to stress that there are no fiat on- or off-ramps; the funds must already be in the form of crypto-assets and transferred to a regular exchange (sometimes erroneously referred to as a centralised exchange) to be converted back to fiat. Within DeFi, the most popular service at present is decentralised exchanges (DEX). A DEX is a peer-to-peer marketplace where transactions occur directly between crypto-asset users, utilising smart contracts and distributed applications or dApps, to facilitate trades. DEX are privacy-friendly and more anonymous than regular exchanges, as there is no need to provide personal information one's crypto-asset information. DEXs are highly susceptible to hacks and funds being stolen due to the transparency of the transaction information offering exploitation opportunities. Between June 2022 and May 2023, there were over $890 billion in transactions on the available DEX (see https://www.dune.com/dex), of which over 50% is thought to come from stolen crypto-assets (Chainalysis 2023, p. 45) (Table 3.2).

Despite the positive aspects of crypto-asset technology allowing law enforcement to leverage, there are still several technical challenges to overcome. Firstly, the challenge of attributing a crypto-asset public address to a real-world person is not straightforward. In Bitcoin alone, there are 2^{160} possible public addresses, more than

[17] The second question might be answered by tracking the changing destination of illicit funds over time, mapped against the introduction of legislation regulating crypto-assets for the purposes of AML.

Table 3.2 Destination of illicit funds

	2017 (%)	2018 (%)	2019 (%)	2020 (%)	2021 (%)	2022 (%)
Exchanges	68	79	89	81	77	68
DeFi	1	1	1	9	11	18
Mixers	4	6	4	9	9	8
P2P	11	11	4	1	1	1
Other	16	4	2	1	3	6

Source: Chainalysis (2023, p. 44). This was the only year that this very useful table was produced. Unfortunately, no data is available for 2023 and 2024

all the grains of sand on the world's beaches; therefore, it is possible for a tech-savvy criminal to make sure that every transaction they make uses different public addresses. Secondly, the technology is not standing still, and introducing regulation or enforcement to one area may have unintended consequences and drive criminals to embrace newer aspects of the technology. An example could be the use of privacy-enhancing coins (PECs), which are digital assets that use additional cryptographic techniques to make blockchain analytics and attribution even more complex. Thankfully, Silfversten et al. (2020) identified limited use to date of PECs for illicit transactions. This is due to the accessibility, ubiquity, and ease of use of regular crypto-assets, but they warn that a criminal might be driven to PECs if the regulation of regular crypto-assets makes them too unattractive for criminal use. Thirdly, even if impugned funds are traced to an exchange, that exchange must be in a friendly jurisdiction and be compliant with standard rules so that a court order can be served, or an FIU power utilised (Chap. 7), to reveal the real-world identity behind the transaction and/or freeze and seize the asset (Furneaux 2018; Interpol 2020; White 2020). This last point can be succulently summarised as questioning whether the regulation of the crypto-asset system off-ramps provides sufficient and effective coverage.

Having seen how crypto-assets have been misused for crypto-crime and crypto-laundering, the book will now proceed to the introduction of AML regulation on crypto-assets.

References

Albrecht C, Duffin KM, Hawkins S, Morales RVM (2019) The use of cryptocurrencies in the money laundering process. J Money Launder Control 22:210–216

Antonopoulos AM (2016) The internet of money: a collection of talks by Andreas M. Antonopoulos: volume 1, 1st edn. CreateSpace independent publishing platform

Antonopoulos AM (2017) The internet of money volume two: a collection of talks by Andreas M. Antonopoulos: volume 2, 1st edn. Merkle bloom LLC

Antonopoulos AM (2019) The internet of money volume three: a collection of talks by Andreas M. Antonopoulos: 3. Merkle bloom LLC

Apodaca R (2017) How Bitcoin works: a technical overview for beginners–Bitzuma. https://bitzuma.com/posts/how-bitcoin-works/. Accessed 21 Aug 2025

Attorney General's Cyber Digital Task Force (2020) Cryptocurency: enforcement framework. US Department of Justice, Washington, D.C
Bartlett J (2015) The dark net. Windmill Books, London
Binance (2019) What is Byzantine Fault Tolerance?
Bleakley C (2020) Poems that solve puzzles: the history and science of algorithms, Illustrated Edition. OUP Oxford, New York
Blockchain Council (2020) Certified Blockchain expert training course. Blockchain Council, California
Brenig C, Accorsi R, Müller G (2015) Economic analysis of cryptocurrency backed money laundering. 23rd ECIS Münster, Germany (S 1–18)
Buterin V (2014) Ethereum Whitepaper. https://ethereum.org/en/whitepaper/. Accessed 21 Aug 2025
CEPOL (2020) 09/2020/onl Darkweb and cryptocurrencies
Chainalysis (2025) The 2025 crypto crime report. Chainalysis, New York
Chainalysis (2023) Crypto Crime Report:2023
Choo K-KR (2015) Cryptocurrency and virtual currency: corruption and money laundering/terrorism financing risks? In: Handbook of digital currency. Elsevier, pp 283–307
Christopher CM (2014) Why on earth to people use bitcoin. Bus & Bankr LJ 2:1
Ciphertrace (2023) Crypto crime and anti-money laundering
Clark R (2020) UK jurisdiction taskforce publishes legal statement on status of Cryptoassets and smart contracts—Observations from Ireland. C L P 27:3–9
Clohessy T (2019) Blockchain: the business perspective. NovoRay, Galway
Custers BH, Pool RL, Cornelisse R (2019) Banking malware and the laundering of its profits. Eur J Criminol 16:728–745
Dash M (2011) David O'Keefe: the king of hard currency. In: Smithsonian Magazine https://www.smithsonianmag.com/history/david-okeefe-the-king-of-hard-currency-37051930/. Accessed 24 Nov 2021
Davies G (2002) A history of money: from ancient times to the present day, 3rd ed., with revisions. University of Wales Press, Cardiff
de Andrade MD (2017) Legal treatment of crypto-coins: the dynamics of bitcoins and the crime of money laundering. Braz J Pub Pol'y 7:44
Demetis D (2010a) Technology and anti-money laundering: a systems theory and risk-based approach. Edward Elgar, Cheltenham
Demetis D (2010b) The nature of money, Recorded Lecture
Duff C (2019) "Dirty money"–an overview of the Irish anti-money laundering landscape. C L P 26:85–90
ElBahrawy A, Alessandretti L, Rusnac L et al (2020) Collective dynamics of dark web marketplaces. Sci Rep 10:18827
Europol (2024) Internet organised crime threat assessment (IOCTA) 2024. Publications Office of the European Union, Luxembourg
Europol (2025) Serious and organised crime threat assessment–the changing DNA of serious and organised crime. European Union Agency for Law Enforcement Cooperation, The Hague
Europol (2020) Internet organised crime threat assessment. European Union Agency for Law Enforcement Cooperation, The Hague
Europol EC3 (2021) Bitcoin guide for investigators: following the money. Europol, The Hague
Federal Bureau of Investigation (2024) Cryptocurrency fraud report 2023. In: Internet Crime Complaint Centre (IC3), Washington
Finck M (2018) Blockchain regulation and governance in Europe. Cambridge University Press, Cambridge, United Kingdom; New York, NY, USA
Franco P (2015) Understanding bitcoin: cryptography, Engineering and Economics. Wiley, West Sussex
Furneaux N (2018) Investigating cryptocurrencies: understanding, extracting, and analyzing Blockchain evidence. Wiley, Indianapolis, IN

Gatti M (2019) The byzantine generals problem and bitcoin's solution. In: The Cryptonomist. https://en.cryptonomist.ch/2019/08/04/byzantine-generals-bitcoin-solution/. Accessed 21 Aug 2025
Gifari A, Anggorojati B, Yazid S (2017) On preventing bitcoin transaction from money laundering in Indonesia: analysis and recommendation on regulations. In: 2017 international workshop on big data and information security (IWBIS). IEEE, pp 143–148
Goldfeder S, Kalodner H, Reisman D, Narayanan A (2018) When the cookie meets the blockchain: privacy risks of web payments via cryptocurrencies. Proc Pri Enhan Technol 2018:179–199
Gonçalves MM (2019) How cryptocurrencies enable money laundering. Malmo University, Malmo
Goodman M (2015) Future crimes: everything is connected, everyone in vulnerable and what we can do about it. Corgi, London
Grabosky P (1998) Crime in cyberspace. In: Combating transnational crime: concepts, activities and responses, pp 195–208
Grabosky PN (2001) Virtual criminality: old wine in new bottles? Soc Leg Stud 10:243–249
Hughes E (1993) The Cypherpunk's Manifesto. https://nakamotoinstitute.org/static/docs/cypherpunk-manifesto.txt. Accessed 21 Aug 2025
Interpol (2020) Criminal finances and cryptocurrencies. Virtual
Irwin ASM, Dawson C (2019) Following the cyber Money Trail: global challenges when investigating ransomware attacks and how regulation can help. J Money Launder Control 22:110–131
Ishii Y (2019) Blockchain technology and anti-money laundering regulations under international law. /insights/volume/23/issue/1/blockchain-technology-and-anti-money-laundering-regulations-under. Accessed 21 August 2025
Lamport L, Shostak R, Pease M (1982) The byzantine generals problem. ACM Trans Program Lang Syst 4:20
Leishman A (n.d.) What Is the Byzantine Generals Problem? In: River Financial. https://river.com/learn/what-is-the-byzantine-generals-problem/. Accessed 21 Aug 2025
Mabunda S (2018) Cryptocurrency: the new face of cyber money laundering. In: 2018 international conference on advances in big data, computing and data communication systems (icABCD). IEEE, pp 1–6
Maddox N (2020) Bitcoin as Property? C L P 27:143–146
Meighan S (2004) Ireland's response to internet child pornography: a critical examination. In: M.Sc. In international police science. University of Portsmouth
Moiseienko A, Izenman K (2019) Gaming the system: money laundering through online games. RUSI Newsbrief 39:5
Nakamoto S (2008) Bitcoin: a peer-to-peer electronic cash system. 9
Netflix (2018) Cryptocurrency
Poole RM (2018) The Tiny Island with Human-Sized Money. https://www.bbc.com/travel/article/20180502-the-tiny-island-with-human-sized-money. Accessed 21 Aug 2025
Popper N (2016) Digital gold: the untold story of bitcoin. Penguin
Revenue Commissioners (2020) Tax and Duty Manual–Taxation of Cryptocurrency Transactions (Reviewed April 2020). In: Taxation of Cryptocurrency Transactions (Reviewed April 2020). https://www.revenue.ie/en/tax-professionals/tdm/income-tax-capital-gains-tax-corporation-tax/part-02/02-01-03.pdf. Accessed 21 Aug 2025
Silfversten E, Favaro M, Slapakova L, et al (2020) Exploring the use of Zcash cryptocurrency for illicit or criminal purposes. RAND Corporation
Smit JP, Buekens F, du Plessis S (2011) What is money? An alternative to Searle's institutional facts. Econ Philos 27:1–22
Spithoven A (2019) Theory and reality of cryptocurrency governance. J Econ Issues 53:385–393
TRM Labs (2025) 2025 crypto crime report. TRM Labs, San Francisco
van Wegberg R, Oerlemans J-J, van Deventer O (2018) Bitcoin money laundering: mixed results? An explorative study on money laundering of cybercrime proceeds using bitcoin. J Financ Crime 25:419–435

Weatherford J (1997) The history of money: from sandstone to cyberspace. Crown Publishers, Inc., New York

Weber M, Domeniconi G, Chen J, et al (2019) Anti-money laundering in bitcoin: experimenting with graph convolutional networks for financial forensics. arXiv preprint arXiv:190802591

Werbach K, Braman S, Jaeger PT (2018) The Blockchain and the new architecture of trust. MIT Press, Cambridge, MA

Whelan K (2018) Should central banks be concerned about virtual currencies? 19

White G (2020) Crime dot com: from viruses to vote rigging, how hacking went global, New Edition. Reaktion Books

Chapter 4
Regulating Crypto-Assets: AML Systems and Enforcement

Crypto-asset technology, initially embraced by a niche cadre of cypherpunks and cyber-libertarians, has achieved almost universal public acceptance in a relatively short period of time (Popper 2016). It is seen as important for the health of the rapidly expanding global economy, especially in online trade and commerce (Bartlett 2015, pp. 80–81). However, as this book has previously discussed (Chap. 3), like all technology, it can be exploited for illegal uses (FATF 2013, 2014, 2020a; Gensler 2018; Houben and Snyers 2018, 2020; O'Sullivan 2020; Popper 2016). This crypto-asset-enabled cyber-criminality, especially crypto-laundering, is of growing interest and concern to civil society.

4.1 Choices to Be Made

Authorities need to decide whether to ignore, isolate (ban), integrate, or regulate the technology (Carney 2018; Ellul et al. 2020, p. 2).

Given that Bitcoin was launched in 2009, the evidence of widespread crypto-asset criminal misuse and the attention given by international organisations, such as the FATF, ignoring their regulation is no longer a viable option (Albrecht et al. 2019, p. 215).

Some jurisdictions, such as China, Bolivia, Mexico, and Turkey, have outwardly banned crypto-asset use outright.[1] There may be many reasons for deciding to take this path; however, doing so is not considered the best option as it disregards all the potential benefits of the technology, and it may be a futile exercise as the technology is freely accessible through any internet-connected device (Bartlett 2015, pp. 80–81; Twomey 2013). There is also evidence available via blockchain analytics to show

[1] https://www.euronews.com/next/2022/08/25/bitcoin-ban-these-are-the-countries-where-crypto-is-restricted-or-illegal2 (Accessed: 21 August 2025).

S. Meighan, *Money Laundering and Crypto-Assets*, Contributions to Finance and Accounting, https://doi.org/10.1007/978-3-032-13481-3_4

substantial crypto-asset usage in the countries that have banned its use. The reasons for banning the technology may be unrelated to the technology itself. Take, as an example, China.[2] They began as a crypto-asset pioneer and are still a major contributor to Bitcoin mining. They ban their citizens from holding crypto-assets; however, it is speculated that this ban is for political reasons, such as population control, preventing outward capital flows, and because China is thought to be developing its own Central Bank Digital Currency (Academy of European Law 2021). Currently, the public can hold fiat money issued by a Central Bank in the form of banknotes and coins, but only financial institutions hold electronic central bank money in the form of *reserves*. A *central bank digital currency* (CBDC) would be an electronic form of central bank money that could be used by households and businesses to make payments and store value (Bank of England 2020, p. 7). It could be based on the same technology as a crypto-asset, but it would be issued by a central authority that falls outside of our definition of a crypto-asset as set out in Chap. 1.

Some jurisdictions have fully embraced and integrated crypto-assets into their financial system by:

1. Offering themselves as crypto-asset sanctuaries that heavily invest in and offer business support to companies developing the technology, for example Malta[3] and Ireland.[4]
2. Not taxing crypto-asset earnings, e.g. Belarus, Germany, and Malaysia.[5]
3. Replacing their fiat currency with crypto-assets, e.g. El Salvador.[6]
4. By introducing a CBDC to supplement the fiat money supply—countries such as the United Kingdom are considering this (Bank of England 2020).

4.2 Regulating Crypto-Assets

Most countries, even those that have gone down the integration path, have decided to regulate certain aspects of crypto-assets to guard against illicit activities, ensure financial stability, and protect the investing and consuming public (Ellul et al. 2020; Foley et al. 2019; Forsman 2020; Gensler 2018; Silfversten et al. 2020). The latter two of these reasons can be considered as *prudential* regulation and supervision,

---

[2] https://www.bbc.com/news/technology-58678907
https://www.ft.com/content/430ffad7-d95a-4c85-bc62-c26c65bfb379
https://www.euronews.com/next/2021/11/20/bitcoin-ban-these-are-the-countries-where-crypto-is-restricted-or-illegal2 (Accessed: 21 August 2025).

[3] https://www.bloomberg.com/news/articles/2018-04-23/how-malta-became-a-hub-of-the-crypto-currency-world-quicktake (Assessed: 21 August 2025).

[4] https://www.gov.ie/en/speech/50cac-speech-to-blockchain-ireland-week-2021/ (Assessed: 21 August 2025

[5] https://decrypt.co/43513/countries-that-dont-tax-bitcoin-gains (Assessed: 21 August 2025).

[6] https://www.rte.ie/news/world/2021/1123/1262555-bitcoin-el-salvador/; https://www.bbc.com/news/world-latin-america-59368483 (Assessed: 21 August 2025).

which is beyond the scope of this book. Therefore, only the regulation that guards against cyber-laundering will be considered.

There are several factors to consider when introducing regulation on new technology.

Firstly, governments must balance the need to prevent the illicit activity with the necessity to allow a sufficient degree of freedom for the technology to develop and its positive aspects to emerge (Carney 2018; Connell 2018; Gensler 2018; Haffke et al. 2020; McCarthy 2019). Responsible regulation must therefore rest on a frank and common-sense determination of how people are using and misusing the technology, with regulation focusing on the crimes being committed with the technology and not on the technology itself (Connell 2018; Fairfield 2018; McCarthy 2019).

Secondly, crypto-asset technology is rapidly developing, meaning that it may easily bypass or outpace any regulation introduced. Regulatory responses must be adaptive enough to spurn advances that aim to defeat the regulation introduced while being specific enough to capture with legal certainty the criminal activity being regulated (Paesano 2019, p. 5).

Thirdly, while there is a broad consensus on the need to regulate crypto-assets to prevent illicit use, such as crypto-laundering, there is inconsistent legislative implementation. This has the potential to leave regulatory gaps that might be exploited by criminals undertaking a form of international arbitrage.

Fourthly, there is no point in introducing regulation until the technology is sufficiently understood by legislators and law enforcement. It is important to properly define the aspects and operation of the technology upon which is being regulated and then working forward from these basic principles to a position where the potential AML risks can be understood and examined so the regulation can mitigate the risk identified (Al-Tawil and Younies 2021; Clark 2020; Ellul et al. 2020; FATF 2014; Holman and Stettner 2018; Houben and Snyers 2018, 2020; McCarthy 2019; Twomey 2013; White 2020).

Finally, there are many challenges to regulating crypto-assets in a jurisdiction other than the one in which the controlling entity is located.

When regulating new technology, there are generally two approaches to controlling illicit activity: either introduce new laws or adapt existing ones. Regarding crypto-laundering and the regulation of crypto-assets for the purpose of AML, the majority view has been to adapt the existing AML framework to encompass crypto-assets or bring them into the scope of current legislation. This approach is not without criticism, and many have argued that adapting twentieth-century banking laws to account for new technology is insufficient and stretches the existing legislation to such an extent as to create unintended gaps in the policy regime (Academy of European Law 2021).

The remainder of this chapter will discuss and analyse regulating crypto-assets for AML, following the same format as in Sect. 2.2.2. and outlined in Fig. 2.3; the international dimension (the FATF), the supranational dimension (the EU), and finally, the national dimension (Ireland). The chapter will then consider the crypto-asset services that have previously been identified as being the most likely to be exploited by criminals:

1. Fiat *on-* and *off-ramps* such as exchanges, P2P exchanges, and crypto-ATMs.
2. Intermediary services such as DeFi, mixers/tumblers, unhosted wallets, and gambling sites.

4.2.1 The International Dimension: The FATF and the Regulation of Crypto-Assets

The development and growing general acceptance of internet-based payment methods, such as crypto-assets, were taken seriously by the FATF because the technological benefits—speed, low cost, cross-border, disintermediation, pseudonymity—could be readily exploited by criminals to bypass traditional AML controls to launder criminal proceeds (FATF 2021a, pp. 11–12).

The FATF's Recommendation 15 requires countries and financial institutions to identify and assess the money laundering risks that may arise in relation to new products, business practices, and delivery mechanisms for both new and pre-existing products and to take appropriate measures to manage and mitigate those risks (Financial Action Task Force 2019). The consistent approach of the FATF has been to bring new and emerging technologies into the scope of the existing AML regime and impose the traditional KYC, CDD, transaction monitoring, and STR reporting obligations on people and businesses using the new technology; crypto-assets are no different.

Since June 2014, the FATF has published several key documents to address the growing threat of crypto-laundering and review the actions implemented (Table 4.1). Most importantly, in October 2018, the FATF adopted changes to its AML standards to explicitly define and bring crypto-assets into the scope of risk-based AML regulation for the first time.

Table 4.1 Key FATF crypto-asset discussion papers

June 2014	Virtual Currencies: Key Definitions and Potential AML/CFT Risks (FATF 2014)
June 2015	Guidance for a Risk-Based Approach to Virtual Currencies (FATF 2015)
October 2018	Amendment of the FATF recommendations to include crypto-assets (VAs) and virtual asset service providers (VASPs)
June 2019	New interpretative note 15—New technologies
June 2020	12 Month Review of the Revised FATF Standards on Crypto-assets and Virtual Asset Service Providers (FATF 2020b)
September 2020	Crypto-assets Red Flag Indicators of Money Laundering and Terrorist Financing (FATF 2020a)
July 2021	Second 12 Month Review of the Revised FATF Standards on Crypto-assets and Virtual Asset Service Providers (FATF 2021b)
October 2021	Updated Guidance for a Risk-Based Approach to Crypto-assets and Virtual Asset Service Providers (FATF 2021a)
July 2024	Targeted Update on Implementation of the FATF Standards on Virtual Assets And Virtual Asset Service Providers (FATF 2024)

Crypto-assets are referred to as *virtual assets* and are defined as:

> a digital representation of value that can be digitally traded, or transferred, and can be used for payment or investment purposes (Financial Action Task Force 2019).

Transfer means to conduct a transfer on behalf of another natural or legal person that moves a transaction from one virtual asset address or account to another (Financial Action Task Force 2019). The FATF definition of a crypto-asset does not include digital representations of fiat currencies, securities, and other financial assets that are already covered elsewhere in the FATF recommendations.

Those exchanges that deal with certain crypto-assets activities are referred to as *virtual asset service providers (VASPs)* and are defined as:

> any natural or legal person who, as a business, conducts one or more of the following activities or operations for or on behalf of another natural or legal person:
>
> 1. Exchange between crypto-assets and fiat currencies
> 2. Exchange between one or more forms of crypto-assets
> 3. Transfer of crypto-assets
> 4. Safekeeping and/or administration of crypto-assets or instruments enabling control over crypto-assets
> 5. Participation in and provision of financial services related to an issuer's offer and/or sale of a crypto-asset
> (FATF 2019).

An important distinction to make is that the FATF does not aim to regulate the technology that underlies crypto-assets or VASP activities but rather the natural or legal persons conducting crypto-activities on behalf of other natural or legal persons (FATF 2021a, pp. 31–32). Crypto-assets are defined in a technologically neutral and expansive manner.

The FATF recommendations require VASPs to be regulated, licensed, and subject to effective monitoring and supervision by a competent authority.

In June 2019, a new Interpretative Note to Recommendation 15 was issued, which emphasised the application of a risk-based approach and the full AML regime to the crypto-asset activities that are captured by the VASP definition (FATF 2021a, pp. 7–9).

The October 2021 guidance document was the result of several previous iterations and a comprehensive industry and public consultation process. The guidance is split into three main sections. Firstly, and rather helpfully, it outlines the development of the AML regulation of crypto-assets and VASPs to date and summarises the main positive reasons for imposing AML regulation on the new technology. Secondly, it shows how and which crypto-assets and VASPs are covered by the FATF recommendations. Thirdly, it describes how the FATF AML regime applies to VASPs and other obliged entities that deal in certain crypto-assets.

The guidance states that the definition of a crypto-asset is meant to be interpreted broadly and functionally to cover a wide range of activities and to accommodate technological advancements and innovative business models. The definition of a crypto-asset is technologically neutral and is to be applied to the basic characteristics of the asset and not the technology it employs (FATF 2021a, pp. 22–24).

The FATF guidance also states that the definition of a VASP should be read broadly and functionally to determine if an entity falls within the scope of the AML regime (FATF 2021a, pp. 24–31).

The guidance explicitly states that VASPs must comply with the requirements of Recommendation 16, the so-called *travel rule*. The VASP is obligated to obtain, hold, and submit originator and beneficiary information associated with crypto-asset transfer. Again, this is phrased in a technologically neutral manner, and the exact workings of the scheme are not prescribed. This rule should also be applied when a VASP transfers crypto-assets to entities and services not captured by the AML requirements, for example peer-to-peer or unhosted wallets. The travel rule raises the question of how on earth a VASP obtains this information and how they technically implement the travel rule on a technology that was intended to be pseudonymous?

The FATF definitions appear to bring the vast majority of fiat *on-* and *off-ramps* (the *real-world friction points*) into scope and subject them to AML regulation. However, they are not sufficiently wide to capture all crypto-activity, especially P2P exchanges, mining, and certain on-chain activities such as DeFi, mixers/tumblers, and unhosted wallets. In Chap. 3, it was seen that a large proportion of *on-chain* criminal proceeds are sent to these services for possible eventual conversion to fiat currency. The definitions have already been surpassed by the technology, as they do not apply to assets that can be used as collectables, such as non-fungible tokens (NFTs), or those that can be used in exchange for some service or access to a system (utility tokens), offering potential crypto-laundering typologies that are outside the scope of AML regulation. An NFT is a type of crypto-asset that is unique rather than interchangeable and is, in practice, used as a collectible rather than as a payment or investment instrument. They can also be referred to as crypto-collectibles (FATF 2021a, p. 24). Examples may include partial shares in real-world art items or truly digital items that are appealing to collectors. In theory, they could be used for money laundering in the same way as art and real-world collectables.

4.2.2 The Supranational Dimension: The EU and the Regulation of Crypto-Assets

On 19 June 2018, the EU adopted European Parliament and Council Directive (2018/843/EU) amending Directive (EU) 2015/849 (5AMLD), which amended and expanded certain parts of 4AMLD and, for the purposes of the book, purportedly introduced:

> substantial [regulatory] improvement to better equip the Union to prevent the financial system from being used for money laundering by limiting the anonymity related to crypto-assets and VASPs (Duff 2019, p. 86; European Commission 2021).

The EU, recognising the money laundering risk presented by crypto-assets, treats VASPs as *obliged entities* with the same AML obligations as traditional financial institutions. They must register with local authorities, report suspicious transactions, and obtain information about their customers (Holman and Stettner 2018; O'Sullivan 2020, p. 24; Paesano 2019, pp. 2–3). Some have argued that this continued expansion of the AML system adds further complexity to an already broken system (Odedra 2020).

Previously, the EU referred to a crypto-asset as a *virtual currency* and defined it as a:

> digital representation of value that is not issued or guaranteed by a central bank or a public authority, is not necessarily attached to a legally established currency and does not possess a legal status of currency or money but is accepted by natural or legal persons as a means of exchange which can be transferred, stored and traded electronically (5AMLD).

A VASP was narrowly defined as:

> providers engaged in exchange services between [crypto-assets] and fiat currencies (5AMLD).

The preamble to 5AMLD, although not legally binding, offered insight into the intention of the legislators. Recitals 8 and 9 state that businesses engaged in certain crypto-asset activities, especially exchange services between crypto-assets and fiat currencies, were under no EU AML obligations to identify suspicious activity, meaning criminals could exploit the anonymity provided by the technology and transfer the proceeds of crime freely into the EU financial system. These recitals also acknowledged that it is possible to transact in crypto-assets without utilising the services of a VASP, meaning a lot of crypto-related activity will be outside the scope of AML regulation. Recital 10 acknowledged that crypto-assets are mostly used as a means of payment but could also be used for other purposes and find broader applications, such as means of exchange, investment, store-of-value products, or use in online casinos. The stated objective of 5AMLD was to cover all the potential criminal uses of crypto-assets at the time, that is 2018.

It was acknowledged by the EU that 5AMLD, as it stood, was insufficient for the way in which crypto-assets are contemporaneously used and misused. As part of the proposed EU AML reform package (Sect. 2.2.4), the EU signalled its intent to widen the scope of AML regulation on crypto-assets and implement the required FATF travel rule. According to the EU, these proposals will ensure a coherent EU framework for dealing with crypto-assets that comply with FATF requirements and reduce regulatory fragmentation—the so-called enemy of effective crypto-laundering enforcement.

The *Markets in Crypto-assets* (MiCA) regulation (EU) 2023/1114 is a part of a wider digital finance package, which focuses primarily on prudential supervision, which is beyond the scope of this book, but it does introduce new definitions of crypto-assets and VASPs.

Definition Article 3 of MiCA defines a *crypto-asset* as "a digital representation of value or rights which may be transferred and stored electronically, using *digital ledger technology* or other similar technology".

Digital ledger technology is defined as a type of technology that supports the distributed recording of encrypted data—a blockchain—of which crypto-assets are one of the major applications.

Definition The EU redefines a VASP as a *crypto-asset service provider (CASP)*, which is defined as any person whose occupation or business is the provision of one or more crypto-asset services.

The services are the same as those defined in the FATF definition. Therefore, there is no substantial difference between a VASP and a CASP, just another example of superfluous and misaligned terminology, which is unhelpful from a legal perspective. In effect, CASPs have become obliged entities and subject to the entire gamut of AML regulation.

To give effect to the travel rule required by the FATF (cf. Recommendations 15 and 16), the EU decided to recast Regulation (EU) 2015/847 on information accompanying transfer of funds (the "TFR"). The TFR, as currently enacted, demands that an obliged entity, when transferring funds over €1000, ensure that details of the payer and payee accompany the transaction. Identifying information. Art. 2(2) of the regulation applies to traditional wire transfers involving fiat currency or its digital/virtual representation (bank notes, coins, scriptural money, and electronic money).

The recast TFR lays down rules on the identifying information about originators and beneficiaries that must accompany transfers of crypto-assets where at least one of the payment providers or CASPs is established in the Union (Art. 1 TFR recast). Art. 3 defines an originator as

> A person that holds an account with a CASP and allows a transfer of crypto-assets from that account, or, where there is no account, that gives a transfer of crypto-asset order.

It further defines a beneficiary as

> A person that is the intended recipient of the transfer of crypto-asset.

The recast regulation applies to transfers of funds, in any currency or crypto-asset valued at more than €1000, which are sent or received by a CASP or an intermediary payment service provider established in the Union but excludes the transfer of funds using a payment card, an e-money instrument, a mobile phone, or any other similar digital device once several conditions apply (Art. 2 TFR recast).

The CASP of the originator must ensure that the transfer of the crypto-asset is accompanied by (but does not have to be directly attached to the transaction) the name of the originator, the originator's account number (where an account is used to process the transaction), the originator's address, official personal document number, customer identification number or date and place of birth. The name of the beneficiary and the beneficiary's account number (if it exists) must also accompany the transaction.

Before transferring the asset, the CASP shall verify the accuracy of the originator based on documents, data, or information obtained from a reliable and independent source. If no account number is used, the CASP shall ensure that the transfer of crypto-assets can be individually identified, and the public address identifiers of the originator and beneficiary are recorded.

The CASP is precluded from executing the transfer until it fully complies with this article (Art. 14 TFR).

The beneficiary's CASP must ensure that the required information is included in, or follows, the transfer of the asset, and they must have a system in place to detect when that information is missing. They must then verify the information before making it available to the beneficiary, if the transfer or series of transfers exceeds €1000, when a cash or anonymous electronic money pay-out is requested, or where the CASP has reasonable grounds for suspecting money laundering (Art. 16 TFR).

The beneficiary CASP shall consider missing or incomplete data when assessing if the transaction is suspicious as the basis for making a report to the FIU (Art. 18 TFR).

The technical feasibility of implementing this rule for VASPs will be challenging and, given the nature of blockchain and DLT, perhaps impossible (Academy of European Law 2021).

As they stood, the definitions used in 5AMLD were hopelessly narrow and outdated. The definitions set out in MiCA bring the EU's definitions in line with the FATF recommendations, which is welcome, but still leaves many crypto-asset services outside the scope of AML, as was seen in the previous subsection. It is also argued that the EU's definitions create legal uncertainty and leave loopholes that allow some crypto-asset users and intermediaries to escape AML regulation (Haffke et al. 2020, p. 138).

The creation of uniform AML standards across the Union, as set out in the AML package, may go some way to dealing with this position if the legislators are aware of the expansion of the technology and how it can be misused by criminals. However, if certain activities and users are out of scope of AML, there exists the potential for criminals to take advantage for the purposes of money laundering.

4.2.3 The National Dimension: Ireland and the Regulation of Crypto-Assets

The EU's 5AMLD brought crypto-assets into the scope of AML and imposed certain obligations on the businesses that provide certain services relating to them. As required by EU membership, Ireland transposed 5AMLD into national law with the enactment of the *Criminal Justice (Money Laundering and Terrorist Financing) (Amendment) Act 2021*; the provisions of this act were commenced on 23 April 2021.

The definitions provided in Irish law are broadly in line with the FATF recommendations and EU law.

Definition Ireland refers to crypto-assets as virtual assets and defines them as "a digital representation of value that can be digitally traded, or transferred, and can be used for payment or investment purposes but does not include digital representations of fiat currencies, securities, or other financial assets" (S. 24 Criminal Justice Money Laundering and Terrorist Financing) Act, 2010 as amended).

Definition A VASP means a (legal or natural) person who, by way of business, carries out one or more of the following activities for, or on behalf of, another (legal or natural) person:

1. Exchange between crypto-assets and fiat currencies.
2. Exchange between one or more forms of crypto-assets.
3. Transfer of crypto-assets, that is to say, conduct a transaction on behalf of another person that moves a virtual asset from one virtual asset address or account to another.
4. Act as a custodian wallet provider.
5. Participation in, and provision of, financial services related to an issuer's offer or sale of a virtual asset or both (ibid., *S. 24*).[7]

A VASP does not include a designated person that is not a financial or credit institution and that provides virtual asset services in an incidental manner and is subject to supervision by a national competent authority, other than the Central Bank. A custodian wallet provider means an entity that provides services to safeguard private cryptographic keys on behalf of its customers, to hold, store, and transfer virtual currencies. The reference to a virtual currency appears to be a drafting error that follows the EU definition and was taken out of context.

As the Irish definitions are based on those espoused by the FATF, the criticisms discussed above equally apply in Ireland, e.g. insufficient AML coverage of certain criminal usage.

VASPs are defined as *designated persons* (the Irish version of an obliged entity) for the purposes of the *Criminal Justice (Money Laundering and Terrorist Financing) Act, 2010 as amended*, and are therefore subject to all of the general AML obligations contained in Part 4 of the act, and the specific crypto-related obligations set out (Section 25, Sections 106A to 106Y).

Each VASP must be registered with the Central Bank of Ireland (CBI). A legal or natural person who carries on the business of a VASP without an authorisation commits a criminal offence (ibid., Section 106E). VASPs that were in existence prior to the introduction of the legislation are allowed to continue operating under a transitional provision once they have made an application for registration to the CBI (ibid., Section 106F). The Bank must take steps to ensure that the persons operating the VASP are *fit and proper* (ibid., ss. 106G-M). The ultimate beneficial owners of the VASP must be identified (ibid., Section 106 N). The CBI may revoke all or part of the authorisation at any time (ibid., Section 106P). The CBI may issue a direction

[7] The definitions of Virtual Asset and VASP are due to be replaced when parts of (EU) 2023/1113 the EU Transfer of Funds Regulation are transposed into Irish Law. In that case, these definitions will be replaced by crypto-assets and cryptoasset service providers (see Chap. 2), but the legal effect will be minimal.

to the VASP to cease carrying out all or specific crypto-asset business (ibid., Section 106Q). The CBI is the competent authority for the AML supervision of VASPs and implements a graduated approach to supervision where more intensive supervision is directed towards VASPs and services at a higher risk of money laundering.

VASPs will be subject to the following AML requirements. Failure to comply with these is a serious criminal offence that may be dealt with by the criminal justice system or may result in civil enforcement action under the CBI's Administrative Sanctions Procedure:

1. Carrying out a money laundering risk assessment of their business.
2. Performing KYC and CDD on their customers.
3. Subject higher-risk customers to EDD.
4. Carrying out ongoing TM of their customers' activities.
5. Reporting STRs to the FIU where money laundering is suspected.
6. Maintaining, reviewing, and implementing AML policies, procedures, and controls.
7. Providing ongoing AML training to all staff
8. Retaining appropriate records for the required statutory period (Central Bank of Ireland 2021; Lawlor and Ritchie 2021)

The Irish approach to the regulation of VASPs is summarised in Fig. 4.1.

As with the international and transnational regulation, the vast majority of on- and off-ramps (real-world friction points) are subject to Irish AML regulations; however, there are significant gaps around certain on-chain activities that have the potential to be leveraged by criminals for the purposes of crypto-laundering.

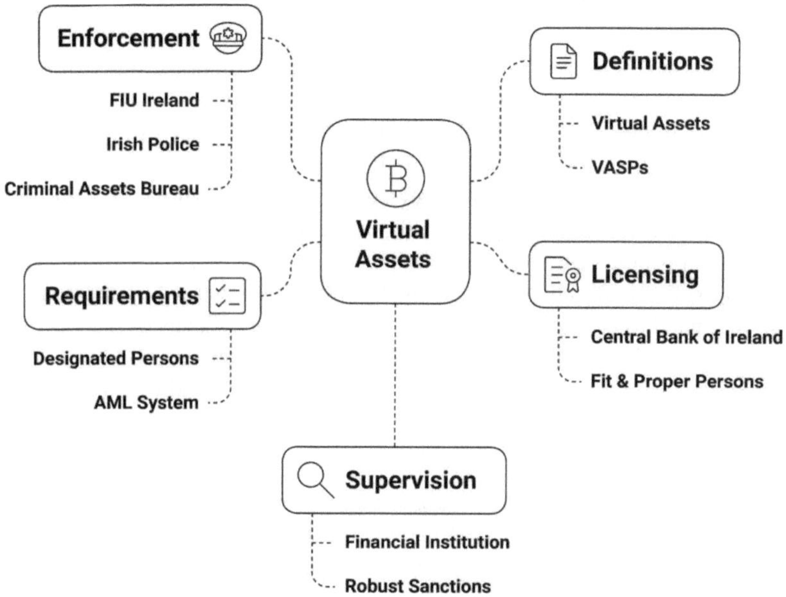

Fig. 4.1 Summary of Irish crypto-asset AML regulation

This is now an appropriate juncture to examine the types of VASPS in operation today. All VASPs legally operating in Ireland are required to be authorised by the Central Bank of Ireland, implement a risk-based approach to AML, perform KYC/CDD/TM, and report suspicious transactions to the FIU. Some VASPs may only perform one or two of the services listed in the legal definition; however, many provide multiple crypto-asset services to their customers (often in conjunction with eMoney, payment, and transfer services). These *full-service* VASPs allow the user to set up an account much like a regular bank account. This account can receive credits by way of electronic transfers from other credit and financial institutions (including from third parties). It can also receive crypto-asset transfers, including those that do not come through a VASP (via unhosted wallets), making AML controls redundant. The account allows the user to purchase many different types of crypto-assets (cross-chain activity) and place the value from these in their account. The balance of the account can be transferred to other accounts, to other crypto-asset public addresses (including unhosted), or can be spent using an issued debit card. The potential for criminal exploitation of these accounts to launder illicit proceeds of crime is readily apparent.

The appropriateness and effectiveness of the Irish position is one of the main questions of this book and will be examined in detail in Chap. 6 when discussing the case study of FIU Ireland. What will be required is sufficient data, including an examination of the STRs received by the FIUs from VASPs, to understand the phenomenon of crypto-laundering and its pursuit and detection.

4.3 Observations

Taking the main discussion points from the preceding sections, one can synthesise a table of the main crypto-asset services and entities that are used by criminals to commit cyber-laundering and tabulate their AML significance (Table 4.2), whether they are regulated for the purposes of AML, and what controls are in place if they are within the scope of current AML regulation. This will allow the framing of the discussion on any conclusions this book might make on the regulation of crypto-assets for the purposes of AML.

Regarding the material discussed in this chapter, several key themes or areas emerge that need to be considered when examining the efficacy of the current legislative framework for regulating crypto-assets for the purposes of AML. These will be considered when discussing the case study of FIU Ireland (Chap. 6 and 7) and when drawing conclusions from this book (Chap. 9). The key themes can be listed as follows:

1. The suitability of imposing existing laws on crypto-asset technology (Academy of European Law 2021; Pol 2018, 2019, 2020).
2. The sufficiency of coverage given by the current AML regulations to the crypto-asset activities of crypto-launderers.

Table 4.2 Exploitation of on–/off-ramps for crypto-laundering[a]

Crypto-asset service	Overview	AML implications	Regulated for AML
Crypto-asset exchanges	Platforms facilitating the buying, selling, and trading of crypto-assets	High risk of money laundering and illicit activities due to perceived anonymity, technology, and global accessibility	Yes
Exchanges in high-risk countries	Exchanges operating in jurisdictions with higher levels of AML/CFT risks	Increased risk of money laundering, weak regulatory oversight, and potential facilitation of illicit activities	May claim to have AML controls, but not effective or operational
High-risk exchanges	Exchanges with a history of AML-related issues, regulatory violations, or weak compliance measures	Higher risk of money laundering, facilitation of illicit transactions, and regulatory enforcement actions	May claim to have AML controls, but not effective or operational
Mixers/ tumblers	Services designed to enhance the privacy and anonymity of crypto-asset transactions	Potential facilitation of money laundering and obscuring the source of funds	No
Darknet marketplaces	Underground online platforms for illegal goods and services, often accepting crypto-assets	Higher risk of money laundering, illicit transactions, and facilitation of illegal activities	No
Unhosted wallets[a]	Crypto-asset wallets that are not managed or controlled by a third-party service provider	Difficulties in tracking transactions and identifying wallet owners	No
Gambling sites	Online platforms offering gambling and betting services with crypto-assets	Potential for money laundering, fraud, and illegal gambling activities	Yes
Decentralised exchanges (DEX)	Platforms facilitating peer-to-peer trading without intermediaries	Challenges in implementing AML controls due to decentralised nature	No
Crypto-ATMs	Physical machines allowing users to buy or sell crypto-assets	Potential for anonymous transactions and misuse for money laundering	No—But complying with stringent AML controls makes them an unattractive business proposition for legal operators
Privacy-enhanced coins (PECs)[b]	Crypto-assets that incorporate advanced privacy features, such as Monero	Potential for money laundering and obscuring the source of funds	No

(continued)

Table 4.2 (continued)

Crypto-asset service	Overview	AML implications	Regulated for AML
Non-fungible tokens (NFTs)	Unique digital assets representing ownership or proof of authenticity of a specific item or piece of content	Potential for use in money laundering and illicit activities, especially if associated with high-value assets	No
Intermediary services	Services providing intermediary functions in crypto-asset transactions, such as escrow services or OTC (over the counter) trading	Potential for facilitating money laundering, illicit transactions, and unauthorised activities	Varies by platform, service provided, and country operating in

[a]Adapted from industry papers and reports, and several key crypto-asset textbooks (Carlisle 2024; Chainalysis 2020; Ciphertrace 2021; Elliptic 2020; Furneaux 2018, 2024)
[b]Note that PECs and Unhosted Wallets are shown as not being regulated for AML in the table. They are being subjected to more stringent AML controls when the first EU AML Regulation comes into effect in 2027, however, their encrypted nature and lack of visibility (see →Chap. 3) means they are effectively unregulated

3. The level of data that is available to law enforcement and its implications for the investigation of crypto-laundering.
4. The challenges faced by law enforcement agencies conducting crypto-asset investigations.
5. The rapid pace at which the technology evolves.
6. The training needs of law enforcement.
7. The possibility that regulation may have unintended consequences on criminal tactics.

References

Academy of European Law (2021) Annual conference on financial compliance in the EU 2021
Al-Tawil TN, Younies H (2021) The implications of the Brexit from EU and bitcoin. J Money Launder Control 24:137–149
Albrecht C, Duffin KM, Hawkins S, Morales RVM (2019) The use of cryptocurrencies in the money laundering process. J Money Launder Control 22:210–216
Bank of England (2020) Discussion Paper–Central Bank digital currency: opportunities, challenges and design 57
Bartlett J (2015) The dark net. Windmill Books, London
Carlisle D (2024) The crypto launderers: crime and cryptocurrencies from the dark web to DeFi and beyond. Wiley, Hoboken, NJ
Carney, M., 2018. The future of money: a speech given by mark Carney, governor of the Bank of England to the inaugural Scottish economics conference, Edinburgh university 2 march 2018.. Bank of England
Central Bank of Ireland (2021) Virtual asset service providers. Central Bank of Ireland, Dublin
Chainalysis (2020) The 2020 geography of cryptocurrency report: analysis of geographic trends in cryptocurrency adoption, usage, and regulation (September 2020)

Ciphertrace (2021) Cryptocurrency crime and anti-money laundering report

Clark R (2020) UK jurisdiction taskforce publishes legal statement on status of crypto-assets and smart contracts—Observations from Ireland. C L P 27:3–9

Connell D (2018) Do EU regulations combating money laundering and the financing of terrorism adequately tackle cryptocurrencies? The case of Ireland. I J E L 21:68–90

Duff C (2019) "Dirty money"–an overview of the Irish anti-money laundering landscape. C L P 26:85–90

Elliptic (2020) Financial crime typologies in crypto-assets: the concise guide for compliance leaders. Elliptic, London

Ellul J, Galea J, Ganado M, McCarthy S, Pace GJ (2020) Regulating Blockchain, DLT and smart contracts: a technology regulator's perspective. ERA Forum 21:209–220

European Commission (2021) Anti-money laundering and counter terrorist financing [WWW Document]. URL https://ec.europa.eu/info/business-economy-euro/banking-and-finance/financial-supervision-and-risk-management/anti-money-laundering-and-counter-terrorist-financing_en. Accessed 21 Aug 2025

Fairfield J (2018) Cryptocurrencies: oversight of new assets in the digital age. Library of Congress, Washington

Financial Action Task Force (2013) Guidance for a risk-based approach prepaid cards, mobile payments and internet-based payment services. FATF-GAFI, Paris

Financial Action Task Force (2014) Virtual currencies—key definitions and potential AML/CFT risks. FATF-GAFI, Paris

Financial Action Task Force (2015) Guidance for a risk-based approach virtual currencies. FATF-GAFI, Paris

Financial Action Task Force (2019) International standards on combatting money laundering and the financing of Terrorism & Proliferation: the FATF recommendations. FATF-GAFI, Paris

Financial Action Task Force (2020a) FATF report: virtual assets red flag indicators of money laundering and terrorist financing. FATF-GAFI, Paris

Financial Action Task Force (2020b) 12 month review of the revised FATF standards on virtual assets and virtual asset service providers. FATF-GAFI, Paris

Financial Action Task Force (2021a) Updated guidance for a risk-based approach to virtual assets and virtual asset service providers. FATF, Paris

Financial Action Task Force (2021b) Second 12-month review of revised FATF standards–virtual assets and VASPs. FATF-GAFI, Paris

Financial Action Task Force (2024) Virtual assets: targeted update on implementation of the FATF standards on VAs and VASPs. FATF-GAFI, Paris

Foley S, Karlsen JR, Putniņš TJ (2019) Sex, drugs, and bitcoin: how much illegal activity is financed through cryptocurrencies? Rev Financ Stud 32:1798–1853

Forsman M (2020) 30 years of combating money laundering in Sweden and internationally—does the system function as intended? Sveriges Econ Rev 1:24–55

Furneaux N (2018) Investigating cryptocurrencies: understanding, extracting, and analysing Blockchain evidence. Wiley, Indianapolis, IN

Furneaux N (2024) There's no such thing as crypto crime: an investigative handbook, 1st edn. John Wiley & Sons, Incorporated, Newark

Gensler G (2018) Cryptocurrencies: oversight of new assets in the digital age. A Speech Given to the Committee on Agriculture, United States House of Representatives July 18, 2018. Library of Congress, Washington

Haffke L, Fromberger M, Zimmermann P (2020) Cryptocurrencies and anti-money laundering: the shortcomings of the fifth AML directive (EU) and how to address them. J Bank Regul 21:125–138

Holman D, Stettner B (2018) Anti-money laundering regulation of cryptocurrency: U.S. and global approaches [WWW document]. Allen & Overy, LLP. URL https://www.allenovery.com/en-gb/global/news-and-insights/publications/the-international-comparative-legal-guide-to-anti-money-laundering. Accessed 21 Aug 2025

Houben DR, Snyers A (2018) Cryptocurrencies and Blockchain 103
Houben DR, Snyers A (2020) Crypto-assets–Key developments, regulatory concerns and responses 77
Lawlor D, Ritchie G (2021) Virtual asset service providers in Ireland. Simmons & Simmons LLP, Dublin
McCarthy J (2019) Fintech: the legal and regulatory significance for Irish banking. C L P 26:139–146
O'Sullivan J (2020) After the gold rush. Gazette Law Soc 114:20–25
Odedra D (2020) The fault in our SARs: the importance of realignment towards actionable intelligence | Arachnys. URL https://www.arachnys.com/the-fault-in-our-sars-the-importance-of-realignment-towards-actionable-intelligence/. Accessed 21 Aug 2025
Paesano F (2019) Working paper 28: regulating cryptocurrencies: challenges and considerations. Basel Institute on Governance
Pol RF (2018) Anti-money laundering effectiveness: assessing outcomes or ticking boxes? J Money Launder Control 21:215–230
Pol RF (2019) Anti-money laundering ratings: uncovering evidence hidden in plain sight. J Money Launder Control 22:836–857
Pol RF (2020) Response to money laundering scandal: evidence-informed or perception-driven? J Money Launder Control 23:103–121
Popper N (2016) Digital gold: the untold story of bitcoin. Penguin
Silfversten E, Favaro M, Slapakova L, Ishikawa S, Liu J, Salas A (2020) Exploring the use of Zcash cryptocurrency for illicit or criminal purposes. RAND Corporation
Twomey P (2013) Halting a shift in the paradigm: the need for bitcoin regulation. T C L R 16:67–89
White G (2020) Crime dot com: from viruses to vote rigging, how hacking went global, New Edition. ed. Reaktion Books

Chapter 5
Socio-Technical Systems Theory in AML Context

> *Playing a part is, deep down, about seeing yourself as a part, a tiny part of a much larger whole, that, if you play your part perfectly, can be greater than the sum of the parts ... Iago in Japan is simple ego, the readiness to throw a whole exquisitely designed mechanism into chaos by focussing in on one small part of it.*
>
> *(Iyer 2020, pp. 31, 77).*

Systems theory begins with a simple but profound observation. Any entity of interest, whether a living organism, a social construct, or a complex phenomenon, can be understood as a *system* delineated by its *boundary* that distinguishes it from its more complex *environment*. The interplay between system, boundary, and environment provides a foundational lens through which systems theory frames all subsequent concepts.

Consider a single-celled organism such as an amoeba. Its cellular membrane delineates what belongs to the organism (the internal cytoplasm, organelles, and genetic material) and what lies outside in the environment (nutrients, toxins, and other organisms). Through this membrane, the amoeba exchanges matter and information with its environment to regulate its internal processes and to maintain its stability in the face of external change. In essence, the system transforms its *inputs* into *outputs* that are useful to the environment, least it will not survive.

Systems can also be made up of systems. While the single cell is a complete system in itself, complete with its own boundary and environment, it rarely operates in isolation. Cells come together and aggregate into tissues, organs, individuals, groups, organisations, and so on. Each level forms a distinct system whose boundary encloses all of the subordinated subsystems. Each level in the *hierarchy* retains the system, boundary, environment triad while exhibiting emergent properties (*synergy*) and feedback dynamics that cannot be fully explained by reductive analysis.

Systems theory can be applied to complex human constructs such as criminal activity and organisations that aim to prevent and detect criminality. As these involve the interaction of people and technology, coming together in a structured manner to

S. Meighan, *Money Laundering and Crypto-Assets*, Contributions to Finance and Accounting, https://doi.org/10.1007/978-3-032-13481-3_5

perform tasks, *socio-technical* systems theory is proposed as being most appropriate for this book, and to understand crypto-laundering and its pursuit and detection by the FIU.

Socio-technical Systems Theory is a versatile framework for deconstructing complexity (*wicked problems*) and designing strategic interventions. It can provide a holistic framework for uncovering interdependencies, anticipating emergent behaviour, and designing effective interventions across complex, multi-level environments.

5.1 A Theoretical Scaffold

The theoretical framework is a natural extension of the literature review from the previous chapters. While the purpose of the literature review is, among other things, to highlight the state of the current academic knowledge around the regulation of crypto-assets for the purpose of AML, including any gaps and shortcomings therein, the theoretical framework outlines the perspective taken to answer the chosen research questions. It will detail the theories and concepts used to address or make sense of the problem under investigation (Lempriere 2019).

Engagement with theory is a crucial element of any research. A key question for researchers, regardless of their tradition or philosophical stance, is what role does theory play in their research? Walsham (1995) sets out three distinct uses of theory: as an initial guide to design and data collection; as part of an iterative process of data collection and analysis; and as a final research product. This book will use theory in all three ways. There is no doubt that theory primes and influences the data collection and analysis phases of any research, but there is a danger that it can negatively influence and restrict the researcher by narrowing their focus to that espoused by the chosen theory. It is therefore desirable to preserve a degree of openness to the field of data, and a willingness to modify initial assumptions and theories (Walsham 2006, pp. 324–325, 1995, pp. 76–77), which the author has attempted to do in this book through iterative rounds of data analysis.

To think systemically, one must first understand why it is important to understand systems in the first place, and then what exactly a system is (Betley et al. 2021).

5.2 Why Systems?

While science, logic, and reductionism have contributed to some complex problems being managed, there is a growing realisation that the use of classical scientific methods that rely upon specialisation and compartmentalisation in an "attempt to reduce complexities to their constituent [parts] and build an understanding of the wholeness through knowledge of its parts is no longer valid" (Skyttner 2005, pp. 36–37)—akin to the Japanese concept of *Iago* as seen at the start of this chapter.

Problems cannot be understood, addressed, resolved, or improved without engaging in a cyclical and iterative process, with real progress only coming when the richest understanding of the whole is achieved (Reynolds and Holwell 2020, p. 310).

To make sense of complexity and avoid problematic interventions, one must, inter alia, examine the problem:

1. While focusing on and having cognisance of the bigger picture
2. From multiple perspectives, including being respectful of those different from our own
3. In terms of wholes and relationships rather than looking at individual constituent parts in isolation
4. Moving up and down levels of abstraction (between parent and child systems)
5. Being mindful of undesirable, latent system behaviours produced by the complex system's internal structure (Churchman 1968; Bawden 1998; Midgley 2008; Chapman 2004; Meadows 2009; Cabrera and Cabrera 2018; Jackson 2019)

Systems theory offers a way to achieve this.

Systems theory (Wiener 1948; Von Bertalanffy 1950; Boulding 1956; Von Bertalanffy 1968; Bogdanov and Dudley 1996, among many others) has been proposed as a way to understand the world and as a method to help policymaker and decision-maker when describing and tackling *wicked* problems (Jackson 2019; Midgley 2021). It does this by attempting to understand people and their environment holistically, as part of interacting systems, and from multiple perspectives (Ramage and Shipp 2020, pp. 3–4). It acknowledges the complexity and uncertainty of a situation where the first step is to establish and agree what the problem is, agreeing that there is no single solution to it, and resolving or managing the situation rather than the identified "problem" (Reynolds and Holwell 2020, pp. 8–9). Systems theory offers a common language across methods, disciplines, and contexts that facilitates interdisciplinarity and provides opportunities for exploiting commonalities with other systems (Meadows 2009, pp. 1–2, 6; Demetis 2010b; Cabrera et al. 2020).

The idea of a system as a whole and thinking holistically can be found in both Western and Eastern philosophy, where many:

> philosophers have considered the concept that ideas, people, or things must be considered in relation to the things around them to be fully understood (M'pherson 1974).

A detailed examination of systems theory is outside the scope of this book; however, it can be said that it has a rich, diverse background in history, religion, and philosophy.

As far back as 300 BCE, Aristotle considered that "the totality is not, as it were, a mere heap, but the whole is something beside the parts" (Metaphysics, Book VIII, 1045A.8–10), often clichéd as "the sum of the parts is more than the whole".

In the eighteenth century, the philosopher Frederick Hegel considered the nature of systems and stated that:

1. The whole is more than the sum of the parts
2. The whole defines the sum of the parts
3. The parts cannot be understood by studying the whole
4. The parts are dynamically interrelated or independent (Skyttner 2005, pp. 49–50).

Despite the concept of holism existing in many guises for millennia, it was not until the early twentieth century that it re-emerged as a counterpoint to the predominant scientific doctrine of reductionism which argues that if a phenomenon can be explained at a lower level, explanations at a higher level can be deduced; that the environment (surrounding entities, interrelations, etc.) is irrelevant; and (ideally) the observer is not involved in the process leading to a desired neutral and objective process (Skyttner 2005, pp. 14–15).

Systems theory is an interdisciplinary field that explores complex systems in nature, science, and society by using interdisciplinary concepts and foundations that are applicable to all types of systems. It can be used to explore a problem domain where the observer (the researcher or author) defines a system of interest by setting a boundary and examines systemic properties at various levels and from different perspectives to understand the phenomena being studied (Churchman 1968; Midgley 2008, 2021; Skyttner 2005, p. 55; Senge 2006; Mobus and Kalton 2015; Cabrera and Cabrera 2018). It "steers clear of reductionism" not by ignoring the individual parts, but by looking at their systemic interaction, examining the system-as-a-whole, and exploring the concept of emergence (Demetis 2010b, pp. 40–41). Geoffrey Vickers, a prominent early systems theorist, argued that "systems should be thought of as *tools of understanding* rather than a precise description of reality" (Ramage and Shipp 2020, p. 75, original emphasis), fitting in with a constructionist view.

Ramage and Shipp (2020, pp. xiv–xv) argue that modern systems theory, with its myriad methodologies and approaches, can be traced back to early contributors, such as Smuts and Bogdanov, and two starting branches: (1) General Systems Theory or GST (Von Bertalanffy 1950; Boulding 1956; Von Bertalanffy 1968) and (2) Cybernetics (Wiener, 1948). It can be argued that these two schools have essentially merged at a general level to the extent that, for the purposes of this research, the differences between the two are irrelevant, and common concepts have been appropriated and applied where appropriate.

The Austrian philosopher and biologist Ludwig "Eric" Von Bertalanffy (1901–1972), lecturing and writing on the topic of systems theory as early as the 1920s, was an advocate of an *organismic* approach where the focus is on the whole system of an organism and its relationship to its environment;

> parts of a whole are in intimate connection, such that they cannot exist or be understood independently of the whole (Von Bertalanffy 1968).

He describes GST as an attempt to formulate principles that are relevant to all open systems (be they concrete, conceptual, abstract, natural, or man-made) on the basis that homologies exist between systems from different disciplines allowing knowledge from one system to transfer to another in a different area of research;

> It is the beauty of systems theory that it is … neutral, that is, its concepts and models can be applied to both material and nonmaterial phenomena (Von Bertalanffy 1968).

Systems therefore have general concepts, independent of the scientific areas to which they belonged, and this interdisciplinary approach with its common language can be used as a way to abstract from reality to a simpler form which can be a "tool with which to handle complex systems" and "capture multidimensionality and emergence" (Skyttner 2005, pp. 54–56; Ramage and Shipp 2020, pp. 39–40, 53; Reynolds and Holwell 2020, p. 13).

GST is therefore concerned with the general characteristics of systems, applicable to different areas of study, with a focus on the topics of open systems, boundary, hierarchy, emergence, and the system in relation to its environment (Ramage and Shipp 2020, p. 51).

Cybernetics deals with the theory of control, communication, and information processing in both natural and artificial systems. It is based on the idea that many natural and artificial systems can be described using a common set of principles, especially those concerned with the way that systems receive, process, and respond to information. One of the key concepts in cybernetics is feedback, the process by which a system can observe and analyse its own behaviour and then use this information to adjust its behaviour to adapt and improve its performance over time (Luhmann 2013a; Ramage and Shipp 2020, pp. xviii–xix; SEBoK Authors 2021).

5.2.1 What Is a System?

To understand systems, ironically and in a very un-systemic manner, one must reduce the theory to its constituent components and key properties (a form of systemic reductionism?). Fig. 5.1 shows those components. The fundamental systemic properties are hierarchy, emergence, complexity, self-reference, and communication/

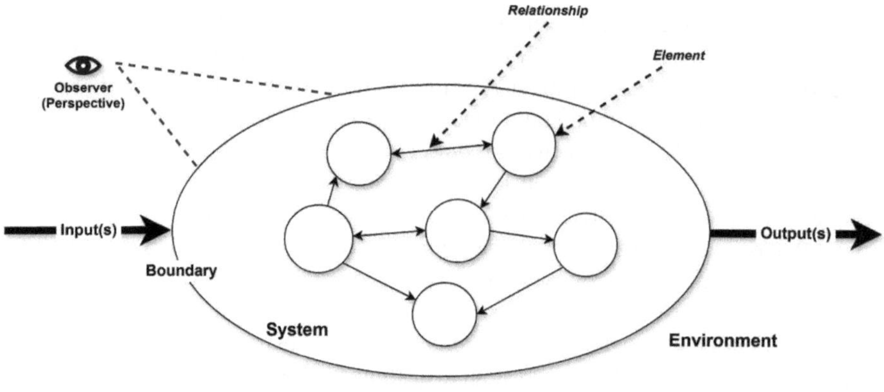

Fig. 5.1 Components of a system

coding. It is vital to remember that each component and property does not exist independently or in a vacuum; they all occur and interact simultaneously in a holistic manner.

Definition A system is defined as two or more coherently structured elements that interact in such a way that it performs a function and produces its own pattern of (emergent) behaviour over time (Checkland 1985; Demetis 2010a, pp. 43–47; Meadows 2009, pp. 2, 11; Skyttner 2005, pp. 56–58; Von Bertalanffy 1968).

Function is generally used for a non-human system and purpose for a human one (Meadows 2009, p. 15). Given the socio-technical make-up of many systems, including both human and non-human elements, the term purpose is preferred in this book and used throughout from here on. Systems may be natural (physical or biological, such as a cell, a tree, or the human body), social (economic or political, such as a work team or a factory), technical (e.g. a hydroelectric plant), or abstract (e.g. the legal system). The system may be:

> buffeted, constricted, triggered, or driven by outside forces, but the system's response to these forces is characteristic of itself, and that response is seldom simple in the real world and often unintended (Meadows 2009, p. 2).

This means that attempts to *solve* complex problems with well-intended interventions (e.g., the introduction of new regulations) oftentimes have adverse unintended consequences, which in turn generate even more problems.

A system element refers to a component that makes up and contributes to the overall functioning of the larger system. They are coherently structured and *communicate* with each other (cf. self-reference and coding). Elements can be any combination of natural, social, abstract, or technical entities, e.g. hardware, software, data, people, teams, processes, procedures, facilities, materials, and naturally occurring entities (water, organisms, minerals) or even systems in their own right (Betley et al. 2021; SEBoK Authors 2021). Systems that contain social and technical elements are referred to as socio-technical systems (cf. socio-technical systems theory). The behaviour of each element has an effect on the system's behaviour; the behaviour of the elements and their effect on the system are interdependent (changes to one affects the others); however, where subgroups of the elements are formed, all have an effect on the behaviour of the system, but none has an independent effect on it (Ackoff 1981). In socio-technical systems, both the technical and social elements need to be considered to understand the system's behaviour and purpose.

The *purpose of the system is what it does* (Beer 2002, p. 218), i.e. the outcome or result it achieves. At a theoretical level, "the purpose of a system is to transform inputs into outputs in an efficient and effective manner" (Meadows 2009). The most critical determinant of a system's behaviour is its true purpose, which may not necessarily be spoken, written, or explicitly expressed but only discovered by observing its output over a period of time. Frustratingly, and adding to the complexity of the phenomena under study, the system's behaviour may be an (undesirable) emergent behaviour not intended by the system's designers (Meadows 2009, pp. 14–17). Changing individual systemic elements usually has the least overall effect on the system. It can generally go on being itself, even with complete substitutions of elements, if its relationships and purpose remain intact. Changes in the relationships and purpose can have dramatic, unintended effects on the overall system, but changing the purpose of a system changes the system profoundly—even if everything else remains the same (Meadows 2009, pp. 15–17).

Systems are goal-seeking where systemic interaction must result in a final state or some equilibrium point being reached (Skyttner 2005, p. 53). This is one of the basic ideas behind systems theory, namely that one thing affects another and events do not happen in a vacuum. Systems are dynamic but paradoxically try to retain their integrity (equilibrium) while adapting to this inevitable change (Perkins 2015). Steady state refers to "the ability of an open system to reach a time-dependent state of equilibrium, whereby the entire system and its components remain constant" (Von Bertalanffy 1950), while recognising that there are many equally valid ways of achieving this state (Emery 2016). *Multifinality* is the idea that a given cause can lead to multiple outcomes or effects, highlighting the non-linear and unpredictable nature of systems. Meadows (2009) argues that complex systems may have many possible states and outcomes, and small changes in initial conditions (or interventions) can lead to vastly different results, which is a major contributor to *wicked* problems.

Systems, especially real-world complex ones, tend to form parts of larger systems and to organise in a hierarchical structure as illustrated in Fig. 5.2 (Skyttner 2005, pp. 65–68). To understand systemic qualities and behaviour, it is necessary to also study the levels above and below the chosen level (Skyttner 2005, p. 55) to identify the interdependencies between the levels to understand how changes at one level can affect the others (Checkland 2000). Systems can be nested within systems, leading to purposes within purposes, where any sub-purpose could conflict with the overall purpose. An essential purpose of *successful* systems is to reduce these conflicts and align individual sub-purposes with the overall purpose (Meadows 2009, pp. 15–16).

The subjective process of defining a phenomenon of interest as a system, or distinguishing it from its environment, allows a researcher to make sense of and to share that understanding with other people as required. The choice of what system to *see:*

> implies the designation of a specific perspective for a particular purpose [which] can change, depending on the purpose of the observer designating the system and operating within his own particular choices (Angell and Demetis 2010, p. 106),

a true example of subjective constructivism, but keeping in mind that:

> no system can be fully described; the issue is always whether the description chosen is appropriate for the task at hand (Angell and Demetis 2010, p. 106).

The observer-relative/dependent act involves making several boundary distinctions as "*no system can exist without a boundary and an environment*" (Angell and Demetis 2010, p. 107; Cabrera et al. 2021, p. 22; Checkland 1999, p. 312; Demetis 2010a, pp. 41–43).

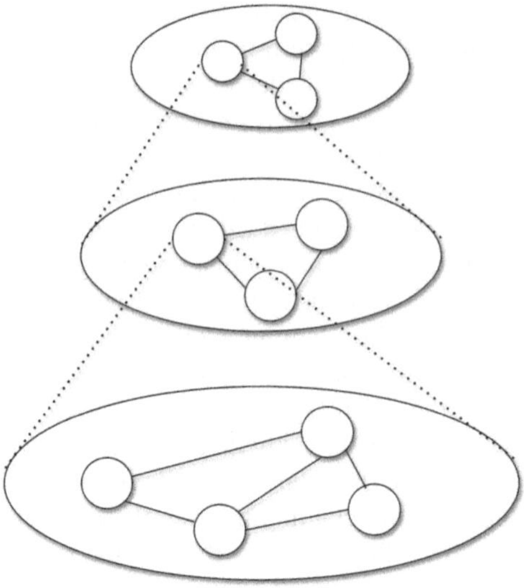

Fig. 5.2 System hierarchy

Demetis (2010a) summarises the definitional process by stating that defining or observing a system:

1. Creates an environment that establishes the difference between the system and the environment.
2. Delimits the system by setting its boundary.

No system can exist without an environment because that is the only way that a system can be defined, that is, distinguished from everything else (Demetis 2010a, pp. 41–43; Luhmann 2013a, pp. 43–70). Such a system, by default and necessity, includes the observer (Midgley 2021). The boundary, playing a crucial role in systemic formation, is ambiguous as it is simultaneously part of both the environment and the system (Angell and Demetis 2005; Demetis 2010a, pp. 47–49).

The environment is defined as everything that is not in the system, but it:

> must not be considered as some sort of inert background, rather as a complex system in itself: *a bubbling soup of interacting systems*, both similar and different, *all continuously changing and affecting each other*" (Angell and Demetis 2010, p. 109, emphasis added).

For every system, "the environment is more complex than the system itself" and to survive the ever-changing environment, it must "exploit its variety and contingency" which systems do by controlling their boundary (Demetis 2010b, pp. 47–51).

Systems can therefore be considered either open or closed, although Angel and Demetis argue that this dichotomy is outmoded and replaced with the concept of self-referential systems (2010, p. 107), discussed below, and it could be stated that the concept is not a dichotomy but a continuum with no system capable of being entirely closed.

A closed system has no interactions with its environment (Von Bertalanffy 1968), and merely outputs into the environment while "an open system is always dependent on its environment with which it can exchange matter, energy, and information" (Skyttner 2005, p. 62) across its boundary through interfaces (Ramage and Shipp 2020, pp. 55–56); they "maintain themselves in exchange of materials with [the] environment, and in continuous building up and breaking down of their components" (Von Bertalanffy 1950, p. 23).

System and environment are therefore structurally coupled, meaning "there is an interaction between the system and its environment, but this does not mean that the evolving structure of the latter can causally determine changes in the former" (ibid.). Bogdanov, one of the first systems theorists, captured this eloquently by stating that:

> a system is not simply a collection or aggregate of components and their relationships. It is also a process, or continuous flux of independent granular processes, concatenated in self-triggering circles of build-up and degradation. It cannot be separated from its environment because it does not simply exist or interact with its environment: it is structurally coupled with its environment and thus evolves its own environment while co-evolving with it (Bogdanov and Dudley 1996).

The environment (or entities therein) acts as a trigger (once perceived by the system) for the subsequent structural changes that occur within the system, and vice versa—systemic changes can affect the environment (Angell and Demetis 2005; Demetis 2010b, pp. 47–49). The purpose of the boundary is to allow for the interactive exchange of (information) feedback between the system and its environment. Changes in the system "feedback across the boundary and modify the environment", a process vital for structural coupling, and feedback essentially constitutes an "exchange of codified information transmitted between the system and the environment". This feedback can be positive or negative. Positive feedback can threaten the system's very existence by "creating havoc among the subsystems and the process that they use to communicate", ultimately leading to the system breaking down into either a new system or it becomes extinct altogether. Negative feedback counteracts any "disruptive processes" in order to reinforce "the relative stability of the system" (Demetis 2010b, pp. 47–51), keeping in mind that all non-living systems tend towards disorder or (negative) entropy (Skyttner 2005, p. 53.)

One major feature of system theory is that of emergence (Boccara 2010). Often referred to as synergy, it is:

> the principle that [systems] exhibit properties which are meaningful only when attributed to the whole, and not its parts. [Those properties exhibited being derived] from its component activities and their structure, but cannot be reduced to them (Checkland 1999).

It is the ability of individual components in a larger system to work together to give rise to a dramatic and diverse behaviour spontaneously and not predetermined due to (simple) interactions between the constituent parts, such behaviour not being a property of any of the individual parts (Demetis 2010a, pp. 46–47; Martin and Helmerson 2014). It is:

> a property of a complex system … [as it] arises out of the properties and relations characterising its simpler constituents, [but] is neither predictable from, nor reducible to, these lower-level characteristics" (Honderich 2005, p. 224).

In short, emergent system behaviour results from the interactions and relationships between the system elements, rather than the behaviour of individual elements. In general, the more complex a system is, the more difficult it is to predict its emergent behaviour, which causes difficulties when planning any systemic interventions.

Systems, especially socio-technical ones, are complex. Complexity can be considered "a measure of how difficult it is to understand how a system will behave or predict the consequences of an intervention" that changes it in some way (SEBoK Authors 2021). Similar to how we define *wicked* problems (see Chap. 1), complex systems can be characterised by:

> a large number of elements, many interactions between those elements, the attributes of the elements are not always predetermined, interaction between elements is loosely organised, the system is probabilistic in its behaviour, the system evolves over time, its subsystems are purposeful and generate their own goals, the system is subject to behavioural influences, and the system is largely open to the environment (Skyttner 2005, p. 106).

Other contributors to systemic complexity are, obviously, emergence, especially if it is unintended or unpredictable, e.g. after an intervention. Sheard and Mostashari (2011) categorise the contributors to systemic complexity as follows:

1. *Structural complexity*—elements, relationships, emergent behaviour.
2. *Dynamic complexity*—the changing behaviour of the system over time.
3. *Sociopolitical complexity*—the effect of individuals, stakeholders, and groups.

These are especially relevant when one considers the *bubbling mass of systems* in the environment in which it is impossible to monitor all interactions, giving rise to a major contributor of intra-system complexity (Angell and Demetis 2010, p. 113; Demetis 2010a, pp. 47–49, 51–54).

Self-reference is one of the most important systems theory concepts. It refers to the ability of a system to refer to itself. Luhmann (1995, 2013a, 2008a, b) argues that systems, such as social systems, are self-referential as they function based on their own operations, rather than external factors. This is not to say that the system does not still interact with its environment, which contains various external factors that create challenges and opportunities for the system. Luhmann states that self-reference is a fundamental systemic property as it is what allows the system to maintain its autonomy and operate in an independent manner. The system produces its own reality by generating a framework for its purpose that is based on the system itself and its own (internal) operations. He adds that a self-referential system can only communicate with itself, and that this communication is what allows the system to make decisions based on its own reality. Luhmann emphasises the importance of self-reference to make sense of complex systems. Angell and Demetis (2010) argue convincingly that by appreciating self-reference and complexity, one can better understand and respond to today's wicked problems.

Closely related to the concepts of communication and self-reference is coding. In systems theory, coding refers to the processing or translation of information into a form that can be understood and processed by the system. It is essential for the functioning of the system as it facilitates efficient communication and decision-making within it, albeit in a self-referential way. Luhmann (1995, 2013b) argues that social systems, such as organisations, function using shared codes (schemas) as common understandings and meanings (a self-referential reality). These binary codes allow for communication and decision-making within the system, and they are essential for its functioning.

The preceding pages have defined, outlined, and discussed the key systems theory concepts and properties that are necessary to allow systems theory to be applied to a real-world system of interest. Boulding, one of the co-founders of the GST movement, considered the world multifariously as "a physical, biological, social, economic, political, communication, and evaluative system" (Ramage and Shipp 2020, pp. 65–66) and applied systems theory to the social sciences. Similarly, Miller used systems theory to describe all living systems as:

> a description of living structure and process in terms of input and output, flows through systems, steady states, and feedback, which will clarify and unify the facts of life (Miller 1976, p. 315).

As this book proposes to apply systems theory to AML, it is necessary to have a framework to do so that takes account of the socio-technical make-up of our system of interest and the fact that AML is made up of organisations.

5.3 Organisations and Phenomena as Systems

In their 1966 book, *The Social Psychology of Organisations*, Katz and Kahn applied systems theory to model and describe organisations as open systems. The socio-technical approach is extremely useful as it views:

> organisations in a way that emphasises the interrelatedness of the functioning of the social and technical subsystems of the organisations and the relation of the organisation as a whole (including emergent behaviours) to the environment in which it operates … recognising that organisations are made up of people that produce an output using some technology, and that each affects the operation and appropriateness of the technology as well as the actions of the people who operate it" *(*Pasmore et al. 1982*, p. 1182).*

The output is valued by customers and users external to the organisation and located in its environment *(*Griffith and Dougherty 2001*, p. 206).*

The theory recognises that the coupling of social and technical elements derives mutual benefits, or reciprocity, which in turn shapes both subsystems (Emery 1980*;* Ropohl 1999). Glass (1996) agrees by stating that organisations can be considered as:

> complex open systems that are deeply influenced by and influencing their environments where … actions can give outcomes, which are unexpected and opposite to those intended.

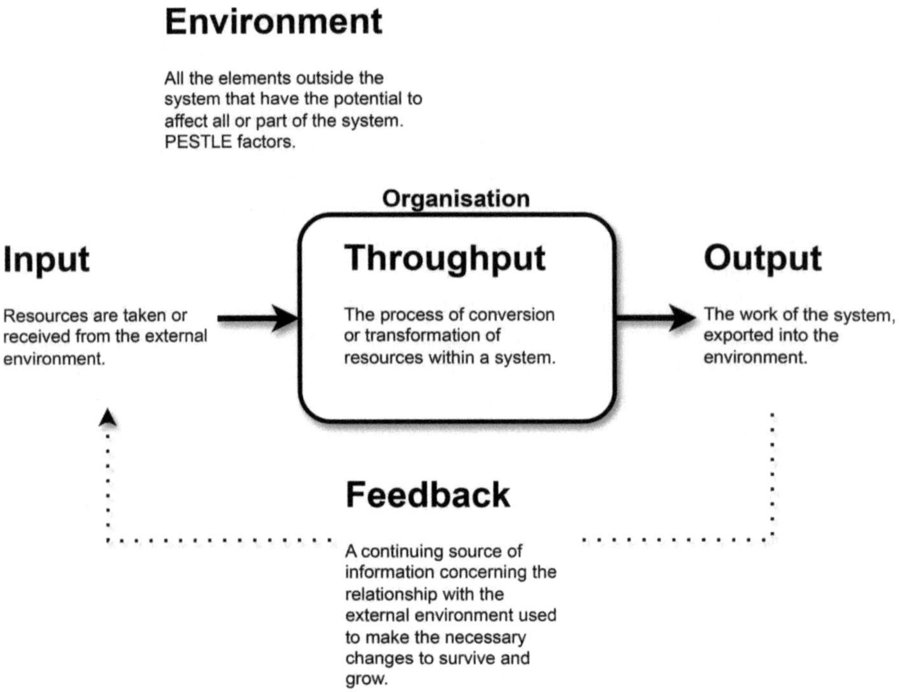

Fig. 5.3 Model of an organisation as a system

Katz and Kahn (1966) described a model (Fig. 5.3) that interprets organisational actions in terms of input, throughput, and output, taking cognisance of the (structurally coupled) relationship between the environment and the organisation's functioning, including its ability to change and adapt to environmental changes (Boulding 1956; Katz and Kahn 1966; Ramosaj and Berisha 2014).

In essence, all organisations are ultimately involved in the transformation of resources (inputs) into goods or services (outputs) and are made up of interrelated elements which are intertwined with their environment (Worthington et al. 2018, pp. 4–6).

Inputs are described as resources taken or received from the external environment; throughput as the process of transforming those inputs within the system; outputs as being the work of the system exported back into the environment; feedback as a continuing source of information concerning the relationship with the external environment and used to make necessary changes in order to survive and thrive; and the environment as all of the elements outside the system that have the potential to affect all or part of the system (Katz and Kahn 1966).

While the environment can exert a degree of control over the organisation, it cannot be controlled by it; however, over time, through constant interaction, the environment affects the organisation, and the organisation, in turn, affects the environment (Skyttner 2005, p. 64).

As part of the strategic management process, it is necessary to analyse an organisation's environment (including anticipated future changes) at local, national, supranational, and international levels. One suggested way of doing this is examining what is referred to as the *PESTLE* factors, namely political, economic, sociocultural, technological, legal, and (ethical and ecological) environment (Worthington et al. 2018, pp. 6–10).

PESTLE analysis is a useful shorthand for considering the various elements in the environment, especially those that might not often be considered. However, it should be remembered that each PESTLE factor/element is actually a system in its own right and can be considered using systems theory as outlined above.

The Katz and Kahn model is useful when looking at an organisation of interest at a systemic macro-level. Therefore, it can also be used to explore a complex phenomenon as well.

However, one also needs to look inside the organisation at a micro- or subsystem level, knowing that all organisations are made up of technology and people combined. Socio-technical systems theory achieves this ambition.

5.4 Socio-Technical Systems Theory

Socio-technical systems theory is an organisational theory, built upon general and open systems theory (Von Bertalanffy 1950), that conceptualises a system as being made up of two constituent and interrelated social and technical subsystems, with the goal of achieving joint optimisation between the two (Abbas and Michael 2022). Joint optimisation is the degree of fit between the two subsystems, resulting in an optimum state and benefits for the overall socio-technical system (Abbas and Michael 2022; Emery 2016).

Socio-technical systems theory originated from post-war research by the Tavistock Institute into coal mining and associated labour studies that were led by Trist, Bamford, and Emery (Emery 2016; Trist and Bamforth 1951). It was a response to the prevailing paradigm of the time where people were seen as an expendable part of the industrial machine, having narrow skills, and working in a "command and control" autocratic management regime. Joint optimisation views people as a participative resource to be nurtured and developed, complementary to the technology, managed in a participative, collegiate manner (Trist 1981).

Bostrom and Heinen (1977a) conceptualised a socio-technical systems theory framework (Fig. 5.4) for describing and understanding complex systems. It:

> assumes that an organisation … can be described as a socio-technical system … [which is] made up of two *jointly* independent, but correlative *interacting* systems—the social and the technical … [where] the outputs of the [organisation] are the result of joint interactions between these two systems" (Bostrom and Heinen 1977a, p. 17 original emphasis).

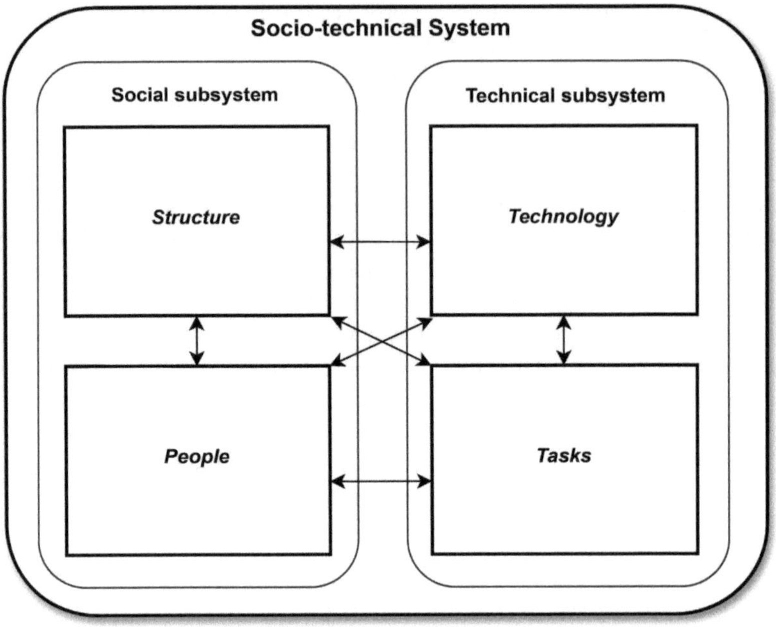

Fig. 5.4 Socio-technical system model

The environment of this socio-technical system is made up of:

> the context, surroundings, and conditions within which the open socio-technical system operates and is situated (Abbas and Michael 2022).

The technical system is concerned with the processes, tasks, and technology needed to transform inputs into outputs (Bostrom and Heinen 1977a, p. 17). This subsystem is further broken down into *Technology*—the hardware and software (algorithms) that make up and control the system—and *Task*—the procedures that govern how the system is used and operated (Abbas and Michael 2022; Bostrom and Heinen 1977a).

The social system is concerned with the attributes of people (e.g. attitudes, skills, values), the relationships among people, the reward systems among people, and the authority structures (Bostrom and Heinen 1977a, p. 17). This subsystem is broken down into *Structure*—the formal organisation and management of the system including policies, procedures, rules, and regulations—and *People*—which represents how the people who use and operate the system communicate, relate to each other, share information, and resolve difficulties (also known as the informal structure) (Abbas and Michael 2022; Bostrom and Heinen 1977a, b). It is important to remember that all the elements of the model are structurally coupled and interact with each other.

To intervene in an organisation is to be viewed as a strategy to improve its function, recognising that "decision-making, data collection, data manipulation, and data transmission" are key tasks in the organisation where "changes cause more changes within other variables", or "secondary effects", in the organisation (Bostrom and Heinen 1977a, pp. 18, 24–25).

While the theory originally focused on heavy industry, it has since been applied to a range of more modern disciplines such as "office-based work and services", business, management, and complex information systems, while remaining faithful to its original core principles (Davis et al. 2014; Morris 2009; Mumford 1983, 2006).

As discussed above, the Katz and Kahn (1966) model of an open system can be used to describe an organisation, or a phenomenon of interest, as an open system at a relatively macro-level. The Bostrom and Heinen (1977a, b) model can be used to describe a socio-technical system, especially how the technology and people interact. This can be considered as a more micro-level view of the organisation or phenomenon. It is proposed to combine two of these models to more adequately capture both the macro- and micro-levels of any organisation or phenomenon being studied. This model can be used for any system of interest but will be used in this research to look at the crime of crypto-laundering and its pursuit and detection through the work of the FIU (Fig. 5.5).

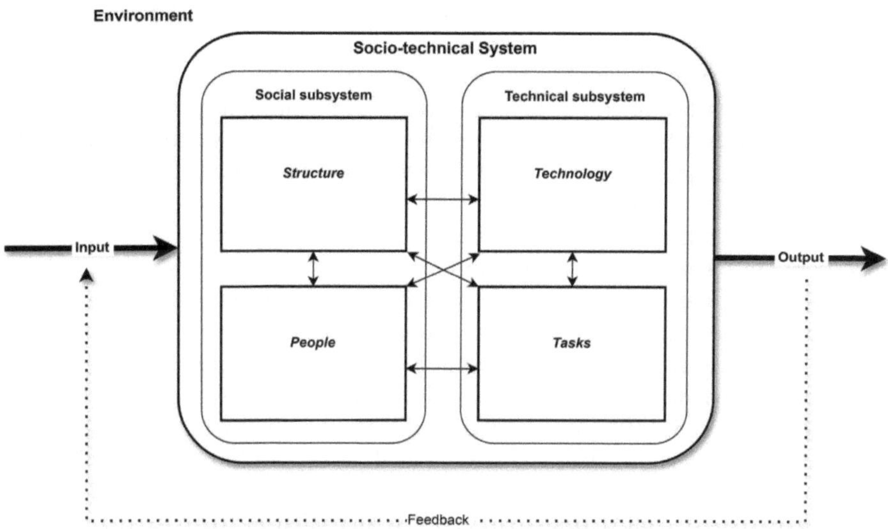

Fig. 5.5 Combined socio-technical system model

5.5 Criticisms of Systems Theory

While systems theory offers the most appropriate methodology for studying how FIU Ireland handled the introduction of crypto-asset AML regulation (Chap. 6), it is important to note and be mindful that the theory has been subject to several criticisms, which are summarised as follows.

There is no accepted grand theory, or single framework of systems (a unification of methods), leading to a pluralistic myriad of systems approaches (Cabrera 2006; Cabrera and Cabrera 2018), necessitating a "pick-and-choose" multi-methodological approach (Midgley 2008, 2021) which could be faulted for a lack of academic rigour.

Systems theory has been accused of being too vague, rigid, and inflexible to handle real-world situations (Weick 1995), and of lacking consideration of power dynamics (Clegg 1989), human behaviour, and decision-making (Checkland 1999; Flood and Romm 1997). It has also been reproached for putting too much focus on the processual character of systems (Seidl and Schoeneborn 2010) and not being applicable to rapidly changing, unpredictable situations (Checkland 1985).

Ironically, systems theory can be accused of a form of reductionism with an overextension of the "whole-part" relationship analogy (Strauss 2002) and the danger of subjectively focusing on parts of a system of interest while missing its holistic nature (Maturana and Varela 1991).

Systems theory can be said to tend to immunise itself against criticism in a self-referential way (Seidl and Becker 2006).

The Katz and Kahn systems model was described in one short paper, and although it has many citations in respected high-quality academic journals, there does not appear to have ever been a critical examination of its suitability carried out. To balance this, the model is simple, straightforward, and the systems theory principles are readily apparent from it.

Specifically, regarding socio-technical systems theory, Kelly (1978) maintains that there are inherent flaws related to the concept of joint optimisation and that earlier studies focused on the social subsystem to the detriment of the technical one. The focus on the social subsystem, which was rearranged "around an existing technology in order to approximate joint optimisation," viewed technology as constant, which as we have discussed throughout this research, is simply incorrect (Pasmore et al. 1982, pp. 1185, 1195). What is required is equal focus on the technical subsystem and its ever-changing nature (Pasmore et al. 1982, p. 1200), while avoiding an "anti-technology" perspective (Coiera 2007) which could "result in limited application of core socio-technical principles" (Abbas and Michael 2022).

These identified theoretical shortcomings need to be acknowledged and kept firmly in the mind of the researcher. This allows the avoidance of potential traps in thinking, leading to a more robust understanding of the real-world situation, problems, and interventions being researched. For the reasons set out earlier in the chapter, the author contends that systems theory, particularly socio-technical systems theory, is best suited for this book as will be demonstrated in the remaining chapters.

5.6 Application of Systems Theory to AML

It is the contention of this book that the AML regime, and crypto-laundering as a complex phenomenon, can be conceptualised as a complex socio-technical system. The AML system is made up of many coherently organised elements that interact to perform a function, ostensibly the prevention, disruption, detection, investigation, and prosecution of money laundering. Each individual element is a system in its own right with inputs, outputs, feedback, and systemic properties. It is possible to explore the system from many different levels or layers, e.g. international, supranational, and national. The systems are structurally dependent upon each other, are heavily influenced by the changing environment, and exhibit emergent behaviour.

The AML system generates its own reality by creating a framework for understanding and detecting money laundering activities. This framework is self-referential in that it refers to the AML system itself and its own (internal) operations, e.g. the process of identifying and reporting suspicious transactions, and the use of financial intelligence. Furthermore, communication within the AML system is also self-referential, e.g. when an obliged entity reports an STR to the FIU, it must refer to the same AML system, laws, and regulations to understand and communicate about the suspicious activity (see Sect. 2.2.5.2 on the construction of suspicion). The meaning of the suspicious activity, and the action to be taken is generated by this process of self-referential communication using binary codes such as suspicious/false positive, criminal indicator present/no criminal indicator, sufficient/insufficient evidence, guilty/not guilty, forfeit/return (Fig. 5.6).

It is important to remember that the systems about to be outlined in more detail below are subjectively defined by the author based on his professional experience as a police manager (and later leader), a financial investigator, a technologist, and a trained barrister who worked as a senior manager in FIU Ireland, combined with all of his personal beliefs, opinions, biases, and worldview.

5.6.1 The Irish AML System

The Irish AML can be conceptualised as a complex socio-technical system (see Fig. 5.6). Each box represents a component part of the system with its own inputs, outputs, and systemic behaviours. Shown on the diagram are the information/communication flows between elements, where it is apparent that one system's output is another's input. Also shown is the self-referential schema that each element uses to process its inputs to make valuable output (determined by the feedback received?) for the wider system and, ultimately, the external environment. It is interesting that each element is looking at different codes, and this is one possible contributor to the complexity of the system, with the potential for supposedly cooperating elements being at crossed-purposes.

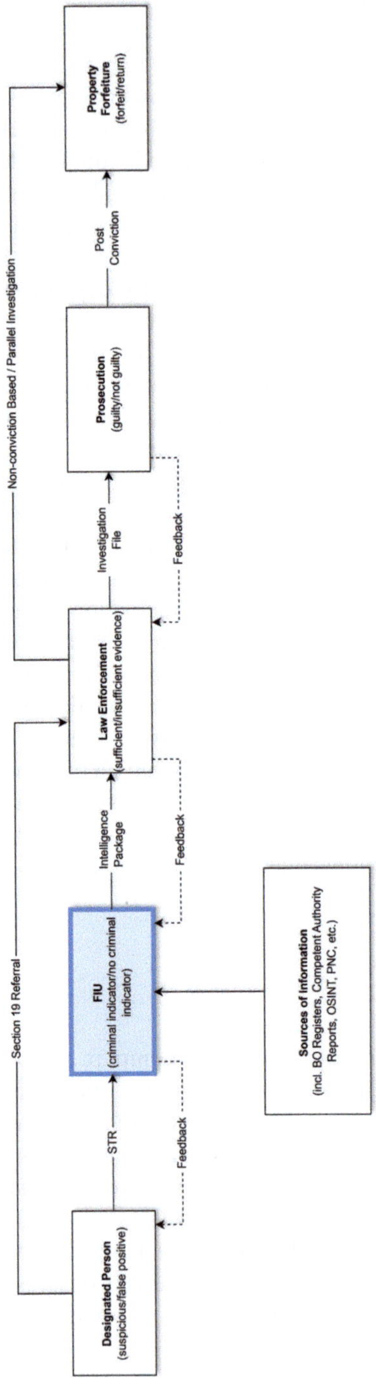

Fig. 5.6 Irish AML system

As expected, the environment is more complex than the individual system. The previous chapters in this book showed that different layers or levels exist, e.g. international and supranational, that are a level above the county's system. In this upper layer, we have the FATF and the EU. As the (self-proclaimed) international standard-setting body, the FATF takes input in the form of expert opinion, country submissions, and other feedback to output its methodology, its recommendations, its country MER reports, and its position papers. These form the backbone of instructions to the lower-level national systems to implement an AML regime. The EU sits in between the FATF and the individual country at the supranational level. It takes the FATF output as its input and processes it to generate legislation in the form of directives which it imposes on member states, such as Ireland. These systems monitor their own output and how the lower-level systems are using it, all in a self-referential manner. Moving down to the country system, the government of the country receives instructions from the FATF and the EU to set up a series of preventative and repressive mechanisms and organisations with the aim to prevent, disrupt, detect, investigate, and prosecute criminal activity and to seize the proceeds of crime. The country system is monitored by the international/supranational systems with various inspections, mutual evaluation reports, and other information being fed back as required.

Examining the Irish AML system itself in more detail, one can see that the first element of note is that of the obliged entity. It obtains its customers' information in the form of account opening documentation which is processed by performing KYC and CDD/EDD. It monitors all customer transactions on an ongoing basis, seeking explanations for any unusual activity detected. Where abnormal customer activity is discovered, the MLRO must decide if the activity is *suspicious* or a *false positive*. Where an activity is or transactions are classified as *suspicious*, they will output information directly to law enforcement where a crime has occurred (in the form of a crime report under Sect. 19 Criminal Justice Act, 2011) or as an STR to the FIU where there is suspicion that the customer is engaging in money laundering.

The FIU's role is to analyse the STR received from the obliged entity, enhanced with other information, e.g. beneficial ownership (BO) registers, open-source intelligence (OSINT), information from the Irish Police National Computer (PNC) called PULSE,[1] utilisation of their coercive powers, other STRs, and any other information available. Where a *criminal indicator* is apparent, it will develop and output that information in the form of an intelligence package to the relevant law enforcement agency, usually the police, who may initiate a criminal investigation. Feedback is provided to the obliged entity at the appropriate point, sometimes in general form because of their participation in a public–private partnership or recipient of FIU outreach.

Where an investigation is conducted and there is *sufficient evidence* of a criminal offence having occurred, the police submit a file to the Director of Public

[1] PULSE is the Irish Police National Computer and is an acronym for *Police Using Leading Systems Effectively*.

Prosecutions who may direct a criminal investigation in the Courts. At the end of the courts' process, the person will be found *guilty* or *not guilty* and there may be post-conviction criminal forfeiture if the threshold to *forfeit* is satisfied. Alternatively, or sometimes in parallel, the FIU may transmit information to CAB for non-conviction based forfeiture.

The Irish AML system and processes described briefly above are included for completeness and to give context to the focus of this book, the Irish FIU, which is the subject of a comprehensive interpretative case study in Chap. 6. However, it is first necessary to apply the systems theory principles discussed in this chapter to that organisation. This work should only be taken as an initial view, which will be refined as this book progresses and further data is analysed.

5.6.2 FIU Ireland as a Socio-Technical System

Systems Theory has been used previously to present a coherent interdisciplinary theoretical framework to the demanding research domain of AML (Angell and Demetis 2005; Demetis 2010a, b). Those studies focused on the generation of STRs by private sector financial institutions, in particular a Greek bank. Other studies have been conducted on the effective use of socio-technical systems theory as an approach to understand and improve the prevention and detection of money laundering (Al-Qatawna 2010; Campbell-Verduyn and Goguen 2017; Canhoto 2021; Desmond et al. 2019; Gonçalves 2019). This book explores the phenomenon of crypto-laundering and investigates what use the Irish FIU makes of the STRs it receives, particularly those related to crypto-assets, using the concept of two inter-related and structurally coupled socio-technical systems. The first is FIU Ireland of which an initial socio-technical model is described in Fig. 5.7. The second is the crypto-laundering system, which will be determined by examining the operation of the FIU, the crypto-STRs received in 2021, and interviews with experts (see Chaps. 6 and 7).

The regulation of crypto-assets for the purposes of AML is concerned with the people and technology that interact and mutually coexist. The use of the Katz and Kahn (1966) *organisation as a system* model in conjunction with the socio-technical systems theory framework developed by Bostrom and Heinen (1977a) best captures the interaction between the social and technical components to give the deepest understanding of the research problem. This position is justified as follows, while keeping in mind that:

> all definitions and conceptualisations are limited but can be considered fit for the purpose of research if these limitations are recognised, and one does not assume its universal validity (Boell and Cecez-Kecmanovic 2015, pp. 4965–6).

Firstly, it has been satisfactorily established that money laundering and AML are structurally coupled socio-technical systems (Angell and Demetis 2005; Demetis 2010a, b). Crypto-assets are a complex interdisciplinary problem domain covering

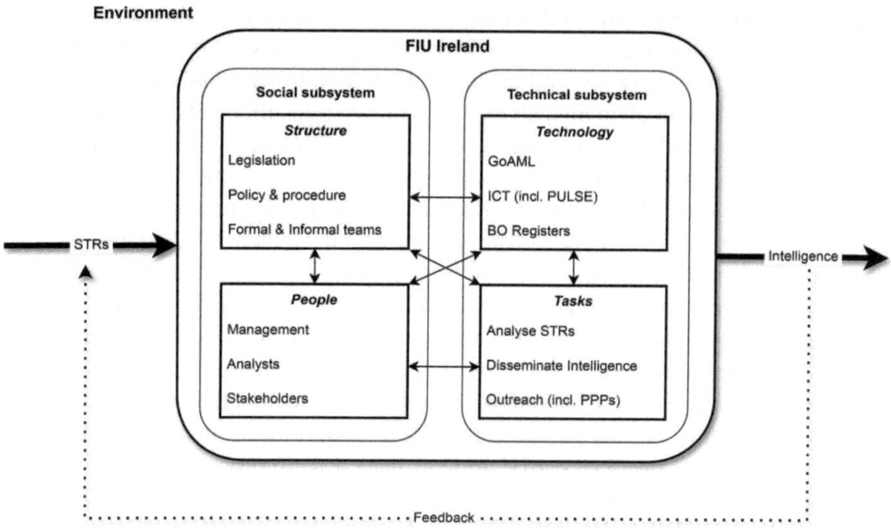

Fig. 5.7 Socio-technical systems model of FIU Ireland (first impression)

cryptography (mathematics), software and network engineering, and economics. An understanding of criminology and law is required to explore the regulation of crypto-asset technology. Similarly, "AML is a demanding research domain that is interdisciplinary at its core" (Demetis 2010b, p. 36). Individually, all three domains—money laundering, AML, and crypto-assets—are complex systems. However, when they are viewed as an integrated whole, their complexity is intensified. The socio-technical lens is required as one examines the intersection of the domains and the complexity of that intersection.

Secondly, it is not useful from an ontological standpoint to totally separate technology from the social actors who created and use it. Lee argues that:

> research in the [systems] field examines more than just the technological system, or just the social system, or even the two side by side; in addition, it investigates the phenomena that emerge when the two interact (Lee 2001, p. iii).

Both the social and technical aspects are in continuous interaction, producing emergent phenomena which make the resulting system more than the sum of the parts and require the study of all three aspects (Meadows 2009, p. 2).

Thirdly, taking the socio-technical approach overcomes the deterministic shortcomings of examining either part in isolation.

Fourthly, it examines the unidirectional relationships between technology and social actors which allows for understanding the role technology plays in society.

As was seen earlier, the FIU is a part of the larger Irish and even larger International and Supranational AML systems. As an organisation, it can be conceptualised as a system using the Katz and Kahn (1966) model which shows STRs received as inputs, the analysis of STRs as the throughput, and the disseminated intelligence packages as the output. The environment includes all of the other elements outside the system that have the potential to affect it. Feedback can include the information that is provided to the designated persons who make STRs (as outreach, presentations, training, and during public–private partnerships). The FIU is made up of constituent elements, all of which are systems themselves, and is deeply influenced by its external environment, which is ever-changing due to technological advancements, such as crypto-assets, and legislation changes, such as the expansion of AML regulations, to include entities that deal with crypto-assets. As a socio-technical system, described using the Bostrom and Heinen (1977a) model, it is made up of a combination of social and technical elements. Its stated purpose is to prevent and detect money laundering, which it does by transforming STRs received from the private sector (inputs) into actionable intelligence for law enforcement (outputs). The effectiveness, or otherwise, will be examined in the case study and discussion afterwards (see Chapters 6, 7, and 8). The technical components of the FIU system include the hardware, software, and algorithms that are designed to analyse and process the STRs. FIU Ireland uses a technology called GoAML, a UNODC software product, to perform its main purpose, i.e. receive STRs, analyse all information available, determine if the information is indicative of money laundering or other criminality, and, if so, disseminate intelligence reports to law enforcement. FIU Ireland also utilises other technology to fulfil its role. The social component includes the people who use and interact with the FIU, such as FIU analysts, managers, and stakeholders, e.g. MLROs and law enforcement. They interpret the information generated by the technical subsystem and make decisions on how to progress activities that have been designated as *suspicious* and indicative of money laundering. The structural component is made up of the formal and informal roles and relationships that govern how the FIU operates. The formal part is made up of the policies, procedures, and legislation, while the informal side is determined from the interaction of the people that operate the system, including FIU management and national (e.g. the Irish cross-departmental Anti-money Laundering Steering Committee or AMLSC), supranational (e.g. the EU), and international bodies (e.g. other FIUs and the FATF).

External to the FIU is its ever-changing and evolving environment which represents the broader context in which it operates and includes PESTLE factors, such as the global economy, cultural considerations, and the political and legal systems, that influence the operation of the FIU. Included in this environment is the money laundering socio-technical system, which has adapted over recent years to accommodate crypto-laundering through the misuse of crypto-assets. That system will be explored in detail in Chap. 8, but one can initially apply concepts from the socio-technical systems framework developed by the author. Its technical component refers to the technology, especially crypto-assets, that is used to perform the task of moving and concealing the proceeds of criminal conduct using the myriad of methods available. It also crosses into civil society with tasks such as misusing the legitimate financial sector to move money, obfuscating the financial trail, and concealing its illicit origins. The social subsystem contains the people and organisations involved in the money laundering process, for example, organised criminal organisations, money launderers, and corrupted/compromised insiders. These people use their connections and influence (formally and informally) to facilitate money laundering at every stage. Another crossover with civil society can be found in the structural subsystem. In here are the policies and legislation put in place to prevent and detect illicit activity, of which the criminal is well aware and is anxiously attempting to circumvent, e.g. by the use of new technologies or an insider. This model will be developed through the remainder of this book.

5.7 Alternative Theories Considered

The previous sections described and outlined the rationale for the selection of socio-technical system theory to make sense of the phenomenon under investigation in this book, crypto-laundering. While choosing this approach, various other academic theories were explored, which will now be discussed briefly.

Money Laundering and AML have been explored and described using, among others: Economic Theory, Game Theory, Psychological Theory, Network Theory, Sociological Theory, and Design Theory.

Economic theory views money laundering as a criminal activity that distorts resource allocation and results in negative societal outcomes, in essence a form of market failure (Business Insider 2011; Ferwerda 2009; Masciandaro et al. 2007).

Game theory views money laundering as a decision made by each involved party based on their perceived risks and rewards (Araujo 2010; Bååth and Zellhorn 2016; Jayantilal et al. 2017).

Psychological theory views money laundering as a result of faulty individual cognitive biases leading them to make decisions that are not in their best interests (Isa et al. 2015; Saeidi 2021).

Network theory conceptualises money laundering as (dirty) money flowing through legitimate and criminal networks with a focus on key actors and pathways that are ripe for targeted intervention (Al-Abdullah 2015; Keyan and Tingting 2011).

Sociological theory views money laundering as a criminal activity that is enabled or facilitated by social structures and cultural norms (Constantine 2021; Dodd 2005; Sanjaya et al. 2020).

Money laundering could be considered under any of the traditional criminological schools of thought, e.g. positivist criminology, strain theory, or crime control (Newburn 2017).

While each of the above theories was interesting and described money laundering and the people involved in it to various extents from its own observing perspective and epistemological outlook, there was insufficient socio-technical focus to consider how money laundering and AML evolve and is affected by crypto-asset technology.

The author strongly considered some of the theories captured under the information systems (IS) superset of theories for this research. IS can be defined as a formal, socio-technical, organisational system designed to collect, process, and store data, and distribute information (Piccoli 2012, pp. 25–32). It consists of all the elements that work together to accept an input, process it, and produce an output in an organised manner (Cordella and Iannacci 2012, p. 13; Kranzberg 1986, p. 550; Oz and Sousa 2014, pp. 10, 12), which addresses the information processing needs of individuals and organisations (Majchrzak and Markus 2013, p. 1). There are five main components or elements within an information system:

- *Hardware*, the physical computers, networks, and support equipment.
- *Software*, algorithms that direct the physical computer to function in useful ways, especially in the transformation of data to information.
- *Data*, the raw materials of information systems.
- *Processes*, the policies that govern the real-world operation of the information system.
- *People*, the users of the information system, or those affected by it.

The first three can be broadly captured as technology and are what many people consider to be *information technology*. The remaining two components, processes and people, move information systems from the more technical or computer science sphere to take account of the organisational, human, and social elements at play (Bourgeois et al. 2019, pp. 4–8).

The inputs and outputs of an IS are data and information, respectively. Data, from the Latin *datum*, means a raw fact, which can take the form of a number, a statement, or a picture. It is important to stress that data is not information, but it is the raw material in its production. Data alone is rarely useful and must be manipulated or transformed into *information*, which is defined as facts or conclusions organised in such a way that they have contextual meaning or value, beyond the value of the facts themselves and retain an observer-sensitivity (March and Smith 1995; Oz and Sousa 2014, p. 8; Reynolds and Stair 2017, pp. 4–6).

The transformation from data to information, accepting that this is observer-dependent and a product of cognition and observation, can be carried out by algorithms, "a series of steps that are performed to solve an information problem". In IS, they are the hidden methods (software) that computers (hardware) apply to process data into information and solve real-world problems for society (Bleakley 2020, p. 1).

Finally, and very system-like, the IS provides a feedback mechanism to monitor and control its operation and to make sure that it continues to meet its goals and objectives (Reynolds and Stair 2017, p. 7), whether they are those intended or otherwise.

Information systems can be used to explore crypto-assets very satisfactorily. As was previously seen, crypto-assets reflect a complex interdisciplinary problem domain covering cryptography (mathematics), software and network engineering, and economics.

Crypto-assets fulfil the definition of an information system and, by extension, that of a system. The components of the system work together to process the informational needs of its users to meet the goal of asset/value transfer; such transfer can represent a legal transaction or an illicit one, depending on the motivation and goals of the user (see Affordances below).

The *hardware* consists of computers, mobile phones, networks, and peripheral devices such as "cold" hardware wallets. The *software* is the open-source algorithms that are available on the Internet that perform the vital tasks of operating the peer-to-peer distributed network and the distributed ledger. The *people* are the actors prevalent in the crypto-asset system, namely the internet platform providers, the people who control the underlying software (codebase and programmers), the users of crypto-assets, the media, and the government/regulators. The *data* is the digital 1 s and 0 s that make up the public address, private keys, wallets, transactions, blocks, blockchain, etc. As it stands, the data has little use until it is transformed into information that is useful for the user's goals, i.e. the value of the crypto-asset. In the case of crypto-assets, the "tokens" or "coins", and the processes for transferring them to other people, can be considered as digital information that is given value by the users of the crypto-asset. It is the potential to transfer this value that attracts criminals to exploit the technology for illicit purposes such as money laundering and cybercrime. The information is the unspent transaction that is unlocked by a private key, intrinsically worthless but given value nevertheless by the participants in the system, and that value only exists in the information system (Bleakley 2020, p. 216). IS was rejected by the author as it was problematic to usefully describe the socio-technical AML system in interaction with crypto-assets as an IS to answer the research questions based on the data available.

The other main contender for an alternative theory considered for use by the author was Affordance Theory (Gibson 1966, 1977, 1979; Norman 1988, 1999, 2013). This theory is popular in the field of (information) systems and was considered as it is very useful for examining how people use (and misuse) technology and how that technology affects individuals and organisational users (Volkoff and Strong 2017; Wang et al. 2018).

Affordance theory takes a socio-technical and systematic perspective that "allows specificity about the technology while simultaneously incorporating the social and contextual elements" (Volkoff and Strong 2017, p. 2). The socio-technical focus is of benefit in examining crypto-asset technology, how it can be misused depending on the intention of the user, and how that misuse potentially affects a wider (information) system such as AML.

The concept of an *affordance* refers to what a particular user with a particular goal could achieve with a piece of technology. Closely related to this is the concept of a *constraint* (also known as an *anti-affordance*), which refers to the ways in which a user can be prevented from accomplishing a particular goal when using that technology. Affordances are distinct from the features of the technology and from the attributes of the user; they are the relationship between both, referred to as the *action potentials* that are "afforded by" the technology to users with certain characteristics and purposes, or as Gibson puts it "needs control the perception of affordances and also initiate acts" (1982, p. 411). The value in exploring the relational concepts of affordances becomes obvious when understanding two facts: (1) users do not always realise the apparent potential of a technology when they use it, and (2) users often use technologies in ways never intended by their inventor or designer.

Studying the relationships between technology and the human actor also allows us to understand that what one user with particular capabilities and purposes can or cannot do with a technology may be very different from another user (Majchrzak and Markus 2013; Wang et al. 2018, pp. 56–57).

Affordances would have been extremely useful to describe how certain actors with certain motivations could exploit crypto-assets for criminal purposes. However, the author replaced affordance theory with socio-technical systems theory as it better described the interaction of organisations, people, and information based on the data that was available for this book.

Consideration was also given to exploring this research through the alternative theories of Foucauldian Governmentality (McGrath 2019; Rose et al. 2006; Wong 2013), Responsive Regulation (Ayres and Braithwaite 1992), and Power Relations (Backhouse et al. 2006).

While none of the alternative theories discussed above were explicitly used, their study by the author may have influenced his thought process and, as a result, examples that could be attributed to these theories may be seen in places throughout the book.

References

Abbas A, Michael K (2022) Socio-technical theory: a review, in: Papagiannidis, S. (Ed.), TheoryHub Book

Ackoff RL (1981) The art and science of mess management. Interfaces 11:20–26

Al-Abdullah M (2015) An actor-network theory approach in investigating the information systems perspective of anti-money laundering compliance through a case study of the foreign account tax compliance act (FATCA) implementation in a Jordanian local bank. Virginia Commonwealth University

Al-Qatawna JS (2010) Multi-stakeholder enquiry for securing e-business environments: a socio-technical security framework. (PhD Thesis). Sheffield Hallam University

Angell I, Demetis D (2010) Science's first mistake: delusions in pursuit of theory. Bloomsbury Academic, London

Angell I, Demetis D (2005) Systems thinking about anti-money laundering: considering the Greek case. J Money Laund Control 8:271–284

Araujo RA (2010) An evolutionary game theory approach to combat money laundering. J Money Launder Control

Ayres I, Braithwaite J (1992) Responsive regulation: transcending the deregulation debate. Oxford University Press, Oxford

Bååth D, Zellhorn F (2016) How to combat money laundering in bitcoin? An institutional and game theoretic approach to anti-money laundering prevention measures aimed at Bitcoin

Backhouse J, Hsu CW, Silva L (2006) Circuits of power in creating de jure standards: shaping an international information systems security standard. MIS Q 30:413–438

Bawden RJ (1998) The Community Challenge: The Learning Response, Keynote Paper Annual Conference of the Community Development Society, Athens, Georgia. Reprinted in. New Horizons in Education

Beer S (2002) What is cybernetics? Kybernetes 31:209–219

Betley E, Sterling EJ, Akabas S, Paxton A, Frost L (2021) Introduction to systems and systems thinking. Lessons in Conservation 11:9–25

Bleakley C (2020) Poems that solve puzzles: the history and science of algorithms, illustrated Edition. OUP Oxford, New York

Boccara N (2010) Modelling complex systems. Springer Science & Business Media

Boell S, Cecez-Kecmanovic D (2015) What is an information system?

Bogdanov A, Dudley P (1996) Bogdanov's Tektology: 1996. Centre for Systems Studies, University of Hull

Bostrom RP, Heinen JS (1977a) MIS problems and failures: a socio-technical perspective, part II: the application of socio-technical theory. MIS Q 1:11–28

Bostrom RP, Heinen JS (1977b) MIS problems and failures: a socio-technical perspective. Part I: The Causes. MIS Q 1:17–32

Boulding KE (1956) General systems theory—the skeleton of science. Manag Sci 2:197–208

Bourgeois D, Smith J, Wang S, Mortati J (2019) Information Systems for Business and beyond. Open Textb

Business Insider (2011) The Economics of Money Laundering [WWW Document]. URL https://www.businessinsider.com/the-economics-of-money-laundering-2011-6?op=1. Accessed 21 Aug 2025

Cabrera D (2006) Systems thinking, doctoral dissertation. Cornell University

Cabrera D, Cabrera L (2018) Systems thinking made simple: new Hope for solving wicked problems, 2nd edn. Odyssean Press

Cabrera D, Cabrera L, Cabrera E (2020) An Evolving Evidence-base and Literature Review of the Universal Patterns and Atomic Elements of Complex Cognition. Cabrera Research Lab, Ithaca, NY

Cabrera D, Cabrera L, Midgley G (2021) The four waves of systems thinking. In: The Routledge handbook of systems thinking. Routledge, London

Campbell-Verduyn M, Goguen M (2017) The mutual constitution of technology and global governance: bitcoin, blockchains, and the international anti-money-laundering regime. In: Bitcoin and Beyond. Routledge, pp 69–87

Chapman J (2004) System failure: Why governments must learn to think differently. Demos

Canhoto AI (2021) Leveraging machine learning in the global fight against money laundering and terrorism financing: an affordances perspective. J Bus Res 131:441–452

Checkland P (2000) Systems thinking, systems practice: includes a 30-year retrospective. J-Oper Res Soc 51:647–647

Checkland P (1999) Systems thinking. Rethink Manag Inf Syst 45–56

Checkland P (1985) From optimizing to learning: a development of systems thinking for the 1990s. J Oper Res Soc 36:757–767

Churchman CW (1968) The systems approach. Dell Publishing Company

Clegg S (1989) Frameworks of power. Sage

Coiera E (2007) Putting the technical back into socio-technical systems research. Int J Med Inform 76:S98–S103

Constantine JH (2021) Business Ethics and sociology of money laundering

Cordella A, Iannacci I (2012) Information systems and Organisations. London School of Economics

Davis MC, Challenger R, Jayewardene DN, Clegg CW (2014) Advancing socio-technical systems thinking: a call for bravery. Appl Ergon 45:171–180

Demetis D (2010a) Technology and anti-money laundering: a systems theory and risk-based approach. Edward Elgar, Cheltenham

Demetis D (2010b) A systems theoretical approach for anti-money laundering informed by a case study in a Greek financial institution: self-reference, AML, its systemic constitution and technological consequences, PhD Dissertation. London School of Economics

Desmond DB, Lacey D, Salmon P (2019) Evaluating cryptocurrency laundering as a complex socio-technical system: a systematic literature review. J Money Laund Control 22:480–497

Dodd N (2005) Laundering "money": on the need for conceptual clarity within the sociology of money. Eur J Sociol Eur Sociol 46:387–411

Emery F (2016) Characteristics of socio-technical systems. In: the social engagement of social science, a Tavistock anthology, volume 2. University of Pennsylvania Press, pp 157–186
Emery F (1980) Designing socio-technical systems for "greenfield" sites. J Occup Behav:19–27
Ferwerda J (2009) The economics of crime and money laundering: does anti-money laundering policy reduce crime? Rev Law Econ 5:903–929
Flood RL, Romm NR (1997) Critical systems thinking: current research and practice
Gibson JJ (1982) Reasons for realism: selected essays of James J. Gibson. Lawrence Erlbaum Assoc Incorporated
Gibson JJ (1979) The theory of affordances: the ecological approach to visual perception. Houghton Miffin, Boston
Gibson JJ (1977) The concept of affordances. In: Perceiving, acting, and knowing: toward and ecological psychology. Lawrence Erlbaum associates, New Jersey
Gibson JJ (1966) The senses considered as perceptual systems. George Allen & Unwin Ltd., London
Glass N (1996) Chaos, non-linear systems and day-to-day management. Eur Manag J 14:98–106
Gonçalves MM (2019) How cryptocurrencies enable money laundering. Malmo University, Malmo
Griffith TL, Dougherty DJ (2001) Beyond socio-technical systems: introduction to the special issue. J Eng Technol Manag 18:207–218
Honderich T (2005) The Oxford companion to philosophy. OUP Oxford
Isa YM, Sanusi ZM, Haniff MN, Barnes PA (2015) Money laundering risk: from the bankers' and regulators perspectives. Procedia Econ Finance 28:7–13
Iyer P (2020) A beginner's guide to Japan: observations and provocations
Jackson MC (2019) Critical systems thinking and the management of complexity: responsible leadership for a complex world. Wiley Blackwell, Hoboken, NJ
Jayantilal S, Jorge SF, Ferreira A (2017) Portuguese anti-money laundering policy: a game theory approach. Eur J Crim Policy Res 23:559–574
Katz D, Kahn RL (1966) The social psychology of Organisations. Wiley
Kelly JE (1978) A reappraisal of sociotechnical systems theory. Hum Relat 31:1069–1099
Keyan L, Tingting Y (2011) An improved support-vector network model for anti-money laundering, in: 2011 fifth international conference on management of E-commerce and e-government. IEEE, pp. 193–196
Kranzberg M (1986) Technology and History: "Kranzberg's Laws.". Technol Cult 27:544–560
Lee AS (2001) Editor's comments. MIS Q 25:iii–vii
Lempriere DM (2019) How to write a theoretical framework–the PhD Knowledge Base. PhD Proofread. URL https://www.thephdproofreaders.com/structuring-a-thesis/what-is-a-theoretical-framework/. Accessed 14 Aug 25
Luhmann N (2013a) Introduction to systems theory. Polity, Cambridge, UK; Malden, MA
Luhmann N (2013b) Theory of society, volume 2. In: Theory of society, volume 2. Stanford University Press
Luhmann N (2008a) Law as a social system. Oxford University Press, Oxford
Luhmann N (2008b) The autopoiesis of social systems. J Sociocybernetics 6:84–95
Luhmann N (1995) Social systems. Stanford University Press
Majchrzak A, Markus ML (2013) Technology Affordances and Constraints in Management Information Systems (mis) 5
March ST, Smith GF (1995) Design and natural science research on information technology. Decis Support Syst 15:251–266
Martin A, Helmerson K (2014) Emergence: the remarkable simplicity of complexity [WWW Document]. The Conversation. URL http://theconversation.com/emergence-the-remarkable-simplicity-of-complexity-30973. Accessed 14 Aug 25
Masciandaro D, Takats E, Unger B (2007) Black finance: the economics of money laundering. Edward Elgar Publishing
Maturana HR, Varela FJ (1991) Autopoiesis and cognition: the realization of the living. Springer Science & Business Media

McGrath J (2019) Regulating white-collar crime in Ireland: an analysis using the lens of governmentality. Crime Law Soc Change 72:445–465
Meadows DH (2009) Thinking in systems: a primer. Earthscan, London
Midgley G (2021) An introduction to systems thinking for tackling wicked problems
Midgley G (2008) Response to paper "systems thinking" by D. Cabrera et al.: the unification of systems thinking: is there gold at the end of the rainbow? Eval Program Plann 31:317–321
Miller JG (1976) The nature of living systems. Behav Sci 21:295–319
Mobus GE, Kalton MC (2015) Principles of systems science. Springer, New York
Morris A (2009) Socio-technical systems in ICT: a comprehensive survey
M'pherson PK (1974) A perspective on systems science and systems philosophy. Futures 6:219–239
Mumford E (2006) The story of socio-technical design: reflections on its successes, failures and potential. Inf Syst J 16:317–342
Mumford, E., 1983. Designing human systems for new technology: the ETHICS method. Manchester Business School
Newburn T (2017) Criminology, 3rd edn. Routledge, London New York
Norman DA (2013) The design of everyday things, Rev. and expanded ed. ed, Design. MIT Press, Cambridge, MA
Norman DA (1999) Affordance, conventions, and design. Interactions 6:38–43
Norman DA (1988) The psychology of everyday things. Basic Books, New York
Oz E, Sousa K (2014) Management information systems, 7th edn. Course Technology, Stamford, CT, USA
Pasmore W, Francis C, Haldeman J, Shani A (1982) Sociotechnical systems: a north American reflection on empirical studies of the seventies. Hum Relat 35:1179–1204
Perkins M (2015) Introduction to systems theory
Piccoli G (2012) Essentials of information Systems for Managers: text only, reprint edition. John Wiley & Sons, Hoboken, NJ
Ramage M, Shipp K (2020) Systems thinkers, 2nd edn. Springer
Ramosaj B, Berisha G (2014) Systems theory and systems approach to leadership. Ilir Int Rev 1:59–76
Reynolds G, Stair R (2017) Fundamentals of information systems, 9th edn. Course Technology, Mason, OH
Reynolds M, Holwell S (eds) (2020) Systems Approaches to Making Change: A Practical Guide, 2nd edn. Springer
Ropohl G (1999) Philosophy of socio-technical systems. Soc Philos Technol Q Electron J 4:186–194
Rose N, O'Malley P, Valverde M (2006) Governmentality. Annu Rev Law Soc Sci 2:83–104
Saeidi H (2021) Impacts of psychological behaviours of managers on money laundering: evidence from Iran stock exchange. J Money Laund Control
Sanjaya AW, Nurjaya IN, Djatmika P, Ruba'i M (2020) Sociological implication of pro parte dolus pro parte culpa form of fault in the formulation of passive money laundering. Res Soc Dev 9
SEBoK Authors (2021) Foundations of systems engineering, Version 2.4. ed. International council on systems engineering (INCOSE), San Diego, CA
Seidl D, Becker KH (2006) Organizations as distinction generating and processing systems: Niklas Luhmann's contribution to organization studies. Organization 13:9
Seidl D, Schoeneborn D (2010) Niklas Luhmann's autopoietic theory of organisations: contributions, limitations, and future prospects. Univ Zurich Inst Organ Adm. Sci IOU Work Pap
Senge PM (2006) The fifth discipline: the art and practice of the learning organization, Rev. and updated ed. Random House Business Books, London
Sheard SA, Mostashari A (2011) 6.2. 1 complexity types: from science to systems engineering, in: INCOSE International Symposium. Wiley Online Library:673–682
Skyttner L (2005) General systems theory: problems, perspectives, practice. World scientific

Strauss DF (2002) The scope and limitations of Von Bertalanffy's systems theory. South Afr J Philos 21:163–179

Trist, E.L., 1981. The evolution of socio-technical systems. Ontario Quality of Working Life Centre Toronto

Trist EL, Bamforth KW (1951) Some social and psychological consequences of the longwall method of coal-getting: an examination of the psychological situation and defences of a work group in relation to the social structure and technological content of the work system. Hum Relat 4:3–38

Volkoff O, Strong DM (2017) Affordance theory and how to use it in is research. In: The Routledge companion to management information systems. Routledge, pp 232–245

Von Bertalanffy L (1968) General system theory: foundations, development, applications. G. Braziller

Von Bertalanffy L (1950) An outline of general system theory. Br J Philos Sci

Walsham G (2006) Doing interpretive research. Eur J Inf Syst 15:320–330

Walsham G (1995) Interpretive case studies in is research: nature and method. Eur J Inf Syst 4

Wang H, Wang J, Tang Q (2018) A review of application of affordance theory in information systems. J Serv Sci Manag 11:56–70

Wiener N (1948) Cybernetics or control and communication in the animal and the machine. Technology Press

Weick KE (1995) Sensemaking in organizations. Sage

Wong L (2013) Money-laundering in Southeast Asia: liberalism and governmentality at work. Contemp Polit 19:221–233

Worthington I, Britton C, Thompson E (2018) The business environment: a global perspective, Eighth edition. Pearson, Harlow, England New York

Chapter 6
The Case of FIU Ireland

6.1 Introduction to the Case Study

This case study explores the operation of the Irish Financial Intelligence Units, FIU Ireland, at a time of regulatory change, namely from 2020 to 2023. The time frame covers the period immediately before and after the introduction of legislation in April 2021 to bring crypto-assets and virtual asset service providers (VASPs) within the scope of anti-money laundering (AML) regulations, or alternatively the introduction of crypto-laundering regulations.

The months prior to April 2021 saw frenzied discussions about the dangers of crypto-asset misuse and the rise of crypto-laundering, which provoked a response from civil society in the form of expanding the AML system to include crypto-assets (Chap. 4). The case study seeks to understand the phenomenon of crypto-laundering and the role the Irish FIU plays in its comprehension, pursuit, and detection. It is important to stress that the Irish FIU could be substituted for any global FIU; therefore, the lessons learned are applicable in any other jurisdiction.

At all times, the questions of the suitability of the FIU to handle crypto-laundering and the organisational consequences of the expansion of the FIU's role are paramount.

The description of the case study is sensitised by socio-technical systems theory, so the disparate data collected through observations, interviews, focus groups, document analysis, and the exploration of 2719 crypto-related STRs that were submitted to FIU Ireland in 2021 can be considered together (a detailed analysis of these crypto-STRs will be provided in Chap. 7). To avoid confusion, any STR that references crypto-assets will be called a crypto-STR.

The results from this case study form the basis for the theoretical contribution of this book, where the development from a specific case and its data allows for additional analytical work to be carried out in order to develop two systems-oriented

S. Meighan, *Money Laundering and Crypto-Assets*, Contributions to Finance and Accounting, https://doi.org/10.1007/978-3-032-13481-3_6

visualisations that allow further inductive progression to identify patterns, theoretical dimensions, and abstractions (Chap. 9).

6.1.1 Crypto-Laundering

Before delving into the case study, this is a useful juncture to consider a quick recap of the main phenomenon being researched. *Crypto-laundering* is a crypto-asset-specific variant of cyber-money laundering, i.e. laundering the proceeds of crime through crypto-related digital assets. If the source of funds is criminal in nature, then any possession, transfer, conversion, etc. of those funds raises potential crypto-laundering criminal offences, where the criminal's main aim is to clean the funds and break the link with the predicate offence that generated them. Crypto-assets can be considered a system where it is first necessary to convert fiat currency to crypto-assets to use their perceived value within the system. This conversion is currently carried out almost exclusively through businesses called VASPs. Apart from some limited use cases, it is necessary to reconvert crypto-assets back to fiat currency to enjoy the fruits of the crime or to reinvest in more serious criminality. Again, this conversion is carried out by VASPs. It is vital to remember that crypto-assets themselves are not illegal and have many legitimate uses.

The criminal launderer seeks to hide their illicit transactions in plain sight among the many legitimate transactions, making the job of detecting suspicious activity more difficult, akin to finding the proverbial needle in a haystack. The identification of a suspicious transaction—or what the private sector regulated entity perceives to be a suspicious transaction—should trigger the making of an STR to the FIU, which may cause a money laundering investigation to be commenced and, ideally, lead to the criminal being deprived of their ill-gotten gains. This fulfils the three main purposes of an AML regime—criminalising money laundering, denying criminals the use of criminal proceeds, and protecting the legitimate financial system (Chaps. 2 and 3).

6.1.2 The Role of FIUs in the AML System

Financial intelligence units (FIUs) are the link between the private and public sector partners in the AML system, and the link between the preventative and repressive AML measures put in place to address money laundering (Fig. 2.4).

Under FATF Recommendation 29 (App. 1) and Art. 32 of 4AMLD (App. 3)—to be replaced by Art. 19 of 6AMLD (App. 2)—each county is required to establish an FIU to prevent, detect, and effectively combat money laundering and terrorist financing. The FIU is mandated as the single agency in a country responsible for receiving and analysing reports relevant to suspicions of money laundering or related criminality. Where appropriate, the FIU then disseminates reports of *financial intelligence* to competent authorities for investigation and prosecution. Each

FIU should be operationally independent, autonomous, and have sufficient resources to fulfil its mandate. Their structure varies by jurisdiction: ranging from administrative FIUs (e.g. Belgium), law enforcement (e.g. Ireland), or hybrid (e.g. the Netherlands) models. However, regardless of structure, their role and function remain the same:

- Prevention and detection: detect suspicious activity by analysing STRs/SARs for patterns or indicators of money laundering using all sources of information available to them.
- Dissemination: share *financial intelligence* with competent authorities so that investigations, prosecutions, and asset seizure might take place.
- Coordination: act as the bridge between the private sector, law enforcement, and international partners.

The work of the FIU is shaped and dependent on FATF standards, EU legislation, and national AML legislation. It must be stressed that FIUs are not investigative bodies but merely hold and process *financial intelligence* at the suspicion stage before an investigation, evidence gathering, and prosecution take place. These roles will be expanded upon later in this chapter.

6.1.3 Data Sources

The primary data sources for this book were semi-structured interviews with FIU and AML experts, and a download of 2719 crypto-asset-related STRs received by FIU Ireland in 2021. These were combined with several focus groups and the author's observations from working in the FIU over 2½ years. Secondary sources included a review of all legislation, policy, procedures, and industry reports pertaining to the FIU and the regulation of crypto-assets.

Each interviewee gave their informed consent to participate in this research. To preserve their anonymity and prevent respondents from being identified by their respective roles or titles, each participant was assigned a random number (R1, R2, …). To give the reader context of the contribution being made, a general description of the person's expertise is included at each mentioned intervention.

The research for this book was carried out in accordance with the highest academic standards and approved by the University of Hull.

6.2 FIU Ireland

This case study will first examine the establishment, role, legislative framework, and structure of FIU Ireland, paying particular attention to how the existing AML structure was modified and expanded to account for the introduction of legislation to regulate crypto-assets for the purposes of AML. It will then look at how FIU staff are trained, especially in dealing with crypto-STRs.

The system of interest is the FIU organisation itself. It consists of many socio-technical elements which interact in such a way to perform a function—purportedly the analysis of STRs—but which may exhibit emergent behaviour, different from its intended purpose, which can then be considered its actual purpose. The system is part of the larger hierarchical AML system. It is itself made up of many social and technical sub-systems. The inputs to our system are STRs, including crypto-STRs, received from the designated persons who have identified suspicious activity carried out by their customers. The FIU system should provide feedback to the reporting entities to ensure the system remains viable. The outputs of our system are the intelligence packages created when a suspicion of money laundering, or crypto-laundering, is substantiated. This intelligence package will, hopefully, lead to a criminal investigation and possible asset seizure. This system of interest is located within an ever more complex environment, and by necessity is distinguished from it by the author taking a certain perspective based on his own knowledge, experiences, background, and biases. The case study will then look in detail at the functioning of the FIU and how it has dealt with crypto-laundering in particular. By doing so, it is hoped to get a greater understating of this new phenomenon, which can be considered a *wicked* problem (Chap. 1).

6.2.1 Establishment of FIU Ireland

Each EU member state is required by Art. 32(1) of 4AMLD to establish an FIU in order "to prevent, detect, and effectively combat money laundering and terrorist financing" (App. 3).[1] As was seen previously, the FIU is the crucial link between the public sector criminal investigators and the private businesses and persons required by law to carry out AML checks on their customers and report suspicious activity to the FIU. It is also the link between the preventative and repressive measures of the AML system.

The book identified that there are concerns around the effectiveness of the current AML system and the expansion of it to regulate crypto-assets for the purpose of AML, as the additional workload created has the potential to overwhelm the scarce FIU resources and raises questions about whether the STR model is effective for a new, fast-moving technology such as crypto-assets (Chap. 2).

The need for an FIU, instead of sending information about suspicious activity directly to law enforcement, was discussed with several of the interviewees. R1, an experienced FIU manager, stated:

> the whole AML framework falls down if you take the FIU out … the reason being is that the FIU is involved at an early stage when the STRs aren't confirmed crimes, they are only

[1] To be replaced by Art. 19 6AMLD (App. 2).

> suspicions. We protect the people named in the STRs by not recording them on the criminal database.

The protection discussed here lies at the heart of the FIU's operation. Only personnel inside the FIU have access to the full FIU database (which is strictly confidential) and are acutely aware that the information needs to be further developed before it is sent to law enforcement. R10, a senior FIU manager, also states that the FIU offers support to reporting entities, including VASPs:

> The FIU is not seen as the police; this allows a good relationship to be developed between the designated person and the FIU. Given that the FIU in Ireland has no supervisory role, the designated person is likely to speak more freely with the FIU once that relationship has been developed. This allows for better cooperation and reporting of incidents at an early stage… Regarding crypto-assets, each VASP was met in person prior to their registration to onboard them to the FIU reporting system, GoAML. In many cases, this was the first discussion the entities had with the public sector regarding AML, which they stated was very valuable.

R7, a crypto-AML supervisor, echoed the importance of this type of cooperation, which helps to filter out the "overreporting and other nonsense" before it reaches the police. Defensive reporting and reporting of so-called junk STRs have long clogged up the system and take resources away from work that might be better directed to genuine STRs that indicate true money laundering. Although it must be accepted that many, many junk STRs are still filed and clog the system. Indeed, some might argue that these account for the majority of submissions.

R9, an experienced FIU manager, concurs with the previous respondent and states:

> The FIU will analyse STRs indicating suspected money laundering and only send to the police what they believe to be necessary. They also store the balance of the reports not sent out to the police as intelligence if the police ever come looking for intel to assist their investigations. The FIU deals with a lot of other bodies as well. So, without an FIU there would just be passing the buck to the police to do all the donkey work.

Other interviewees responsible for the investigation of money laundering agreed that the FIU was vital and acted as an essential "intelligence store for financial investigators" (R5, an experienced AML professional). The FIU was also considered to provide a mechanism for obtaining information—and using this in its analysis—not normally available to law enforcement "like Egmont, and bank account information from the newly formed central register", information that "can add valuable assistance to an investigation that didn't necessarily come from an STR" (R8, a money laundering investigation manager).

It is important to stress that the information sent to law enforcement on their request is not in raw format and has been enhanced by FIU analysis and comments before it is provided to the requester. The type of intelligence provided is usually a profile of a person's financial accounts and assets, their expected legitimate income, and any foreign accounts they may have. Legitimate income is important, as Irish legislation contains a presumption that any unexplained wealth can be considered the proceeds of criminal conduct when conducting a money laundering investigation. Currently, information requests sent back to the police will also include crypto-asset information where applicable.

The Irish Financial Intelligence Unit, known as FIU Ireland, was established in May 1995 following Ireland's transposition of the first EU AML Directive (1AMLD). Subsequent EU legislation, strongly influenced by the recommendations of the FATF, has further defined and expanded the role and functions of this organisation. R11, an international AML expert, states that although the FATF and EU:

> standards are not 100% perfect ... it's amazing that we got all the nations in the world to agree to a common AML framework. However, it is the implementation of these standards at the country level that is a problem and causes criminals to seek gaps in legislation in a form of criminal law arbitrage.

Regarding crypto-assets, this allows criminals to seek countries that have yet to regulate crypto-assets for the purposes of AML or have implemented a regime with narrow definitions that allow activity to take place in an unregulated manner. It can also include using VASPs in unfriendly countries that are not known to cooperate with other countries and will not respond to law enforcement requests for assistance. Both of these are forms of location-based arbitrage. It is also perceived that some VASPs are less stringent on AML controls than others. This makes them attractive to criminals who may seek out these entities over those that are known to have more stringent AML controls (arbitrage between exchanges).

FIU Ireland is a police-based FIU that is embedded within the Garda National Economic Crime Bureau of An Garda Síochána, Ireland's National police service. The reasons for Ireland adopting this type of FIU (i.e. a police-based configuration instead of a purely intelligence-based bureaucracy) are perhaps lost in time. As R9, a senior FIU manager, commented:

> As far as I can remember ... the then Superintendent (in Economic Crime) ... was very much aware of the necessity to understand what was going on in the financial and the banking worlds vis-a-vis how was money being moved, legally and illegally ... he saw it as an opportunity for the Gardaí to have the financial intelligence unit. It was his foresight that caused the Gardaí to put their hands up and take it. On top of that, there was probably a reluctance from anyone else to take it. So, probably, one balanced out the other in the end.

This comment is interesting, as it shows an acknowledgment and awareness by the Irish police that illegal funds were being filtered unmolested through the legitimate financial economy, often without police knowledge or understanding. The foresight of that senior police officer is to be commended; however, the sting in the tail is an acceptance that no other Irish public sector body wanted to take on the onerous task of running the FIU. R10, a senior FIU manager, similarly reflects:

> The FIU was left with An Garda Síochána because nobody else wanted it. It was seen as a law enforcement issue by the powers that be. However, it was probably a good decision in the end as the police already had the investigative and analytic skills, they just needed to develop their financial knowledge i.e., how the financial world worked.

Regardless of the reasons why, today's financial investigators, such as R8, see the benefits of having a police-based FIU as the staff's "knowledge and background of investigating crime", having access to criminal databases, and having a knowledge of what is reasonable to send onto the police for investigation knowing their capabilities is a tremendous advantage and stops the police being flooded with unactionable information. Police in the FIU are also seen as less of a barrier "between the investigation team and the intelligence" than a non-police structure. "It makes sense having Garda (police) investigators in that office" (R8, money laundering investigation manager). Police feel they are able to speak more directly with other police officers, as they come from a similar background and understanding of purpose.

6.2.2 *Role of FIU Ireland*

FIU Ireland's primary responsibility is to carry out, on behalf of the Irish State, all of the functions of an EU FIU as set out in the EU's 4AMLD. It is worth noting that despite the majority of the FIU's functions being specified in the *Criminal Justice (Money Laundering and Terrorist Financing) Act, 2010 as amended*, some key roles are not explicitly outlined, requiring that reference must also be made to the text of 4AMLD, in particular Art. 32 (App. 3).

FIU Ireland's main function is twofold and will be outlined in brief here before each component is discussed in detail below.

Firstly, the FIU receives STRs from designated persons, including VASPs. It then carries out an analysis of the information in the STR and seeks to develop that information to see if it likely discloses a money laundering offence. This is done by accessing information:

1. Already in its possession
2. Within the various beneficial ownership registers
3. From open source intelligence (OSINT)
4. Using the coercive powers of sworn analysts to demand information from a variety of sources

There are several additional analysis steps to be completed when dealing with crypto-STRs. Recall how every transaction that ever took place is recorded on the publicly available blockchain, and that there is no link to the real-world identity of the person sending or receiving the crypto recorded. In this situation, crypto-assets are simultaneously private and public. On one hand, real-world identities are private and not readily ascertainable from viewing the open blockchain. On the other hand, every transaction is available to any person who chooses to examine its origin. This includes FIU analysts who, as part of analysing a crypto-STR, may seek to:

1. Trace and map value moving through the crypto-asset system.
2. Cluster addresses in a manner that may provide a window into otherwise anonymous and criminal activity.
3. Associate pseudonymous crypto-information with a real-world user (attribution)

While these tasks may be carried out manually, given the volume of data currently associated with each blockchain (e.g. as of May 2025, the Bitcoin blockchain currently contains 5 ½ terabytes of data), the use of proprietary, commercially available blockchain analysis software is now commonplace. The operation of these blockchain analytics tools will be discussed in detail in Chap. 8.

Where a criminal indicator is present, an intelligence package is prepared and disseminated to law enforcement for possible criminal investigation. Law enforcement is broadly defined, and includes Irish and worldwide police services, and other bodies with investigative responsibilities for money laundering and its predicate offences.

It is important to note that there is not a one-to-one relationship between disseminations and STRs; a dissemination can be made up of information from a wide variety of sources. It is also important to note that FIUs are not an investigative authority.

Secondly, FIU Ireland acts as an intelligence store, or repository, for a vast amount of information that may be useful for ongoing or future criminal investigations. This information can be made available to law enforcement on request subject to data protection requirements, etc.

Staff at FIU Ireland also contribute to the development of National and European AML policy. Senior representatives of FIU Ireland sit on the Anti-money Laundering Steering Committee (AMLSC) and represent Ireland at various international fora, such as the EU, the FATF, and the Egmont Group of FIUs. The AMLSC somewhat successfully ensures Ireland's AML policies remain compliant with EU and international standards (especially 5AMLD and the introduction of crypto-asset AML regulation, of which FIU Ireland staff contributed to the implementation of the new legislation and national policy). The AMLSC is a multi-departmental and multi-agency committee, chaired by the Department of Finance, which strives to provide a national, cross-sectoral forum for the oversight and active review of Ireland's AML/CFT framework. Staff at the FIU have been recognised as experts in anti-money laundering and have been selected to take part in FATF country evaluations. The author was part of the mutual evaluation of Indonesia (2021–2023), with responsibility for IO7 (Money Laundering) and IO8 (Asset Seizure). The Head of the FIU at the time of this research was a FATF accessor who worked mainly with the Inter-Governmental Action Group against Money Laundering in West Africa (GIABA) and some EU countries, which had been found to have significant AML structural difficulties (e.g. Albania).

FIU Ireland staff conduct a large number of outreach activities to designated persons each year, including, in recent times, to VASPs seeking registration in Ireland and onboarding to GoAML for STR creation. Outreach also consists of presentations to and engagement with individual companies, specific sectors, and to larger compliance events that are held in Ireland and Europe. FIU Ireland contributes to and supports five public-private partnerships (PPPs):

1. The Joint Intelligence Group (Irish Domestic Banks)
2. The International Joint Intelligence Group (International Banks operating in Ireland)

3. The Joint Practice Group (Accountancy AML Supervisors and Accountants and Tax Advisors in practice)
4. The Financial Intelligence Taskforce (FinTechs and VASPs operating in Ireland)
5. Europol's European Financial Intelligence Public Private Partnership (EFIPPP)

The Fintech group was set up by the author during his time at FIU Ireland as a direct response to the introduction of 5AMLD and the need to engage directly with VASPs regarding their reporting obligations and the quality of crypto-STRs submitted to the FIU (Chap. 8).

FIU Ireland delivers STR/intelligence package handling and money laundering training courses to law enforcement personnel in advance of them receiving intelligence from the FIU, and this recently includes specific information on intelligence packages that contain crypto-asset information. This was necessary as the police were often not familiar with how to action and deal with the intelligence packages received from the FIU. In some cases, the intelligence was mishandled or ignored. By creating a pool of trained investigators throughout the country, this problem was somewhat alleviated; however, the volume of material being disseminated outweighs the number of trained investigators. FIU Ireland also works closely with the various AML supervisors (see Chap. 8 for an example of this cooperation regarding crypto-STR reporting). As Ireland has a dual-reporting requirement whereby each STR must also be submitted to the Revenue Commissioners (the Irish Tax Authorities, responsible for the investigation of all tax matters), regular meetings are held with them to ensure that STRs are properly addressed.

6.2.3 Legislative Framework

The legislative framework for Ireland's AML regime, including the role and function of FIU Ireland, is set out in the much-amended group of acts[2] that are included in the following collective citation: the *Criminal Justice (Money Laundering and Terrorist Financing) Acts 2010 to 2021*, hereinafter referred to as the 2010 Act.

Two examples of recent significant legislative changes affecting the FIU are as follows. Firstly, in 2018, FIU Ireland was given statutory legitimacy following the transposition of 4AMLD—after operating on an ad hoc basis for nearly 23 years. R9, a very experienced senior FIU manager, argues that despite operating in a legal vacuum for that period, FIU Ireland:

> had its own identity within the police and the lack of legal status didn't cause any real difficulties.

However, R9 conceded this lack of legal status meant it was:

[2] The following acts constitute Ireland's AML regime: the Criminal Justice (Money Laundering and Terrorist Financing) Acts 2010, the Criminal Justice Act 2013, the Criminal Justice (Money Laundering and Terrorist Financing) (Amendment) Act 2018, and the Criminal Justice (Money Laundering and Terrorist Financing) (Amendment) Act 2021.

hanging on the coat tails of the police and obviously often suffered. There were a lack of staff and a lack of resources, a lack of budget. Yeah, it probably wasn't ideal.

Considering this concession, it cannot be said that an organisation such as an FIU can operate effectively without a legal underpinning which has now (eventually) been provided. This also gives rise to concerns about how operationally autonomous the FIU in Ireland actually is. Congruent with FATF Recommendation 29 and Art. 32(2) of 4AMLD, each FIU is required to be operationally independent and autonomous. This is defined in a way that bestows the FIU with the authority and capacity to carry out its functions freely, including the ability to take autonomous decisions to analyse, request, and disseminate specific information. This presents an obvious issue for FIU Ireland as it is almost totally reliant on An Garda Síochána for its allocation of human, IT, and financial resources. Can it be said that any organisation is autonomous where they have no financial autonomy? If an organisation's budget is cut by say 50%, then what is the point of operational independence?

The answer to both questions is obviously no, and does present a paradox when discussing an FIU that can determine the scope of its work but is totally reliant on another party to provide the means to do that work. R9, a senior FIU manager, accepts the majority of this position but is not entirely convinced:

Autonomy is a big challenge for us, but somebody somewhere always has to control the finances. Nobody has ever shown me an FIU that does not rely on a parent organisation for funding and resources. Our main problem is not deciding what work we do, our main difficulty today and into the future is our resources, when the resources are controlled by HRM (the HR section of the police) with so much of a pull of them from other sections and front line policing units. … the FIU don't have the autonomy to do our own stand-alone hiring. It going to be a challenge into the future.

Surely, this is a perfect example of a lack of FIU autonomy? Another FIU manager, R10, seems more attuned to the issue and says that:

the situation is not perfect. We need more staff and IT resources. We rely totally upon An Garda Síochána, we are not always a priority and don't get what we need to do our job. The need for a stand-alone FIU with its own budget, HR capability, and IT support is vital going forward, especially with the expansion of the number of entities reporting into us and the increasing complexity of those reports when discussing new technology such as crypto-assets and crypto-laundering.

A common discussion point throughout the period of observation was the need for an independent multi-agency model for FIU Ireland, similar in structure to the Criminal Assets Bureau (CAB), where staff from the police and other law enforcement bodies could work together.

The second recent and significant legislative change occurred in April 2021, when crypto-assets and VASPs were brought into the scope of AML regulation for the first time, resulting from the transposition of 5AMLD into Irish law (the focus of this book). FIU Ireland staff assisted in the implementation of the new legislation by providing comments on the drafts, discussing the requirements at the government level, and providing implementation guidance to VASPs. However, by assigning additional responsibilities to the FIU, a significant strain on its resources followed, and this required considerable upskilling in the new area of crypto-laundering.

The creation of additional reporting entities creates additional STRs, which, added to the already increasing number of STRs received annually, presents a strain on the scarce resources in the FIU. Given that this was a new technology, there were significant knowledge and training gaps that had to be addressed. The specialised onboarding of VASPs also drew from the FIU's scarce resources and detracted from their analysis work, which created bottlenecks at later stages. Nevertheless, bringing this modern method of value transfer under the AML requirements "was necessary, right, and absolutely required to address the challenges of money laundering through crypto-assets" (R11, international AML expert).

6.2.4 Structure of FIU Ireland

FIU Ireland is headed by a Detective Chief Superintendent, who is supported by a senior management team consisting of a Detective Superintendent (Deputy Head of FIU) and a Detective Inspector (Head of Operations) (Fig. 6.1). FIU Ireland is divided into three main functional areas, each of which is supervised by a detective sergeant: the money laundering intelligence unit (this was the original section of FIU Ireland and is still referred to as the FIU), the Terrorist Financing Intelligence Unit (TFIU), and the International Relations and Policy Unit (IRPU). The functions of each section will be described when the analysis of STRs is examined presently.

FIU Ireland is staffed by members of An Garda Síochána (sworn police officers) and civilian police staff (unsworn), who have been specially appointed in writing by the Garda Commissioner.[3] Civilian staff are referred to as *civilian analysts*, whereas police officers are titled as *sworn analysts*. Sworn analysts retain all of their police powers and privileges in addition to a number of supplementary FIU powers that are granted upon their appointment to the FIU. Throughout the duration of the case study, in addition to the senior management team, there were approximately 20–25 personnel working in FIU Ireland. A police forensic accountant was also appointed to the FIU and available to assist in the analysis of larger and more complex projects as needed.

All interviewees identified the need for additional human and IT resources within the FIU to cope with the ever-increasing workload being imposed on them. As one can see, the number of staff within the FIU is extremely small. This comes into sharp focus when one sees how many STRs are received each year and how complicated they are becoming with the introduction of new technology, such as crypto-assets. As the FIU cannot directly hire expert AML staff, they must provide training to the meagre number of general staff that are allocated to them by their parent

[3] Section 40A(2) of the 2010 Act.

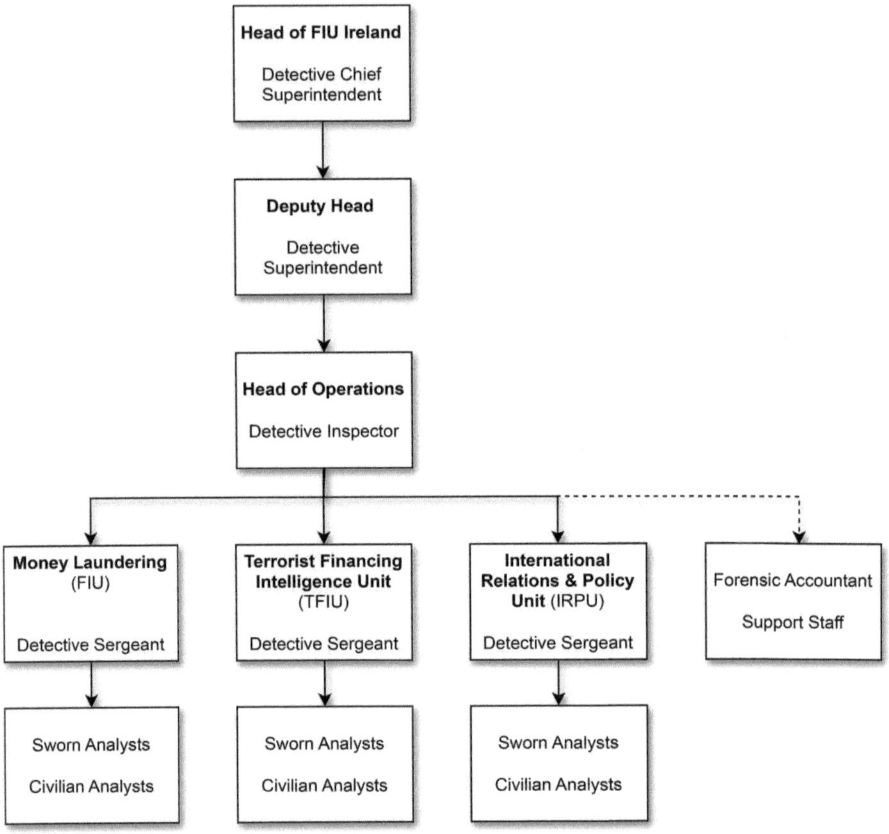

Fig. 6.1 FIU Ireland Organisation chart

organisation. These new staff require specialised training that is delivered in-house by the FIU itself, which is yet another demand on its scarce human resources.

6.2.5 Training of FIU Staff

Upon allocation to the FIU, new staff members undertake a comprehensive induction course that covers AML legislation, reporting requirements, the use of GoAML, and the FIU's policies and procedures. They are also required to undertake external courses provided by the EU, FATF, the Egmont Group, the Basel Institute, and other external training providers. For their probationary period, new staff are assigned a peer mentor and work closely, shadowing this person for their first few weeks until deemed competent to work on their own. Each FIU staff member is under the supervision of a highly skilled detective sergeant at all times. The direct hiring of specialised staff would alleviate the need for some of this basic training and allow new staff to immediately contribute to the FIU's daily work.

Management at FIU Ireland was aware of crypto-assets and crypto-laundering from 2017, arising from their attendance at various national and international meetings. As a result, a small number of staff were selected to receive intensive training on crypto-assets, crypto-laundering, and blockchain analytics. This training was provided by Europol, external universities, and commercial companies that provide blockchain tools to law enforcement. FIU Ireland has access to a number of these tools for analysing crypto-STRs.

This type of selective, specialised training means that the level of understanding of crypto-assets in general, and crypto-laundering in particular, among the other FIU analysts and money laundering investigators is uneven at best. Some FIU staff are very aware of crypto, crypto-laundering, and how to analyse crypto-STRs to determine if crypto-laundering is indicated. Many of those interviewed have taken a personal interest in the subject and have completed several training and academic courses, many independent of the FIU (R1, R2, R3, R4, R5, R7, and R11).

R6, a crypto-laundering investigator, states:

> it's easy to watch somebody's money on the computer (on the blockchain) and use the tools that are available. Even the open source ones are fantastic. I've learned to use them by teaching myself and picking things up as I've gone along.

However, this ad-hoc path to training can lead to different approaches from people within the same organisation, which is not always ideal. According to R1, an experienced FIU manager, FIU Ireland is:

> definitely not there yet, it is such a new area that we're catching up on so we're relying on the likes of say Europol to run training and companies that provide the analysis software to support us … and that goes against the grain … of how we usually deal with things in house … but we can't do this without a private entity.

Other staff members have limited knowledge but are working to improve their skill set (R8, money laundering investigation manager), whereas some employees will actively try to pass off any cases received involving crypto-assets to a more "tech-savvy" colleague (R13, criminal investigator). This spread of knowledge is not unexpected due to the specialised nature of crypto-laundering; however, it illustrates that awareness, knowledge, training, and resources are needed across the entire public sector, especially within FIU Ireland.

Having given a general overview of the establishment, structure, and function of FIU Ireland, the duties of FIU Ireland can now be examined in greater detail, particularly the receipt, analysis, and storage of STRs and crypto-STRs.

6.3 Receipt of STRs and Other Information

FIU Ireland is the Central Authority responsible for receiving and analysing STRs, and other information relevant to money laundering or terrorist financing for the purposes of preventing, detecting, and investigating suspected money laundering and terrorist financing.[4] Each designated person is obliged to make an STR to FIU Ireland if they "know, suspect, or have reasonable grounds to suspect", on the basis of information obtained in the course of carrying out a business as a designated person, that a person (usually their customer or the person with whom their customer is transacting with) has been or is engaged in an offence of money laundering.[5]

A designated person is defined[6] as a natural or legal person acting in the course of a specific business carried on by the person in Ireland, such as a credit or financial institution, or a VASP. This definition also includes some of the so-called gatekeeper professions, such as lawyers, accountants, auditors, and also some of the cash-intensive businesses with a high risk of being exploited for money laundering, such as bookmakers and dealers in high-value goods. The STR must be made as soon as practicable and include the following details:

1. The reason on which the designated person's knowledge, suspicion, or reasonable grounds are based (referred to as the reason for suspicion)
2. The identity, if known, of the person suspected to be involved in the money laundering
3. The whereabouts of the property, which is the subject of the money laundering
4. Any other relevant information (e.g. account numbers, addresses, transactions, etc.)[7]

As can be seen, the STR is made mainly on the basis of scrutinising information gathered by the designated person in the course of their business (including automatic banking transactions), but the legislation allows any circumstances to be used to substantiate the suspicion, e.g. an OSINT search for negative media.[8] The fact that a person cannot or refuses to complete KYC and CDD is sufficient to ground a suspicion of money laundering.[9]

Unlike the United Kingdom, Ireland does not operate a consent regime whereby permission must be obtained from the FIU to proceed with a transaction that is deemed suspicious. R10, a FIU manager, states: "a consent regime would overwhelm the FIU, just like it has in the UK, and take the focus away from STR work". R9, another FIU manager, emphatically agrees stating:

> the system in the UK … really takes a lot of pressure and the onus off the financial entities and puts it on to the FIU. From my knowledge, in the UK FIU the majority of their time is dealing with [consent requests] rather than dealing with the SARs that they're getting. So, it's not a system I would particularly like.

4 Section 40B(1) of the 2010 Act. All references to money laundering from this point onwards can also be taken to include a reference to terrorist financing.

5 Section 42 of the 2010 Act.

6 Section 25(1) of the 2010 Act.

7 Section 42(2) and (6) of the 2010 Act.

8 Section 42(3) and (5) of the 2010 Act.

9 Section 42(4) of the 2010 Act.

The fact that two FIU managers are adamant in not wanting a consent regime to be implemented in Ireland is perhaps an indication that this would overwhelm the already scarce resources within the FIU and need additional investment of resources. A consent regime could alleviate concerns around the dissipation of criminal proceeds before an STR is made, but evidence from the United Kingdom on the success of this is somewhat unsubstantiated. Instead, in Ireland a designated person who makes an STR should not proceed with the transaction or service connected with the report unless it is (a) not practicable to delay or stop the transactions or service from proceedings, or (b) the designated person is of the reasonable opinion that the failure to proceed may result in the person who is the subject of the report suspecting that a report may have been made.[10] In practice, due to the nature of transaction monitoring in the quickly moving financial world, especially within VASPs, and given the nature of crypto-asset technology, almost all reports are made after the fact of the suspected transaction or service. This can equate to a lost opportunity for law enforcement to freeze any suspected proceeds of criminal conduct before they are dissipated.

A designated person is potentially exposed to a money laundering or AML regulatory prosecution if they allow a transaction to proceed and it is later proved to be money laundering. Prosecutions such as this are extremely rare and usually constitute part of a wider AML failure. A designated person who fails to make a report commits an offence and is liable on summary conviction to a fine not exceeding €5000 and/or imprisonment for a term not exceeding 12 months, or on conviction on indictment to a fine and/or imprisonment for a term not exceeding 5 years.[11] In practice, due to the subjective nature of the concept of suspicion, prosecutions of this nature are difficult to sustain. They are seldom initiated, and then only as part of a suite of allegations that include substantive money laundering and other AML regulatory offences.[12]

In Ireland, there are two reporting requirements regarding money laundering. A designated person will oftentimes submit two identical reports, which increases the workload of the FIU and has the potential to create a duplication of efforts. At other times, an organisation will make an incorrect report, representing a potential loss of information for the FIU and render the police unaware of how to proceed with the material received. Therefore, it is important to distinguish the two.

Section 19 of the Criminal Justice Act, 2011, came into force after the STR regime was established. It obliges any person, not just designated persons, to notify An Garda Síochána (not FIU Ireland) of any relevant offence, which includes money

[10] Section 42(7) of the 2010 Act. STRs are extremely confidential and disclosing their existence (tipping-off), save in limited circumstances, is a serious criminal offence (Section 49 of the 2010 Act).

[11] Section 42(9) of the 2010 Act. This is therefore a serious "arrestable offence" which carries with it powers of search, arrest, and investigative detention (see Meighan (2025) or App. 4 for a summary of Irish police powers applicable to the investigation of money laundering).

[12] See, for example: https://www.breakingnews.ie/ireland/solicitor-arrested-after-search-of-offices-by-gardai-launches-court-challenge-1284654.html (Accessed: 21 August 2025).

laundering and most predicate offences. A person who fails to make a section 19 report commits an offence.[13] The interplay of section 19 and STR reports causes consternation and confusion for many designated persons. Many people submit both reports (STRs and section 19 s), which causes duplication of efforts and often leads to the FIU:

> informing the police of something they are already aware of, which defeats the purpose of the STR regime. The submission of both reports is another example of defensive reporting and often a tell-tail sign that the MLRO is not really sure of the reporting requirements (R10, a FIU manager).

The difference between the two reports is their threshold and where the report is submitted. STRs are mere suspicions of money laundering which must be analysed by the FIU and developed into an intelligence package for dissemination to law enforcement for possible investigation. Section 19 reports are crime reports, i.e. a crime has occurred. They are submitted directly to An Garda Síochána for investigation. One problem with section 19s is that there is no central depository to submit them. The legislation is silent on this, which means they are often submitted to any police station in the country, often by email and without context for local police. Contrary to this, the FIU is a convenient central office with an established reporting mechanism that is easy to use. It seems to offer a simpler submission mechanism and could be seen as the path of least resistance.

R1, a FIU manager, suggests the police could establish a "central receptacle within the police to report the section 19s, so they can be filtered out to" a trained single point of contact within each Division, who could liaise with the FIU before sending the report for investigation. Apart from trying to educate designated persons on the difference between the two reports (a further draw on scarce FIU resources), it would be very helpful if the legislators amended section 42 of the 2010 Act in future revisions to remove the reference to "knows … a person has engaged in money laundering" and make explicit reference to section 19. This would remove the ambiguity where the two different pieces of legislation conflict with each other.

FIU Ireland and the Central Bank of Ireland have clearly stated that the correct report must be submitted. Where a section 19 report has been made, an STR should not also be submitted, and vice versa. The submission of the STR does not fulfil the section 19 statutory obligation, and if a section 19 is made as an STR, it may not be covered by the reporting protections provided by the 2010 Act. In summary, confirmed criminality and suspected criminality outside money laundering are not suitable for STR reporting. This research did not have access to all the crypto-related section 19 s submitted to An Garda Síochána, which is a limitation of this work and an avenue of potential future research.

[13] Section 19(2) of the Criminal Justice Act, 2011 states that a person who fails to make a report is guilty of an offence under this section shall be liable (a) on summary conviction, to a €5000 fine or imprisonment for a term not exceeding 12 months or both, or (b) on conviction on indictment, to a fine or imprisonment for a term not exceeding 5 years or both.

Each class of designated persons should have a competent authority prescribed for the purpose of supervising and monitoring the effectiveness of the AML measures implemented. These supervisors should have the power to impose penalties and financial sanctions for any identified AML failures. Note that AML failures are also serious criminal offences that can be prosecuted by the police. These offences are sent to the FIU before they are transmitted to the investigative authority. It is another drain on the FIU's meagre resources. It should be acknowledged that these reports might contain useful information that assists in the analysis of other STRs, but this requires FIU staff to analyse them in the first place.

VASPs only became designated persons and subject to the AML requirements on 23 April 2021. Their AML supervisor is the Central Bank of Ireland. R4, an AML supervisor, argues:

> it's absolutely right that [VASPs] were brought into the AML sphere. I think like any institution that allows for the transfer of funds, they are potentially at risk to be used for nefarious purposes. And they bring something different in terms of the type of product but it's the same risk, it's the risk that they are services which will be used to move funds that have come from a criminal background. The problem, I think with VASPs is because of the anonymity within the services they provide. It's an easy win, potentially for criminals at this point in time. And so, it's about getting [VASPs] up to speed as quick as possible on the risk side and making sure they manage that correctly.

R1, a FIU manager, feels a certain degree of sympathy for how VASPs have been thrust into the AML system:

> the more I look at it, the more I feel a little bit sorry for the VASPs … that after developing their technology and business model, fighting for business, they then had to integrate into the (AML) framework.

This point was discussed in Chap. 4 about the danger of regulation stifling technological development, but in this case, the regulation came after the development.

All VASPs are required to register with the Irish Central Bank.Firms that were not established and carrying on business as a VASP in Ireland prior to this April 2021 cannot operate until an authorisation has been issued. However, VASPs that were already operating in Ireland prior to that date—and subject to AML requirements—are allowed to continue carrying on the business of a VASP once they have applied for an authorisation. No firms were authorised in 2021. Those who submitted STRs to the Irish FIU did so either voluntarily before April 2021 or as part of the "grandfathering" arrangement post April 2021. Since then, only nine firms have received authorisation—four in 2022, and five in 2023.[14] The Central Bank of Ireland has not published figures on how many VASP applications it has received. Based on meetings attended by the author and informal discussions with Central Bank officials and VASPs engaging with the FIU to onboard to GoAML, it is estimated to be around 70–80 firms. Not all of these applicants progressed their applications fully. R4, an AML supervisor, states:

[14] https://registers.centralbank.ie/DownloadsPage.aspx (Accessed: 21 August 2025).

> a lot of firms fell away when we started to work with them in terms of looking at what they had and what they needed to have AML-wise... A lot of VASPs are technology-led companies, and therefore their natural mindset is around new technologies, it's around making things faster, more convenient, and not necessarily around the money laundering risks they're running by doing that... This leaves approximately 30 to 40 that are still there in the system waiting to be approved or seeking registration... the split is 60/40, 60% new entrants and 40% previously operating in Ireland as a VASP.

In 2021, 11 firms registered on FIU Ireland's GoAML database as VASPs. Of these, only four actually submitted any STRs in 2021, and then over 97% of all these crypto-STRs were from one entity. At the end of 2023, there were 27 firms registered as VASPs on GoAML. Only nine submit STRs, and then two VASPs make up the majority of all crypto-STRs to the FIU. This is extremely concerning, as it shows that a large number of VASPs operating in Ireland have not submitted any STRs to the FIU, which gives rise to concerns of non-compliance with the AML legislation, a lack of awareness that the activities of a VASP are now regulated, and concerns around the quality of the crypto-STRs actually submitted.

The majority of VASPs operating in Ireland in 2021 were those that either relocated to Ireland post-Brexit or those that had an e-money licence and looked to expand their regulated operations. Prior to onboarding, each VASP had a series of separate meetings with senior staff in the FIU and the Central Bank of Ireland to explain Irish law, requirements, and FIU Ireland's expectations (discussed by R1, R4, R7, R10). The number of VASPs entering the Irish market is worrying for two reasons. Firstly, for the non-submission of STRs that we mentioned, and secondly, those VASPs that are submitting STRs are doing so in such a volume that threatens to over-stretch the limited resources of the FIU to the breaking point.

The supervisory approach taken by the Central Bank of Ireland with VASPs is similar to that used with other credit and financial institutions. As R4, an AML supervisor, mentions, the supervision approach looks:

> at whether a VASP meets all of its obligations under the Criminal Justice Act in a way that is appropriate for their firm and that is effective. However, governance is governance, it doesn't matter whether you're a VASP, or whether you are a credit institution or a credit union.

R7, another AML supervisor, added in the context of the supervisory approach taken of VASPs, "we're only looking at them against the regulations and only from an AML/CTF point of view". While the KYC and CDD requirements are the same for VASPs and traditional institutions, there are additional challenges to supervising—such as understanding where the money has come from or is going to an unhosted private address without further details of who owns that address. R4 expands this as follows:

> VASPs have customers and you can see the transactions. But it's very difficult for them to understand whose part of that transaction ... so they know their own customer, but where is the money going? ... This is a challenge both for the firms themselves and for the regulators so we can see if we are accurately and effectively capturing suspicious transactions.

This last point is one of the main difficulties for VASPs performing KYC and transaction monitoring, and, in general, knowing the counterparties to their customer's transactions. Users can have any number of public keys that are not known to the VASP, and using one set of public keys is not inherently tied to their activity using another set or their real-world identity. Within the transaction that is visible on the blockchain, there is no link to the real-world identity of the person at the other end of their customer's transaction.[15] R7 is more concerned with the lack of AML knowledge of the VASPs themselves. They stated that some of the AML:

> policies and documents presented to us were [downloaded] from the internet or copied from another entity. There's lots of "copy and paste" and a lot of stuff from up there (the internet). So, their understanding isn't great on the money laundering AML point of view. So, a lot of them do not understand this.

The author has seen an example of this in his work, where an AML policy template was downloaded from the Internet by a VASP. The template referenced UK legislation, the incorrect jurisdiction, and was not VASP specific, i.e. it referred to an e-money setup. On the other hand, during PPP meetings attended by the author, many VASPs complained that the AML requirements on them are too strict, cost too much to implement, and are ineffective. However, this is robustly rebutted by the public sector agencies. As R9, a FIU manager, argues:

> A lot of these entities I suppose … started out with an idea, a business idea… All of a sudden it did work, really well. And then they had to start thinking about compliance, AML, data protection and all that. They probably were not aware of these at the beginning of the of the journey. They've had to try, and play catch up and I think it's actually having a detrimental effect on their work because what happens is regulators will turn around and say you're not complying therefore you can't do business until you start complying. I don't think it's the case of rules being too strict only that VASPs often never even thought about them at the start.

STRs are made to the FIU via a website (www.fiu-ireland.ie). They are stored on an IT system called GoAML, which is an integrated database and analysis system developed by the UNODC and currently used by FIUs in over 60 countries.[16] FIU Ireland requires STRs to be submitted under one of two broad categories:

1. Regular STRs which concern suspicious activity that has a nexus to Ireland,
2. STR.EUs, usually submitted by designated persons located in Ireland but passporting their services to other EU countries, where there is no nexus to Ireland.

The second type of report was introduced in 2021 to deal with the rapidly increasing number of these reports, most of which are submitted by e-Money institutions and VASPs. In its first year of operation, 1995, FIU Ireland received 199 STRs; each was received in the post in hard copy and entered into a large leather-bound ledger.[17]

---

[15] See for example *US v. Sterlingov (2024)* summarised in App. 5.

[16] See http://www.fiu-ireland.ie or https://unite.un.org/goaml/ (Accessed: 21 August 2025).

[17] These two leather-bound ledgers were rediscovered by the author when the FIU was packing up and preparing to move to a new premises in 2022. They are now on display in the author's office. The first STRs concerned the murder of Veronica Guerin (see Chap. 2) and were handwritten by

Table 6.1 Breakdown of VASP submissions to FIU Ireland (2021–2023)

		STR	STR.EU	Total
2021	Total	35,239	3473	38,712
	VASPs	300	716	1016
		0.9%	20.6%	2.6%
2022	Total	35,751	11,670	47,421
	VASPs	6625	5138	11,763
		18.5%	44.0%	24.8%
2023	Total	52,223	16,776	68,999
	VASPs	23,843	5729	29,843
		45.7%	34.1%	43.3%

In 2021, the year in which AML regulation of crypto-assets and VASPs was introduced, there were 38,712 reports received, of which 1016 (2.6% of total) were from VASPs (see Table 6.1). The following year, there were 38,712 reports with 11,763 (24.8%) from VASPs, and in 2023, there were 68,999 reports received with 29,843 (43.3%) from VASPs. As is obvious from this breakdown of STRs received, the increased workload from VASPs is very significant and requires additional FIU staff, which have not been provided.

In 2020, FIU Ireland began publishing the number of STRs received per annum (Fig. 6.2). Additionally, Table 6.2 shows a breakdown of STRs by which sectors submitted them. The information was published on the FIU Ireland website and represents provisional figures as of 10 January 2023. As can be seen, the submission of STRs by some sectors (e.g. the legal, accountancy, and real estate sectors) is far lower than one would expect, given the relative size and risk associated with some low reporting sectors. One limitation of this study is that the time frame of the available STR data was limited to 2021; however, a multi-year longitudinal study is suggested for future research.

Now that the process by which STRs and crypto-STRs are submitted to the FIU has been analysed, the next step is to examine what the FIU does with these reports.

6.4 Analysis of STRs and Crypto-STRs

FIU Ireland's analysis function consists of conducting:

1. An *operational analysis* that focuses on individual cases and specific targets of suspected money laundering
2. A *strategic analysis* that addresses money laundering trends and patterns.[18]

the Head of the FIU (when this book's research was taking place) when he was one of its first sworn analysts.

[18] Section 40B(2) of the 2010 Act.

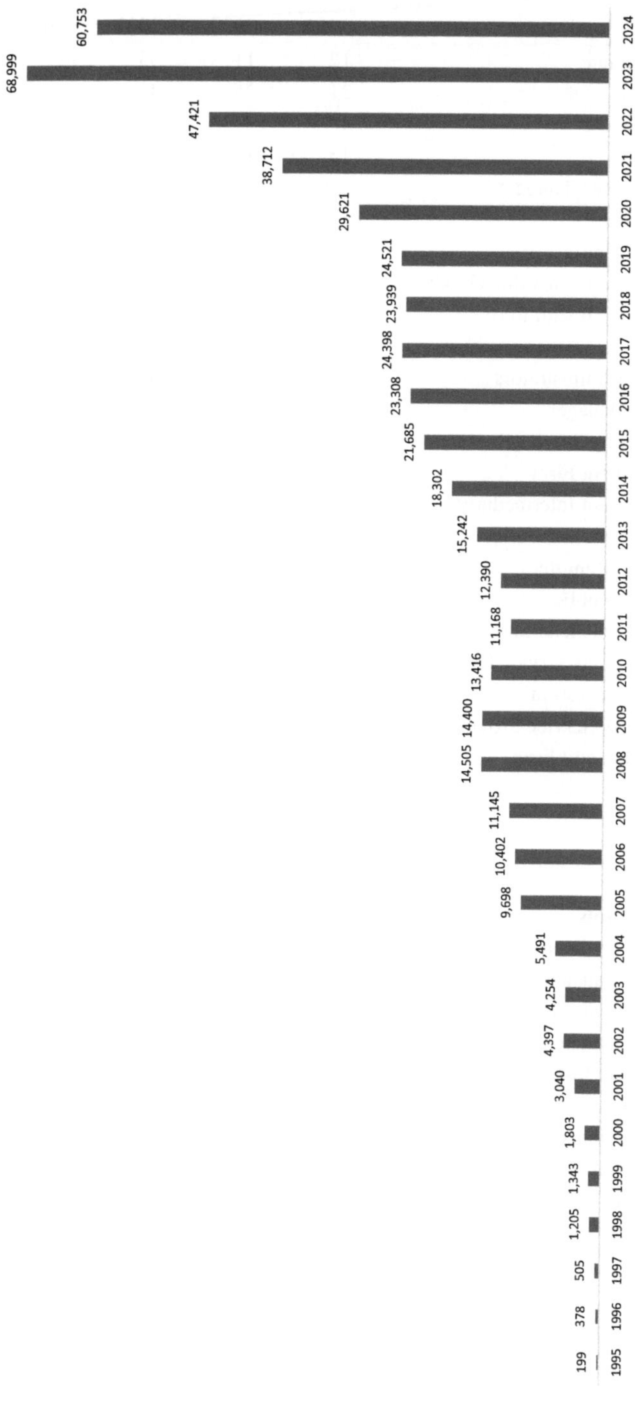

Fig. 6.2 STRs submitted to FIU Ireland (1995–2024)

Table 6.2 Breakdown of STRs by sector 2019–2023

		2019	2020	2021	2022	2023
STR	Accountant	17	11	33	9	15
	Auditor	21	25	4	1	0
	Auctioneer	4	2	5	0	6
	Bank	15,031	19,322	23,323	18,785	19,161
	Bureau de Change	189	50	46	108	119
	Car Dealer	118	61	86	49	25
	Credit Union	6047	5829	4993	4246	4007
	Dealer in High-value Goods	35	56	59	130	97
	E Money Institution	28	351	1382	931	1303
	Fund	13	17	41	26	30
	Fund Administrators	43	35	45	35	42
	Fund Manager	77	48	28	10	11
	Gambling Service Provider	255	349	559	1224	503
	Investment Firm	26	17	21	57	61
	Investment Intermediary	1	1	2	2	1
	Life Insurance Company	356	279	123	52	29
	Money Remitter	94	91	58	41	48
	Notary Public	0	0	1	1	3
	Other Financial Service Provider	324	316	417	555	483
	Other Fund Service Provider	7	9	9	18	13
	Payment Institution	1685	2637	3247	2338	2050
	Property Service Provider	1	1	0	0	0
	Retail Credit Firm	99	92	428	480	348
	Solicitor	8	8	12	13	6
	TCSP	19	6	12	12	15
	VASP	0	0	300	6625	23,843
	Other	23	8	5	3	3
	Sub-totals	**24,521**	**29,621**	**35,239**	**35,751**	**52,222**
STReu	E Money Institution	0	0	1944	4881	9157
	Fund Manager	0	0	51	70	81
	Investment Firm	0	0	0	54	180
	Life Insurance Company	0	0	289	407	467
	Payment Institution	0	0	476	1120	1160
	VASP	0	0	716	5138	5729
	Other Financial Service Provider	0	0	0	0	2
	Sub-totals	0	0	3476	11,670	16,776
	Totals	**24,521**	**29,621**	**38,715**	**47,421**	**68,998**
	% Difference (Year on Year)		21%	31%	22%	46%

1. Designation is selected by reporting entity at time of registration.
2. STReu is a specific report, usually submitted by entities passporting their services to other EU countries, where there is no nexus to Ireland. They are disseminated to the appropriate jurisdiction of the attention of the authorities in that EU country.

The results of any strategic analysis undertaken are usually presented on the FIU website, during outreach or training events, and during public-private partnership meetings. Crypto-STRs are processed in the same manner as regular STRs, with some additional processing as discussed earlier. One recalls from Chap. 5 that a system's true purpose is what it does, what outcome or result is achieved by transforming its inputs into outputs useful to the wider environment in an efficient and effective manner. For the FIU to be useful, it must produce outputs that are considered valuable, i.e. intelligence packages that lead to criminal investigations, prosecutions, and asset forfeitures. But is this what is happening?

All STRs and crypto-STRs received are processed and analysed according to the following process (Fig. 6.3). Incoming STRs are initially examined by the FIU's civilian analysts. These STRs are randomly allocated daily. Each STR is handled by one analyst, but some are subject to spot checking by a supervisor. The civilian analysts operate as part of the quality and compliance team for the GoAML database. Each STR is inspected to ensure the quality and layout of the report is sufficient to be accepted into the database and be analysed. Unacceptable reports are rejected and returned to the reporting entity for amendment and resubmission. One issue identified during this research was that there is no legal obligation on the reporting entity to resubmit a rejected STR or crypto-STR. These are chased up manually, which is another drain on the FIU's resources and potentially represents a loss of valuable intelligence if the report is never resubmitted. The database then links and merges existing persons, entities, and/or accounts already on the GoAML system to ensure that the widest picture possible is available. Some civilian analysts have received crypto-awareness training. Ideally, all crypto-STRs should be processed by these personnel, but this is not always possible due to the volume of STRs received and the random initial allocation process. The current version of GoAML is not designed to handle crypto-asset-specific information, e.g. public addresses, transaction hashes, and crypto-balances. These are captured in regular banking-type fields, such as account number, or in a free-text narrative, which misses opportunities to *link and merge* across the database of STRs.

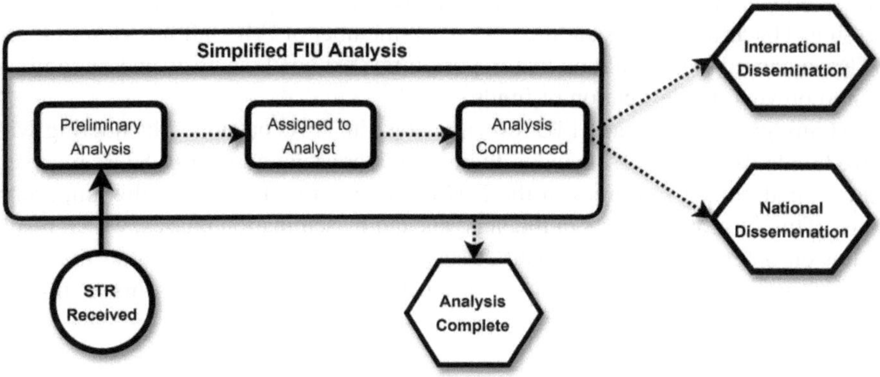

Fig. 6.3 Simplified FIU analysis process

Once these initial checks are passed, the STR is assigned a status of *preliminary analysis*, and the civilian analyst will check the central police database, PULSE,[19] to see if any additional criminal information is known. At this stage, only Irish databases are checked as the civilian analysts don't have access to any international systems. The civilian analyst must then determine the most appropriate section within FIU Ireland to send the STR (i.e. to the money laundering or TF section). They will examine the provided data in the report and pay particular attention to the *reason for suspicion* fields. These are free-text fields where the money laundering reporting officer (MLRO) working in the regulated entity (designated person) outlines their subjective opinion on why they found their customer's activity or transaction(s) to be suspicious. STRs that are identified as potentially relating to terrorist financing or terrorist activity are sent to the Terrorist Financing Investigation Unit (TFIU). These STRs are prioritised, given a status of *assigned to analyst*, and immediately assigned to one of the specialised police officers (sworn analysts) within the TFIU. These officers liaise closely with their colleagues in the Irish security services and anti-terror police units. STRs originally sent to the TFIU and found not to have a TF indicator but are indicative of money laundering are sent back to the money laundering section to be processed as normal. STRs appearing to relate to money laundering with an Irish nexus are given a status of *assigned to analyst* and sent to one of the police officers (sworn analysts) based in the money laundering section of FIU Ireland. Given the ever-increasing volume of crypto-STRs, this might be an opportune time to set up a separate unit to handle all crypto-related STRs.

Reports that do not fall within the parameters of money laundering, TF, or suspected criminality are closed by the civilian analyst and assigned a status of *analysis complete*. These reports are archived and are not further analysed unless new information comes into FIU Ireland—such as an additional STR, new open source information, or additional information from law enforcement.

One final point about the civilian analysts is that although the small number is dedicated and hard-working, the work is monotonous and tedious. There should be ways to automate some of these steps and train the analysts to perform more meaningful work (leverage technology). Given the small number of staff, it also means that holiday and sickness leave creates a bottleneck of reports requiring initial processing. This is a major risk to the FIU, as no member of FIU staff has viewed these STRs, meaning there could be lost opportunities for quick analysis and dissemination to prevent the dissipation of funds.

At any given stage, each FIU sworn analyst in TFIU or money laundering will have hundreds of STRs assigned to them. The increasing number of STRs received and limited human resources in the FIU often lead to a backlog at this important stage. This can cause delays in the analysis and dissemination phases, which result in law enforcement being informed of suspicious activity sometime after the event and often when funds have been dissipated. This often represents a missed

[19] Police using leading systems effectively (PULSE) was introduced in 1999 and has been continually developed and expanded since.

opportunity to seize and confiscate the proceeds of criminal conduct. With newer, faster methods of value transfer, such as crypto-assets, this delay is amplified, as will be seen when we examine the 2021 crypto-STRs in detail presently. Currently, the FIU police analysts decide in which order to tackle their backlog. While, the FIU has put in place a triage or prioritisation scheme to identify the most important STRs at the initial stage, this decision is currently left to the discretion of the individual analyst at the later stages, which is less than optimal.

The issue of junk STRs needs to be considered at this point. These are reports submitted by designated persons defensively and without proper scrutiny. In many cases, they will never progress to a criminal investigation, but consume the valuable time away from FIU staff. One solution would be to direct the designated persons not to submit what analysts would refer to as junk-STRs as well as defensive STRs, but this is not possible. As one of the interviewees, R1 an FIU manager, mentioned:

> There is no supervisory function within the FIU. The FIU can't stop people submitting their STRs, we can't say look, we don't want that. But if you're getting thousands and thousands of STRs and you have limited resources, you have to put controls in place to identify the pertinent ones. And the more STRs that come in, the staff in the FIU are overwhelmed … You just can't see the wood for the trees. There's too many [STRs] and there's not enough people, you know, it grinds the systems to a halt, so we end up just kind of running to a standstill.

So far, what has been seen at the two initial stages of the analysis phase in FIU Ireland is too few staff dealing with too many STRs, ever-increasing workloads, especially due to the reports being submitted by VASPs, and dealing with too many junk STRs that will never progress from the FIU. All these factors mean the efficiency of the FIU as a system is below par. If a system's purpose is what it actually does, then one could say the true purpose of the FIU is a bureaucratic quagmire that merely stores useless reports? Or is the FIU's purpose and function saved if it disseminates some quality reports that lead to prosecution and asset seizure despite the massive waste built in?

Each sworn analyst will analyse their reports in a similar manner; however, each section will obviously have a very different focus because of the differences between money laundering and TF (see Chap. 2). When the sworn analyst begins their analysis, they mark the status of the STR as *analysis commenced* and begin to ascertain if they can develop the intelligence and show that a criminal indicator is present. Crypto-STRs require additional analysis as discussed above. Generally, but not always, crypto-STRs are sent to a trained analyst. Due to the volume of STRs received, this is not always possible, which is not ideal and supports the setting up of a crypto-section within the FIU. Each police officer in the FIU has access to the central beneficial owner registers established by the State for the purposes of Art. 30(3) and 31(4) of 4AMLD.[20] Some FIU staff also have access to blockchain analysis tools. The sworn analyst may rely upon their additional FIU powers to demand

[20] Section 40C(1) of the 2010 Act. These include the register of beneficial ownership of corporate/legal persons (maintained by the Companies Registration Office), the register of trusts (maintained by the Revenue Commissioners), and the register of bank accounts and safety deposit boxes (main-

information. They may, for the purposes of "preventing, detecting, investigating, or combating money laundering or terrorist financing", request any person to provide them with information held under any enactment giving effect to Art. 30(1) or 31(1) of 4AMLD.[21] The sworn analyst may also request in writing (usually through the secure "Message Board" feature on GoAML) any "financial, administrative, or law enforcement information" that they require to carry out their functions from:

1. A designated person
2. A competent authority (AML supervisor)
3. The revenue commissioners
4. The social welfare authorities

A designated person, but not any of the others, commits a criminal offence if they fail to comply with such a request without a reasonable excuse.[22] R10, a FIU manager, discussed receiving complaints about the scope and breadth of this power to demand confidential information from designated persons:

> Many designated persons have criticised the breath of this FIU power which unlike other similar powers has no judicial oversight. The Law Society of Ireland has stated that it will not comply with such a request unless backed by a court order. The balance, I guess, is that it is for intelligence purposes only and any criminal investigation will have to uplift evidence using a judge issued warrant.

R1, a FIU manager, and R8, a money laundering investigator, have some sympathy for the position that the powers are too broad, but state that this is necessary and is a requirement imposed on Ireland by European legislation. R8 and R9 are both satisfied with the powers available to the FIU and financial investigators in Ireland, but both point out that there needs to be a more harmonious approach across Europe in the application of powers, e.g. FIU freezing powers and European investigation orders. There is no time limit specified for such requests to be answered. When a designated person has made a report to FIU Ireland, they are required "as soon as practicable" to respond to any request for additional information.[23]

By virtue of their coercive powers, the police analyst also has access to other sources of information, such as Europol and Interpol, immigration and passenger information, passport details, mobile phone subscriber details, driving licence

---

tained by the Central Bank of Ireland). There are plans to develop an interconnected Europewide system of all the registers in each member state.

[21] Section 40C(2) of the 2010 Act.

[22] Section 40C(3) of the 2010 Act. Failure to comply is an offence punishable on summary conviction to a fine of €5000 and/or a term of imprisonment not exceeding 12 months, or on conviction on indictment to a €500,000 fine and/or a term of imprisonment not exceeding 3 years. As the term is less than 5 years, this is not an *arrestable offence* and has no coercive investigative powers attached to it.

[23] Section 42(6A) of the 2010 Act. Failure to do so is a serious criminal offence that attracts, on conviction on indictment, an unlimited and/or a term of imprisonment not exceeding 5 years. This makes a breach of this section an "arrestable offence" with the associated powers of search, seizure, arrest, detention, etc.

details, insurance claims, land registry, credit ratings, as well as OSINT. The analyst is trying to develop the information in the report to determine if it appears likely that money laundering or a criminal offence has occurred. R1, a FIU manager, states the FIU analysts are trying:

> to raise the STR from a suspicion of money laundering to a more concrete criminal intelligence level, which is a higher level (threshold) needed to send it out to law enforcement. The analyst will do a check of the police database. If there's criminality involved … the STR becomes intelligence nearly instantly, if not it would require more work done on it.

One means of further raising the STR is to determine the legitimate income of the person named in the STR and examine any unexplained wealth. It is presumed in Irish law that such assets, i.e. those which is out of proportion with the income and expenditure of the person, are the proceeds of criminal conduct.[24] If there is no criminal indicator present, the STR is marked as *analysis complete*, archived, and retained for future intelligence—this is the fate of the majority of STRs.

Where a criminal indicator is present, the analyst prepares an intelligence package for dissemination to law enforcement. This will contain all information the FIU has about the suspect, including any accounts, crypto-transactions, their criminal involvements, and their legitimate income and assets (where known). Law enforcement includes not only the police,[25] but also other investigative agencies, e.g. the Criminal Assets Bureau (CAB) or the Department of Social Protection (Social Welfare). Interestingly, given the detail set out in the Irish legislation, there is no mention of disseminating STRs or intelligence packages in the Irish law. This lack of legal backing may give rise to a legal challenge in the future if a person mentioned in an intelligence package and who is not convicted, makes a claim that their data protection rights were infringed, as their sensitive personal data were shared without a legal basis. What the FIU currently reply upon is Art. 32(3) of 4AMLD, which states:

> the FIU shall be responsible for disseminating the results of its analyses and any additional relevant information to [law enforcement] where there are grounds to suspect money laundering, associated predicate offences, or terrorist financing.

Any STRs that contribute to a dissemination are marked with a specific status depending on their intended destination. Intelligence packages sent to a national police unit (e.g. GNECB for international money laundering OCGs, or one of the specialised investigative bureaus, depending on the crime-type of the predicate offence—drugs, prostitution, TF, etc.) or an external Irish investigative body (e.g. social welfare inspectors, CAB) are marked as *national dissemination*. Intelligence packages sent to local police officers, specially trained in money laundering, are marked as *divisional dissemination*. FIU Ireland has not released figures on the number of disseminations per year for operational reasons. Regardless of where an

[24] Section 11(4) of the 2010 Act.

[25] Cases that appear to be the most serious, have a public interest, or involve international OCGs are usually sent to the specialised Money Laundering Investigation Unit attached to GNECB, who have a close working relationship with the FIU.

intelligence package is sent, it is up to the receiving investigator to decide whether or not the matter progresses to a full criminal investigation. This decision should be based on the contents of the intelligence package, local knowledge about the subject, and the policing objectives in the area.

Feedback is sought from law enforcement regarding what happened with each intelligence package, as FIU Ireland, where practical, is required to provide feedback to designated persons on the effectiveness and follow-up to reports made to it.[26] Due to the volume of reports received and the nature of disseminations to law enforcement, it is not possible to give individual feedback on a single STR save in exceptional circumstances. FIU Ireland provides general feedback during its outreach activities, during PPP meetings, and as part of its strategic analysis function. These points are reinforced by R1 and R10 in their capacity as FIU managers. As they said:

> The priority in the FIU is to get information to the police as soon as possible; feedback is probably down the list of priorities given the number of staff we have. We could probably make this better and get better quality STRs if we had more time to do this (R1).

> There is a feeling that the lack of feedback is an excuse used by industry to excuse poor STRs, these guys know their business and their customers, so they should know what is suspicious in the first place. I wonder if they would be overwhelmed if they got a piece of feedback for every STR submitted? (R10).

A question worth considering at this point is, given all the work that is carried out by the FIU, why can the intelligence package disseminated not be used as it is by the police in their investigation? One might presume the package contains all of the information required to prosecute the suspect for a money laundering offence? The intelligence package is made up of confidential information obtained from the STR (itself gathered from information gathered in the ordinary course of business and not intended to be incriminatory) and additional information that was harvested in the analysis process. It is not lawfully obtained evidence to the required criminal standard (beyond a reasonable doubt). Intelligence is used in a criminal prosecution as a "road map" to identify where potential evidence exists. The investigator is then required to use their police powers to gather that evidence and other evidence identified throughout the investigation with an intent to arresting, detaining, and questioning the suspect (App. 4). The result of the investigative process is a file being sent to the DPP that outlines how the evidence shows, and can be used in court, that the suspect has a case to answer. Ultimately, only a judge can convict a person of money laundering after going through the stringent criminal justice process. The conviction of a person for money laundering, when the case originated from an FIU intelligence package, is the ultimate vindication of the decision by the MLRO to nominate their customer as a suspect and make a report to the FIU. As discussed, each stage in the process is merely building upon or filtering that suspicion until it is confirmed by the judge upon conviction.

[26] Section 42(11) of the 2010 Act.

It is not known how many of these disseminations result in money laundering prosecutions. This is a difficulty, as prosecuting money laundering is one of the three key activities of any money laundering regime, and one cannot establish its effectiveness in the absence of data. Therefore, one must make connections between different pieces of data as an indication of efficacy. As shown in Fig. 2.4, money laundering investigations are initiated by the police as a result of receiving:

1. An FIU intelligence package (made up of one or more STRs)
2. A section 19 report
3. A complaint from an injured party.

It is also possible for the police to carry out a financial investigation when conducting a criminal investigation into any of the predicate offences, e.g. drug trafficking. However, anecdotally, it seems that most money laundering investigations in Ireland are initiated by way of an STR. R8, a money laundering investigator, estimates that "95% of his work is initiated from STRs gotten from the FIU".

The author obtained the number of money laundering offences (by individuals) that are directed by the DPP, and the number of cases (individual summonses and charge sheets) that are brought before the courts each year.[27] Taking these two data sources together gives an indication of the level of money laundering prosecution in Ireland (Fig. 6.4). Accounting for various factors (investigation lag time, different sources of investigation initiation, etc.), we can see that since 2010, 2367 individuals were prosecuted for 3566 money laundering offences, which compare reasonably well with Ireland's European counterparts. During the same period, the FIU received and analysed 373,112 STRs, suggesting less than 1% led to a money laundering prosecution. Could this be a cause of concern, an indication of an inefficient system, or both?

6.4.1 *International STRs*

Given the cross-jurisdictional nature of money laundering, FIU Ireland regularly receives reports, including those concerning suspected crypto-laundering, that have no connection or nexus to Ireland. The majority of these are crypto-related, as will be evidenced presently. These reports and STR.EUs are dealt with directly by the International Relations and Policy Unit (IRPU)[28] and processed according to a different workflow than outlined above. In such instances, the Irish FIU acts as a *mailbox* on behalf of the FIU in the jurisdiction most connected with the STR. These reports are disseminated to the relevant foreign FIU, and no further analysis takes place in Ireland. STRs received from a foreign jurisdiction are processed as if they

[27] This information was obtained using a request made to the entities concerned under the Freedom of Information Act, 2014.

[28] The IRPU also develops internal policies and procedures, and handles most of the stakeholder engagement and outreach.

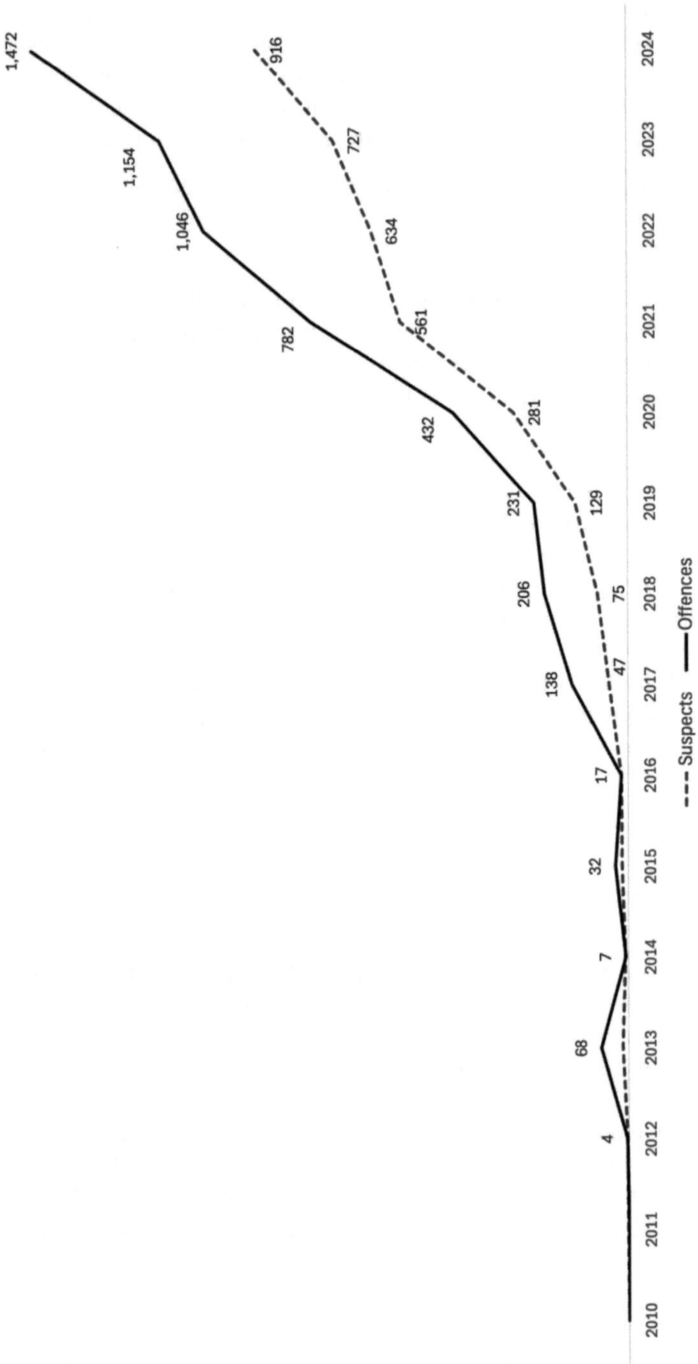

Fig. 6.4 Money laundering prosecutions (2010–2024)

were received from an Irish regulated entity. In compliance with its obligations under Art. 52 and 53 of 4AMLD, the Irish FIU complies with requests for information from other FIUs and sends requests for information when analysing its own reports.

FIU Ireland uses FIU.net, a secure system maintained by the EU Commission, to securely share FIU Intelligence with other EU FIUs (including Europol) and the Egmont Secure Web (ESW) when dealing with third country FIUs.[29]

R1, who is a FIU manager, feels this *mailbox* function is "a waste of our limited resources", is complicated by having different types of FIU with no standardisation of reporting across countries or between FIUs, and the danger that multiple entities are getting the same reports giving rise to concerns that nobody takes action, as everyone assumes someone else is doing the work, or multiple analysis of the same information by multiple entities. R4, an AML supervisor, disagrees. They state that they:

> appreciates this is a massive challenge for FIUs. But unfortunately, that's the way the system is, that's how it is at the moment. So, is it efficient and ideal? No, I don't think it is. I think STRs should go directly to the nexus (country) of where the suspicion is. However, I think there are some advantages in the Irish FIU and Central Bank understanding firms operating from Ireland and what they are seeing.

R5, an AML professional, suggests the solution is sending the STR "directly to the country where the suspicion exists" rather than just to FIU Ireland, meaning the designated persons needs to do some meaningful work on the report, rather than take the easiest option of submitting to FIU Ireland with the view that "its reported, our job is done. Move on to the next one".

6.5 Intelligence Store

During the course of operations since 1995, the FIU has compiled an enormous amount of data from the receipt and analysis of nearly 500,000 STRs. While the majority can be considered junk STRs, there exists a potential value for financial investigators in Ireland and across Europe. For that reason, FIU Ireland can compile and provide a requested intelligence package (as opposed to what we have been discussing previously, referred to as a spontaneous dissemination), where justified, to other FIUs, Europol, and other investigators.[30]

In 2021, FIU Ireland responded to nearly 2000 such requests from Irish investigators. This represents another significant strain on the FIU's scarce resources. Due to the increase in STRs and crypto-STRs received in 2022 and 2023, submitted by VASPs operating across the EU, the number of police requests will likely increase.

---

[29] Sections 40E, 40F, and 40G of the 2010 Act. Data protection issues are addressed in sections 40H and 40I.

[30] Sections 40CA, 40D, 40DA, 40E, 40F, 40G, 40H, 40I of the 2010 Act.

This has the potential to reduce the FIU's operating efficiency, reduce the quality of FIU analysis, and lead to even fewer money laundering investigations taking place.

There is also an inherent tension between AML and Data Protection Law, which has not yet been resolved, even at the European level (Wiewiorówski, 2020). The retention of personal data for an indeterminate time is likely to fall foul of GDPR at some stage.

6.6 Recap of Current Situation in FIU Ireland

Before moving on to the main piece of analysis from the FIU case study, the examination of crypto-related STRs received at the FIU in 2021, it is useful to draw together some of the salient points discussed thus far.

While FIU Ireland plays a crucial regulatory role, its current composition and resourcing present serious operational challenges. Since its establishment in May 1995, it has operated within the National Police Service. Despite being placed on a statutory footing in 2018, the FIU remains totally reliant upon its parent organisation for all personnel and IT resources, which brings its operational autonomy into question. The FIU is struggling to fulfil its primary function, as backlogs exist at every level of the analysis process. Its limited resources are further stretched when one examines the additional work (e.g. in-house and external training, outreach, answering requested disseminations, policy development, international commitments, etc.) that the FIU staff perform. It is also apparent that the FIU is not leveraging technology to its full advantage.

The exponential increase in STRs received and the extension of the AML system in 2021 to include crypto-assets have the potential to detrimentally impact the operational efficiency of the FIU. There is an urgent need for additional personnel and technology within the FIU. This would enable the development of a dedicated crypto-STR analysis unit, which is required to progress the rapidly increasing volume and complexity of crypto-STRs from VASPs and other entities. If the FIU is to uphold its mandate effectively and grapple with its mounting workload pressures and ever-evolving financial crime trends, strategic investments and innovation are urgently required.

References

Meighan S (2025) Money laundering in Ireland: context, history and the law. Clarus Press, Dublin

Wiewiorówski W (2020) Opinion 5/2020 on the European Commission's action plan for a comprehensive policy on preventing money laundering and terrorism financing. European Data Protection Supervisor, Brussels

Chapter 7
Analysis of Crypto-Related STRs

In 2021, FIU Ireland received a total of 38,712 reports (regular and crypto-related) from designated persons reporting suspicious activity by their customers they thought might be money laundering or terrorist financing. Of those, 2719 reports were received from 57 entities regarding crypto-assets (7.02% of total reports received in 2021). These reports were extracted from the GoAML database and analysed according to a stringent methodological process. The aim was to develop models to understand the phenomenon of crypto-laundering, and its pursuit and detection by the FIU. These models were theoretically sensitised by *socio-technical systems theory*.

7.1 General Analysis

The crypto-asset-related reports can be broken into three distinct categories: crypto-STRs from VASPs (300 reports from 4 entities, or 0.8% of total reports received in 2021), crypto-STR.EUs from VASPs (716 reports from 2 entities, or 1.8% of total reports received in 2021), and STRs relating to crypto-asset usage from non-VASPs (1703 reports from 51 entities, or 4.4% of total reports received in 2021). Figure 7.1 shows this broken down diagrammatically.

A number of preliminary examinations of this data took place, which are described as follows.

The first examination carried out on the STR data was to determine what happened with each report following FIU analysis (see Fig. 6.3 for analysis process, and Fig. 7.2 for visual breakdown). Based on the analysis, 38.5% of the 2719 were found not to reach the criteria for dissemination (i.e. no criminal indicator was present) and were archived for intelligence, with no further action being carried out. These reports formed part of the FIU's intelligence store that is available to law enforcement on request if required, or part of their *junk* STR store, depending on the

S. Meighan, *Money Laundering and Crypto-Assets*, Contributions to Finance and Accounting, https://doi.org/10.1007/978-3-032-13481-3_7

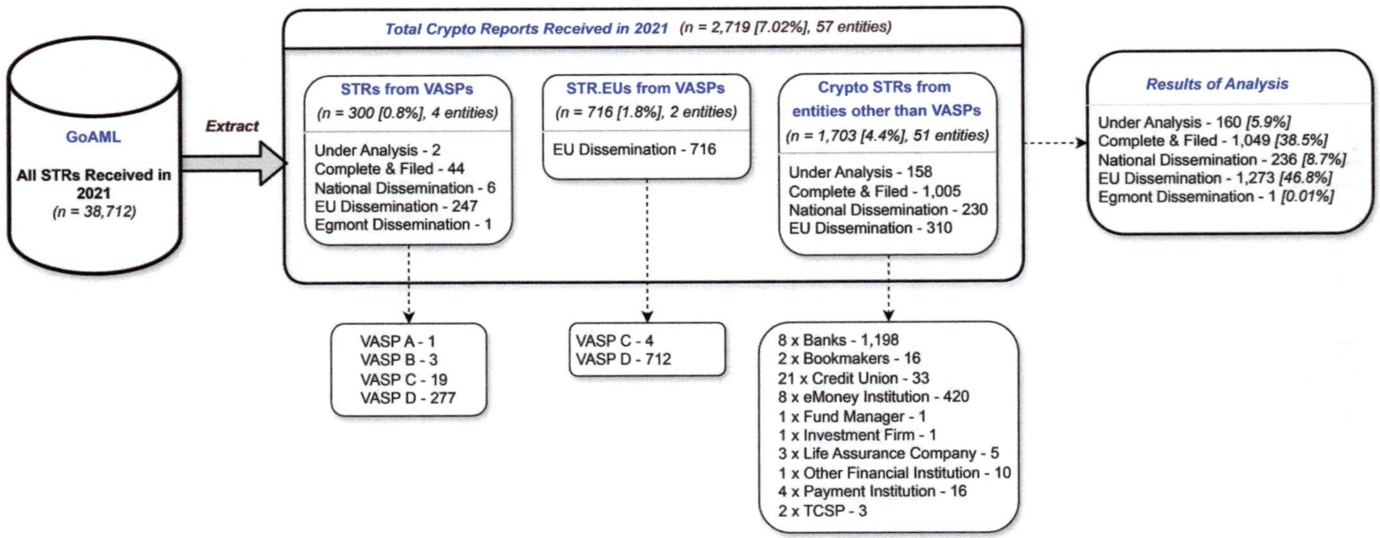

Fig. 7.1 Breakdown of crypto-STRs received at FIU Ireland in 2021

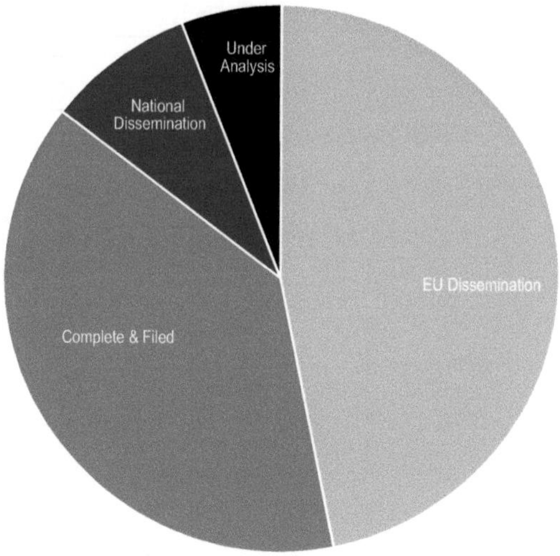

Fig. 7.2 Distribution of 2716 crypto-STRs after processing

perspective taken. 160 or 5.9% were still being analysed at the time of extraction. 55.5% of the reports were analysed and disseminated as intelligence packages to law enforcement for consideration of a full criminal investigation: 236 (8.7%) to Irish investigators, 1273 (46.8%) to other EU FIUs, and just 1 (0.01%) to the UK FIU via the Egmont network. This is not surprising as many UK VASPs relocated to Ireland and other EU countries post-Brexit. The analysis shows that many of the crypto-STRs received (1274 or 46.8%) had no nexus to Ireland, which is not unexpected given the inherent make-up of crypto-asset technology and their lack of geographic restriction. It does raise the question of AML efficiency with excess bureaucracy where submission to FIU Ireland necessitates forwarding the STRs to another FIU for further action (cf. *mailbox* function discussed earlier in Chap. 6). This can create delays in processing STRs, leading to bottlenecks at various stages of the process, and ultimately leading to a delay in getting reports to law enforcement, meaning a possible hold-up in acting.

A breakdown of where those intelligence packages (often made up of more than one STR) were sent to is shown in Fig. 7.3. It also illustrates that the dissemination rate of over 50% was quite high when compared to traditional STRs, which are usually in the 5–20% range based on the experience of different FIUs.

The second examination determined the breakdown of reports submitted by VASPs and non-VASPs. 1016 reports (37.3% of total crypto-reports) were filed by VASPs and the remainder (1702 or 62.6%) by non-VASP designated persons (Fig. 7.4). This figure must be slightly reduced as some of the STRs captured in the extraction were found not to be related to crypto-assets upon further analysis. With the non-crypto reports discounted, the ratio between VASPs and non-VASPs was 51.1–48.9%. This is unusual; during the period of this research, only four VASPs submitted STRs compared to over 3000 registered non-VASPs. This trend shows that a smaller number of specialised entities (VASPs) are submitting the same

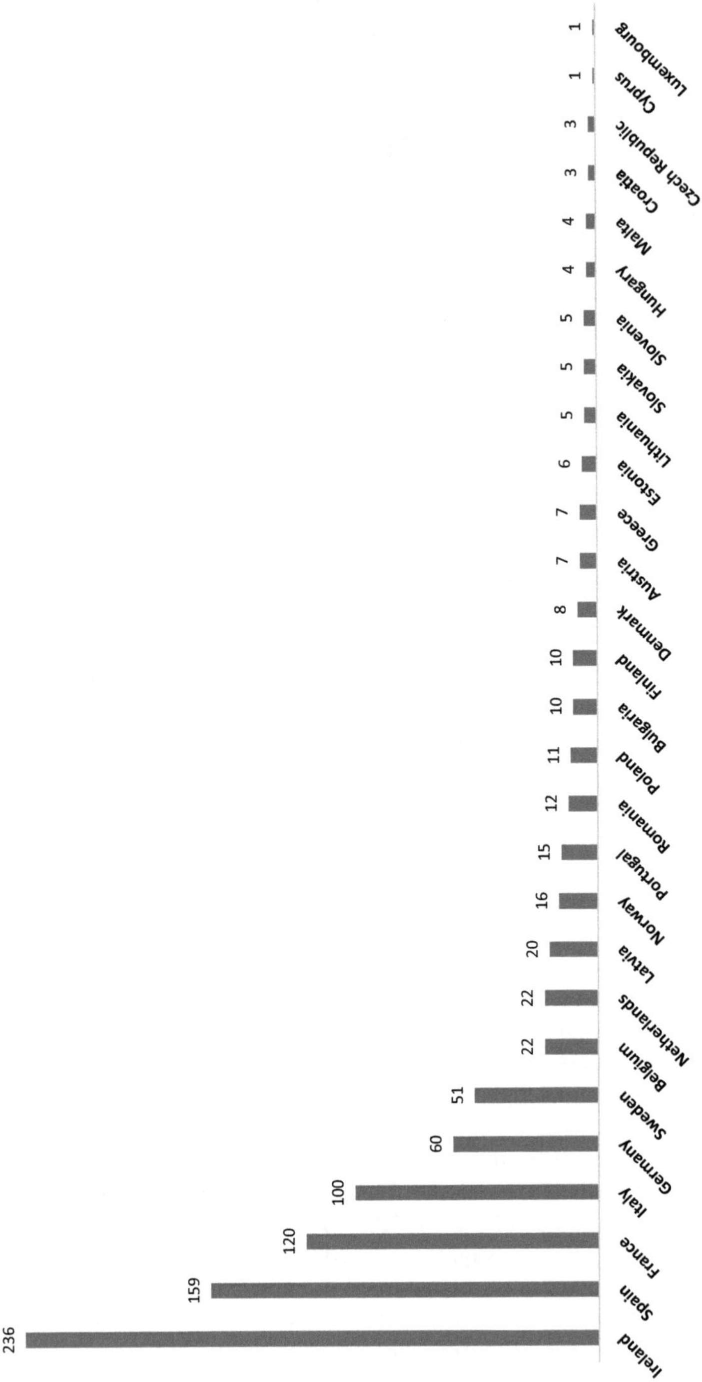

Fig. 7.3 Destination country of disseminations from crypto-STRs in 2021

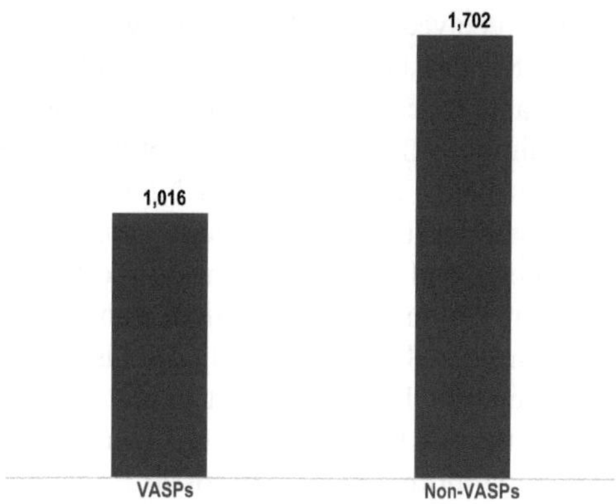

Fig. 7.4 2021 Breakdown of crypto-STRs submitted by VASPs and non-VASPs

number of STRs as the remainder of the entire population of non-VASP entities. If the number of VASPs increases, this will correlate to a dramatic increase in STRs received at FIU Ireland (this trend was already observed in 2022 and 2023 as can be seen on Table 6.1), which has the potential to overwhelm the already scarce resources of the FIU. An increase in specialist crypto-STRs may also necessitate the creation of an enhanced specialised crypto-unit within the FIU, which could change the previous focus of the FIU, which has traditionally been credit and financial institutions.

The third examination examined the volume of text placed in the free-text *reason for suspicion* fields of the crypto-reports submitted to FIU Ireland. Recall how GoAML operates off three main constructs: a person, an account, and a transaction. When a designated person makes a report to FIU Ireland, these three constructs are populated into pro forma fields with financial data that the designated entity has in its possession as a result of its KYC, CDD/EDD, and transaction monitoring activities. The *reason for suspicion* is one of the few free-text fields. Its importance is that it enables the reporting entity to outline their subjective reason for their suspicion. The "reason for suspicion" is a mandatory 4000 character limit free-text field, while the "Action" field is discretionary with a similar 4000 character limit. This field permits the expansion of the reason for suspicion and to set out any activity that the reporter undertook after their suspicion was formed (e.g. blocked the account, de-risked their customer). In total, this provides the reporting entity 8000 characters, or roughly 500–1000 words, to set out their suspicion of money laundering to the FIU. R10, an FIU manager, states that:

> The reason for suspicion is vital for the analyst to understand why the report was made to the FIU in the first place. Without this, we are only looking at a transaction without any context which makes developing the STR very difficult if not impossible. Vague reasons don't help either; what is needed is some detail to outline why the MLRO made the report in the first place. Of course, I am not saying that a report has to be such and such a length, but the MLROs that take time and put effort into writing a comprehensive reason for suspicion mean an STR that is better to analyse and, probably, more likely to result in a dissemination.

In the 2719 crypto-reports received in 2021, the average number of words used was 300 and the median was 281, far short of the maximum allowed and, in most cases, not sufficient to give the analyst context when analysing the STRs. The maximum value was 958 and the minimum value was 10. Some of the shorter reports were bereft of detail in these important fields, e.g. “Customer buying crypto currency—on job-seeker’s allowance”, “substantial funds into account—customer advised it was gains from selling crypto currency”, and “Customer transferred funds of €10,000 from his bank account to our Credit Union”. Customer then transferred €10,000 to another bank to purchase crypto currency. Unusual activity on this member’s account”.

None of these reasons enable the FIU analyst to understand why the reports are considered suspicious by the MLRO and usually means no further action can be taken. To examine this issue more deeply, Microsoft Excel’s built-in data analysis tool was used to generate a histogram to visualise the distribution of word counts (Fig. 7.5). The histogram was divided into discrete bins (0–100 words, every 50 words between 100 and 650, and everything more than 700 words) representing different word count intervals. This was necessary to assess the frequency of reports falling within each range. The histogram analysis determined that the vast majority of reports (approximately 60%) fall within the 150–550 word count range, which indicates a tendency towards very brief reasons for suspicion being given by designated persons when making reports to the FIU. In effect, providing little justification for the suspicion. When dealing with crypto-STRs, the information provided was curt. Due to the limitations of GoAML crypto-specific information often has to be entered into the free-text fields, which is not always done. There were only 47 reports with more than 650 words and none with more than 958 words. Overall, this seems to indicate a practice where limited reasons for making the report are given by the designated person. This situation means the FIU analysts must extrapolate the reason why the report was made in the first place and omits vital crypto-related

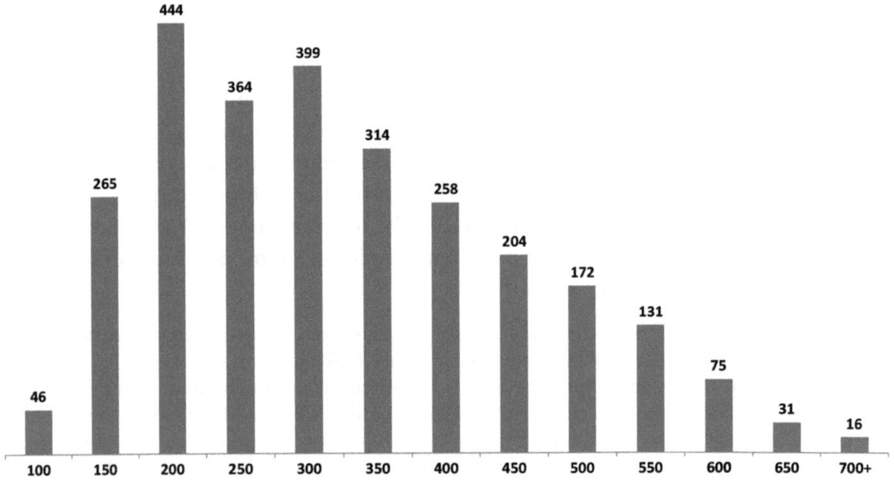

Fig. 7.5 Histogram of wordcount in *reason for suspicion* field

information. It may also be that the FIU has not expressly set out its expectations for this important field during VASP onboarding and outreach activities. This is an area for action that may give an immediate improvement in the quality of crypto-STRs (Chap. 8). While not examined, it would be interesting to see if the same situation applies to non-crypto STRs.

A piece of future research concerning crypto-STRs would be to evaluate the correlation between the length of the STR narrative and the quality of the report. Of course, how we measure quality would need to be determined, e.g. a report that is disseminated and leads to a money laundering prosecution and conviction, or a report that has sufficient information for analysis regardless of its dissemination status.

Of the 2719 STRs, none were for terrorist financing (TF). Given the prevalence of crypto-assets being used for TF (Chap. 2), it certainly appears unusual that none of the reports made to FIU Ireland in 2021 were for suspicions of TF. Although not the focus of this research, it could indicate that designated persons are not aware of the risks or do not have sufficient effective monitoring rules for TF activity involving crypto-assets.

The interviewees were asked about their opinion of money laundering through crypto-assets or crypto-laundering. Some answered based on the crypto-STRs that they had seen, while others answered from their experiences in investigating these crimes. Most agreed that crypto-laundering is simply money laundering using a different type of (pseudonymous) asset for value transfer, i.e. crypto-assets instead of cash. R1, an FIU manager, states:

> money laundering is money laundering whether they use cash or whether they use crypto-assets. But the difficulty with crypto-assets is regulation. And law enforcement is just catching up because there's a little bit of an information gap or we're learning about them (crypto-assets) and we're plugging the gaps. And as we plug those gaps, the criminals are moving on to something new or something shiny.

R5, an AML professional, agrees:

> the aim and process (of money laundering) is the same, the only difference is the techniques and tools underlying. It doesn't matter what form the proceeds are in. Money laundering is very simple, it is establishing a person's legitimate income, then looking at their actual possessions … My job is to come up with a range of what this unexplained wealth is … Anything unexplained above their legitimate income is potentially the proceeds of criminal conduct. Whether it is or not is ultimately up to a judge but can be established by the police through evidence gathering, interviewing suspects, and inferences drawn during a detention.

Some cases are more straightforward, e.g. a student account receives the proceeds of an invoice redirection fraud—which is obvious criminality and there is no need to complete a financial profile of the money mule in that case. R8, a money laundering investigation supervisor, states:

> I suppose it's very same, but obviously it's just the method by which the money laundered and layered is different. The main difference will be that it is in the form of a cryptocurrency. So if you're not skilled in that area, it's more difficult to investigate. But in terms of is there a difference? No, I don't believe those are the major differences. We see. It's a new avenue.

It is now appropriate to offer some general comments about the reports analysed. 2719 crypto-STRs were extracted from GoAML and imported into NVivo as a dataset. A number of cycles of coding were performed, with codes initially informed by socio-technical systems theory (structure, people, technology, task, environment). Additional codes were then identified from passing through the data and grouping them into several broad categories. The majority of STRs were reasonably well structured and contained sufficient detail for FIU analysis, albeit a more involved task than if more information had been provided in the free-text fields. There was also sufficient detail to extrapolate the two socio-technical systems models laid out in Chap. 8. From the analysis, crypto-asset misuse supports all forms of regular criminal activity—drugs, gambling, CSEM, and human trafficking. Criminals well versed in social engineering and the use of spoofed telephone numbers use crypto-assets to lure fraud victims. Analysis of the crypto-STRs shows that crypto-launderers are not wedded to crypto-asset technology; one could say that crypto-launderers simply operationalise crypto-assets as a method of value transfer, and consequently, they view crypto-assets as useful due to specific features that they find attractive. Similarly, the use of privacy-oriented tools such as VPN, TOR, and the dark web allows for a greater sense of anonymity and comfort. R10, an FIU manager, states:

> In my experience, criminals will use the most convenient method of transferring criminal proceeds that is available to them. If it is technology based and offers an enhanced sense of privacy, is quick, and is able to transfer across borders, all the better. At the moment, I think this is why crypto-assets are attractive to criminals and we are seeing an increase in crypto-asset misuse. Equally, during Covid-19, we saw criminals revert to cash, which shows that they are not tied into any one method but will constantly change their methods to account for the prevailing situation.

Based on the knowledge gained from the literature review and a thematic analysis of the interview data, a number of issues were identified that make crypto-STRs more difficult to analyse and crypto-laundering more difficult to investigate as compared to non-crypto STRs and money laundering. Firstly, there was a period prior to the regulation of crypto-assets where criminals were free to use the new technology in an unregulated manner. R1, an FIU manager, states:

> Over the last 10 or 15 years, the (AML) frameworks put in place are working and are really helping to deal with money laundering in the traditional sense. The problem is crypto-assets come in after we're playing catch-up. Initially, criminals had free rein and we're playing catch-up, waiting for regulation to come in. And the problem is, it's like trying to put the genie back in the bottle.

R11, an international AML expert, agrees that "the period where criminals operated in an unregulated area really gave them a head start and advantage over FIUs and law enforcement". Secondly, there is still a knowledge gap or lack of understanding regarding crypto-assets by law enforcement. The time lag caused by a lack of training and time needed to upskill again gives criminals an advantage. R8, a money laundering investigator, states:

> In terms of my knowledge of crypto-assets, to date it wouldn't be great, but it is slowly improving. I think, as an organisation, we need to upskill in this area massively as it is the highest risk for future money laundering offences. This gap gives criminals a massive advantage until we catch up.

Thirdly and finally, the cross-jurisdictional nature of crypto-assets, and the ease with which they cross borders—unlike bank transfers, for example—complicates matters, as multiple FIUs, police forces, prosecutors, etc. are involved. R10, an FIU manager, states:

> It is really difficult when multiple jurisdictions are involved. You can see that a lot of our crypto-related STRs have no nexus in Ireland, so we send them off to another FIU, but we don't know what happens to them. Do the other FIUs presume we have done something with them, is anything done at either end? Are criminals escaping because of the bureaucracy in sending information to different agencies in different countries?

R11, an international AML expert, agrees:

> Despite the efforts of international agencies such as Egmont, Europol, and Interpol, any analysis or investigation is complicated when there are multiple jurisdictions involved. There are language difficulties, differences in law, and differences in attitudes to offences, especially when new technology such as crypto-assets is involved. The crime might not even be a crime in the other jurisdiction. When you have more than one jurisdiction working on a case, it becomes much more difficult.

On a simple practical level, R6, a money laundering investigator, recounts his experience in dealing with VASPs in different jurisdictions:

> A good amount of them are based outside of the Irish jurisdiction. So it's a lot harder to uplift material from them. You have to do mutual legal assistance requests which can take up to 2 years to get basic information back. I do feel that the VASPs want to help. However, there is a large number of them that do not reply to us. From an email you get an automated message, and you can't contact a real person and talk to them.

Despite having sufficient detail for FIU analysis and for constructing the socio-technical models, the 2719 STRs were not without fault and issues of concern around VASPs were identified. According to R1, an FIU manager:

> I would suggest while the quality of crypto-STRs is slowly getting better, it's still poor. A problem with them is … I think the AML standard isn't there and provides incomplete information with not a lot of follow-up on their part. For example, I've seen STRs where a customer is providing, say, a West African ID document when the customer's address is in Ireland, and their phone number is in Germany and the address in Ireland might not exist. The transaction monitoring systems can't keep pace with the speed of transactions and the entity covers themselves and report to FIU [defensively].

This suggests a lack of AML awareness on the part of some VASPs, who make defensive STRs that are missing vital information for FIU analysis. The example given by the respondent suggests that not even basic information is always checked, which is a difficulty when designated persons are the first line of defence in the AML system. The fact that transaction monitoring systems are struggling to keep up with the speed and volume of crypto-transactions is also worrying. This means reports will be made to the FIU after the fact and any opportunities for early investigative interventions are lost. R4, an AML supervisor, continues in the same vein but with some optimism for the future:

> I suspect, at the moment, there's a lot of defensive STRs going in despite the fact they (VASPs) know they're under our scrutiny. They know they're being watched. And so for them, there's sort of an element of, well, let's put loads of stuff into it so that it looks like we're doing the right thing. I hope that when you start to focus on a new sector or new types of firms … the quality gets better overtime and the quantity potentially drops, but I know there are certain firms and VASPs in Ireland submitting rather a lot of STRs, and I can't imagine that they are all genuine and proper STRs.

R7, another AML supervisor, opines:

> some VASPs would be reporting just for a numbers game but would have no idea of why they are reporting … while often 'real' STRs are not reported at all. This arises from a lack of (crypto-laundering) knowledge, some firms have excellent policies and procedures in written form, but they are not operationalised.

This comment is concerning for a number of reasons. Firms may have excellent written policies in place; however, they are simply not implemented due to a lack of understanding or focus on the underlying motive for AML controls. This is an example of *box-ticking* compliance at its worst and contributes to junk STRs clogging up the FIU and diverting scarce resources from the analysis of actual crypto-laundering cases. Many VASPs appear to submit crypto-STRs merely on the basis that law enforcement made a request to them for information (e.g. data protection request or service of a court order), which is not a correct use of an STR. R6, a crypto-investigator, recalls one crypto-laundering case where they made a request for information to a VASP. The FIU had no STRs on the suspect, so they went directly to the company for assistance. On foot of their request, the VASP "subsequently made multiple reports to the FIU that were terrible, there was no basic information such as personal details of the account holder and their wallet addresses".

Essential crypto-related information that would be considered to be basic (e.g. a Bitcoin public address, account information, customer due diligence information, etc.) is often unreported by designated entities, which creates additional bureaucracy as the FIU must then use its coercive powers to seek the required information. It is accepted that while VASPs would and should have this information, other traditional reporting entities might not. R9, an FIU manager, defends VASPs by saying that they:

> are making every effort to comply with the legislation and the regulations. I think they themselves are finding it very difficult to do that. Some of them have grown very, very quickly, and they just can't keep up with the speed of opening new accounts, the amount and the volume of transactions they have. I think it's leaving huge loopholes in the system. We're aware of VASPs who are a long way behind in their reporting systems. But then again, we're also aware of some banks, regular banks, that are a long way behind in their reporting … [many VASPs] grow so quickly, and then they found it hard to get the resources to manage their AML and compliance side of the house especially struggling to get the right people in to do that work.

The primary issue made apparent by the analysis of the 2719 crypto-STRs is a significant time lag between the suspicious activity occurring and submission to the FIU. This raises concerns that VASPs might feel the need to "investigate" cases on their own, to defend their actions or lack thereof, before submitting a (typically substandard) report to the FIU.

Analysis of the STRs submitted by VASPs and non-VASPS will be conducted separately. This is to determine whether any differences exist in technological understanding, risk appetite, and level of detail provided.

7.2 Insights from VASP Reporting of STRs

Analysis of the STRs submitted by VASPs identified a strong understanding of the underlying crypto-asset infrastructure and operation. This is to be expected due to the technology-based nature of these entities and their business model. Many VASPs have also employed ex-police officers and ex-FIU analysts to work in their compliance and fraud prevention operations. These persons were often at the forefront of crypto-asset investigation in the public sector. For example, one such individual was hired away from Europol's EC3 Cyber Centre by a major VASP. This was after they had developed the training manual for law enforcement officers that details the track and trace protocol for crypto-assets. Similar recent investments by VASPs should improve the quality of their STRs over time. This is a topic for future research.

One interesting reflection emerged from R4, an AML supervisor, on a potential collaboration between traditional credit and financial institutions and VASPs, which could bridge the VASP's lack of AML knowledge, educate financial institutions on crypto-asset technology, and potentially offer opportunities for mutual benefit:

> the VASP's area of expertise is crypto...they understand crypto, but I'm not sure they understand the (money laundering) risks as well as a credit institution; a credit institution will understand the money laundering and terrorist financing risk, but actually, they are still learning about crypto so they don't have the full picture. These are the differences between traditional finance and crypto finance... on one side they understand the risk, but on the other they don't really understand the product... if they could share and talk to each other, it might help.

This comment is insightful, given that FIU Ireland deals with a number of public–private partnerships. None have suggested this crossover, which could lead to mutual opportunities being missed.

The crypto-STRs submitted by VASPs generally demonstrated the use of sophisticated processes to identify customer IP and MAC addresses, the use of VPN software, and interaction with mixers, tumblers, gambling sites, TOR, and dark web marketplaces. From this, the research concluded that commercial blockchain analysis tools were being utilised by many VASPs, but that information was not being provided to the FIU in the crypto-STR. These reports looked very much like traditional STRs and often omitted any crypto-asset technology information, such as addresses used, and transaction identities.

Evidence of cross-chain activity, which is the transfer of assets from one type of crypto-asset to another, was readily apparent in the crypto-STRs. For example, the proceeds of an invoice redirection fraud were converted to bitcoin at an exchange, co-mingled with the proceeds of additional frauds, and then converted to other crypto-assets before being withdrawn in fiat cash. There was no STR reporting involving privacy-enhanced coins like Monero or ZCoin. This raises significant concerns over a potential black hole in reporting. These privacy-friendly crypto-assets utilise additional cryptographic techniques to disguise publicly available blockchain information (Furneaux, 2018), which further impedes law enforcement efforts. Police worldwide have serious concerns about a growing dark crypto-laundering community promoting their use and moving the field of crypto-laundering to a space of undetectability. Of course, even if crypto-STRs were received concerning privacy coins that were made, the FIU and law enforcement currently have no way to break the strengthened encryption and attribute the impugned transaction.

Assessment of the crypto-STRs submitted tends to show that the VASP reviews the entire transactional behaviour and external business conduct of the reported customer before submitting an STR to the FIU. In the cases analysed, there were many instances where basic information was missing from the submitted reports, e.g. current balances, other accounts held at the same institution, and serial numbers of account opening documents. This lack of information adds further delay to the analysis process as the FIU analyst must request this missing information from the VASP. In many cases, the customer was de-risked and removed as a customer as a result of an STR being filed with the FIU, and this was often done prior to the report being made, giving rise to potential "tipping off" and delay in submission concerns.

It is readily apparent from the crypto-STRs submitted that VASPs are operating in a similar manner to a bank account, i.e. a user sets up an account, provides the appropriate identification documentation, and uses the account as a vehicle to store and transfer value. R3, a crypto-laundering investigator, confirms that this is the case, despite "Bitcoin not being designed to work in that way". This is generally good for the AML system, as we see the majority of users working through a regulated fiat/crypto friction point and not through unregulated points that the crypto-asset technology allows, e.g. direct public address to public address transfer of value. It means the majority of clients operate via a regulated service. Despite this positive manner of operation, crypto-assets are still considered attractive to cyber-launderers.

As the free-text fields of an STR are completed by the MLRO, the terminology, formatting, and language used in the 2716 crypto-STRs clearly illustrate when a new MLRO is appointed. This is because each MLRO's own individual reporting style, presentation of information, and risk level of suspicion is reflected in the STR. This is concerning, as it signifies that the underlying institutional reporting procedures are not well established, and something so fundamental in terms of money laundering risk communicability like the STR can change dramatically from one MLRO to another.

In many instances, the reason for submission is wholly unsubstantiated, even when one accounts for the necessary subjective nature in the construction of money laundering suspicion. Also present is an obviously incongruent degree of understanding of what constitutes money laundering among MLROs. Some display a rudimentary knowledge of key concepts such as layering and rapid transfers without any understanding that the source of funds must be criminal in nature. In some cases, customers were reported for breaking up their legitimately held assets into multiple crypto-assets, holding them for a short time, and recombining them back in one place before converting their assets back to cash. Such behaviour is certainly indicative of money laundering layering and integration, but only if the source of funds is illegal in the first instance.

The majority of VASPs entering the Irish market are relocating from the UK and slowly transitioning to the Irish AML regime. Evidence of this is the frequent reference to UK legislation (e.g. requesting consent to carry out a transaction when Ireland does not operate a consent regime), incorrect terminology, "cut and paste" from reports submitted to the UK FIU, and no understanding of the crime reporting requirement under section 19 of the Criminal Justice Act, 2011.

STRs were often submitted too late for any action to be taken by the police, i.e. the funds had already dissipated to zero, which raises a question of when should customer accounts be frozen/blocked. In some instances, 60–100 transactions occurred over a normal period (i.e., not rapidly), but a delay in submission of the STR meant that the balance of the account at the time of submission was zero. This could indicate an issue with transaction monitoring or role creep, where the level and intensity of "investigation" by the VASPs is too detailed, takes too long, and is not disclosed to the police. Particularly in the context of role creep, some VASPs see themselves as the primary investigators; this can exacerbate delays in reporting to the FIU/police.

Many VASPs are made up of different entities, some with different MLROs for each entity; this makes it more challenging to handle different aspects of their business. For example, one VASP has one e-money entity for its fiat business that also interacts with its VASP entity for its crypto-business. This results in different and multiple reports to the FIU from transactions that often cross-reference each other, creating unnecessary duplications in analyses and investigations. Depending on where the particular entity is located, this can result in multiple STRs being made to different FIUs. Some, such as R4, an AML supervisor, are against this multiple licensing:

> This is interesting because we've had some discussions internally on this … the reality is, it's one business. And the reality is, they tend to be the same people who are operating all the entities [with] … the one MLRO. Our approach is changing from requiring multiple authorisations to a more functional model. I hope that over time that will help and there won't be duplication in STRs and there won't be confusion.

Having looked at the crypto-STRs made by VASPs, the research will now examine the ones submitted by non-VASPs.

7.3 Insights from Crypto-STRs Submitted by Non-VASPs

Crypto-STRs from non-VASPs will now be reviewed. Traditional credit and financial institutions demonstrated that a much less developed appreciation of the risk of crypto-laundering was observed in the analysed STRs (at least in 2021, though the explosion of crypto-STRs made in 2022 and 2023 might indicate increased alertness). In many cases, STRs were made merely because their customer had purchased crypto-assets through an exchange—even well-known and regulated ones. In some instances, STRs were made because a business was operating as a VASP. In one situation, STRs were submitted because a business was providing blockchain education. While it was evident that the traditional entities were becoming more risk-tolerant of crypto-assets towards the end of 2021, this new-found broadmindedness of crypto-assets seems to have been reversed in 2023 with one major US Bank declining to take part in all crypto transactions—in effect de-risking crypto-assets entirely:

> … because fraudsters are increasingly using crypto assets to steal large sums of money from people … [and] declining these transactions is one of the ways of keeping [customers and their] money safe.[1]

A trend observed in the analysis of the crypto-STRs was that all VASPs need a credit or financial institution to hold and transact their fiat funds. This produces an interesting fiat/crypto interface for financial investigators to explore. Traditional transaction monitoring systems were often confused by payments to and from exchanges. These would involve medium to large transactions to a bank account in a foreign jurisdiction, usually activity outside that expected of their customer. Several STRs showed interesting, although not illegal, activity. In some cases people were pooling funds from multiple places and family members to purchase crypto-assets for investment purposes. In some cases, it was apparent that people had taken large loans to invest in crypto-assets, some of which were investment scams.

Another trend observed was that the STRs also showed that some early (non-criminal) adopters of crypto-asset technology generated staggering profits. This aroused suspicion of behaviour outside their expected, legitimate income; it also gave rise to tax evasion concerns (a predicate offence for money laundering in Ireland). In one case, an STR was made because the branch official was suspicious of money laundering, as the account was being used for crypto-investment and not being used for its intended purpose. This raises an interesting KYC question: how should crypto-asset use, including transacting large volumes of money, be retrospectively applied to any account opened prior to the late 2010s? At the very least, this would require an update of transaction monitoring rules and the customer's profile, which does not appear to have happened in 2021.

---

[1] Chase Bank UK (https://www.ft.com/content/e02ffd47-18a9-4017-b6fc-2ea388f85f2a, accessed: 4 May 2025).

Another trend observed was that other non-financial businesses and professions similarly struggled in determining their risk appetite for crypto-activity. Entities were presented with customers who had earned large profits from crypto-investment and made STRs as they were unable to verify their customers' source of funds. Oftentimes, as with traditional banks, STRs were made merely on the basis that their customer was involved with crypto-assets in some way. Like the traditional financial and credit institutions, analysis of the 2021 crypto-assets shows that some DNFBPs struggled to understand crypto-assets and that lack of knowledge resulted in the unnecessary filing of junk STRs with the FIU, further clogging up the system.

7.4 Leading the Way: Noteworthy 2021 Crypto-STRs

From the analysis of the 2719 crypto-STRs, the following six (anonymised) STRs were identified as examples of excellent reports that were easy to analyse and understand, required minimal expansion, and were rapidly disseminated. These were selected by R10—a senior FIU manager who oversaw the crypto-analysis process in 2021—from the 236 crypto-STRs that were developed into intelligence packages and disseminated to Irish police officers. In a time of increased pressure on the scarce FIU resources, these examples are illustrative of what can be achieved when the AML regime works as intended. The reports are not perfect in all respects, e.g. the length of time the activity occurred before reporting, delay in reporting, etc. A limitation of this book is that it has not been able to access whether any criminal investigations have been conducted and the results, if any, of the same. This would be a suggestion for further research in this area.

STR 1

Our TM systems flagged this transaction as a potential scam based on several risk factors:

- New customer (VASP account details provided)
- An atypical customer profile (age and demographics)
- Bitcoin address activity
- Customer demeanour, observed as being on the phone while using the Bitcoin kiosk

Upon contacting the customer, we confirmed they were the victim of a phone extortion scam claiming to be from the social welfare department. The customer was advised to deposit cash at the Bitcoin ATM.

Scam summary:

- The customer received a call from an Irish mobile phone number.
- A pre-recorded message played claiming that their personal details had been used for illegal activity. The customer was asked to press 1 to speak with an agent.

- After pressing 1, the customer was forwarded to someone who asked for additional personal data (which was handed over)
- The customer was then advised that their personal details had been discovered as part of an ongoing criminal investigation (specifics unclear).
- The customer was asked to confirm what their local garda (police) station was, including the number. The scammer arranged a suitable time for the local garda station to call back. The customer received a phone call from the same number as their local garda station.
- The customer was advised there was a risk of losing their funds if they didn't act.
- The scammer advised the customer to withdraw money from the bank and deposit the money into a "protected government account" temporarily. The customer was assured they would have access to the funds the following day. The customer was instructed to deposit the cash at a Bitcoin ATM Kiosk. The customer was sent a QR code (destination bitcoin address) via WhatsApp. The customer was guided through the process of purchasing bitcoin at the ATM by a human operator acting as *tech support*.

Note: the scammers are spoofing garda (police) station numbers and are ensuring that the customer is familiar with this number to add credibility to the scam. The customer was advised of an active criminal investigation, and their details were compromised and somehow connected to the crime.

This report included all account numbers, personal details of the customer, IP/MAC addresses, etc. to allow the criminal investigator to trace the criminal and follow the money on the blockchain. The funds had already been transferred to a different VASP, but details for this VASP were provided, which allowed an immediate outreach to that entity. The report was received within 4 weeks of the incident having occurred. Unfortunately, the second VASP was in an unfriendly jurisdiction, and a request for information and assistance from FIU Ireland went unanswered. This meant that the funds were not recovered.

STR 2

The reported customer registered for a VASP account in June 2019 and has since had a total fiat account turnover of 710,256.00 GBP.

Between June 2019 and January 2021, the reported user received 109 Bitcoin deposits totalling a value of 67.14273902 Bitcoins (approx. 2.7 million GBP) into their VASP account from external Bitcoin addresses. This is out of profile for the customer profile, the source of funds is unknown. The user also received 3 Bitcoin deposits totalling 0.581842 Bitcoins (approx. 15,000.00 GBP) that were sent internally to the account of another of our customers who was previously reported to the UK's National Crime Agency. This is deemed as high risk.

During this period, the user made transfers totalling 5.993619 Bitcoins (approx. 180,000.00 GBP) from the user's account to external Bitcoin addresses. It is noted, there are multiple connections to mixer services, also known as tumblers, blenders, shufflers. These anonymising tools are used to combine numerous cryptocurrency payments into a single transaction. Given the nature of mixers, we hold concerns that the customer attempted to disguise the original source of funds, as mixers are often used by criminals to hide the origin of funds.

The customer has used their VASP debit card to make payments to [another online bank], [an online auction site], and [a money transfer service].

In conclusion, based on the findings of the investigation, such as the high turnover of funds and the use of a mixer to conceal the origin of funds, we have reasonable grounds to suspect that the reported user has utilised the account facility to launder the proceeds of crime and, as a result, money laundering has occurred. The user's account has been permanently suspended as a result of this review.

This report contained all the required information including customer details (name, address, date of birth, account opening information), IP/MAC addresses, and mobile phone numbers/devices. The duration this activity occurred before a report was made is concerning. Reference to the internal *investigation* may also be an indicator of the reason for the delay and some role creep into the FIU/police function. Sufficient information was provided to allow the FIU to perform some blockchain analytics before the case was disseminated to the police for investigation.

STR 3

We believe that the reported suspect's account balance is criminal property due to the reasons set out below. The reported user registered for a VASP account in July 2018 and has a current balance of 912.45 GBP.

Between 10/12/2018 and 09/07/2019, the reported user received nine cryptocurrency deposits totalling a value of 0.02 Bitcoins (approx. 685.49 GBP) and 8.674448555 Ether (approx. 20,000.00 GBP) into their VASP account from external cryptocurrency addresses. Of the above deposits, two totalling 0.02 Bitcoins (approx. 675.00 GBP) were classified as high risk due to their connections to a known Ponzi scheme [name given and open source reports support this contention]. Upon receipt of digital assets, the suspect immediately converts them to fiat to spend via card payments. For example, a total of 1124.32 EUR was spent this way (Names of stores given). We therefore believe that the reported user has benefited from the proceeds of crime. Given the strong links to Ponzi schemes and the immediate disbursement of funds, we believe the suspect opened their account to facilitate money laundering. The user's account has been permanently suspended as a result of this review.

The reported user has [a small value retained in their VASP account]. Given the details outlined above, we suspect that these funds may be the proceeds of crime. We seek a defence against the Proceeds of Crime Act to transfer these funds to an external fiat account and cryptocurrency address to be nominated by the reported user.

There is no consent regime in Irish legislation; this leaves the VASP with a dilemma of what to do with the funds remaining. This report contained all the information required to develop a high-quality intelligence package (personal information, transaction information, IP addresses, crypto-addresses, etc.). However, it was submitted after the suspicious activity had occurred and the majority of funds had been dissipated, which represented a lost opportunity for law enforcement intervention. The provided details allowed the funds to be traced to another exchange.

STR 4

A customer attempted to top up their account using external credit cards. The uploads would begin with a small amount and would then rapidly increase in quantity, indicating that test transactions were first made before the card was maxed out. We suspect that the user purchased stolen credit cards (perhaps on a dark net marketplace) and attempted to top up this suspected money mule account.

All required information was provided including crypto-addresses and credit card numbers. This STR was interesting as it showed a modus operandi being used for crypto-assets that would previously be used for stolen and cloned credit cards, i.e. a small test withdrawal before use. With the information provided in this STR, it was possible to use a blockchain analysis tool to identify the dark net marketplace used. The FIU is of the opinion that the VASP used the same tool to identify the marketplace, but there was no mention of this in the STR. The customer was de-risked after the STR was made.

STR 5

The accounts were registered with addresses in [an EU country]. The users were all [Asian] nationals with North American phones. The email addresses are all similar and appear to be "throwaway" accounts. The user's selfies taken to verify the customer's identity had been taken by a third party who can be seen in the picture. All reported users shared the same devices.

This STR alerted the FIU to a money mule recruiting operation. From analysis it was possible to see the organised crime structure behind the money mule scam (herders, controllers, directors). This STR shows poor KYC by the VASP who engaged with the FIU after the STR was made to enhance their KYC and TM rules to prevent future reoccurrences. Unfortunately, in this case, the impugned funds were traced to a VASP in an unfriendly jurisdiction; it was not possible to recover the funds.

STR 6

This is an investigation into the substantiated fraudulent activity (and subsequent money laundering of the proceeds of the fraudulent activity) of a former employee [within the reporting VASP]. They abused their employment status and knowledge to engineer and perpetrate a scheme to defraud customers for their own financial gain, which continued beyond their termination.

Over 18 months, the ex-employee misdirected funds from customers to his own VASP account. Their MO was to select customers seeking technical support with account or trading issues. They would request a manual deposit to their own VASP account for verification purposes and would then supply their own account as if it were the customer's, meaning any payments would be received in their own account. Post-termination the suspect continues this activity using the knowledge they obtained during their time as an employee. The suspect also lured customers with promises of preferential investment rates and early access to non-existent investment schemes.

This STR contained all the details needed to develop a comprehensive intelligence package. When received by law enforcement, it was reported back to the FIU that the material had already been received in the form of a section 19 report, and an investigation was initiated. This report shows the danger of the *insider threat* and the difficulties with having two reporting requirements in Ireland.

As can be seen from these selected crypto-STRs, if the FIU is provided with the pertinent information by the VASP in a timely manner, the FIU has the potential to take action to disseminate intelligence to law enforcement quickly and recover funds if possible. In some cases, the STRs alerted the FIU, which in turn alerted law enforcement and the wider AML community, of new methods of committing crypto-laundering (see STR1, for example). However, it should be emphasised that even high-quality STRs are effectively useless if they are confined to a backlog due to the staffing constraints present in the FIU.

7.5 Final Observations

This case study researched the internal operations of FIU Ireland from 2020 to 2023. The time span covered the period immediately prior to and after the introduction of legislation in April 2021 that regulated crypto-assets for the purposes of

AML for the first time. The case study sought to understand the phenomenon of crypto-laundering and the role the Irish FIU plays in its understanding, pursuit, and detection based on the data collected. The description of the case study was sensitised by socio-technical systems theory so that the disparate data collected through observations, interviews, focus groups, document analysis, and the exploration of 2719 crypto-related STRs submitted to FIU Ireland in 2021 could be considered together in an academically rigorous manner.

It is now possible to summarise the key findings that emerged from the specific case of FIU Ireland as follows:

- There is a need to have an FIU acting as the link between the private sector reporting entities and public sector investigators. The FIU purportedly acts as a filtering mechanism to sift out irrelevant information, to add value to reports disseminated, and to provide expertise to both sides as required. Due to comprehensive oversight of the wider AML system, the FIU is well positioned to understand crypto-laundering.
- Crypto-assets are being used to support the laundering of funds created by all forms of criminal activity. Regulating the fiat/crypto interfaces and expanding the AML rules to the entities (e.g. VASPs) operating in that space was a good response to the current way in which crypto-assets are misused. This will require periodic evaluation as criminals adapt to use the technology in different ways: for example, the use of privacy-enhanced coins or bypassing regulated VASPs. Currently, these entities operate in a similar fashion to bank accounts and this mode of operation is well suited to the current AML rules.
- The expansion of the AML regime to crypto-assets has created an additional workload on the limited resources of the FIU. Additional training to understand the new technology, outreach to assist the reporting entities and criminal investigators, and managing and analysing the massive increase in STRs received—which have been generated almost entirely by crypto-STRs submitted by VASPs—has stretched the resources and affected the operational efficiency of the FIU. The submission of junk or defensive STRs and crypto-STRs needs to be addressed, as these create further strain on the system. The majority of crypto-STRs submitted to FIU Ireland in 2021 had no nexus to Ireland whatsoever; the Irish FIU acted as a mailbox and forwarded these reports to other FIUs for analysis in a bureaucratic fashion.
- To effectively manage the increased workload caused by the proliferation of VASPs, the FIU needs to be truly operationally autonomous and have its own budget and resources. FIU Ireland does not currently have this; it is neither autonomous nor operating at its full potential. Staff shortages cause delays in the analysis of STRs and the dissemination of intelligence packages. This in turn causes additional inefficiencies and represents lost investigative and asset recovery opportunities. These delays also have the potential to cause reputational damage to the FIU and Ireland's AML system in general. Ireland is seen as a global financial hub seeking to attract foreign direct investment from multinational companies to drive our economy, so any reputational damage is unwelcome and has a negative impact.

- Opportunities to collaborate with the private-sector entities that provide blockchain analytics and other expertise should be fully exploited. There is a need to create further awareness of crypto-laundering both within the FIU and the wider public sector. Pursuit of this goal requires further knowledge, training, and resources, which have not yet been provided to the FIU or the police.
- Crypto-STRs are disproportionately responsible for the increased volume of STRs received by the FIU. The majority are submitted by a very small number of entities. Many VASPs have never submitted an STR to the FIU. This raises a number of questions. Firstly, are those VASPs submitting numerous reports doing so defensively, or are they submitting superfluous reports to create the appearance of complying with AML rules? Secondly, why are the other VASPs not seeing the same risks and submitting STRs in the same numbers as their counterparts?
- Considering that less than 1% of the STRs and crypto-STRs submitted to the FIU contribute to money laundering prosecutions, the true function of the FIU system appears to be an inefficient, bureaucratic storage facility for reports. Many of the reports are of no value and were filed defensively by designated persons who have no true awareness of the money laundering risk or perhaps are too wary of negative regulator intervention. Ireland's prosecution of money laundering compares well with our European counterparts, which raises questions about the efficiency of the entire AML system.
- High-quality crypto-STRs should contain all relevant real-world and crypto-related information (see Chap. 6 for further discussion on this). Should a report be deficient, this creates an additional time burden on the FIU, which has to seek the missing information as part of their analysis. This creates further bottlenecks and delays that represent lost investigative opportunities and provides criminals the necessary time to disperse funds. Crypto-STRs, due to the nature of crypto-asset technology, are made after the fact, which misses opportunities for early law enforcement intervention. The speed and volume at which crypto transactions are generated are creating difficulty for the transaction monitoring carried out by VASPs and, in turn, the FIU.
- Although it was not a focus of this research, it is surprising that there were no crypto-STRs received by FIU Ireland in 2021 that reported suspicions of terrorist financing. This reporting deficit gives rise to concerns of a VASP blind spot for this type of criminality.

Given the right resources, the FIU is qualified to investigate crypto-STRs and comprehend crypto-laundering. The consequences of the expansion of the FIU's role could potentially render it functionally inadequate. As the majority of money laundering prosecutions in Ireland are generated from an FIU intelligence package, creating a blockage at this important part of the wider AML system has the potential to render the entire AML system ineffective. Currently, focusing AML efforts on the real-world friction points (on- and off-ramps of the crypto-asset system) is appropriate and reflects the manner in which criminals are misusing crypto-assets. This pattern of behaviour requires continued observation and will need to be addressed should criminals adopt an alternative method of crypto-asset use. This might include setting up their own criminally funded crypto-asset for nefarious use, adapting the use of privacy-friendly assets such as ZCash or Monero, or swapping cold storage wallets (on USB keys, for example) as a means of value transfer outside of the AML-regulated system.

The conclusion of this case study forms the basis for the next chapter, where the book transitions from the specific case of FIU Ireland and its data to develop two systems-orientated visualisations. These will enable further inductive progression for identifying patterns, theoretical dimensions, and abstractions.

Reference

Furneaux N (2018) Investigating cryptocurrencies: understanding, extracting, and analysing blockchain evidence. Wiley, Indianapolis

Chapter 8
AML Socio-Technical Systems Models

Life is not accumulation; it is about contribution.

~ Stephen Covey

Money laundering research tends to be very descriptive and uses case examples to illustrate points made. This approach was seen in the previous chapter when describing the Irish FIU. What is now required is to build up a theory or framework of what the data collected during this research (the 2719 crypto-STRs, the interviews, the focus groups, the document analysis, the observations) collectively tells us.

This book uses the theoretical scaffold of socio-technical systems theory, which is well described and supported in the academic literature, to organise and categorise the data; this can help us achieve a higher-level understanding of the phenomenon of crypto-laundering from:

1. The criminal perspective: what are they doing? How are they doing it? Who is involved?
2. The civil society perspective: What is the FIU doing, in cooperation with which people and resources, to address the complex issue of crypto-laundering?

This chapter begins with a quick review of the key systems concepts previously discussed in Chap. 5. It then moves from the specific case study and its data, described in detail in the previous two chapters, to build two socio-technical systems models for describing the phenomenon studied, crypto-laundering, and its pursuit and detection from the perspective of the FIU. These two models will be described using the author's own *2D socio-technical systems framework* that was developed by combining the well-known Katz and Kahn (1966) and Bostrom and Heinen (1977a, b) models. These constructions will provide a common framework if disparate groups come together to examine the phenomenon in future research and this could aid designated persons to recognise suspicious activity involving crypto-assets and file high-quality, actionable STRs.

The chapter will then examine how these two models interact with each other and their common environment: what components they share, and what mutual

S. Meighan, *Money Laundering and Crypto-Assets*, Contributions to Finance and Accounting, https://doi.org/10.1007/978-3-032-13481-3_8

dependencies affect them both. This will be presented using a newly developed *3D socio-technical systems model* developed by the author from the 2D systems diagram created in Chap. 5.

This model is one of the key theoretical contributions of this book. The chapter will then describe three instances where the use of this new 3D approach achieved results in the AML field. As an aside, the chapter will then discuss a new approach to identifying bad behaviour through the medium of crypto-assets, randomness. The chapter concludes with a discussion on the wider general implications and limitations of this new approach.

8.1 Socio-Technical Systems Modelling

The crypto-laundering system has evolved from the (main) money laundering socio-technical system, which has adapted over recent years as technology emerged to accommodate value transfer and the committing of crime through new, emerging technology such as ICT and crypto-assets. Systems theory has been proposed as a useful theory through which a deeper understanding can emerge and can help us address complex, wicked problems, such as crypto-laundering and its pursuit and detection.

Recall that a system is two or more coherently structured elements that interact with each other to perform a function (Meadows 2009). Socio-technical systems theory is built upon von Bertalanffy's concept of an open system where there is a flow (input, transformation, and output) and interaction between system components and their more complex environment, resulting in the system's evolution or modification (Von Bertalanffy 1950). This perspective recognises that a system's survival is dependent on how it interacts with the ever-changing environment in which it is situated. In effect, environmental factors influence the way a system behaves (Mumford 2006). To understand complex issues, like crypto-laundering, the interaction between the system and these external factors needs to be understood (Mumford 2003). Organisations, such as the FIU, and complex phenomena such as crypto-laundering, can be successfully conceptualised as systems (Angell and Demetis 2005; Katz and Kahn 1966). This approach is enhanced when utilising a socio-technical approach that considers the social/human and technical elements in combination (Emery 2016; Ropohl 1999; Trist and Bamforth 1951). The socio-technical approach, therefore, is a useful method of viewing organisations and phenomena in a way that:

> emphasises the interrelatedness of the functioning of the social and technological subsystems … and the relationship of the (system) as a whole to the environment in which it operates. It recognises that systems are made up of people that produce products or services using some technology, and that each affects the operation and appropriateness of the technology as well as the people who operate it (Pasmore et al. 1982, p. 1182).

This method can be simplified by recognising that the socio-technical approach is concerned with the mutual benefits derived from the interaction of the technical and social elements (Emery 1980), but also a way to appreciate tensions, gaps, problems, and unintended consequences between them. The socio-technical framework utilised by this research was proposed by Bostrom and Heinen (1977b) and is focused on three primary dimensions: the social subsystem—is made up of *people* and *structure* components—and is comprised of the people and human factors in the system. In an organisation, this includes the individuals and groups, their relationships, structure, values, power dynamics, and manner of working. The technical subsystem is made up of "technology" and "tasks" components. It refers to the tasks, tools, techniques, and technology used by the social subsystem to transform the system's inputs into outputs that are, hopefully, useful to the environment. Finally, the environment refers to the wider surroundings and context in which the system of interest is situated (Bostrom and Heinen 1977b). Remember that each subsystem is connected to each other subsystem and to the external environment; the system as a whole is itself connected to the external environment. In Chap. 5, the author combined the frameworks developed by Katz and Kahn (1966) and Bostrom and Heinen (1977a, b) to allow complex organisations and phenomena to be simultaneously diagrammed at both the macro-level (open system with inputs, transformation, outputs, feedback) and the micro-level (internal socio-technical system). This new approach is useful. It allows a complex organisation like the FIU, or a complex phenomenon, like crypto-laundering, to be described in a systems-sensitised manner.

These models will now be generated and presented as two theoretical contributions to this research. Each system will be discussed individually; this enables a full understanding of each subsystem and its ancillary connections. The chapter will later explore how these two models interact with each other and their environment.

8.1.1 Crypto-Laundering Socio-Technical Systems Model

Chapter 3 identified how crypto-laundering is a crypto-asset-specific variant of cyber-laundering (using the internet and ICT to launder criminal proceeds) involving *cleaning* the proceeds of crime through the crypto-asset system. In some instances, the predicate crime is committed in the real world or *off-chain,* and the proceeds need to be converted to crypto-assets to be obfuscated. In other cases, the proceeds of cyber-criminality are already in the form of crypto-assets or *on-chain* and are ready to be laundered through the crypto-asset system without prior conversion from fiat currencies. In the majority of situations, there is still a requirement to convert the sanitised funds back to fiat currency to enjoy or reinvest them. It is accepted that some criminals have found alternative routes to value transfer without going through an exchange, e.g. the exchange of NFTs, hardware cold wallets, and passwords. This usage may increase as regulation tightens up the usage of exchanges. Despite the method chosen by the criminal, the aim of money laundering is to obscure any links to the predicate offence that generated the profits and legitimise the funds through the normal business, banking, and crypto-asset channels. When successful, this frustrates the AML efforts by law enforcement and civil society and effectively *makes crime pay*. The laundering process simply removes the link between the predicate offence and the final legitimate appearance of the funds by comingling the transactions in plain sight among the billions of (almost identical) legitimate transactions that take place daily (Fig. 2.1). In effect, money laundering is a simple process that is difficult to detect. One must find the proverbial needle in a haystack, or more accurately, the needle in a stack of other identical needles.

Thus, the function of our crypto-laundering system can be described as the cleaning of *dirty money*. It does this by taking the proceeds of crime as an input and outputting them as apparently legitimately obtained funds after an internal laundering transformation. This process involves not only crypto-assets, but also the interface with the fiat world, e.g. VASPs and the traditional banking system. This system provides feedback in the form of knowledge of *successes*, or more importantly *failures*, whereby criminals learn what works and how to circumvent the AML rules put in place to address this type of nefarious behaviour. The author has seen this type of information shared on dark web bulletin boards, encrypted mobile devices, and, more recently, Telegram groups. This feedback potentially gives law enforcement an insight into how criminals are exploiting the crypto-asset system, and this knowledge can be leveraged for investigations or future study. A dark-web-based examination in this important area is suggested as an avenue for future research.

The social subsystem (*people* and *structure*) consists of the people and organisations involved in the crypto-laundering process. Analysis will begin with the people involved in crypto-laundering. The initial, and most obvious place, to start is with the *criminal* who commits the predicate offence. Without this behaviour, there would be no proceeds of criminal conduct to launder. As evidenced in the literature review, almost every crime is committed to generate profit. As an example, drug trafficking creates enormous profits that allow the criminal to lead a lavish lifestyle and to reinvest in further and more serious criminality. The proceeds created represent power to the criminal. During his time as a criminal investigator, the author has observed many such occurrences. A criminal, or a small-scale family grouping, will start selling a trivial amount of drugs in their locality; as their business expands, their lifestyle improves. The generated profit is used to buy more drugs and in turn expand their territory. This brings them into contact with other criminals who may band together and form a larger Organised Crime Group (OCG), but more likely will result in conflict and violence. The profits of drug trafficking are then used to purchase weapons and enforcers. A gang feud develops, which can result in murder and other types of mayhem. In many cases seen by the author, the OCGs utilised crypto-assets in one way or another—sometimes as a method of value exchange, sometimes to purchase illegal firearms, and sometimes as a speculative asset to generate the appearance of legitimate wealth. Naturally, all of these OCGs result in the erosion of the rule of law and tie up scarce police resources. This cycle recently played out in Dublin with the Hutch-Kinahan feud from 2015 to 2018, which resulted in 18 murders and many other serious international crimes that are still under investigation.

The second type of person in this substructure is the *crime victim*. With crimes such as investment frauds and cyber-criminality, like ransomware attacks, there is a victim who parts with their hard-earned, legitimate money, usually through threat, coercion, or deception (often through sophisticated social engineering) on the part of the criminal. Investment frauds involving crypto-assets and the lure of achieving massive returns in a short time frame (greed?) were prevalent during the period that FIU Ireland was being observed as part of the case study in the previous chapter. Crime victims are an important element to consider; without them, there would be no profits to launder in the first place. This puts a premium on prevention, which is often missing in any discussion on serious and organised criminality.

As money laundering relies upon the legitimate business and banking system, the third type of person in this substructure can be captured under the heading of *customer*. There is always a need to involve a legitimate bank, credit institution, VASP, or other intermediary in the laundering process; in order to do so, one must be a customer of that entity. Sometimes, the criminal will open an account themselves either using their real details (this is ill-advised should they wish to avoid law enforcement) or with fraudulent details. The 2719 crypto-STRs analysed for this research contain multiple instances where the criminal opened an account using either fake or fraudulently obtained genuine documents and details, and so identity impersonation becomes a critical component of onboarding. As one will see shortly, the customer could also be a person recruited to operate as a money mule who uses their legitimately opened account for criminal purposes.

Whichever form the customer takes, it is this customer-entity relationship that allows the impugned funds to enter the legitimate business and banking systems and allows the illicit money to be obscured among the billions of daily transactions. The analytical differentiation between *criminal* and *customer* is an important ontological distinction in the crypto-laundering system, as there are occasions where the distinction collapses (i.e. the criminal *is* the customer) and others where the criminal-to-customer pathways are more complex.

Staff also need to be included as another category of persons who can be involved in crypto-laundering, equivalent to what in cybersecurity would be referred to as *insider threats* (Whitelaw et al. 2024). In some of the crypto-STRs that were analysed, it was apparent that a staff member inside the AML-regulated entity was assisting the money launderer. This included actions such as providing data to bypass AML controls or using their knowledge to deceive customers into parting with their funds. This effectively resembles a transposition of the bank teller role in traditional money laundering schemes into the member of staff in a VASP, as the digital equivalent of an insider in crypto-laundering. The insider can either be operating in full cooperation with the criminal launderer or under duress after the criminal has compromised them in some way, e.g. by possessing evidence of criminal or immoral activity they are threatening to disclose to their family or employer.

The last category of people that can be included in this section—based on the literature review and the case study of FIU Ireland—can be collectively called *facilitators*. These are people who either knowingly or unknowingly assist the launderer. This might include professionals in the business world, such as lawyers, accountants, and estate agents. In the case of crypto-assets, the main facilitator of crypto-laundering evidenced in the crypto-STRs is the VASP itself, without this precluding the involvement of additional facilitators, which will be considered below.

The people in the crypto-laundering subsystem interact, in both formal and informal structures, to allow for money laundering to occur and operationalise it across a variety of potential pathways. As previously noted, these structures—groups of people—can either do so inadvertently or in full knowledge of what is happening. The first structure to consider is that of the *OCG*. In Irish law, a *criminal organisation* means:

> a structured group, however organised, that has as its main purpose or activity the commission or facilitation of a serious offence, i.e. one for which a person may be punished by imprisonment for a term of 4 years or more. It must include three or more persons, not randomly formed for the immediate commission of a single offence. The group exists notwithstanding the absence of any or all of the following:
>
> (a) Formal rules or formal membership, or any formal roles for those involved in the group
> (b) Any hierarchical or leadership structure
> (c) Continuity of involvement by persons in the group.[1]

Based on the crypto-STRs submitted in 2021, it appears there are many well-structured OCGs operating in Ireland, which are comprised of Irish, Eastern European, and West African groups. These alliances are well-organised and commit a variety of offences. Their primary focus is on economic crimes—especially invoice redirection frauds, CEO frauds, and romance frauds. The crypto-STRs show that *money mule* accounts are routinely used to receive the impugned funds before they are laundered through the crypto-asset system and transferred as value up to the higher echelons of the OCG. The STRs received relate mostly to the activity of money mules, mule herders, and controllers; this necessitates a "follow the money" investigation to identify those at the more prominent levels of the OCG, which is where the funds are ultimately being directed. This approach allows civil society to criminalise the behaviour of those directing and leading the criminal structures and provides opportunities to trace the accumulated criminal funds. While these OCGs have a permanent footrprint in Ireland, the main leadership is often located abroad. This configuration creates jurisdictional difficulties for law enforcement: police respect borders, criminals exploit them. The crypto-STRs evidence that both genuine and bogus *companies* are used to purchase goods, which are shipped to the OCG's home country in the form of trade-based crypto-laundering.

Many of the investment frauds that were identified through the crypto-STRs were structured in a similar way to traditional *Ponzi Schemes* (another example of *old wine in new bottles* perhaps?). These are included in this subsystem based on what was seen in the 2719 crypto-STRs analysed. As the people subsystem includes

[1] Section 70 Criminal Justice Act, 2006 as amended.

customers, one must include the entity under which the customer accounts are held. In crypto-assets, this structure is either the regulated entity that handles the exchange of fiat for crypto-assets or vice versa (*VASPs*). This entity is vital for purchasing and selling crypto-assets and must be included in a consideration of crypto-laundering—without a VASP, it is extremely difficult to launder crypto-assets. One should also include other AML-regulated entities that hold and transfer funds, such as credit and financial institutions. Many VASPs interact with these and, indeed, have their own accounts with regulated banks and financial institutions. Finally, one needs to consider the concept of *suspicion* in this structure subsystem. As examined earlier, this is a construction whereby VASP customers are identified acting in an abnormal or unexpected way, which has aroused a suspicion of money laundering. If an account is deemed suspicious, the MLRO may report the matter to the FIU or police, giving the criminal a cause for concern that they might be caught. For this reason, the criminal wants to avoid detection by employing tactics such as money mules and insiders, for example. It is easy to see that people crypto-laundering do so in formal and informal structures. The model allows the aforementioned network of linkages and groupings to be easily seen.

The technical subsystem consists of the technology used by the people (operating in informal and formal structures) to carry out a particular task. The main technology referred to in crypto-laundering is obviously *crypto-assets* (public addresses, wallets, transfers, etc.), and the main task is to *transfer value* from one person to another, or to oneself through a concurrent holding of multiple wallets (see Chap. 3). Recall that the criminal is trying to break the link between the profits generated by a criminal act and the crime itself. This process involves utilising the legitimate crypto-asset system. What makes a crypto-laundering transaction different is the source of the funds. The criminal attempts to exploit the crypto-asset architecture to rapidly move funds, often across borders, and utilises techniques to conceal the funds' criminal origins, thereby legitimising them. Based on the data gathered in the previous chapter, it is possible to examine some of the technology and tasks that the criminal is performing to achieve their goal.

Grounded on the crypto-STRs analysed, evidence of the use of *crypto-ATMs* to convert the proceeds of criminal conduct to crypto-assets was obvious (on-ramps). Some crypto-STRs also refer to criminal misuse of *crypto-debit cards* to spend the illicit proceeds (off-ramp); therefore, these two instances of crypto-asset technology are included in the model. Criminal use of other technology, such as *VPNs*, *mixers/tumblers*, and interaction with the *dark web/TOR,* was evident from the crypto-STRs submitted. This reveals how criminals are exploiting privacy-enhancing technologies (PETs) in an attempt to hide their tracks and frustrate the efforts of law enforcement to detect them. A concern not evident from the analysis, but raised during the interviews, makes it prudent to include *privacy-enhanced coins (PECs)* in this subsystem. This is a significant finding. It is important to emphasise that the lack of crypto-STRs for PECs, coupled with corroborated intelligence that they are being used, is a significant *black-hole* in the AML intelligence picture. Is this because they are not being seen—that is, the technology is so successful it cannot be detected—or is it because of knowledge gaps by AML professionals, such as

MLROs, who are scrutinising their customers' transactions and don't know what they are looking for?

The use of two other non-crypto technologies was apparent in the primary data. The first was the use of payment *card terminals* to receive payments from crime victims, and the immediate transfer of those funds into a crypto-asset via a VASP. These devices are readily available from numerous suppliers and allow a person to receive credit and debit card payments from customers. The second technology employed was the use of *QR codes* by criminals to send to victims of ransomware attacks and investment frauds. These QR codes contained the public crypto-asset addresses of wallets that were scanned at crypto-ATMs; funds were then lodged directly to a criminally controlled public address and rapidly dissipated to other accounts. In one batch of crypto-STRs received at FIU Ireland, it was apparent the OCG was operating a help-desk/call-centre where victims who were having trouble converting their money to crypto-assets were assisted to complete the transaction.

The tasks in this model can be amalgamated as *fiat-crypto exchange*, *transfer value*, and *crypto-fiat exchange*. The crypto-STRs received at FIU Ireland showed that the method used often involved a combination of regular financial tasks and crypto-tasks, such as receiving transfers from a bank account, external card loads, and the misuse of point-of-sale card terminals. On the last point, crypto-STRs showed examples of criminals purchasing legitimate credit card details on the dark web; these were most likely obtained because of a data breach and sold by other criminals for a profit. The card terminals were used to type in the stolen credit card details for bogus purchases that obtained funds for the criminal, which were quickly converted to crypto-assets for laundering.

Based on the significance of money, as the common element of crime, money laundering, and AML, both the ways in which money is generated and how it is used to purchase illegal goods and services need to be carefully considered in the model. Crimes such as fraud, cybercrime, drug trafficking, weapons trafficking, CSEM—collectively referred to as *profit generation*—are the predicate offences that generate the dirty money. The *purchase of illegal goods and services*, such as drugs and firearms, also needs to be considered. This is illegal activity itself (profit generation), but dealing with the proceeds made by selling these illicit goods is also crypto-laundering on the part of the seller.

Another task of interest is how transactions are *obscured* and concealed from law enforcement through the rapid movement of funds, crypto-to-crypto transfers, mixers/tumblers, privacy software, and international transfers—often to unfriendly jurisdictions.

The final task to consider here can be referred to as *victimisation,* an abstract category to represent the variable ways in which potential victims are selected and subjected to deception. Evidence from the primary data shows that crypto-assets, especially their potentially huge return on investment, were often used to lure crime victims into parting with their hard-earned cash. Reports in regular and social media of persons who got rich quickly, often enhanced with fraudulent (often AI-generated) celebrity endorsements, fuelled the attraction of crypto-assets and a fear of missing out, which the criminals expertly exploited to their advantage.

From this discussion, one can now present the crypto-laundering socio-technical systems model as the second theoretical contribution of this book (Fig. 8.1).

As shown in the model, the subsystems interact with each other and with their environment. This represents how people come together in formal and informal structures to perform a specific task with the technology. As an example, an OCG (structure), made up of criminals at different levels in a hierarchy (people), sets up an investment fraud to generate profit (task) by luring or victimising (task) a crime victim (people) to transfer funds (task) into a crypto public address (technology) under the control of the criminal (people). The impugned money enters the crypto-laundering system when the victim goes to a crypto-ATM (technology) and converts their fiat into crypto-assets (task) and transfers the value (task) to the public address (technology) belonging to the criminal (people). The criminal (person) then sends the value (task) to a mixing service (technology) and converts it to another type of crypto-asset (technology) in order to break the link with the crime victim. Higher levels of the OCG (structure) control the ultimate destination crypto address (technology) and convert the stolen funds (task) back to fiat through a VASP (structure) located in an unfriendly jurisdiction into a bank account held by them. The benefit

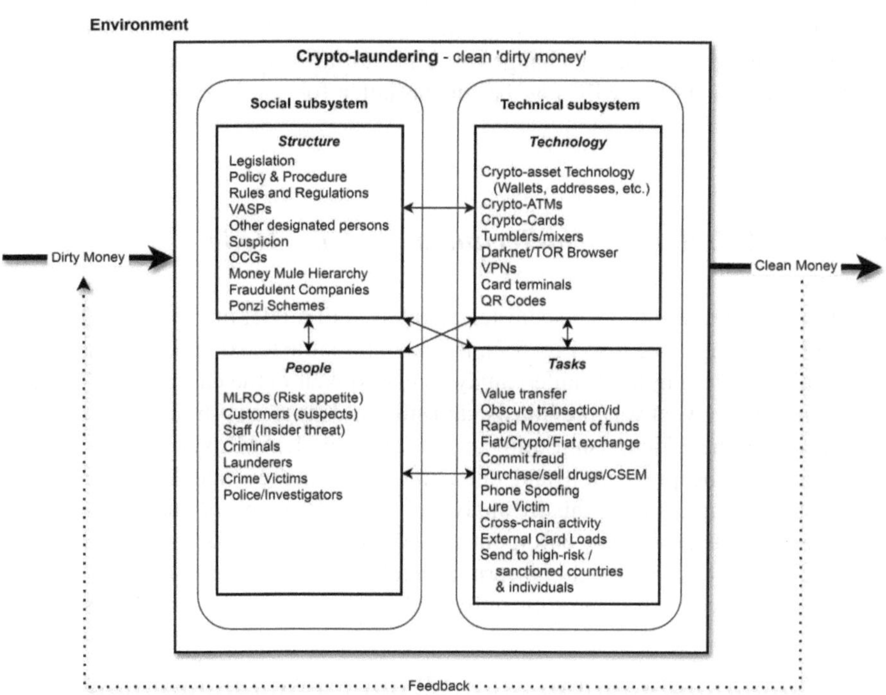

Fig. 8.1 Crypto-laundering system model

of using a socio-technical system sensitised model is that the people and technology are both addressed, and there is a clear pathway to describe issues as they arise.

External to the crypto-laundering system is its ever-changing and evolving environment. This represents the broader context in which it operates and includes PESTLE factors such as the global economy, cultural considerations, and the political and legal systems. These potentially influence the criminal. In particular, it highlights how they attempt to avoid the measures put in place to prevent and detect crypto-laundering. Crypto-laundering has been conceptualised as a complex socio-technical system. One must remember that its surrounding environment is more complex than the individual system and is itself made up of "a bubbling soup of interacting" and structurally coupled complex systems (Angell and Demetis 2010, p. 109). Maturana and Varela (1991) state that the environment can trigger (produce perturbations that systems are aware of) systems to act in a different way. When a system and another aspect of the environment (usually another system) are *highly differentiated*, they may develop relations between each other (structural coupling), such that over time their frequent interactions lead to both systems coming to rely on each other (Jackson 2019, p. 65; Midgley 2000, p. 55). These couplings are *highly selective* as they do not refer to the entire environment, but only to the parts that are connected to each other. In other words, there are parts of the external environment that have no effect on the system defined and being studied by the observer (Luhmann 2013, p. 85). Examples of such structurally coupled systems are money and money laundering, money laundering and AML, and crypto-laundering and the Irish FIU. The FIU is the system that aims to prevent and detect crypto-laundering and has adapted because of changes to legislation bringing crypto-assets under AML regulation. Focus will now be on the latter for use in developing the second model.

8.1.2 FIU Ireland Socio-Technical Systems Model

Recalling the first impression socio-technical system model of FIU Ireland, briefly outlined in Chap. 5 (see also Fig. 5.7), it is now possible to expand upon that socio-technical model using the detailed analysis undertaken in the case study (Chap. 7); bear in mind that what was previously said still holds true. FIU Ireland is a complex system within the wider Irish, European, and worldwide AML systems. Its purpose is to assist in the prevention and detection of all money laundering (including crypto-laundering). It does this by analysing the STRs received and disseminating intelligence packages[2] to law enforcement and providing feedback to the designated persons. The FIU provides this informal feedback in the systemic sense; in most instances, it provides the reporting entity with general comments on what happened

[2] An intelligence package is the output from the FIU to the relevant law enforcement agency. It is the result of the FIU analysis and is made up of the information contained in one or more STRs, enhanced with additional information obtained by the FIU analyst.

to the STR that it had initially reported. Be aware, this is not individual feedback, but rather more general feedback in the form of aggregate statistics and general observations. This information is available on the FIU website (www.fiu-ireland.ie) and is presented during public-private partnership meetings and outreach presentations. The designated entities oftentimes complain that they receive no specific feedback from the FIU. More than two decades since the introduction of FIUs, the hard reality is that meaningful feedback on the route of each STR (a digital progression footprint per se) is not provided by FIUs. In the absence of this feedback, designated persons continue reporting as has previously been done without any incorporation of lessons learned from the FIU. This itself can be considered feedback in a systemic sense as the system becomes a self-referential bureaucracy.

The complex, socio-technical FIU system is itself made up of constituent social and technical subsystems. The social subsystem will be reviewed first. The *people* involved in the FIU system are the managers, the sworn and unsworn analysts, and the forensic accountant who work in the FIU itself. It also includes the FIU's main stakeholders, such as the individual MLROs in the designated entities who scrutinise their customers' activity, identify any abnormal behaviour, and decide to make a (crypto-) STR to the FIU, and the law enforcement (crypto-laundering) investigators in Ireland and abroad who receive the disseminated intelligence packages and conduct a criminal investigation.

The customers (or suspects) who are reported to the FIU can be included under this subsystem, as they are intrinsically linked with the analysis of the submitted STR by the FIU and may become a suspect disclosed in an intelligence package. This subsystem also includes the individual software engineers who customise, support, and maintain the GoAML system (an off-the-shelf package from the UNODC), and the data scientists from the various commercial blockchain analytic tool companies used by the FIU. The formal *structures* of the FIU become apparent by examining how the people working within the FIU are organised and carry out their duties according to its policies, procedures, and legislative framework (including staff manuals, training documents, etc.). As shown previously, the FIU's organisation chart and the various sections within it both can be considered formal teams and indeed further FIU subsystems if one so desired to focus at a lower level of granularity. Internal informal teams might come together on an ad hoc basis for work or social purposes—such as collaborating on a complicated STR or addressing an issue with a part of the FIU's work. External informal teams can be perceived when one observes the interaction of the people mentioned above when they interact with outside entities such as the AMLSC, public–private partnerships, the EU, the FATF, and outside sources from which crypto-asset information is sourced and depends on. Designated entities that are subject to the AML legislation, such as VASPs and other entities—for example credit and financial institutions, which are made up of customers (suspects) and MLROs, should be included in these structures. Finally, as with the crypto-laundering model, one must include the concept of *suspicion* in this structure subsystem. This is the entire premise of the AML system, where VASP customers are identified by MLROs acting in an abnormal or unexpected way, giving rise to a suspicion of money laundering, and becoming the subject of a report to the FIU, which may give rise to a criminal investigation. Within the FIU system, these people, operating within formal and informal structures, interpret the information generated by the technical subsystem and make decisions on how to progress STRs and transform them into intelligence packages. These suspicions of money laundering are further substantiated if it appears to the FIU analyst that a criminal indicator is present or that the MLRO's suspicion was justified.

Focus will now be on the technical subsystem. The FIU uses various IT and ICT systems (technology) such as GoAML, PULSE, the Beneficial Ownership registers, and the commercial blockchain analysis tools to perform its tasks in relation to pursuing crypto-laundering. This subsystem also includes *crypto-assets* (public addresses, wallets, transfers, etc.), as they themselves are used to transfer value by the criminals. The combination of people using technology allows the FIU to perform its tasks of *analysing STRs*, *disseminating intelligence* packages, and performing *outreach*. It is worth considering some of the tasks that are performed by the FIU during their analysis function. Firstly, we can consider ***suspect profiling.*** This is where the person named in the crypto-STR is checked against the criminal database, their legitimate income is determined using FIU powers and available information, and assets that the person has in their possession are examined to determine if there is any criminality or if the person is living beyond their legitimate means. The purpose of this task is to confirm if the reported person is a suspect for money laundering that requires notification to a law enforcement authority. The FIU may engage with stakeholders to request that they obtain the source of funds from their customer, confirm the customer's KYC documentation, or provide a history of the customer's transaction history. This may also provide additional analytic opportunities to identify the account that the suspect was transacting with within another designated entity. Secondly, there is *attribution*, where a known public address is examined to see if the real-world person who owns the address can be ascertained. Various techniques are used, including OSINT and the utilisation of commercial blockchain analysis tools. The use of these resources makes it possible to audit the asset trail and, hopefully, identify other members within the criminal organisation. Commercial tools are also useful because they give an indication if the public address was involved in criminal activity through a process called *address dusting*, which will be discussed in detail later in this chapter. Finally, the FIU can perform *crime prevention* tasks such as requesting telecommunication providers to block certain voice over internet protocol (VOIP) numbers and websites. They can also request an AML-regulated entity to perform a SWIFT/SEPA recall and return the funds to their rightful owner. This last task is particularly useful in invoice redirection and investment frauds if the report is made in a timely manner to the FIU. In 2022, for example the FIU and financial entities reversed fraudulent transactions to the value of over €5 million, which was returned to the injured parties. The analysis of this function and the recovery of funds would be a recommended future project.

From this discussion, as was the process with the first model, it is possible to present the crypto-detection 2D socio-technical systems model, the third theoretical contribution of this book (Fig. 8.2).

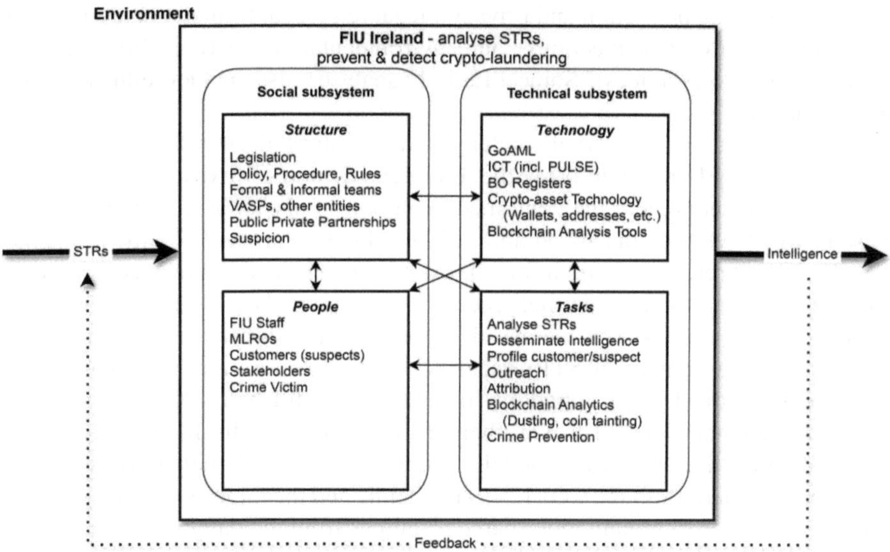

Fig. 8.2 FIU Ireland system model

To show how the model encapsulates the system, analysis of one of the aforementioned 2719 crypto-STRs will be used to illustrate a typical example of an MLRO (person) working in a VASP (structure) according to the AML legislation (structure). They noticed one of their customers (person) behaving in a suspicious manner (structure) and submitted a crypto-STR to the FIU (task). The FIU staff received the STR and analysed it (task) using their computer systems (technology). The analyst used blockchain investigation tools (technology) to attribute the crypto public address (technology) to a real-world person, and their criminal activity (task), via KYC documentation retained at a VASP (structure). The tool indicated the public address (technology) interacted with a mixing service, which was identified through a process of coin tainting/address dusting (task). This information was disseminated (task) to a police investigator (people) for investigation. In the meantime, because of their analysis, the FIU identified a potential invoice redirection victim (people) and carried out a SEPA recall, recovering the funds—crime prevention (task). Feedback was provided to the MLRO and the crime victim.

The ever-changing, complex environment in which FIU Ireland (and crypto-laundering itself) is located can be explored using PESTLE analysis. This type of analysis can provide an understanding of the external factors that may affect FIU Ireland's operations, enabling managers to make informed decisions and implement timely adaptations to changes in the external environment. PESTLE stands for political (e.g. regulation and legislation, government stability, government policies—including at an international and transnational level), economic (e.g. economic growth, exchange rates, inflation rates), social (e.g. demographics, cultural attitudes, technological literacy), technological (e.g. technological advancements, cybersecurity, data protection and privacy), legal (e.g. legal framework, compliance requirements, enforcement actions), and environmental factors (e.g. climate change risks, sustainable practices). Some PESTLE analyses also include ethical factors and standards.[3]

The most significant external challenges that occurred during this research were the United Kingdom's exit from the European Union (Brexit), the COVID-19 worldwide pandemic, and the continued evolution of crypto-asset technology. All these factors have been discussed above. The salient points will be drawn together here for ease of reference. Brexit forced several financial and FinTech companies to relocate to Ireland to maintain their access to the EU market through various passporting of services rules. This increased the number of designated persons in Ireland and, in turn, the number of STRs received by the FIU. As these companies had migrated from the United Kingdom (indeed, many still had UK operations and senior management located there), their understanding of the Irish AML system (especially the differences from the UK system) was obviously below par with what would be expected. Both the COVID-19 pandemic and the migration of a significant number of entities to Ireland took scarce resources from the daily job of the FIU.

COVID-19 changed work practices in almost every industry as society balanced maintaining business continuity with the protection of its staff. This meant working from home, which sometimes resulted in lower-quality work and an increase in poor-quality STRs. It also increased some cybersecurity and fraud risks, which again resulted in an increased workload on the FIU. Finally, crypto-asset technology continues to evolve, which means the FIU and law enforcement are in a continual battle to stay on top of their awareness, training, and resources to tackle cyber-criminality. The final model in Fig. 8.2 is not dissimilar to the one first advanced (Fig. 5.7). This is to be expected because the role and work of the FIU is well known and established, even when dealing with new value transfer methods such as crypto-laundering. It is recognised that the perturbation of the new regulation being introduced has affected the operation of both systems. As crypto-laundering tries to circumvent AML rules, the FIU uses these regulations to prevent and detect crypto-laundering. It is a sequence not unlike the cycle of criminality that was discussed in Chap. 1.

The complex phenomenon of crypto-laundering and the attempts to address it (AML) have been deconstructed by presenting two customised theoretical frameworks in the socio-technical tradition. These two models help to organise the phenomena being studied as open, complex, socio-technical systems and reflect on their internal and external interactions. The internal interaction looks at how the social and technical components or subsystems interact, as demonstrated in the Bostrom and Heinen (1977a, b) models above. The external interaction of these models was outlined as a simple input/output and feedback function (Katz and Kahn 1966). By presenting both using the author's 2D socio-technical systems model, both perspectives are simultaneously apparent. Each model was developed

[3] https://libguides.library.usyd.edu.au/c.php?g=508107&p=5994242 (Accessed: 21 August 2025).

independently of the other, albeit we contended that they are structurally coupled within a complex, changing environment (and each of them can also be perceived in each other's environments).

The following section examines how the two models can be visualised in a way that describes the interaction between the structurally coupled models. This will be an expansion of the author's 2D model and another of the main theoretical ontributions of this book, which can be applied to other research domains.

8.2 3D Model to Understand and Address Crypto-Laundering

As noted above, the author's 2D socio-technical framework captures a single socio-technical system operating in a complex environment well. But according to systems theory, the environment is made up of many other systems, some of which are structurally coupled to the system of interest being observed. The 2D model does not offer a way of conceptualising two models simultaneously, such as crypto-laundering and its pursuit and detection. Analytically, this differentiation is significant; theoretically, it allows us to interconnect socio-technical systems at a higher order of observation. Merely presenting the two models side-by-side, without any connections between them, omits to capture the fact that they are structurally coupled systems that "mutually influence each other … in the sense that their relationship achieves some stability and they come to rely upon each other" (Jackson 2019, pp. 33, 65). There needs to be a way to explore that mutual dependence, or the space between the two models.

Unlike the Western notion of neutral or empty space, the Japanese have the concept of MA represented by the kanji character 間. This literally translates as *a gap* or *a space*. To the Japanese, it represents "a continuous flow, alive with interactions and ruled by a precise sense of timing and pacing" or, in a very socio-technical, systematic way, "the complex network of relationships between people and [technology]" (Genosko 2005, p. 157). This in-between space "gives shape to the whole" (Fletcher 2001, p. 370) and offers a way to "recover the human dimensions and proportions … lost to technological [development]" (Genosko 2005, p. 158). It is the contention of this research that this concept accurately describes the concept of structural coupling between two socio-technical systems. There are elements common to both models, and there are multiple connections between them.

This book, as its fourth theoretical contribution, contends that the combined systematic interaction of two structurally coupled systems of interest (described using the author's combined model) can be visualised if one considers them as planes in three-dimensional space (Fig. 8.3). The entirety of the 3D space represents the external environment, the *bubbling soup* of other systems that may interact with and affect our two systems of interest. Each plane can be labelled as "System 1" and "System 2"; each contains the interrelated social and technical subsystems as

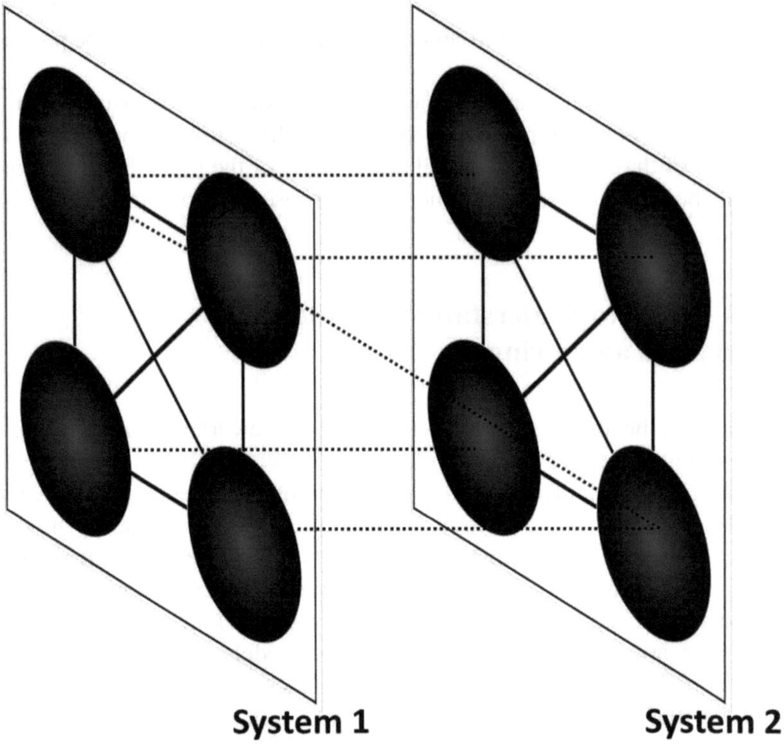

Fig. 8.3 3D Model of two structurally dependent socio-technical systems (only showing some connections)

outlined by Bostrom and Heinen (1977b), and each has the input-throughput-output-feedback process described by Katz and Kahn (1966)—both of which are described using the author's 2D socio-technical framework.

If the two systems are structurally coupled, there are linkages between each of the subsystems, for example "structure 1" to "structure 2", "technology 1" to "technology 2", and so on. There can also be linkages between any of the subsystems in "System 1" and a different subsystem in "System 2", e.g. "structure 1" to "tasks 2", and so on (see Fig. 8.3 for a simplified diagrammatic interpretation of this concept). This contention makes sense when we consider that our two socio-technical systems models interact with each other in many ways, e.g. criminals try to understand AML controls to defeat them, and civil society tries to understand criminal behaviour to control it. This is very useful as one assesses the two models of crypto-laundering and their detection. They both exhibit significant interconnectedness regarding components or processes (subsystems) that overlap. Because the models are structurally dependent, advances or adaptions on one model necessitate corresponding changes in the other to maintain effectiveness. This is one of the key principles of systems theory. This overlap concept underscores the interdependence and structural coupling of the two models.

The interaction between the two systems of interest is therefore a complex web, or mess, of connections. On the one hand, this represents one of the limitations of taking this approach. The number of linkages to be considered has massively increased when observing one system alone in comparison to two structurally coupled systems interacting with each other and their environment. As noted in Chap. 1, the increase in linkages can lead to an intensification in complexity, which could potentially ameliorate the advantages of using systems theory to understand complex phenomena and wicked problems in the first place. On the other hand, one proposed way to cut through some of this complexity is to focus on the elements within the two models that are shared or overlap. One main example to illustrate this point is that value transfer (function), in the form of a crypto-transaction (technology), is the focal point for both models.

Criminals seek to obfuscate the illegal origins of their funds, and civil society attempts to trace and block suspicious transactions that are hidden in plain sight among the many millions of almost identical legitimate transactions flowing through a VASP every day. In effect, the social dimensions of financial behaviour are intertwined and captured in this model with the technical elements of the crypto system, which is exactly what was the desired goal in adopting socio-technical systems theory as a model.

Other examples of commonality between the two models include crypto technology itself, regulatory frameworks (structure), and detection efforts (task). On one side, the criminals understand these as they try to avoid detection and understand the systems put in place to catch them, while civil society tries to put in place stronger measures to detect crypto-laundering.

When one analyses some of the tasks in both models, this paradigm is more easily seen. The FIU tries to attribute a transaction to a real-world identity, while the criminal tries to obfuscate and hide it. The criminal tries to victimise people to generate profit, while the FIU's activities assist in the prevention of this crime to protect the public—the responsibility for financial crime awareness is a particularly complex issue worthy of further study on its own. The criminal tries to generate profits from their illicit usage, and the FIU tries to deny and deprive the criminals of their ill-gotten gains.

This proposed new 3D model is useful for this book, as it has previously approached the phenomena of crypto-laundering and its detection as two separate entities. Here, we can reflect more about the latent space between them. By considering them in combination, one can potentially reduce the complexity of the problem to a new kind of abstraction of the crime and its detection. Crypto-laundering is a crime whereby the criminal conceals the origins of their illegally obtained funds using crypto-asset transactions and technology. Criminals exploit this technology, its pseudonymous nature, and other privacy-enhancing techniques to obfuscate the trail of illicit funds, making it challenging for law enforcement to trace and attribute criminal activities and funds.

Recall that crypto-asset users can have any number of public keys (public addresses) and their activity using one set of public keys is not inherently tied to their activity using another set, nor to their real-world identity, which is not recorded within the blockchain transaction (cf. *United States v. Sterlingov,* 2024, App. 5). STR reporting serves as one of the main tools for detecting instances of crypto-laundering. VASPs and other AML-regulated entities monitor their customer transactions for suspicious activity indicative of criminal behaviour and, where identified, submit STRs to the FIU.

Recognising both as interconnected phenomena and considering the latent space between them offers law enforcement the opportunity to develop more effective strategies for combatting crypto-laundering. By understanding the modus operandi of criminal laundering and the characteristics of suspicious transactions, analysts and investigators can better leverage STR data to identify crypto-laundering, identify money laundering networks, disrupt illicit OCG activity, hold perpetrators accountable, and seize illicit assets for disposal back to the State.

One of the key tools to bridge the gap between these two models and link crime and detection is the commercially available blockchain tools, such as Chainalysis, TRM Labs, Elliptic, and others. The use of blockchain analysis tools is one way proposed by this research for exploring the interaction of the 3D unified crime and detection models. The space in between and commonalities between the two models can be explored and leveraged by law enforcement. It is useful at this junction to examine how these tools operate.

The commercial blockchain analysis tools all work in a similar manner. To begin, the user types in some crypto-information, such as an address, a wallet, a transaction hash, or some other information they are looking to find into a search box. If the information entered is valid, the tool identifies which crypto-asset it pertains to and then returns various insights that *assist* the crypto-investigator in determining whether the activity around that information is suspicious or not.

An indication of the level of suspicious activity pertaining to the information entered is then displayed (e.g. on a scale from high to low). This is based on the interactions, both direct and indirect, between the information entered by the analyst with crypto-information that has been identified by the company as being involved in criminal activity.

Direct interaction means that funds have been sent from the crypto-information entered directly to the suspicious address in the database without any intermediaries in between. An indirect interaction means there are a number of intermediary steps connecting the crypto-information that the investigation is interested in, and the suspicion information contained in the tool's database. As mentioned in the previous chapter, this is proprietary information; each database will be built up from different sources using a combination of techniques,[4] such as web-scraping, OSINT,

---

[4]An explanation of these *heuristics* and the use of a blockchain analytic tool in a criminal prosecution was recently examined in a recent US case (*US v. Sterlingov*, 2024). An outline of this important case is included in App. 5. For several reasons, the Judge concluded that tool was reliable, and that the prosecution had "demonstrated by a preponderance of the evidence that the blockchain analysis generated by Chainalysis Reactor is the product of reliable principles and methods, and the court accordingly denied the defendant's requests to exclude the testimony and evidence based on that analysis".

collecting the IP data connected with each transaction (e.g. Ren and Heinrich 2022), and the clustering of suspicious addresses based on the concept of address dusting previously discussed. Thus, the use of multiple tools in parallel is recommended to get the best possible picture and avoid missing potential analysis opportunities.

One tool (Chainalysis 2024) classifies its suspicion levels as follows:

- Severe—address entered interacts with CSEM, TF, or with an entity that is subject to sanctions or located in a high-risk jurisdiction.
- High—address entered interacts with another address known to be involved in darknet markets, ransomware, and other criminality such as fraud, drug trafficking, and stealing crypto-funds.
- Medium—address entered interacts with a high-risk exchange, a gambling site, a crypto-ATM service, a P2P exchange, a DeFi exchange, or a mixing service.
- Low—address entered has no direct or indirect interaction with illegal activity the firm has previously identified and stored within its database.

The tool will then show other useful material, such as the current balance associated with the information added (perhaps presenting an opportunity to freeze or seize funds if they are in a regulated exchange in a friendly jurisdiction), the total amount transacted, and the last transfer activity, which shows how recently it was used. Some tools will then show a complete breakdown of how much value was transacted with the illicit service identified. After these initial steps, the tools allow the analyst to expand the various transactions of interest and map the complete path or series of transactions that they are interested in (following the money). An example is shown in Fig. 8.4.

In this example, a wallet had previously been identified as belonging to the person behind the infamous Silk Road Dark Web marketplace. This attribution was carried out by a combination of methods, such as OSINT, address dusting, and other blockchain-specific techniques, such as the analysis of change addresses. The accumulated funds in this wallet are the proceeds of criminal conduct; their possession and further dealing are crypto-laundering. Leveraging the open-source nature of the blockchain, one can see the Silk Road wallet transferred a large amount of funds to

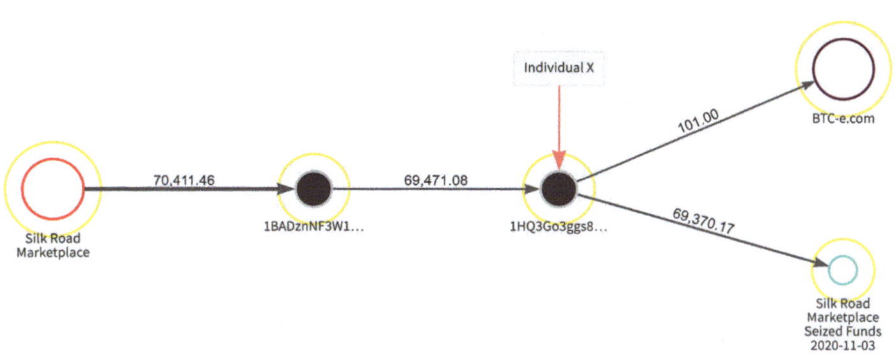

Fig. 8.4 Blockchain analysis diagram. Source: Chainalysis (2020)

the 1BADzn … wallet, which in turn has been sent to Individual X's wallet (1HQ3Go …).

By exploring the blockchain data, one can see that in 2015, individual X converted some funds back to fiat through BTC-e, an untrustworthy cryptocurrency exchange known for criminal behaviour; it was eventually closed by US authorities in 2017 for crypto-laundering. Most of the illicit funds were held by Individual X until recently, when they reached the value of approximately $1 billion. The final node of the diagram illustrates when US authorities recently seized the funds (after a protracted legal process) and transferred them to a government-controlled wallet on 3 November 2020.

This is a perfect example of how visualising crypto laundering and its detection as a unified model and using the appropriate tools to make sense of the commonality between the two models and their complex interconnections, leverages the transparency of the blockchain technology and allows funds to be identified and seized. It also shows how FIU information can be valuable many years after the original crimes have occurred. Unlike regular seizures of criminal assets, of which the author had experience during his time as a bureau officer and head of asset management in Ireland's Criminal Assets Bureau, the forfeiture process is relatively straightforward with crypto-assets. Funds, once identified, are transferred to a government-controlled wallet in the short time it takes for a transaction to take place. At the conclusion of the legal process, the crypto-assets are converted to fiat via a trusted exchange, and the proceeds are remitted to the central exchequer. Concerns and difficulties that arise when dealing with other asset types, such as locating, securing, storing, appointing a receiver, and selling in the open market—which often took months if not years to complete—are greatly simplified with crypto-assets. This is a major benefit for civil society and another example of the double-edged sword of technology discussed in Chap. 1.

The practical contributions of the author's systems theory approach will now be examined. This will reinforce our understanding of the proposed method and communicate the benefits that can be realised.

8.3 Practical Contributions

This section reviews three examples where the author utilised the 3D socio-technical systems model developed by this research to address and understand the phenomenon of crypto-laundering and how it is pursued and addressed. The first concept to be assessed will be how the model was used to improve the content of crypto-STRs submitted to FIU Ireland by VASPs. Next to be evaluated will be an understanding of how the misuse of crypto-laundering cut off one of the main crypto-asset on-ramps in the Irish context. The concluding analysis will look at how the model was used to explore investigative opportunities of activity prior to the committing of a ransomware attack that led to opportunities to identify precursor activity that led to attribution of suspect addresses. Some of these examples are, by necessity, limited in detail to avoid educating future criminals.

8.3.1 *Improving Quality of Crypto-STRs*

One difficulty observed based on the analysis of the 2719 crypto-STRs received by FIU Ireland in 2021 was that very few crypto-STRs contained any crypto-specific information, such as addresses, transaction hashes, wallets, and the like. The crypto-STRs submitted were very much focused on just one customer or one case. While this level of detail is beneficial for the FIU's tactical analysis of an individual person or case, it isn't able to leverage the common elements of both models (crypto-asset technology, customers, suspicion, etc.). This would provide a wider, strategic analysis of STRs to assist FIU Ireland in identifying OCGs that are operating and the ultimate destination of illicit assets. Without the additional crypto-specific information, the FIU was potentially missing opportunities for detecting criminal activity (tactical analysis), network-related information (strategic analysis) by linking STRs, people, and accounts listed in their possession, and leveraging blockchain analytic tools to exploit the recording of all transactions on a public blockchain ledger. The VASPs were effectively treating their suspicious customer and their account in a singular manner and were not providing the necessary information to the FIU to enable them to follow the money and trace the criminal networks. This can be conceptualised as only perceiving one part of the 3D model (the AML side) but not the other (crypto-laundering, the crime).

In June 2022, the author arranged a series of individual workshops with several VASPs and with the FinTech PPP to discuss this issue. The 3D unified model was used as the template for these discussions in order to emphasise the importance of including crypto-specific information in STRs and the mutual benefits thereof. These included fewer follow-up requests by the FIU to the VASP for additional information, which in turn freed up scarce resources on both sides, educated VASPs on the FIU's detection efforts, and allowed the VASPs to demonstrate a greater level of cooperation with the FIU, should they be subject to an AML inspection by their AML supervisor, the Central Bank of Ireland. Fig. 8.5 shows a screenshot of the whiteboard following one of these workshops.

From this picture, it is easy to see that the concepts of treating crime and detection in unison were fully understood. The audience straightforwardly identified commonalities between the two models and then the most important linkages. This workshop also recognised that it was possible to identify how the technology was being misused and what tasks were being carried out by the criminals—using this as the "how" and "what" of a *modus operandi* that would feed into some useful transaction monitoring rules to identify suspicious activity not previously captured. One of the VASP MLROs present in the workshop provided the following feedback anonymously to the author after the workshop:

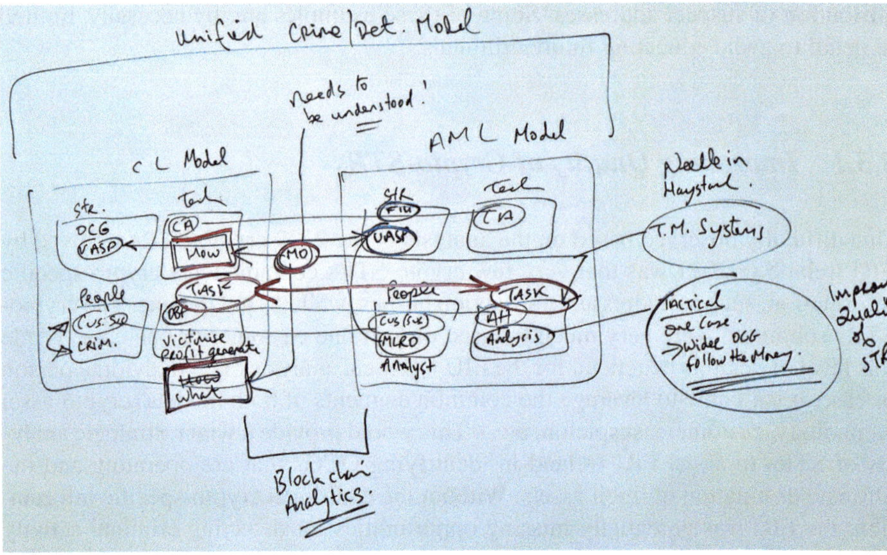

Fig. 8.5 Whiteboard from PPP discussion

> This was a useful exercise to show us how we need to treat the crime and its detection as one. I thought that providing all the relevant information about our customer was sufficient, but I now see that the FIU requires additional information to take their analysis beyond the individual and look at the criminal network behind the criminality. This is information that I have easy access to, and I never thought of including in my STRs.

Another MLRO present stated:

> by explaining why they needed it, using a really easy to understand model, I am more likely to provide the information as I understand why it is being requested and what it is being used for.

R10, an FIU manager, recognised there was some improvement in STR quality following the workshops:

> It was easy to see which MLROs attended the workshops as their STRs became more relevant to our analysis tasks. The inclusion of specific technological information allowed the FIU analyst to take their analysis further to identify linkages and show where assets were dissipated to. Without this information, we either just analysed what we had or had to take valuable time to go back and ask the VASP for the information, which wasn't a good use of our resources.

Using the model as a discussion framework within these workshops allowed a diverse group of people to come together and, using a common and easily understandable language, provided a holistic perspective on the complex issue of crypto-laundering, its pursuit, and detection. It enabled the participants to understand the system as a whole, the interrelationships between its components, and to discuss a complex issue in a sensible manner—the very epitome of the benefits of system theory.

Readers will now consider the second practical contribution of the unified crime/detection systems model. This is an examination of how crypto-ATMs were being exploited by criminals for crypto-laundering and the responses of the FIU and the AML regulator.

8.3.2 *The Exploitation of Crypto-ATMs*

At the beginning of 2023 in Ireland, there were approximately 50 crypto-ATMs in operation. Analysis will first look at how these were being used for crypto-laundering using the crypto-laundering model. Police observed street-level drug dealers (people organised in a hierarchical criminal structure) selling illicit drugs (profit-generating task). The criminal, using a QR code of a crypto public address (technology) and used a crypto-ATM, located oddly enough in the unusual and unexpected location of a local beauty salon, to lodge their daily takings into the machine. The ATM then transferred (task) an equivalent amount of Bitcoin (minus transaction fee) to the public Bitcoin address (technology) under the ownership of the person at the next level up in the organised crime gang (removed from the predicate offence). The funds were then laundered through a series of crypto-addresses, including mixers, where it was eventually re-converted to fiat (task) and spent on luxury goods (task) by those at the higher levels of the OCG. This illustrates how the crypto-laundering model described earlier in this chapter adequately describes this type of criminal activity. Persons interviewed had extensive expertise and numerous examples of this type of criminality. R2, a senior AML investigator, stated that:

> Crypto-ATMs were used to launder the proceeds of street dealing, with street drug dealers going and paying their daily proceeds into the ATM and then passing the profits up the [OCG] food chain.

R3, another crypto-investigator, agreed by stating that crypto-ATMs "make it very easy for people who commit offenses to launder the proceeds of those crimes". R1, a FIU manager, said that crypto-ATMs:

> are a massive challenge—a friction point where fiat can be exchanged for crypto, and vice versa, without stringent AML controls. That is a major money laundering risk.

In this specific instance, there was CCTV and police surveillance that identified the street-level dealers at the lowest level within the OCG. The overarching issue was how to identify the upper echelons of this OCG and ultimately halt the use of this fiat-crypto interface that was being exploited for criminal misuse.

Separately, one must remember that the crypto-ATM (technology) is also included in the detection or FIU model. The crypto-ATM is owned and operated by a VASP (structure), an entity regulated for AML purposes. The MLRO (person) in the VASP should have had controls in place to identify unusual customer behaviour and file a crypto-STR with the FIU if they suspected crypto-laundering was taking place. Of course, given that transactions appeared to be in line with expected usage—indistinguishable from other transactions despite their criminal origin—and the speed/volume of transactions, this was not an easy task to undertake. The technology (the crypto-ATM itself) allowed users to remain anonymous and convert fiat to crypto (task) and transfer it to an unhosted[5] public address (technology). This totally bypassed any AML controls. The criminal was effectively concealing their illicit activity among legitimate transactions. Because of this, there were no crypto-STRs filed by the VASP, but interestingly, there were STRs in FIU Ireland filed by different banks that held accounts belonging to some OCG members and the VASP itself. This is because the VASP could not operate without having a bank account. Due to the volume of reports received by the FIU and its lack of adequate resources (see Chap. 6), all this information was already in the GoAML database, yet it was unconnected! The FIU became aware of the drug-dealing activity when it received a request for assistance from the detectives investigating the case.

By conceptualising this scenario within the 3D model, it was possible to collate the relevant information in the FIU database and envision pathways that were previously obscured. Combined with blockchain analytics, it was possible to construct a chain of transactions from the crypto-ATM to an account held by a senior leader of the OCG. This led to a comprehensive intelligence package being disseminated to a national police unit, which carried out a successful organised crime and money laundering investigation.

The next step was to present the wider, global observations to the AML regulator, the Central Bank of Ireland (feedback). The combined model clearly presented, in an easy-to-understand and jargon-free manner, a criminal pathway that was being exploited for crypto-laundering. As a result of the briefing, the regulators took a considered and nuanced view of the situation. R4, a VASP AML supervisor, summed this up by saying that they too had concerns about the criminal misuse of crypto-ATMs, but:

> have no issue with crypto ATMs as long as they can meet all of their [AML] obligations, however what we have found is that they can't meet all of these obligations, it's just not a viable business model.

The regulator now insists that any crypto-ATM in Ireland must perform complete KYC and CDD of all lodgements and withdrawals, as well as full transaction monitoring of any public addresses used to receive money (this is an indirect implementation of the Travel Rule, see Chap. 2). This type of regulatory intervention and mandate was not congruent with the functioning of crypto-ATMs, and so legitimate VASPs decided not to offer this service, as they were wary of attracting any undue attention from their supervisor. The regulator has not technically banned crypto-ATMs. They have not issued any subsequent authorisations. It is not viable for a

[5] Unhosted wallets allow an additional level of anonymity as they can be independently set up and used without going through a KYC process. It is also possible for a user to have multiple unhosted wallets, which makes attribution a more difficult process—cf. *US v. Sterlingov* (see App. 5).

VASP to offer this type of service. This is due to the newly implemented level of AML controls required and insisted upon by the regulator.

At the time of writing this dissertation, there were no longer crypto-ATMs operating in Ireland. Those operating illegally were seized by the police, and those seeking to operate legally left the market because they could not implement the AML controls required of them. Crypto-ATMs were not banned. Their use, if authorised, will require stringent AML controls, which are not technically feasible or commercially viable to put in place. The synergy of regulators, law enforcement, and legal VASPs collaborating successfully blocked a systemic loophole. This result was made possible due to presenting the information to the Central Bank using our unified model and addressing part of a wicked problem by conceptualising the situation systematically.

The third and final practical contribution of the 3D socio-technical systems model is to capture the phenomenon of ransomware attacks and the subsequent laundering of the proceeds of crime generated. By conceptualising the crime and detection together using the model, new investigative opportunities became apparent to investigators after previously unrelated STRs were linked.

8.3.3 Ransomware Investigation

The use of crypto-assets in ransomware attacks is well known. Crypto-assets are used for several different reasons, both pre- and post-attack. Prior to any attack, they are utilised as a secure method for purchasing anonymous services such as ransomware strains (crime-as-a-service) and other supporting functions, which may include web-hosting, servers, and other required hardware and software. As an example, at the end of 2022, there were estimated to be over 10,000 strains of ransomware available for criminals to purchase using crypto-assets (Santos 2022). Post-attack, crypto-assets are used as the primary vehicle for the transfer of the ransom from the victim to the OCG behind the attack.

In one crypto-STR reviewed in the previous chapter, it was apparent that the OCG had established a help-desk to enable the victim to call and seek assistance in converting their fiat ransom to crypto-assets via a crypto-ATM. The funds are then laundered through the crypto-asset system until they are eventually used by the criminal to commit further criminality, or they are reconverted to fiat to enjoy the fruits of their labour.

R3, a senior crypto and cyber investigator who has recent experience in investigating a massive attack on the Irish health service using a strain of the Conti virus, states:

> the level of anonymity that crypto provides and the ease at which crypto assets can be transferred across borders attracts cybercriminals to their use and causes complications in relation to the progression of these investigations.

Because the ransom is paid in crypto-assets, there is an insertion point for the investigator to trace the funds via the publicly available blockchain and through the use of a commercial blockchain analysis tool. The aim of any crypto-investigation is to track the impugned funds to a regulated VASP and attribute them to a real-world person. The VASP is required by AML legislation to know who their customer is and have details available to provide to law enforcement upon service of the requisite court order. The funds at a VASP also present an opportunity to freeze, seize, and ultimately confiscate the proceeds of criminal conduct. But, what happens if the criminal decides to leave the funds in a wallet and not interact with an exchange to re-convert them to fiat (for example as happened in Fig. 8.4)?

This was the case in a recent investigation where the investigator contacted the FIU for assistance with their investigation. They had ultimately reached an impasse in tracing funds. Using the 3D unified model to graphically illustrate the information available to the investigator and in the FIU databases, it quickly became obvious that there were investigative opportunities available in examining the criminal's behaviour after the ransomware attack.

The assistance of R3 was sought for this investigation. They opined by examining the:

> technical infrastructure behind the attack and the payment methods used, gives an awful lot of leads in relation to our investigations. It will provide us with additional links between investigations. I think, to a certain extent, criminals aren't necessarily as careful in their preparation ... when they purchase servers, software, and stuff like that. There we often find that there's little links present and we try and zoom in on them and take any little bit of evidence and we can try to deanonymize those behind the attack.

By mapping out the process using the 3D combined model, it was possible to develop a pattern of financial activity that occurred pre-crime and search for this in the FIU database.

An account with a VASP was identified that had links to the purchase of Voice Over Internet Protocol (VOIP)[6] disposable phone numbers that were used in the attack. Most of the precursor activities, such as purchasing the software, purchasing servers, and purchasing internet access, are usually paid for in crypto. This effectively gives law enforcement another path to follow in their efforts to attribute the funds and reveal the culprit's identity. This resulted in the development of a comprehensive intelligence package for the detective, who hopes to make arrests soon.

[6] VOIP is a collection of software and hardware that allows telephone use through ICT. A fixed-line telephone number is provided to the user which makes it appear the user is in a particular jurisdiction. Several services on the internet provide anonymous VOIP numbers in exchange for crypto-assets.

Table 8.1 Summary of practical contributions

	Phenomenon	Model application	Outcome
1.	VASP STR quality	3D model used in workshops with VASPs to illustrate commonalities between crime and detection systems; highlighted missing crypto-specific information in submitted STRs.	Improved STR quality from participating VASPs; more crypto-specific details included, reducing FIU follow-ups. Fulfilled the FIU feedback requirement.
2.	Crypto-ATM regulatory intervention	3D model used to present systemic exploitation of crypto-ATMs to regulators; showed friction point risks and structural coupling with FIU detection.	Regulator implemented stringent KYC/CDD for crypto-ATMs; commercial viability dropped, resulting in market exit of ATMs without a formal ban being imposed.
3.	Ransomware precursor detection	3D model mapped ransomware process pre/post attack; identified precursor financial activity linked to VOIP purchases, enabling FIU to link addresses.	FIU identified investigative opportunities pre-attack; the intelligence package led to an active investigation and potential arrests.

8.3.4 Summary of Practical Contributions

Table 8.1 summarises how the socio-technical model developed for this book, translates complex crypto-laundering phenomena into useful and actionable applications; phenomenon → model application → outcome. Using the model allows for key challenges to be linked to its response model-based intervention to achieve an intended policy or operational outcome. The three examples here show how the model can be used in many different AML and other domains.

8.4 Randomness, a New Approach?[7]

Traditional AML approaches rely on triggers such as STRs, crime reports from victims, or investigations into predicate offences (see information deficit discussion in Chap. 2 and Fig. 2.4). However, financial intelligence about crypto-asset transactions is available (for the most part) on an open-source, public ledger. This gives investigators another avenue for money laundering and crypto-laundering investigations using randomness—a provocative investigative technique?

Take, for example Block 855,497 on the core Bitcoin blockchain, randomly selected by the author after using a free blockchain viewing website. This block was mined on 5 August 2024. It contained 6687 individual transactions to a total value of 2222.6156 BTC (at the time of writing, worth just under €225 million). From this

[7] This section is a summary of presentations made by the author to the 41st Cambridge International Symposium on Economic Crime (1–7 September 2024) and the 24th Annual Security Conference, Las Vegas (29–30 April 2025).

block, a single transition was selected, again at random, showing a simple transaction from one user to another, with the change returning to the sender in the normal manner. This wallet was manually mapped, backward and forward, several transactions or "hops" (Fig. 8.6).

This transaction map reveals the transaction data without any context. Each wallet address was entered into a commercial blockchain analytic tool to indicate the nature of these transactions. It should be noted that no attribution was/is possible at this stage. This would involve serving a court order in the VASP to obtain the KYC data they maintain for their customer, if and only if they are in a friendly jurisdiction that will respond. Based on the analysis, the wallet identified was linked to the purchase of child sexual abuse material (CSAM), some of which originated from a darknet marketplace. Based on this, the author notified the relevant FIU of his findings, perhaps identifying a person and criminal activity that would never have been identified.

This experiment demonstrates that it may be possible for FIUs and law enforcement to use random sampling of blockchain data to complement their traditional AML approach. To be clear, this is not being proposed as a substitute for the socio-technical models developed in this book, but to complement traditional methods and identify low-volume, low-value wallets that might otherwise escape AML thresholds and reporting. It is accepted that systematic randomness would be resource-intensive at a time of limited resources, and this experiment could have just been a lucky choice.

The idea presented here may be suitable for future research and development into a supplementary approach for financial intelligence analysis.

8.5 General Applicability and Limitations

This book has made four theoretical contributions. While these contributions were made in the specific context of regulating crypto-assets for the purposes of anti-money laundering, they have a wider and more generalised applicability.

The first contribution was a 2D socio-technical systems framework that combined the research of Katz and Kahn (1966) and Bostrom and Heinen (1977a, b). This allowed any complex phenomenon or organisation to be conceptualised for the first time on a macro- and a micro-level simultaneously. On the macro-level, it allows the organisation or phenomenon to be conceptualised, modelled, diagrammed, and viewed as an open system with inputs, transformations, outputs, feedback, and environmental interactions. On the micro-level, it models the system in a manner that shows the interaction between the equally important social and technical elements within a system. It implies that these subsystems are interdependent and must be considered holistically to understand the entire system behaviour. The focus of this arrangement is therefore to align the social and technical components to achieve optimal system performance. This combined model has general applicability to any research domain and can be used to describe any complex

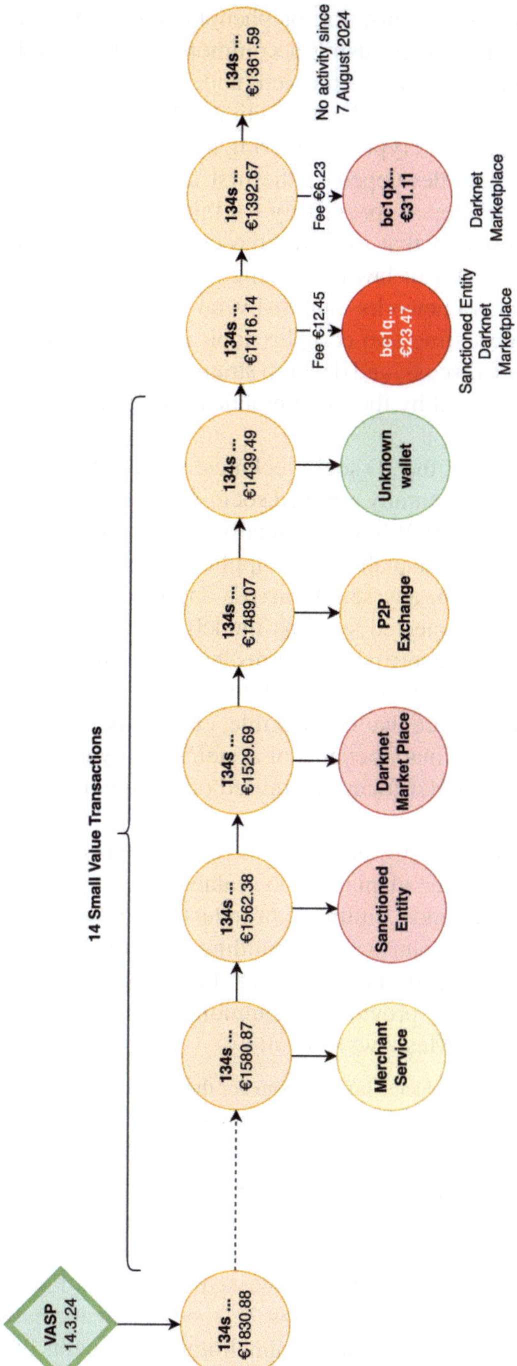

Fig. 8.6 Transaction map of a randomly selected crypto-wallet

organisation or phenomenon. Its usage empowers users to make sense of complex scenarios, understand the organisation or phenomenon being studied, discuss the issue with relevant stakeholders using a common language, and devise effective strategies for addressing the wicked problem under consideration.

The second and third theoretical contributions of this research developed socio-technical systems models of crypto-laundering and its pursuit and detection by the FIU, using the 2D model developed as the first contribution. While these models were conceived and developed specifically for this research, they could be used or adapted in similar research that explores the crime of crypto-laundering and its detection by a public sector or law enforcement body. The fundamental principles underlying these two frameworks can easily be adapted to other criminological fields of study. By presenting two complex topics in a diagrammatic fashion, it is possible to understand, discuss, and develop strategies with a wide multidisciplinary audience, as was evidenced by the three practical instances where the author used the model.

The fourth contribution, the 3D socio-technical systems model, was developed to illustrate two specific, structurally coupled socio-technical models (namely, crypto-laundering and its detection). While specifically developed for this research, its fundamental principles are adaptable and applicable across many domains and scenarios. It can be used in any setting across any research domain that could be conceptualised as interconnected systems models. The model is versatile and, in combination with the first contribution, forms the framework that can be tailored to and implemented in diverse contexts to address a wide variety of challenges. The benefits of the framework are that it is flexible, easy to use, and easy to describe. It exploits all the interdisciplinary benefits of systems theory and socio-technical systems theory when a particular focus is required on the mutual interaction of people and technology (see Chap. 1).

The theoretical contributions made by this research transcend their original purposes (this research) to offer adaptable and scalable frameworks that are applicable across diverse challenges and a multitude of industries and disciplines. It is respectfully submitted that these contributions, building upon the vast benefits of systems theory, are additional "tools of understanding" (cf. Geoffrey Vickers) in the arsenal of the systems thinker that provide "a common language across methods, disciplines, and contexts" (cf. Meadows) and allow

> human intervention to help change interventions for the better and navigate the interrelated dimensions of making more effective strategic decisions in the twenty-first century (Reynolds and Holwell 2020: ix).

As discussed at various points throughout this chapter, the proposed socio-technical systems frameworks, while theoretically robust, may have some potential limitations that need to be acknowledged. These are additional considerations over the limitations of systems theory itself, as discussed in Chap. 3. Firstly, the number of connections in the models, particularly the 3D model, may increase the complexity of the problem under discussion and may ameliorate the benefits of taking a systems theory approach. This is in addition to the intricate nature of (socio-technical) systems theory itself, which could make the models inaccessible or cumbersome for people lacking familiarity or specialised knowledge of systems theory. This would mean that their usage is dependent on extensive guidance and training in their use. Secondly, while these models claim an assumption of general applicability, certain context-specific nuances and intricacies across diverse domains, industries, and disciplines may not be adequately captured. This may compromise the effectiveness of using the proposed models in different scenarios from which they were developed. The third limitation pertains to the claimed assumption that the social and technical subsystems are of equal importance. Depending on the research context, there may be deviations and variability in the significance of each sub-system and its interactions. This could potentially undermine the utility of the frameworks in certain contexts. Fourthly, there is a need for additional empirical validation of these frameworks to further demonstrate their practical utility in real-world situations. This is a suggested avenue for future research, along with the need to capture emergent behaviour and unforeseen consequences of interventions when mapping a phenomenon or organisation using the frameworks. Fifthly, as with all systems theory applications, the frameworks are contingent upon the users' interpretations, biases, background, etc. (observer dependent). This could mean that there is potential for (inadvertent) misinterpretation or misuse of the framework.

This book aimed to understand crypto-laundering and how crypto-assets are regulated for the purposes of AML using a socio-technical systems view of FIU Ireland. It strived to develop a socio-technical model of the crypto-laundering phenomenon and of how it is pursued and detected. It then sought to discuss and understand how these two models interacted with each other and with their shared, complex environment. It is the author's contention that this research has achieved these goals and raised some important points along the journey. They will be discussed in the next and final chapter.

References

Angell I, Demetis D (2005) Systems thinking about anti-money laundering: considering the Greek case. J Money Laundering Control 8:271–284

Angell I, Demetis D (2010) Science's first mistake: delusions in pursuit of theory. Bloomsbury Academic, London

Bostrom RP, Heinen JS (1977a) MIS problems and failures: a socio-technical perspective. Part I: the causes. MIS Q 1:17–32

Bostrom RP, Heinen JS (1977b) MIS problems and failures: a socio-technical perspective, part II: the application of socio-technical theory. MIS Q 1:11–28

Chainalysis (2020) Chainalysis in action: US Government Agencies seize more than $1 billion in cryptocurrency connected to Infamous Darknet Market Silk Road [WWW Document]. Chainalysis. https://www.chainalysis.com/blog/silk-road-doj-seizure-november-2020/. Accessed 21 Aug 2025

Chainalysis (2024) Using field investigation [WWW Document]. https://support.chainalysis.com/hc/en-us/articles/14942573265428. Accessed 21 Aug 2025

Emery F (1980) Designing socio-technical systems for "greenfield" sites. J Occup Behav:19–27

Fletcher A (2001) The art of looking sideways. Phaidon, London; New York

Emery F (2016) Characteristics of socio-technical systems. In: The social engagement of social science, a Tavistock anthology, vol 2. University of Pennsylvania Press, pp 157–186

Genosko G (ed) (2005) Marshall McLuhan: critical evaluations in cultural theory. Routledge, London; New York

Jackson MC (2019) Critical systems thinking and the management of complexity: responsible leadership for a complex world. Wiley Blackwell, Hoboken

Katz D, Kahn RL (1966) The social psychology of organisations. Wiley

Luhmann N (2013) Introduction to systems theory. Polity, Cambridge

Maturana HR, Varela FJ (1991) Autopoiesis and cognition: the realization of the living. Springer Science & Business Media

Meadows DH (2009) Thinking in systems: a primer. Earthscan, London

Midgley G (2000) Systemic intervention: philosophy, methodology, and practice, Contemporary systems thinking. Kluwer Academic/Plenum, New York

Mumford E (2003) Redesigning human systems. IGI Global

Mumford E (2006) The story of socio-technical design: reflections on its successes, failures and potential. Inf Syst J 16:317–342

Pasmore W, Francis C, Haldeman J, Shani A (1982) Sociotechnical systems: a North American reflection on empirical studies of the seventies. Hum Relat 35:1179–1204

Ren & Heinrich (2022) MetaMask stores user IPs and wallet addresses. Do this to avoid getting tracked. Coinmonks. https://medium.com/coinmonks/metamask-stores-user-ips-and-wallet-addresses-do-this-to-avoid-getting-tracked-231d5265a0a5. Accessed 21 Aug 2025

Reynolds M, Holwell S (eds) (2020) Systems Approaches to Making Change: A Practical Guide, 2nd edn. Springer

Ropohl G (1999) Philosophy of socio-technical systems. Soc Philos Technol Q Electron J 4:186–194

Santos DJP dos (2022) Key findings from the 1H 2022 FortiGuard Labs Threat Report | FortiGuard Labs [WWW Document]. Fortinet Blog. https://www.fortinet.com/blog/threat-research/fortiguard-labs-threat-report-key-findings. Accessed 21 Aug 2025

Trist EL, Bamforth KW (1951) Some social and psychological consequences of the longwall method of coal-getting: an examination of the psychological situation and defences of a work group in relation to the social structure and technological content of the work system. Hum Relat 4:3–38

Von Bertalanffy L (1950) The theory of open systems in physics and biology. Science 111:23–29

Whitelaw F, Riley J, Elmrabit N (2024) A review of the insider threat, a practitioner perspective within the U.K. financial services. IEEE Access 12:34752–34768

Chapter 9
Conclusion and Future Directions

9.1 Introduction

This book began as a journey to understand the complex and adaptive phenomenon of crypto-laundering and how crypto-assets are regulated for the purpose of anti-money laundering. It investigated the use of socio-technical systems theory to understand the crime and improve its detection, with a particular focus on FIU Ireland. To achieve its aim, it developed suitable frameworks to understand the interaction between each system and its shared complex environment.

The research sought to answer the following questions:

- Can the existing AML system adapt to appropriately deal with crypto-laundering?
- Are all forms of crypto-crime covered by the rules introduced?
- Is FIU Ireland equipped, structurally and operationally, to meet the challenge of crypto-laundering?
- How can socio-technical systems models help analyse and improve the response to crypto-laundering?

The book utilised a longitudinal, interpretative case study, sensitised by socio-technical systems theory and supported by exclusive access to 2719 crypto-related STRs, interviews, focus groups, observations, and document analysis, to develop integrated models of crypto-laundering and its pursuit and detection by the FIU with a particular focus on financial intelligence.

S. Meighan, *Money Laundering and Crypto-Assets*, Contributions to Finance and Accounting, https://doi.org/10.1007/978-3-032-13481-3_9

9.2 Summary of Key Findings

Foundationally, the first five chapters found that understanding and addressing crypto-laundering is a wicked problem. Its complexity is driven by the adaptive and cross-border nature of the underlying crypto-asset technology. The traditional AML regulatory system struggles to maintain its relevance when disruptive technologies, such as crypto-assets, are introduced. Necessary adaptations to the AML system tend to lag behind criminal innovation. This cycle of criminality tends to repeat, with civil society always chasing evolving criminality and technology misuse. To understand and analyse wicked problems, the lens of socio-technical systems theory offers a way of understanding open, adaptive entities in complex environments.

Chapters 6 and 7 explored the case study of FIU Ireland and its analysis of the 2719 crypto-related STRs received in 2021, the year crypto-AML regulation was first introduced in Ireland. It found that FIU Ireland operates as a socio-technical system. However, it is resource-constrained, dependent on outside assistance that potentially affects its autonomy, and is strained by rising STR volumes and the additional demands introduced by crypto-laundering and its regulation. Of the 2719 crypto-STRs received, 38.5% were archived, 46.8% were disseminated (mostly to EU FIUs), and 8.7% were sent to Irish investigators. This demonstrates the cross-jurisdictional complexity of regulating crypto-assets. It found that VASP-submitted STRs were generally more technically detailed compared with non-VASP reports; however, all entities tend to submit defensive or junk STRs often missing crucial information. These create analysis delays, at the risk of losing investigative and asset recovery opportunities. It also limits the feedback that is provided, accepting that generalised feedback to public–private partnerships and groups is well received and has an impact on STR quality.

Chapter 8 introduced dual socio-technical systems models of the crypto-laundering (criminal perspective) and the FIU detection (civil/regulatory perspective) systems. The models are useful on their own; however, when combined into a 3D model to show structural coupling, overlapping components (VASPs, technology, and regulation), and mutual adaptation, they highlight opportunities to be leveraged. The book used three scenarios to demonstrate the practical usefulness of the model: VASP STR improvement, crypto-ATM closure, and ransomware precursor detection.

9.3 Theoretical Contributions

The book makes four original contributions.

The first is a 2D socio-technical systems framework, combining the work of Katz and Khan (1966) and Bostrom and Heinen (1977a, b), to visualise complex organisations or phenomena simultaneously at their macro-level (open systems) and micro-level (social/technical subsystems). Using this 2D model, the book presents a crypto-laundering and an FIU model as the second and third contributions. One conceptualises laundering, and the other conceptualises its pursuit and detection as socio-technical systems. The final contribution, the 3D combined model, visualises structural coupling between the crime and detection systems in a shared environment, offering a transferable tool for use in understanding and addressing other wicked problems.

9.4 Practical and Policy Implications

The findings of the book present a number of practical and policy implications for several groups.

Firstly, FIUs. There is a need to create dedicated crypto-analysis units to manage the volume and complexity of crypto-related STRs. These units should be properly trained and provided with the appropriate tools to complete their assigned role. If each FIU develops such a unit, there is an opportunity to create a European or global network of crypto-analysts. FIUs need to have the appropriate level of autonomy and resources to address structural bottlenecks. The quality of STRs, especially those that are crypto-related, can be improved through targeted feedback loops and public–private partnerships with industry, academia, and commercial blockchain analysis companies.

Secondly, regulators. There needs to be a continued focus on friction points between the real/fiat and crypto worlds. Fiat–crypto interfaces are an appropriate place to target AML interventions; however, notice should also be taken of emerging methods of avoiding these, such as through unhosted wallets or privacy-enhanced coins. There needs to be a mechanism developed to harmonise cross-border STRs in order to reduce 'mailbox' inefficiencies. The work of the EU's AMLA over the coming years will be interesting to observe in this regard.

Finally, for the wider AML system. Socio-technical modelling, as a diagnostic and training tool, can be adopted for identifying vulnerabilities, monitoring evolving criminal misuse of the technology, and improving overall systemic design. Academia, analytic tool providers, and the blockchain industry should form part of a strengthened strategic collaboration as efforts continue to make the system more effective.

9.5 Limitations

A number of factors naturally limit the research in this book. Its scope is limited to a single jurisdiction, Ireland, as the basis of the case study. However, the findings are applicable to any FATF-aligned jurisdiction, the majority of nations in the world. There is a focus on 2021 data. This timeframe was relevant as it represented the period immediately before and after the introduction of crypto-related AML regulation. It is accepted that the crypto-market and its regulation are rapidly evolving, and new methods of crypto-laundering and avoiding AML controls emerge rapidly. Given the author's background, the perspective taken in this study is naturally from an FIU viewpoint. The limited insight into the private sector, prosecutorial, and supervisory viewpoints is acknowledged. Finally, the 3D model presented is complex, naturally when describing a complex phenomenon. Training is required prior to its utilisation in other problem domains, lest the lack of guided application cause a risk of over-complexity or over-simplification, both of which defeat the purpose of the model.

9.6 Future Research Directions

Throughout the research, a number of future research directions were identified and are summarised here.

1. *Comparative analysis of FIUs*: Applying the book's models to FIUs in other jurisdictions, for comparing and contrasting different jurisdictions using the model as a common framework.
2. *Longitudinal crypto-analysis*: Explore the effect of regulation over time by extending the analysis beyond the dataset of this book.
3. *Effect of privacy coins and emerging technology on AML*: Investigate the blindness of the AML system to privacy-enhanced coins (PECs), particularly relevant with the de facto EU ban on them, which is due to take effect in 2027.
4. *Full STR lifecycle evaluation*: Track STRs as they move through the entirety of the AML system, to determine system cost and effectiveness.
5. *Randomness detection in AML blockchain analysis*: Explore randomised transaction monitoring of blockchain data to overcome criminal strategies and identify transactions that would not be reported otherwise.

9.7 Closing Reflection

Money laundering is not a static problem. It continuously evolves with technology and adapts to regulation. Socio-technical systems theory provides a way to conceptualise the problem and response, not as isolated mechanisms but as structurally coupled systems in a shared environment. Financial intelligence is the golden thread that runs between both models. Crypto-assets present a unique opportunity: their data is immediately available for analysis.

The models developed in this book, along with an understanding of the vital role financial intelligence plays in AML, offer a toolkit for researchers, regulators, and practitioners. They provide a common language and visual framework to understand and respond to crypto-laundering. Unfortunately, this wicked problem has no final resolution. Instead, there needs to be a commitment to understand and respond to the continuous criminal adaptation. With the right tools and knowledge, these responses can be strategic, timely, and effective. This is a never-ending cycle, but one that is worth doing, provided the correct investment of time, money, and highly skilled, motivated people working together.

Ní neart go cur le chéile (A traditional Irish saying translated as 'There is no strength without unity').

References

Bostrom RP, Heinen JS (1977a) MIS problems and failures: a socio-technical perspective. Part I: the causes. MIS Q 1:17–32

Bostrom RP, Heinen JS (1977b) MIS problems and failures: a socio-technical perspective. Part II: the application of socio-technical theory. MIS Q 1:11–28

Katz D, Kahn RL (1966) The social psychology of organisations. Wiley

Appendices

Appendix 1: Financial Intelligence Units (FIUs)—FATF Recommendation 29[1]

1. Countries should establish an FIU with responsibility for acting as a national centre for receipt and analysis of suspicious transaction reports and other information relevant to money laundering, associated predicate offences, and terrorist financing, and for the dissemination of the results of that analysis.[2]
2. The FIU should serve as the central agency for the receipt of disclosures filed by reporting entities, including:
   (a) Suspicious transaction reports filed by reporting entities as required by Recommendations 20 and 23
   (b) Any other information as required by national legislation (such as cash transaction reports, wire transfers declarations/disclosures)
3. The FIU should:[3]
   (a) In addition to the information that entities report to the FIU, be able to obtain and use additional information from reporting entities, as needed to perform its analysis properly

---

[1] Financial Action Task Force (2012) International Standards on Combating Money Laundering and the Financing of Terrorism & Proliferation: The FATF Recommendations (Revised June 2025). FATF-GAFI, Paris.

[2] Considering that there are different FIU models, R.29 does not prejudge a country's choice for a particular model and applies equally to all of them.

[3] In the context of its analysis function, an FIU should be able to obtain from any reporting entity additional information relating to a suspicion of ML/TF. This does not include indiscriminate requests for information to reporting entities in the context of the FIU's analysis (e.g. "fishing expeditions").

S. Meighan, *Money Laundering and Crypto-Assets*, Contributions to Finance and Accounting, https://doi.org/10.1007/978-3-032-13481-3

(b) Have access to the widest possible range[4] of financial, administrative, and law enforcement information that it requires to properly undertake its functions

4. The FIU should conduct:

(a) Operational analysis, which uses available and obtainable information to identify specific targets, to follow the trail of particular activities or transactions, and to determine links between those targets and possible proceeds of crime, money laundering, predicate offences, and terrorist financing.
(b) Strategic analysis, which uses available and obtainable information, including data that may be provided by other competent authorities, to identify money laundering and terrorist financing-related trends and patterns.

5. The FIU should be able to disseminate, spontaneously and upon request, information and the results of its analysis to relevant competent authorities, and should use dedicated, secure, and protected channels for the dissemination.
6. The FIU should protect information by:

(a) Having rules in place governing the security and confidentiality of information, including procedures for handling, storage, dissemination, and protection of, and access to, information.
(b) Ensuring that FIU staff members have the necessary security clearance levels and understanding of their responsibilities in handling and disseminating sensitive and confidential information.
(c) Ensuring that there is limited access to its facilities and information, including information technology systems.

7. The FIU should be operationally independent and autonomous, by:

(a) Having the authority and capacity to carry out its functions freely, including the autonomous decision to analyse, request, and/or forward or disseminate specific information.
(b) Being able to make arrangements or engage independently with other domestic competent authorities or foreign counterparts on the exchange of information.
(c) Having distinct core functions from those of the other authority when it is located within the existing structure of another authority.
(d) Being able to obtain and deploy the resources needed to carry out its functions, on an individual or routine basis, free from any undue political, government, or industry influence or interference, which might compromise its operational independence.

[4] This should include information from open or public sources, as well as relevant information collected and/or maintained by, or on behalf of, other authorities and, where appropriate commercially held data.

8. Where a country has created an FIU and is not an Egmont Group member, the FIU should apply for membership in the Egmont Group. The FIU should submit an unconditional application for membership to the Egmont Group and fully engage itself in the application process.

Appendix 2: Financial Intelligence Units (FIUs)—Chapter III EU 6AMLD[5]

CHAPTER III

FIUS

Article 19

Establishment of the FIU

1. Each Member State shall establish an FIU in order to prevent, detect and effectively combat money laundering and terrorist financing.
2. The FIU shall be the single central national unit responsible for receiving and analysing reports submitted by obliged entities in accordance with Article 69 of Regulation (EU) 2024/1624, reports submitted by obliged entities in accordance with Article 74 and Article 80(4), second subparagraph, of that Regulation, and any other information relevant to money laundering, its predicate offences, or terrorist financing, including information transmitted by customs authorities pursuant to Article 9 of Regulation (EU) 2018/1672, as well as information submitted by supervisory authorities or by other authorities.
3. The FIU shall be responsible for disseminating the results of its analyses and any additional information to relevant competent authorities where there are grounds to suspect money laundering, its predicate offences, or terrorist financing. It shall be able to obtain additional information from obliged entities.

   The FIU's financial analysis function shall consist of the following:

   (a) An operational analysis which focuses on individual cases and specific targets or on appropriately selected information, prioritised on the basis of risk, the type and volume of the disclosures received, and the expected use of the information after dissemination.
   (b) A strategic analysis addressing money laundering and terrorist financing trends, patterns, and evolutions thereof.

4. Each FIU shall be operationally independent and autonomous, which means that it shall have the authority and capacity to carry out its functions freely, including the ability to take autonomous decisions to analyse, request, and, in

[5] Directive (EU) 2024/1640 of the European Parliament and of the Council of 31 May 2024 on the mechanisms to be put in place by Member States for the prevention of the use of the financial system for the purposes of money laundering or terrorist financing, amending Directive (EU) 2019/1937, and amending and repealing Directive (EU) 2015/849.

accordance with paragraph 3, disseminate specific information. It shall be free from any undue political, government, or industry influence or interference.

When an FIU is located within the existing structure of another authority, the FIU's core functions shall be independent and operationally separated from the other functions of the host authority.

5. Member States shall provide their FIUs with adequate financial, human, and technical resources in order to fulfil their tasks. FIUs shall be able to obtain and deploy the resources needed to carry out their functions.
6. Member States shall ensure that the staff of their FIUs are bound by professional secrecy requirements equivalent to those laid down in Article 67, and that they maintain high professional standards, including high standards of data protection, are of high integrity, and are appropriately skilled in relation to the ethical handling of big data sets. Member States shall ensure that FIUs have in place procedures to prevent and manage conflicts of interest.
7. Member States shall ensure that FIUs have rules in place governing the security and confidentiality of information.
8. Member States shall ensure that FIUs have in place secure and protected channels for communicating and exchanging information by electronic means with competent authorities and obliged entities.
9. Member States shall ensure that FIUs are able to make arrangements with other domestic competent authorities pursuant to Article 46 on the exchange of information.
10. By 10 July 2028, AMLA shall issue guidelines addressed to FIUs on:

    (a) The measures to be put in place to preserve the operational autonomy and independence of the FIU, including measures to prevent conflicts of interest affecting its operational autonomy and independence
    (b) The nature, features, and objectives of operational and strategic analysis
    (c) Tools and methods for the use and cross-check of financial, administrative, and law enforcement information to which FIUs have access
    (d) Practices and procedures for the exercise of the suspension or withholding of consent to a transaction, and for the suspension or monitoring of an account or business relationship pursuant to Articles 24 and 25

Article 20
Fundamental Rights Officer

1. Member States shall ensure that FIUs designate a Fundamental Rights Officer. The Fundamental Rights Officer may be a member of the existing staff of the FIU.
2. The Fundamental Rights Officer shall perform the following tasks:

    (a) Advise the staff of the FIU on any activity carried out by the FIU where the Fundamental Rights Officer deems it necessary, or where requested by the staff, without impeding or delaying those activities.
    (b) Promote and monitor the FIU's compliance with fundamental rights.

(c) Provide non-binding opinions on the compliance of the FIU's activities with fundamental rights.
(d) Inform the head of the FIU about possible violations of fundamental rights in the course of the FIU's activities.

3. The FIU shall ensure that the Fundamental Rights Officer does not receive any instructions regarding the exercise of the Fundamental Rights Officer's tasks.

Article 21
Access to Information

1. Member States shall ensure that FIUs, regardless of their organisational status, have access to the information that they require to fulfil their tasks, including financial, administrative, and law enforcement information. Member States shall ensure that FIUs have at least:

(a) Immediate and direct access to the following financial information:

(i) Information contained in the national centralised automated mechanisms in accordance with Article 16
(ii) Information from obliged entities, including information on transfers of funds as defined in Article 3, point (9), of Regulation (EU) 2023/1113 and transfers of crypto-assets as defined in Article 3, point (10), of that Regulation
(iii) Information on mortgages and loans
(iv) Information contained in the national currency and currency exchange databases
(v) Information on securities

(b) Immediate and direct access to the following administrative information:

(i) Fiscal data, including data held by tax and revenue authorities as well as data obtained pursuant to Article 8(3a) of Council Directive 2011/16/EU
(ii) Information on public procurement procedures for goods or services, or concessions
(iii) Information from BARIS as referred to in Article 16, as well as from national real estate registers or electronic data retrieval systems and land and cadastral registers
(iv) Information contained in national citizenship and population registers of natural persons
(v) Information contained in national passports and visa registers
(vi) Information contained in cross-border travel databases
(vii) Information contained in commercial databases, including business and company registers and databases of politically exposed persons
(viii) Information contained in national motor vehicles, aircraft, and watercraft registers
(ix) Information contained in national social security registers

(x) Customs data, including cross-border physical transfers of cash
(xi) Information contained in national weapons and arms registers
(xii) Information contained in national beneficial ownership registers
(xiii) Data available through the interconnection of central registers in accordance with Article 10(19)
(xiv) Information contained in registers of non-profit organisations
(xv) Information held by national financial supervisors and regulators, in accordance with Article 61 and Article 67(2)
(xvi) Databases storing data on CO_2 emission trading established pursuant to Commission Regulation (EU) No 389/2013
(xvii) Information on annual financial statements by companies
(xviii) National migration and immigration registers
(xix) Information held by commercial courts
(xx) Information held in insolvency databases and by insolvency practitioners
(xxi) Information on funds and other assets frozen or immobilised pursuant to targeted financial sanctions

(c) Direct or indirect access to the following law enforcement information:

(i) Any type of information or data which is already held by competent authorities in the context of preventing, detecting, investigating, or prosecuting criminal offences
(ii) Any type of information or data which is held by public authorities or by private entities in the context of preventing, detecting, investigating, or prosecuting criminal offences and which is available to competent authorities without the taking of coercive measures under national law

The information referred to in point (c) of the first subparagraph shall include criminal records, information on investigations, information on the freezing or seizure of assets, or on other investigative or provisional measures, and information on convictions and on confiscations.

Member States may allow the restriction of access to the law enforcement information referred to in point (c) of the first subparagraph on a case-by-case basis, where the provision of such information is likely to jeopardise an ongoing investigation.

2. Access to the information listed in paragraph 1 shall be considered direct and immediate where the information is contained in an IT database, register, or data retrieval system from which the FIU can retrieve the information without any intermediate steps, or where the following conditions are met:

(a) The entities or authorities holding the information provide it expeditiously to FIUs
(b) No entity, authority, or third party is able to interfere with the requested data or the information to be provided.

3. Member States shall ensure that, whenever possible, the FIU is granted direct access to the information listed in paragraph 1, first subparagraph, point (c). In cases where the FIU is provided with indirect access to information, the entity or authority holding the requested information shall provide it in a timely manner.
4. In the context of its functions, each FIU shall be able to request, obtain, and use information from any obliged entity to perform its functions pursuant to Article 19(3) of this Directive, even if no prior report is filed pursuant to Article 69(1), the first subparagraph, point (a), or Article 70(1), of Regulation (EU) 2024/1624. Obliged entities shall not be obliged to comply with requests for information made pursuant to this paragraph when they concern information obtained in the situations referred to in Article 70(2) of that Regulation.

Article 22
Responses to Requests for Information

1. Member States shall ensure that FIUs are able to respond in a timely manner to reasoned requests for information justified by concerns relating to money laundering, its predicate offences or terrorist financing by the competent authorities referred to in Article 2(1), points (44)(c) and (d), of Regulation (EU) 2024/1624 in their respective Member State where that information is already held by the FIU and is necessary on a case-by-case basis. The decision on conducting the dissemination of information shall remain with the FIU.

   Where there are objective grounds for assuming that the provision of such information would have a negative impact on ongoing investigations or analyses, or, in exceptional circumstances, where disclosure of the information would be clearly disproportionate to the legitimate interests of a natural or legal person or irrelevant with regard to the purposes for which it has been requested, the FIU shall not be obliged to comply with the request for information.

   In such cases, the FIU shall provide the reasons in writing to the requesting authority.
2. Competent authorities shall provide feedback to the FIU about the use made of, and the usefulness of, the information provided in accordance with this Article and Article 19(3), and about the outcome of actions taken and of investigations performed on the basis of that information. Such feedback shall be provided as soon as possible and, in any case, in an aggregated form, at least on an annual basis, in such a way as to allow the FIU to improve its operational analysis function.

Article 23
Provision of Information to Supervisors

1. Member States shall ensure that FIUs provide supervisors, spontaneously or upon request, information that may be relevant for the purposes of supervision pursuant to Chap. IV, including at least information on:

   (a) The quality and quantity of suspicious transaction reports submitted by obliged entities.

(b) The quality and timeliness of responses provided by obliged entities to FIU requests pursuant to Article 69(1), the first subparagraph, point (b), of Regulation (EU) 2024/1624.
(c) Relevant results of strategic analyses carried out pursuant to Article 19(3), point (b), of this Directive, as well as any relevant information on money laundering, its predicate offences, and terrorist financing trends and methods, including geographical, cross-border, and emerging risks.

2. Member States shall ensure that FIUs notify supervisors whenever information in their possession indicates potential breaches by obliged entities of Regulations (EU) 2024/1624 and (EU) 2023/1113.
3. Except where strictly necessary for the purposes of paragraph 2, Member States shall ensure that information provided by FIUs pursuant to this Article does not contain any information on specific natural or legal persons nor cases including natural or legal persons subject to an ongoing analysis or investigation or which may lead to the identification of natural or legal persons.

Article 24
Suspension or Withholding of Consent

1. Member States shall ensure that FIUs are empowered to take urgent action, directly or indirectly, where there is a suspicion that a transaction is related to money laundering or terrorist financing, to suspend or withhold consent to that transaction.

   Member States shall ensure that, where the need to suspend or withhold consent to a transaction is established on the basis of a suspicion reported pursuant to Article 69 of Regulation (EU) 2024/1624, the suspension or withholding of consent is imposed on the obliged entity within the period referred to in Article 71 of that Regulation. Where the need to suspend a transaction is based on the analytical work of the FIU, regardless of whether a prior report has been filed by the obliged entity, the suspension shall be imposed as soon as possible by the FIU.

   The suspension or withholding of consent to a transaction shall be imposed by the FIU in order to preserve the funds, to perform its analyses, including the analysis of the transaction, to assess whether the suspicion is confirmed, and, if so, to disseminate the results of the analyses to the relevant competent authorities to allow for the adoption of appropriate measures.

   Member States shall lay down the period for the suspension or withholding of consent applicable to the FIUs' analytical work, which shall not exceed 10 working days. Member States may lay down a longer period where, pursuant to national law, FIUs perform the function of tracing, seizing, freezing, or confiscating criminal assets. Where a longer period of suspension or withholding of consent is laid down, Member States shall ensure that FIUs exercise their function subject to appropriate national safeguards, such as the possibility for the person whose transaction has been suspended to challenge that suspension before a court.

Member States shall ensure that FIUs are empowered to lift the suspension or withholding of consent at any time where they conclude that the suspension or withholding of consent is no longer necessary to fulfil the objectives set out in the third subparagraph.

Member States shall ensure that FIUs are empowered to suspend or withhold consent as referred to in this paragraph at the request of an FIU from another Member State.

2. Where there is a suspicion that a bank account or payment account, a crypto-asset account, or a business relationship is related to money laundering or terrorist financing, Member States shall ensure that the FIU is empowered to take urgent action, directly or indirectly, to suspend the use of that account or to suspend the business relationship in order to preserve the funds, to perform its analyses, to assess whether the suspicion is confirmed, and, if so, to disseminate the results of the analyses to the relevant competent authorities to allow for the adoption of appropriate measures.

   Member States shall lay down the period of suspension applicable for the FIUs' analytical work, which shall not exceed 5 working days. Member States may lay down a longer period where, pursuant to national law, FIUs perform the function of tracing, seizing, freezing, or confiscating criminal assets. Where a longer period of suspension is laid down, Member States shall ensure that FIUs exercise their function subject to appropriate national safeguards, such as the possibility for the person whose bank account or payment account, crypto-asset account, or business relationship is suspended to challenge that suspension before a court.

   Member States shall ensure that FIUs are empowered to lift the suspension at any time where they conclude that the suspension is no longer necessary to fulfil the objectives set out in the first subparagraph.

   Member States shall ensure that FIUs are empowered to suspend the use of an account or suspend a business relationship as referred to in this paragraph at the request of an FIU from another Member State.
3. The imposition of a suspension or the withholding of consent in accordance with this Article shall not attach liability of any kind to the FIU or its directors or employees.

Article 25

Instructions to Monitor Transactions or Activities

Member States shall ensure that FIUs are empowered to instruct obliged entities to monitor, for a period to be specified by the FIU, the transactions or activities that are being carried out through one or more bank accounts, payment accounts, crypto-asset accounts, or other business relationships managed by the obliged entity for persons who present a significant risk of money laundering, its predicate offences, or terrorist financing. Member States shall also ensure that FIUs are empowered to instruct the obliged entity to report on the results of the monitoring.

Member States shall ensure that FIUs are empowered to impose monitoring measures as referred to in this Article at the request of an FIU from another Member State.

Article 26
Alerts to Obliged Entities

1. Member States shall ensure that FIUs are able to alert obliged entities of information relevant for the performance of customer due diligence pursuant to Chap. III of Regulation (EU) 2024/1624. That information shall include:
   (a) Types of transactions or activities that present a significant risk of money laundering, its predicate offences, and terrorist financing.
   (b) Specific persons who present a significant risk of money laundering, its predicate offences, and terrorist financing.
   (c) Specific geographic areas that present a significant risk of money laundering, its predicate offences, and terrorist financing.
2. The requirement referred to in paragraph 1 shall apply for a period laid down in national law, which shall not exceed 6 months.
3. FIUs shall provide obliged entities with strategic information about typologies, risk indicators, and trends in money laundering and terrorist financing on an annual basis.

Article 27
FIU Annual Report

Each Member State shall ensure that its FIU publishes an annual report on its activities. The report shall contain statistics on:

(a) The follow-up given by the FIU to suspicious transaction and activity reports it has received
(b) Suspicious transaction reports submitted by obliged entities
(c) Disclosures by supervisors and central registers
(d) Disseminations to competent authorities and follow-up given to those disseminations
(e) Requests submitted to and received from other FIUs
(f) Requests submitted to and received from competent authorities referred to in Article 2(1), point (44)(c), of Regulation (EU) 2024/1624
(g) Human resources allocated
(h) Data on cross-border physical transfers of cash transmitted by customs authorities pursuant to Article 9 of Regulation (EU) 2018/1672

The report referred to in the first paragraph shall also contain information on the trends and typologies identified in the files disseminated to other competent authorities. The information contained in the report shall not permit the identification of any natural or legal person.

Article 28
Feedback by FIU

1. Member States shall ensure that FIUs provide obliged entities with feedback on the reporting of suspicions pursuant to Article 69 of Regulation (EU) 2024/1624. Such feedback shall cover at least the quality of the information provided, the

timeliness of reporting, the description of the suspicion, and the documentation provided at the submission stage.

Feedback pursuant to this Article shall not be understood as encompassing each report submitted by obliged entities.

The FIU shall provide feedback at least once per year, whether provided to the individual obliged entity or to groups or categories of obliged entities, taking into consideration the overall number of suspicious transactions reported by the obliged entities.

Feedback shall also be made available to supervisors to allow them to perform risk-based supervision in accordance with Article 40.

FIUs shall report on an annual basis to AMLA on the provision of feedback to obliged entities pursuant to this Article, and shall provide statistics on the number of suspicious transaction reports submitted by the categories of obliged entities.

By 10 July 2028, AMLA shall issue recommendations to FIUs on best practices and approaches towards the provision of feedback, including on the type and frequency of feedback.

The obligation to provide feedback shall not jeopardise any ongoing analytical work carried out by the FIU or any investigation or administrative action subsequent to the dissemination by the FIU, and shall not affect the applicability of data protection and confidentiality requirements.

2. Member States shall ensure that FIUs provide customs authorities with feedback, at least on an annual basis, on the effectiveness of and follow-up to the information transmitted pursuant to Article 9 of Regulation (EU) 2018/1672.

Article 29

Cooperation Between FIUs

Member States shall ensure that FIUs cooperate with each other to the greatest extent possible, regardless of their organisational status.

Article 30

Protected Channels of Communication

1. A system for the exchange of information between FIUs of Member States (FIU.net) shall be set up. FIU.net shall ensure the secure communication and exchange of information and shall be capable of producing a written record of all processing activities. FIU.net may also be used for communications with FIUs' counterparts in third countries and with other authorities and with Union bodies, offices, and agencies. FIU.net shall be managed by AMLA.

   FIU.net shall be used for the exchange of information between FIUs and AMLA for the purposes of joint analyses pursuant to Article 32 of this Directive and Article 40 of Regulation (EU) 2024/1620.

2. Member States shall ensure that FIUs exchange information pursuant to Articles 31 and 32 using FIU.net. In the event of a technical failure of FIU.net, the information shall be transmitted by any other appropriate means ensuring a high level of data security and data protection.

Exchanges of information between FIUs and their counterparts in third countries that are not connected to FIU.net shall take place through protected channels of communication.

3. Member States shall ensure that, in order to fulfil their tasks as laid down in this Directive, FIUs cooperate to the greatest extent possible in the application of state-of-the-art technologies in accordance with their national law.

   Member States shall also ensure that FIUs cooperate to the greatest extent possible in the application of solutions developed and managed by AMLA in accordance with Article 5(5), point (i), Article 45(1), point (d), and Article 47 of Regulation (EU) 2024/1620.
4. Member States shall ensure that FIUs are able to use the functionalities of the FIU.net to cross-match, on a hit/no-hit basis, the data they make available on FIU.net, with the data made available on that system by other FIUs and Union bodies, offices, and agencies insofar as such cross-matching falls within the respective mandates of those Union bodies, offices, and agencies.
5. AMLA may suspend the access of an FIU or counterpart in a third country or Union body, office or agency to FIU.net where it has grounds to believe that such access would jeopardise the implementation of this Chapter and the security and confidentiality of the information held by FIUs and exchanged through FIU.net, including where there are concerns in relation to an FIU's independence and autonomy.

Article 31
Exchange of Information Between FIUs

1. Member States shall ensure that FIUs exchange, spontaneously or upon request, any information that may be relevant for the processing or analysis of information by the FIU related to money laundering, its predicate offences, or terrorist financing, and the natural or legal person involved, regardless of the type of predicate offences that may be involved, and even if the type of predicate offences that may be involved is not identified at the time of the exchange.

   A request shall contain the relevant facts, background information, reasons for the request, links with the country of the requested FIU, and how the information sought will be used.

   When an FIU receives a report pursuant to Article 69(1), the first subparagraph, point (a), of Regulation (EU) 2024/1624 which concerns another Member State, it shall promptly forward the report, or all the relevant information obtained from it, to the FIU of that other Member State.
2. By 10 July 2026, AMLA shall develop draft implementing technical standards and submit them to the Commission for adoption. Those draft implementing technical standards shall specify the format to be used for the exchange of the information referred to in paragraph 1.

   Power is conferred on the Commission to adopt the implementing technical standards referred to in the first subparagraph in accordance with Article 53 of Regulation (EU) 2024/1620.

3. By 10 July 2026, AMLA shall develop draft regulatory technical standards and submit them to the Commission for adoption. Those draft regulatory technical standards shall specify the relevance and selection criteria when determining whether a report submitted pursuant to Article 69(1), first subparagraph, point (a), of Regulation (EU) 2024/1624 concerns another Member State as referred to in paragraph 1, third subparagraph, of this Article.

   Power is delegated to the Commission to supplement this Directive by adopting the regulatory technical standards referred to in the first subparagraph in accordance with Articles 49–52 of Regulation (EU) 2024/1620.
4. By 10 July 2028, AMLA shall issue guidelines addressed to FIUs on the procedures to be put in place when forwarding and receiving a report pursuant to Article 69(1), the first subparagraph, point (a), of Regulation (EU) 2024/1624, which concerns another Member State, and the follow-up to be given to that report.
5. Member States shall ensure that the FIU to whom the request is made is required to use the whole range of its available powers which it would normally use domestically for receiving and analysing information when it replies to a request for information referred to in paragraph 1 from another FIU.

   When an FIU seeks to obtain additional information from an obliged entity established in another Member State which operates on the territory of its Member State, the request shall be addressed to the FIU of the Member State in whose territory the obliged entity is established. That FIU shall obtain information in accordance with Article 69(1) of Regulation (EU) 2024/1624 and transfer the answers promptly.
6. Member States shall ensure that where an FIU is requested to provide information pursuant to paragraph 1, it shall respond to the request as soon as possible and in any case no later than 5 working days after the receipt of the request if the FIU is in possession of the requested information or the requested information is held in a database or register which is directly accessible by the requested FIU. In exceptional, duly justified cases, this deadline may be extended to a maximum of 10 working days. Where the requested FIU is unable to obtain the requested information, it shall inform the requesting FIU thereof.
7. Member States shall ensure that in exceptional, justified, and urgent cases and, by way of derogation from paragraph 6, where, pursuant to paragraph 1, an FIU is requested to provide information which is held in a database or registry directly accessible by the requested FIU, or which is already in its possession, the requested FIU shall provide that information no later than 1 working day after the receipt of the request.

   If the requested FIU is unable to respond within 1 working day or cannot access the information directly, it shall provide a justification. Where the provision of the information requested within 1 working day would put a disproportionate burden on the requested FIU, it may postpone the provision of the information. In that case, the requested FIU shall immediately inform the requesting FIU of such postponement. The requested FIU may extend to a maximum of 3 working days the deadline to reply to a request for information.

8. An FIU may refuse to exchange information only in exceptional circumstances where the exchange could be contrary to fundamental principles of its national law. Those exceptional circumstances shall be specified in a way which prevents misuse of, and undue limitations on, the free exchange of information for analytical purposes.

   By 10 July 2028, Member States shall notify the Commission of the exceptional circumstances referred to in the first subparagraph. Member States shall update such notifications where changes to the exceptional circumstances identified at the national level occur.

   The Commission shall publish the consolidated list of notifications referred to in the second subparagraph.
9. By 10 July 2029, the Commission shall submit a report to the European Parliament and to the Council assessing whether the exceptional circumstances notified pursuant to paragraph 8 are justified.

Article 32
Joint Analyses

1. Member States shall ensure that their FIUs are able to carry out joint analyses of suspicious transactions and activities.
2. For the purpose of paragraph 1 of this Article, the relevant FIUs, assisted by AMLA in accordance with Article 40 of Regulation (EU) 2024/1620, shall set up a joint analysis team for a specific purpose and limited period, which may be extended by mutual consent, to carry out operational analyses of suspicious transactions or activities involving one or more of the FIUs setting up the team.
3. A joint analysis team may be set up where:

   (a) An FIU's operational analyses require difficult and demanding analyses with links to other Member States.
   (b) A number of FIUs are conducting operational analyses in which the circumstances of the case justify concerted action in the Member States involved.

   A request for the setting up of a joint analysis team may be made by any of the FIUs concerned or AMLA pursuant to Article 44 of Regulation (EU) 2024/1620.
4. Member States shall ensure that the staff member of their FIU allocated to the joint analysis team is able, in accordance with applicable national law and within the limits of their competence, to provide the team with information available to its FIU for the purpose of the analysis conducted by the team.
5. Where the joint analysis team needs assistance from an FIU other than those which are part of the team, it might request that other FIU to:

   (a) Join the joint analysis team
   (b) Submit financial intelligence and financial information to the joint analysis team

6. Member States shall ensure that FIUs are able to invite third parties, including Union bodies, offices, and agencies, to take part in the joint analyses where

relevant for the purposes of the joint analyses and where such participation falls within the respective mandates of those third parties.

Member States shall ensure that the FIUs participating in the joint analyses determine the conditions that apply in relation to the participation of third parties and put in place measures guaranteeing the confidentiality and security of the information exchanged. Member States shall ensure that the information exchanged is used solely for the purposes for which that joint analysis was set up.

Article 33

Use by FIUs of Information Exchanged Between Them

Information and documents received pursuant to Articles 29, 31, and 32 shall be used for the accomplishment of the FIU's tasks as laid down in this Directive. When exchanging information and documents pursuant to Articles 29 and 31, the transmitting FIU may impose restrictions and conditions on the use of that information, except where the transmission consists of a report submitted by an obliged entity pursuant to Article 69(1) of Regulation (EU) 2024/1624, or information derived therefrom, which concerns another Member State where the obliged entity operates through the freedom to provide services and which includes no link to the Member State of the transmitting FIU. The receiving FIU shall comply with those restrictions and conditions.

Member States shall ensure that FIUs designate at least one contact person or point to be responsible for receiving requests for information from FIUs in other Member States.

Article 34

Consent to Further Dissemination of Information Exchanged Between FIUs

1. Member States shall ensure that the information exchanged pursuant to Articles 29, 31, and 32 is used only for the purpose for which it was sought or provided and that any dissemination of that information by the receiving FIU to any other authority, agency, or department, or any use of this information for purposes other than those originally approved, is made subject to the prior consent of the FIU providing the information.

   The requirements of the first subparagraph of this paragraph shall not apply where the information provided by the FIU consists of a report submitted by an obliged entity pursuant to Article 69(1) of Regulation (EU) 2024/1624 which concerns another Member State where the obliged entity operates through the freedom to provide services and which has no link to the Member State of the FIU providing the information.
2. Member States shall ensure that the requested FIU's prior consent to disseminate the information to competent authorities is granted promptly and to the largest extent possible, regardless of the type of predicate offences and whether or not the predicate offence has been identified. The requested FIU shall not refuse its consent to such dissemination unless this would fall beyond the scope of application of its AML/CFT provisions or could lead to impairment of an investigation, or would otherwise not be in accordance with fundamental principles of national

law of that Member State. Any such refusal to grant consent shall be appropriately explained. The cases where FIUs may refuse to grant consent shall be specified in a way which prevents misuse of, and undue limitations on, the dissemination of information to competent authorities.
3. By 10 July 2028, Member States shall notify the Commission of the exceptional circumstances in which dissemination would not be in accordance with fundamental principles of national law referred to in paragraph 2. Member States shall update such notifications where changes to the exceptional circumstances identified at the national level occur.

   The Commission shall publish the consolidated list of notifications referred to in the first subparagraph.
4. By 10 July 2029, the Commission shall submit a report to the European Parliament and to the Council assessing whether the exceptional circumstances notified pursuant to paragraph 3 are justified.

Article 35

Effect of Criminal Law Provisions

Differences between national law definitions of predicate offences shall not impede the ability of FIUs to provide assistance to another FIU and shall not limit the exchange, dissemination, or use of information pursuant to Articles 31, 32, 33, and 34.

Article 36

Confidentiality of Reporting

1. Member States shall ensure that FIUs have in place mechanisms to protect the identity of the obliged entities and their employees, or persons in an equivalent position, including agents and distributors, who report suspicions pursuant to Article 69(1), first subparagraph, point (a), of Regulation (EU) 2024/1624.
2. Member States shall ensure that FIUs do not disclose the source of the report referred to in paragraph 1 of this Article when responding to requests for information by competent authorities pursuant to Article 22 or when disseminating the results of their analyses pursuant to Article 19. This paragraph is without prejudice to the applicable national criminal procedural law.

Appendix 3: Financial Intelligence Units (FIUs)—Article 32 4AMLD[6]

1. Each Member State shall establish an FIU in order to prevent, detect, and effectively combat money laundering and terrorist financing.

---

[6] Directive (EU) 2015/849 of the European Parliament and of the Council of 20 May 2015 on the prevention of the use of the financial system for the purposes of money laundering or terrorist financing, amending Regulation (EU) No 648/2012 of the European Parliament and of the Council, and repealing Directive 2005/60/EC of the European Parliament

2. Member States shall notify the Commission in writing of the name and address of their respective FIUs.
3. Each FIU shall be operationally independent and autonomous, which means that the FIU shall have the authority and capacity to carry out its functions freely, including the ability to take autonomous decisions to analyse, request, and disseminate specific information. The FIU, as the central national unit, shall be responsible for receiving and analysing suspicious transaction reports and other information relevant to money laundering, associated predicate offences, or terrorist financing. The FIU shall be responsible for disseminating the results of its analyses and any additional relevant information to the competent authorities where there are grounds to suspect money laundering, associated predicate offences, or terrorist financing. It shall be able to obtain additional information from obliged entities. Member States shall provide their FIUs with adequate financial, human, and technical resources in order to fulfil their tasks.
4. Member States shall ensure that their FIUs have access, directly or indirectly, in a timely manner, to the financial, administrative, and law enforcement information that they require to fulfil their tasks properly. FIUs shall be able to respond to requests for information by competent authorities in their respective Member States when such requests for information are motivated by concerns relating to money laundering, associated predicate offences, or terrorist financing. The decision on conducting the analysis or dissemination of information shall remain with the FIU.
5. Where there are objective grounds for assuming that the provision of such information would have a negative impact on ongoing investigations or analyses, or, in exceptional circumstances, where disclosure of the information would be clearly disproportionate to the legitimate interests of a natural or legal person or irrelevant with regard to the purposes for which it has been requested, the FIU shall be under no obligation to comply with the request for information.
6. Member States shall require competent authorities to provide feedback to the FIU about the use made of the information provided in accordance with this Article and about the outcome of the investigations or inspections performed on the basis of that information.
7. Member States shall ensure that the FIU is empowered to take urgent action, directly or indirectly, where there is a suspicion that a transaction is related to money laundering or terrorist financing, to suspend or withhold consent to a transaction that is proceeding, in order to analyse the transaction, confirm the suspicion, and disseminate the results of the analysis to the competent authorities. The FIU shall be empowered to take such action, directly or indirectly, at the request of an FIU from another Member State for the periods and under the conditions specified in the national law of the FIU receiving the request.
8. The FIU's analysis function shall consist of the following:

---

and of the Council and Commission Directive 2006/70/EC. This is the current article that will be superseded by Article 19 of 6AMLD. It is included here as it is what the Irish legislation is currently based on and under which some of its powers are derived.

(a) An operational analysis which focuses on individual cases and specific targets or on appropriately selected information, depending on the type and volume of the disclosures received and the expected use of the information after dissemination.
(b) A strategic analysis addressing money laundering and terrorist financing trends and patterns.

Appendix 4: Summary of Irish Police Powers[7]

The purpose of this high-level overview is to show some of the common police powers available to investigators in Ireland when investigating money laundering and crypto-laundering. For a more in depth examination, see Meighan (2025).

Power to *Freeze* Transaction/Service

Oftentimes the suspected proceeds of criminal conduct are held in accounts maintained by various entities such as banks, credit unions, virtual asset service providers (VASPs), bookmakers, car dealers, estate agents, or jewellery shops. In these cases, the Criminal Justice (Money Laundering and Terrorist Financing) Acts, 2010 to 2021 (hereinafter the '2010 Act'), provides that investigators may obtain a direction or order instructing the entity maintaining the account not to carry out a service or transaction pertaining to those impugned accounts. This is colloquially known as a *freezing* direction or order. The direction or order can be issued to any person and is not limited to so-called *designated persons* under the 2010 Act.

The purpose of such a direction or order is to preserve the impugned property pending enquiries and investigations to be carried out. As a *freezing* order engages constitutionally protected property rights, the 2010 Act provides a number of safeguards to ensure that proper notice of a *freezing* direction or order being in force is given to affected persons, provides protections to entities that comply with an authorisation or order, and provides a mechanism for affected persons to apply to the District Court seeking to revoke the direction or order, or to seek relief in relation to the *frozen* property for the discharge of reasonable living, legal, or business expenses.

To assist financial investigators who may be seeking to *follow the money*, the 2010 Act also provides for an authorisation to be issued to an entity to legally proceed with a service or transaction that otherwise would constitute a money laundering or terrorist financing offence.

---

[7] For a detailed discussion, see Meighan S (2025), Money Laundering in Ireland: Context, History and the Law. Clarus Press, Dublin.

Arrestable Offence

In Ireland, serious criminal offences are defined as arrestable offences. Once an offence fulfils the definition of an arrestable offence, various police powers become available to the officers investigating it. An *arrestable offence* is defined in section 2 of the Criminal Law Act, 1997, as:

> any offence for which a person of full capacity and not previously convicted may, under or by virtue of any enactment or the common law, be punished by imprisonment for a term of five years or by a more severe penalty and includes an attempt to commit any such offence.

Under section 7(3) of the Criminal Justice (Money Laundering and Terrorist Financing) Acts 2010 to 2021, a person who commits a money laundering offence is liable:

(a) On summary conviction, to a fine not exceeding €5000 or imprisonment for a term not exceeding 12 months (or both) or
(b) On conviction on indictment, to a fine or imprisonment for a term not exceeding 14 years (or both)

Money laundering, including crypto-laundering, is therefore an arrestable offence, and all of the following powers are available to police officers investigating this offence.

Search Warrant

Section 10 of the Criminal Justice (Miscellaneous Provisions) Act, 1997, as amended, provides for a search warrant in relation to arrestable offences to search for evidence relating to the offence under investigation. It states as follows:

1. If a judge of the District Court is satisfied by information on oath of a member not below the rank of sergeant that there are reasonable grounds for suspecting that evidence of, or relating to, the commission of an arrestable offence is to be found in any place, the judge may issue a warrant for the search of that place and any persons found at that place.
2. A search warrant under this section shall be expressed, and shall operate, to authorise a named member, accompanied by such other members or persons or both as the member thinks necessary:

    (a) To enter, at any time or times within 1 week of the date of issue of the warrant, on production, if so requested, of the warrant, and if necessary by the use of reasonable force, the place named in the warrant.
    (b) To search it and any persons found at that place.
    (c) To seize anything found at that place, or anything found in the possession of a person present at that place at the time of the search, which that member reasonably believes to be evidence of, or relating to, the commission of an arrestable offence.

3. A member acting under the authority of a search warrant under this section may:
   (a) Require any person present at the place where the search is being carried out to give the member his or her name and address.
   (b) Arrest without warrant any person who:
      (i) Obstructs or attempts to obstruct the member in the carrying out of his or her duties
      (ii) Fails to comply with a requirement under paragraph (a) or
      (iii) Gives a name or address which the member has reasonable cause for believing is false or misleading
4. A person who obstructs or attempts to obstruct a member acting under the authority of a search warrant under this section, who fails to comply with a requirement under subsection (3)(a) or who gives a false or misleading name or address to a member shall be guilty of an offence and shall be liable on summary conviction to a fine not exceeding €3000 or imprisonment for a term not exceeding 6 months or both.
5. The power to issue a warrant under this section is without prejudice to any other power conferred by statute to issue a warrant for the search of any place or person.
6. In this section:
   (a) "Arrestable offence" has the meaning it has in section 2 (as amended by section 8 of the Criminal Justice Act 2006) of the Criminal Law Act 1997
   (b) "Place" means a physical location and includes:
      (i) A dwelling, residence, building, or abode
      (ii) A vehicle, whether mechanically propelled or not
      (iii) A vessel, whether sea-going or not
      (iv) An aircraft, whether capable of operation or not
      (v) A hovercraft

Power of Arrest

Where a member of the Garda Síochána (sworn police officer), with reasonable cause, suspects that an arrestable offence has been committed, he or she may arrest without warrant anyone whom the member, with reasonable cause, suspects to be guilty of the offence—Section 4(3) of the Criminal Law Act 1997.

Power of Entry to Affect an Arrest

Section 6(2) of the Criminal Law Act, 1997, provides a power of entry to search for and arrest a person suspected of committing an arrestable offence. It states that:

for the purpose of arresting a person without a warrant for an arrestable offence a member of the Garda Síochána may enter (if need be, by use of reasonable force) and search any premises (including a dwelling) where that person is or where the member, with reasonable cause, suspects that person to be, and where the premises is a dwelling the member shall not, unless acting with the consent of an occupier of the dwelling or other person who appears to the member to be in charge of the dwelling, enter that dwelling unless:

(a) he or she or another such member has observed the person within or entering the dwelling, or
(b) he or she, with reasonable cause, suspects that before a warrant of arrest could be obtained, the person will either abscond for the purpose of avoiding justice or will obstruct the course of justice, or
(c) he or she, with reasonable cause, suspects that before a warrant of arrest could be obtained the person would commit an arrestable offence, or
(d) the person ordinarily resides at that dwelling.

Powers of Detention

If a person is arrested on suspicion of an arrestable offence, they may be detained in a Garda station for the purpose of investigating the offence. This most likely involves interviewing the suspect and presenting evidence to them. The suspect enjoys the right to silence, but adverse inferences may be drawn in certain circumstances if they refuse to answer certain questions asked of them once a series of sufficient safeguards is put in place. Depending on the circumstance of the case, various lengths of detention period are allowable. There are also a number of reasons why the *clock might stop*, including hospitalisation and on the authority of a doctor who certifies the person as unfit for questioning.

The majority of money laundering suspects are detained under the general power (Section 4 of the Criminal Justice Act 1984) or under organised crime legislation where applicable (Section 50 of the Criminal Justice Act, 2007).

	Section 4	Section 50
Initial period on arrest	6 h	6 h
First extension authorised by superintendent	6 h	18 h
Second extension authorised by chief superintendent	12 h	24 h
First extension authorised by district or circuit court		72 h
Second extension authorised by district or circuit court		48 h
Total	24 h	168 h (7 days)

Appendix 5: United States v. Sterlingov[8]

This case is significant as it is one of the first recorded judgments where a commercial blockchain analytic tool was accepted in a criminal prosecution.

Roman Sterlingov was prosecuted and subsequently convicted of money laundering, operating an unlicenced money transmission business, and money transmission without a licence in relation to his operation of a bitcoin mixer known as *Bitcoin Fog*. He challenged the prosecution's evidence in relation to their use of blockchain analytics using the software programme *Chainalysis Reactor*.

Transferring bitcoin requires three things:

1. A sending address (that has sufficient *unspent* bitcoin associated with it)
2. A receiving address
3. A private encryption key (to *unlock* the unspent bitcoin)

Addresses are hexadecimal strings akin to a bank account number. Users can have any number of public keys, and their activity using one set of public keys is not inherently tied to their activity using another set or their real-world identity.

Every transaction that has ever taken place is recorded on the Bitcoin blockchain. Each transaction record is made up of several important elements:

1. The sending address(es)
2. The receiving address(es)
3. A unique timestamp
4. The transaction ID (or transaction Hash)

Within the transaction, there is no link to the real-world identity of the person sending or receiving the crypto (anonymity, privacy). This is where crypto-assets are both private and public at the same time. On one hand, real-world identities are private and not readily ascertainable from viewing the open blockchain. On the other hand, every transaction is available to any person with an interest in looking. This includes law enforcement who, as part of a criminal investigation, may seek to:

1. Trace (and map) value moving through the system
2. Cluster addresses in a manner that may provide a window into otherwise anonymous activity
3. Associate those addresses with a single user (attribution)—since the sender would need possession of the *private key* to affect the transfer

While these investigative tasks can be completed by hand using pen, paper, and sufficient time, given the volume of data currently associated with the Bitcoin blockchain (currently 5 TB of data), the use of proprietary, commercially available blockchain analytic software is now commonplace. One example of such software is Chainalysis Reactor. This software uses *heuristics*—based on the technical

[8] United States District Court, District of Columbia, Criminal Action No. 21-399 (29 February 2024) Moss J.

makeup of the crypto-asset—to map value movement, assist in attribution, and associate addresses that have interacted with illegal activities and services. Chainalysis gave expert evidence at the trial where Reactor was described as:

> a software product used to cluster [crypto-asset] addresses that are likely controlled by the same entity and to then tie those clusters to particular entities based on the information gleaned from other sources, including by conducting test transactions with those entities, researching open sources, and exchanging information with various [VASPs] and law enforcement agencies.

In this case, Reactor used three different heuristics.

1. First used the co-spend or common spend heuristic. This is based on a unique feature of the blockchain, namely UTXOs. A transaction can therefore contain multiple input and multiple output addresses. When a transaction has multiple input addresses, those addresses are said to be co-spending. Given that the sender requires the private key for each input address, it is very likely that a single entity controls each of them.

   This "flaw" in the technical makeup of Bitcoin was recognised in the 2009 Bitcoin White paper, where it was observed that "some linking is unavoidable with multi-input transaction … the risk is that if the owner of a key is revealed, linking could reveal other transaction that belonged to the same owner".
2. Second is based on observing and tracking a particular entity's on-chain behaviours and patterns. It is opined that every user of crypto-assets leaves behind a digital *fingerprint* of their activities that can be discerned by looking at information that is publicly available on the digital ledger and by conducting test transactions with addresses known to belong to the target entity.

   This heuristic could involve looking at information such as address type used, time zone analysis, OSINT, the amount of fees paid, and change of addresses.

   Peel chain behaviour—Bitcoin does not permit a user to partially spend the value contained in an input address. If a user's input contains more than the intended value (plus transaction fee), that transaction will be represented as having one input and two outputs. One of the outputs represents the transfer of value to the new owner, while the other is transferring the *change* back to a new address that is controlled by the same wallet as the input address.

   Third is the so-called intelligence-based heuristic (proprietary information, which differs from tool to tool). This includes information that the Chainalysis intelligence team gathered from sources such as "data leaks, court documents, Chainalysis data partnerships, exchanges that share their address with Chainalysis, and manual merges due to services changing wallets". Other commercial providers will call this step *direct attribution*.
3. A fourth heuristic was not used in this analysis and not considered by the court.

Sterlingov's defence team argued that the government's blockchain analysis was *junk science* and sought to have it excluded. The judge disagreed with this assertion for several reasons and allowed the blockchain analysis to be shown to the jury.

Firstly, this was not a case where the prosecution's case was solely based on the Reactor software. The prosecution also produced other corroborative evidence inter alia materials found during searches, their own OSINT, financial analysis, etc. to support their case.

Secondly, much of the output from Reactor was replicated manually (pen and paper method) by the investigation team.

Thirdly, the defendant made certain admissions during the investigation that confirmed the Reactor output.

Fourthly, the Reactor software was *deterministic*; given the same inputs, it would consistently produce the same output.

Fifthly, this was not a *black box* case where the court was asked to trust the output that an unknown program produced. The prosecution disclosed ample material to the defence showing how the product worked and allowing them to carry out their own analysis to see if a different result could be achieved by them or their own expert using the Reactor software.

Finally, the judge was also impressed that the software was *under inclusive* and took a *conservative approach* to attribution.

Relying upon Supreme Court jurisprudence, the court found that, rather than exclude it, the correct venue to test the accuracy of the Reactor output was during trial by "vigorous cross-examination, presentation of contrary evidence, and careful instructions on the burden of proof". The judge concluded that Reactor was reliable, and that the prosecution had:

> demonstrated by a preponderance of the evidence that the blockchain analysis generated by Chainalysis Reactor is the product of reliable principles and methods, and the court accordingly denies the defendant's requests to exclude the testimony and evidence based on that analysis.

Glossary

Anti-money Laundering (AML) A series of preventative and repressive legal, regulatory, and operational measures put in place by governments, international organisations, and private entities, to prevent, detect, disrupt, and prosecute money laundering and seize criminal assets.

Crypto-asset Service Provider (*also known as a Virtual Asset Service Provider or VASP*) A natural or legal person who, by way of business, provides one or more of the following services for or on behalf of another person:

1. Exchange between crypto-assets and fiat currencies
2. Exchange between one or more crypto-assets
3. Transfer of crypto-assets
4. Custodian wallet provision
5. Participation in, or provision of, financial services related to an issuer's offer or sale or both.

Crypto-assets (*also virtual assets*) Privately issued digital assets that:

1. are recorded on a cryptographically secured distributed ledger (e.g., blockchain)
2. are not issued or guaranteed by a central bank or public authority
3. **can be used as a medium of exchange, for investment purposes, or to access goods and services.**

Crypto-crime Any crime involving crypto-assets or blockchain technology. Includes both ***on-chain activity*** (e.g., illicit transactions, ransomware payments, smart contract exploits) and ***off-chain*** **crimes** (e.g., fraud, scams, or drug trafficking) where criminal proceeds are converted to crypto-assets.

Crypto-laundering A sub-type of *cyber money laundering* that uses crypto-assets to launder criminal proceeds. It leverages the features of blockchain technology to move funds rapidly, obscure their criminal origins, and disrupt traditional AML detection methods.

Cyber-laundering A sub-type of *money laundering* that uses the internet and digital platforms to launder criminal proceeds. It includes both crypto-asset and fiat channels.

S. Meighan, *Money Laundering and Crypto-Assets*, Contributions to Finance and Accounting, https://doi.org/10.1007/978-3-032-13481-3

Cybercrime A criminal offence involving the misuse or exploitation of digital technology in the planning, commissioning, or concealing of a crime. Traditionally divided into two categories: *cyber-enabled* (crime that targets ICT directly) or *cyber-dependent* (traditional crimes that are amplified through digital platforms).

Financial Intelligence Information about a person's financial activities, transactions, or assets that may indicate involvement in criminality, including money laundering.

Financial Intelligence Unit A national agency responsible for receiving and analysing Suspicious Transaction Reports (STRs) and disseminating *financial intelligence* to competent authorities for investigation or regulatory action.

Friction Point An interface within the financial system where controls can be applied to detect and prevent illicit money flows. In the AML context, this means applying due diligence and transaction monitoring controls to identify the people connected with each transaction as well as the source and destination of the funds. In the crypto-asset system, these friction points are the interfaces between the fiat and crypto systems, the most well-known being exchanges or CASPs/VASPs.

Money A system of exchange tokens or assets, physical or digital, recognised by a community of users as holding value for the purposes of exchange, accounting, or store of wealth.

Money Laundering The process of disguising the criminal origins of money (or assets) to make it appear to have come from a legitimate source.

Socio-Technical Systems Theory A systems theory framework that conceptualises phenomena as made up of interrelated social and technical sub-systems. It focuses on achieving joint optimisation between people, processes, and technology.

Structural Coupling A systems theory concept describing the dynamic relationship between two interdependent systems that influence one another while maintaining their distinct identities. In this book, it refers to the interaction between crypto-laundering and FIU detection systems.

Suspicious Transaction Report or STR (*also known as Suspicious Activity Report or SAR*) A formal report submitted to the FIU detailing a suspicious transaction or activity suspected of involving money laundering or other criminal activity. STRs/SARs are a key input to financial investigations.

System A coherently structured set of two or more elements that interact to perform a function and produce emergent behaviour over time. A system is delineated from its more complex *environment* by an observer-defined *boundary*.

Systems Theory An interdisciplinary framework used to understand complex phenomena as composed of interrelated and interdependent components operating within a larger environment.

Wicked problem A complex, adaptive issue that resists straightforward solutions due to its evolving nature, multiple stakeholders, and deeply interconnected causes. They cannot be definitively solved but only addressed iteratively through adaptive, multidisciplinary approaches such as *systems theory*.

MIX
Papier aus verantwortungsvollen Quellen
Paper from responsible sources
FSC® C105338

If you have any concerns about our products,
you can contact us on
ProductSafety@springernature.com

In case Publisher is established outside the EU,
the EU authorized representative is:
Springer Nature Customer Service Center GmbH
Europaplatz 3, 69115 Heidelberg, Germany

Printed by Libri Plureos GmbH
in Hamburg, Germany